Americans All

Americans All
The Cultural Gifts Movement

Diana Selig

HARVARD UNIVERSITY PRESS
Cambridge, Massachusetts
London, England

First Harvard University Press paperback edition, 2011

Library of Congress Cataloging-in-Publication Data

Selig, Diana.
    Americans all : the cultural gifts movement / Diana Selig.
      p. cm.
    Includes bibliographical references and index.
    ISBN 978-0-674-02829-6 (cloth: alk. paper)
    ISBN 978-0-674-06224-5 (pbk.)
    1. Pluralism (Social sciences)—United States—History—20th century.
2. National characteristics, American—History—20th century. 3. Ethnicity—
United States—History—20th century. 4. Anti-racism—United States—
History—20th century. 5. Social movements—United States—History—
20th century. 6. Social reformers—United States—History—20th century.
7. United States—Intellectual life—20th century. 8. United States—
Politics and government—1919–1933. 9. Progressivism (United States
politics)—History—20th century. 10. United States—Cultural policy.
I. Title.

E184.A1S545 2008
973.91—dc22   2007045730

For my parents

Contents

Illustrations

Acknowledgments

I am delighted to thank the many people who have supported this project over many years. I could not have completed this book without their help. Paula Fass has been a wonderful teacher and mentor since my first semester of graduate studies in the history department at Berkeley. She encouraged this project in its earliest form and offered valuable criticism and inspiration along the way. I have benefited from her high standards for historical research and writing and from the many opportunities she offered me. I am deeply indebted to her intellectual insights, her challenging questions, her exemplary mentoring, and her warm friendship.

Waldo Martin and Kristen Luker also guided and supported this project from its beginnings. I also thank Robin Einhorn, Jon Gjerde, the late Jim Kettner, Mabel Lee, and Jane Stahlhut. My fellow graduate students provided intellectual companionship and personal friendship. I am grateful to David Engerman, Elizabeth Gessel, Erika Lee, Min Lo, Ethan Pollock, Paul Sabin, Jason Scott Smith, Philip Soffer, Jonathan Spiro, and Justin Suran for their part in this journey.

It is a pleasure as well to recognize William Cronon and Susan Lee Johnson, my undergraduate instructors at Yale, who first inspired and nurtured my interest in history and helped me learn how to think and write about the past. They have been models for my own scholarship and teaching. Since I first contemplated graduate studies, Daniel Horowitz has given generously of time and advice.

At Claremont McKenna College, my colleagues in the history department have offered tremendous support. I am grateful for their confidence and good cheer. Lisa Forman Cody read the entire manuscript with exceptional insight during a critical phase of revisions; I am deeply indebted to her incisive critique and extremely valuable suggestions. David Yoo, a superb colleague in American history, has discussed historical questions large and small and offered indispensable help in both research and teaching. Arthur Rosenbaum and Jonathan Petropoulos have supported my work since I first arrived at the college and have helped to make the department an especially friendly and congenial place. I am also grateful to colleagues Carla Bittel, Gary Hamburg, Arash Khazeni, Nita Kumar, Tina Sessa, Theresa Smith, and Deans William Ascher and Gregory Hess. Fellow Americanists at the Claremont Colleges, including Hal Barron, Janet Brodie, Julie Liss, and Stuart McConnell, welcomed me warmly. My students have inspired me with their talent and energy.

At Berkeley, I received financial support from the Department of History, the Allan Sharlin Memorial Award, and the Chancellor's Dissertation Fellowship. At Claremont McKenna, I am grateful for the support of the Gould Center for Humanistic Studies, the Kravis Leadership Institute, and the Dean of Faculty's office. Generous funding in the form of a Spencer Postdoctoral Fellowship from the National Academy of Education provided a leave that allowed me to expand the scope of the project. The community of Spencer fellows offered helpful comments, as did several Academy members, including Patricia Albjerg Graham, Diane Ravitch, and Maris Vinovskis.

I am indebted to archivists and librarians around the country, with special thanks to those at the Social Welfare History Archive and the Immigration History Research Center at the University of Minnesota. Toward the end of this project, Nicholas Montalto and George A. Crispin generously shared their expertise and their personal recollections of Rachel Davis DuBois, while Edward and Carol Davis graciously agreed to look through family photographs of their dear aunt.

I am grateful to the many colleagues who offered comments on earlier versions of this project and shared their work, including Christina de Bellaigue, Hamilton Cravens, David Gamson, Ellen Herman, Jonathan Holloway, Andrew Jewett, Ben Keppel, the late Shafali Lal, Thomas Mertz, Julia Mickenberg, John Nieto-Phillips, Jonna Perrillo, Jennifer Ritterhouse, and Jonathan Zimmerman. I presented aspects of this research at various conferences and gatherings and benefited from conversations with fellow panelists and participants. Members of the Southern California Social History Reading Group also helped sharpen my thinking. Marian Macdonald gave effective editing suggestions. Anonymous readers for Harvard University Press offered generous and insightful comments that improved the book, while Kathleen McDermott skillfully guided it to publication.

I treasure my friends who heard so much about this project along the way and maintained faith in its eventual completion. I owe a great deal to Carina Johnson, Steve Kantrowitz, Marcy Norton, Rachel Sherman, and Ann Vileisis, who as both friends and fellow scholars and writers have provided precious advice and encouragement on this journey. I have been blessed with other friendships that also sustained me as I completed the book. Lauren Augusta, Bethany Dreyfus, Josh Greenbaum, Nancy Kates, Alan Kingstone, Erica Levy, Ash McNeely, Elisa Odabashian, Abigail Smith, Keren Stronach, Catherine Teare, and Hilary Zaid have offered support, diversion, and good company through many dinners, hikes, and visits. Dear friends in faraway places, including Pauline Abernathy, Kate Bernheimer, Karni Govreen-Segal, Rachel Heckscher, Sarah Madsen Hardy, and Christine Walravens, have been generous of spirit.

I am grateful to Poonam Sundar and also to the wonderful staff at Pasadena Day Nursery for the loving child care that has allowed me to work.

My in-laws, Marilyn, Mike, and Shelley Rose, have welcomed me warmly into their family. My brother, Colin Selig, and uncle, Dorian Bowman, offered much-needed humor as they teased me during the years it has taken to complete this project. I cherish the memory of my beloved grandparents, Anna and Bernard Bowman, who shared stories of their past and who supported my educational ambitions.

My partner, Meredith Rose, has offered love and understanding all the way through and made me laugh every day. She followed the various paths of research, helped me think through analysis and presentation, and read multiple drafts. I am grateful for her warm encouragement, her sharp wit, her perceptive questions, and her excellent editorial skills. The arrivals of our daughter, Anya, during the writing of this book, and of our son, Jonah, as the book goes to press, have brought tremendous joy and delight to our lives.

My parents, Edward and Renata Selig, have provided unflagging support throughout the years it took to complete this book. They heroically read the entire manuscript at the end, proving themselves superb editors and insightful critics as well as wonderful parents. They have given generously to both this book and its author. I am profoundly grateful for their love and their confidence in me. I dedicate this book to them.

Americans All

Introduction:
Cultural Pluralism in
Interwar America

Beginning in the mid-1920s and extending through World War II, hundreds of thousands of Americans took part in a vibrant and complex crusade to overcome their own racial and religious prejudices. Students, teachers, and school administrators, from kindergartens in Boston to high schools in Chicago, celebrated the cultural contributions of immigrant and minority groups to American life. Fifth-graders in Palo Alto studied Mexican culture, while New Jersey high school students listened to Italian music, practiced German folk dance, and performed plays about Chinese traditions. Teachers in training in Georgia and Kentucky studied methods to foster white students' understanding of their black neighbors. Mothers and fathers in New York City learned how to instill tolerance in their young children, while Protestant Sunday school instructors in Berkeley urged respect for Jews and Catholics. Along with citizens in other cities and towns across the country, these Americans shared an optimistic prediction that they could shape children's attitudes so as to eliminate prejudice in the next generation. For them, the increasing heterogeneity of American society led not toward nativism and racism but rather toward the celebration of cultural difference.

The antiprejudice crusade that burgeoned in the 1920s and 1930s has been overlooked in both historical scholarship and popular memory. Few people are aware of its extent and vitality. The record shows countless examples of efforts to foster friendly attitudes toward ethnic, racial, and religious minorities through a lively set of projects designed to analyze the origins of prejudice and to teach young people to appreciate America's cultural diversity. Where did these early efforts in multicultural education come from, what did they accomplish, and why did they fade from historical knowledge?

This book explores the crusade against prejudice that flourished between the wars, telling a complex story of achievements and failures. It analyzes the bold and progressive thinking of visionary activists who pioneered new ideas of American identity. It also reveals oversights that ultimately limited the scope of their vision. Their selective interpretation of cultural difference led to a romanticized version of ethnic identity. And they failed especially to address the experiences of African Americans, who faced legal barriers to full citizenship and encountered racism far more entrenched than did more recent immigrants.

Liberal thinkers and educators promoted tolerance through the concept of "cultural gifts," a term they used to describe the contributions of immigrant and minority groups to American life. In an explicit rejection of the melting-pot theory of assimilation, they welcomed heterogeneity as a source of strength for the nation and argued that the distinctive traits of each group were worth preserving and sharing. Advocates insisted that people could be both ethnic and American and that immigrant cultures were compatible with American institutions and traditions. They taught that immigrants and minorities carried gifts that would revitalize American society and enrich the shared culture. Like more conservative commentators, cultural gifts proponents were concerned with social cohesion and harmony. But unlike their conservative counterparts, they argued that harmony could emerge from difference.

The cultural gifts campaign was primarily an urban phenomenon. Its center was New York City, where much of the ideas, materials, and funding originated, spreading first to other cities on the East Coast. The campaign soon reached schools, child study groups, and churches in other parts of the country as well. When *Progressive Education* published a special issue entitled "Minority Groups and the American School" in 1935, accounts came from New York, Philadelphia, Los Angeles, Palo Alto, Portland, Oregon, Santa Fe, Atlanta, and Kirksville, Missouri. In the Northeast and Midwest, programs aimed to dispel stereotypes of European ethnics, Jews, and African Americans. On the West Coast, programs discussed Japanese, Chinese, and Mexican immigrants, while in the Southwest, they attended to Native Americans. Antiprejudice work in the South focused almost exclusively on antiblack prejudice. Despite these variations, activists saw their work as national in scope, for they offered a new understanding of national identity, a new way to think about what it meant to be American. Together, these efforts formed a critical element of the grand project of twentieth-century liberalism: the creation of a unified American identity from a diverse citizenry.

Most of us think of multiculturalism as a late-twentieth-century phenomenon, an outgrowth of 1960s liberalism and the ethnic pride movements of the 1970s. Some scholars have traced it back to the World War II and Cold War years, when many Americans determined to put aside ethnic differences to fight a common foe. But few are aware that the origins of what we now call multiculturalism date to the social and cultural ferment that followed World War I. Elements of these pioneering efforts have echoed down through the decades, reappearing in recent programs for teaching young people about America's diversity. Debates over the methods and aims of the cultural gifts approach foreshadowed today's debates over ethnic studies and multicultural education.[1]

The popular acceptance of pluralism calls into question the assumption that European ethnic identity waned in the interwar years. Recent scholarship has suggested that immigrant white groups began to dissolve as racial categories by the 1930s, replaced by a unitary and all-encompassing Caucasian identity in a process Matthew Frye Jacobson has termed the "consolidation of whiteness."[2] But this process was neither sudden nor uniform. Cultural gifts work did reinforce the new comprehensive category of whiteness; religious goodwill efforts excluded black clergy and congregants, for instance, even as they promoted tolerance for Catholics and Jews, while school programs celebrated European groups alongside "the black and yellow races."[3] At the same time, liberal activists struggled to maintain the salience of Old World cultures. Native-born whites and ethnic leaders worked together to fashion arguments for cultural persistence rather than forced assimilation. Cultural gifts thus represented a resistance to the ethnic—if not the racial—transformations that were taking place in the interwar period.

The widespread nature of the cultural gifts movement also demands that we reinterpret conflicts over ethnoracial difference in the interwar period.[4] This era, after all, is known more for nativist rhetoric than for the promotion of tolerance. The racism of the period was intense and often violent, sanctioned by the state and a broad sweep of social institutions. The "tribal twenties" saw the collapse of Progressive reform after the postwar Red Scare, the passage of immigration restriction, and the push for "100% Americanism." This decade brought lynchings and race riots, the revival of the Ku Klux Klan, hostility toward Catholics and Jews, the establishment of the border patrol to limit Mexican immigration, anti-Japanese agitation on the West Coast, the hardening of Jim Crow segregation, and antiblack discrimination in the North and South. Historians have explained these movements as expressions of cultural anxiety, as old-stock Protestants, fearful that immigrants threatened their cultural and political hegemony, looked for ways to halt the unfolding social transformations and return to what they saw as traditional values. Advocates of the "melting pot" promised that immigrants would conform to Anglo standards, while scientific racists argued for the genetic superiority of northern Europeans and scapegoated the minorities who seemed to threaten American traditions.[5]

When historians do note the emergence of pluralist thinking at the time, they tend to confine those ideas to a select group of elite intellectuals and artists or to ethnic leaders who insisted that group identity was compatible with Americanism. These "moderns" resisted the trend toward nativism and Protestant cultural hegemony. This group included Franz Boas, whose cultural relativism challenged racial hierarchies; philosopher John Dewey; Horace Kallen, author of the theory of cultural pluralism; and advocates of the cosmopolitan ideal, for example, Randolph Bourne.[6] Also included were writers and artists of the "Lost Generation" and the Harlem Renaissance, who offered a counterpoint to repression and conformity.

Yet intellectuals did not labor in isolation. Another group played an important role in discussions of diversity: white, middle-class, native-born Americans who countered the trend toward Anglo cultural domination and the "melting pot." These teachers, ministers, parent educators, and students protested emphatically against racial and religious bigotry. Cultural pluralism was not confined to intellectual debate and scholarly mobilization, not limited to such familiar sites as the pages of the *New Republic,* the debates between Kallen and Bourne, the sociology department at the University of Chicago, or the artistic communities of Greenwich Village. The impulse toward pluralism included the teachers and parents and clergy who brought these ideas to public attention. These activists used new scientific authority to carry their pluralist aspirations into textbooks, lesson plans, parenting manuals, children's literature, and Sunday school projects. Pluralism had a practical effect on child rearing, education, community programs, and religious life. Although it was intimately connected to intellectual and literary elites, it was not their exclusive terrain.

The process of implementing the new ideas was complex, for the social scientists and intellectuals who outlined pluralism in the abstract offered few instructions for how to carry it out. It was up to educators to determine how to apply the scientific findings to social institutions. Their varied interpretations made the cultural gifts project both disputed and dynamic, an arena of conflict as well as fruitful experimentation.

How was it that the cultural gifts vision emerged at the high-water mark of the nativist movement? In 1924, the year that saw the permanent passage of the National Origins Act limiting immigration, writer Horace Kallen used the term "cultural pluralism" in his book *Culture and Democracy in the United States.* The same year, social researcher Bruno Lasker initiated the pioneering study that was published as *Race Attitudes in Children,* a book that became a touchstone for cultural gifts workers. An energetic schoolteacher, Rachel Davis DuBois, began to experiment with assembly programs about immigrant groups at the high school in Woodbury, New Jersey. The Federal Council of Churches and the Central Conference of American Rabbis, through their Committee on Goodwill between Jews and Christians, pledged to work together for mutual understanding. In the South, the Commission on Interracial Cooperation designed educational programs to teach white schoolchildren about black history.

The simultaneous expression of nativism and tolerance was not coincidental. Racial liberals and conservative nativists were responding to the same developments in American society. In the first decades of the century, increasing ethnic and racial diversity gave rise to enormous cultural tensions. Fifteen million immigrants arrived between 1900 and 1920, swelling the size of cities and increasing their heterogeneity. Immigrants and their children formed the majority of the population in many of the nation's largest cities. Many of these immigrants were Catholics and Jews from southern and eastern Europe who brought new religious and cultural traditions, as did Mexican immigrants to the western states. At the same time, the Great Migration brought hundreds of thousands of African Americans from the rural South to the urban North. Other rural Americans also migrated to the cities, making the

American population increasingly urban. An industrializing economy and new forms of transportation and communication contributed to these social transformations. New patterns of work, family life, religion, and cultural expression brought a range of reactions, from confusion and alarm to optimism and hope.

 Nativism and tolerance gave rise to each other, for it was the nativist activity leading up to the immigration restriction laws that stimulated the antiprejudice campaign. Liberal Americans, distressed by the tenor of public debate, seized on cultural gifts as an antidote to anti-immigrant sentiment. As passage of the National Origins Act sharply reduced the influx from southern and eastern Europe, it drained nativism of its urgency and force. The divisive debates over immigration policy gave way to a broader agenda. "To be sure, in 1924 we almost closed our doors to the immigrant, but we have only locked in our problem," activist Rachel Davis DuBois commented a decade later. "These people are here and they are not going to die out. There are too many millions of them. The problem now is to learn to live together in such harmony as will bring out the best in all of us and thus help to build a richer American culture."[7] In a sense, the passage of the restriction laws redirected debate from political to cultural terms, creating room for pluralism to take hold. As Bruno Lasker noted in 1928, there was a "growing sense of need for harmony between groups, now that immigration is shut down."[8] At the same time, black and Mexican migration patterns brought heightened interest in racial attitudes.

With the dramatic reduction of new arrivals, cultural gifts proponents could avoid the challenges that had confronted the settlement house workers of the Progressive Era, whose task had been to incorporate a stream of immigrants still wearing the clothes and customs of their European homelands. By the middle of the 1920s, with the exception of Mexicans in the Southwest, liberal activists were faced with few greenhorns whose ethnic identity was raw and visible. The immigrants they encountered were already adapting to American society, learning English and trying out American habits. Activists could offer a romanticized vision of ethnic cultures because these cultures were becoming more distant each year and no great influx of newcomers complicated their sentimental portrayal of Old World traditions. It was *because* of the success of nativist efforts that the notion of cultural gifts gained widespread acceptance.

At the same time, progressive trends in social science precipitated the crusade against prejudice. Of particular importance was the emerging scientific consensus on race. Liberal activists drew on Boasian anthropology to promote environmentalist understandings of race and culture and to dislodge theories of scientific racism in the popular imagination. As they celebrated the contributions of the various strains that made up American society, they popularized the concept of cultural relativism and argued that no race was inferior to another. Citing the recent work of social science experts, liberal thinkers explained that each group's characteristics emerged not from hereditary traits but rather from its social and cultural heritage.

The new science of the child also provided fertile ground for cultural gifts training. The emerging child study movement sharpened the view of childhood as a distinct time of life, giving rise to scientific study that emphasized children's special emotional and physical needs. The new ideal of childhood captured the imagination of the educated middle class, as reformers claimed that children offered the best hope for a future of racial understanding. "That is the old generation that does not know any better," a Philadelphia high school student remarked, in a discussion of black contributions to American life. "We are the new generation, and we must see that things are different."[9]

To be sure, the link between childhood and racial tolerance was not entirely new to the period after World War I. The notion of the malleable child originated with John Locke and found expression in earlier religious and sentimental literature. Abolitionist writings had targeted young people as most likely to accept the message of racial equality. But the scientific thrust of the post–World War I incarnation of this message invested it with particular urgency and force. Developments in social science—particularly behaviorist psychology—described childhood as *the* formative stage of life for adult personality. New ideas about race and childhood intersected in the then startling conclusion that racial prejudice was not innate, but rather was learned—and could be unlearned—in the early years of life.

The cultural gifts movement was closely linked to international education, which emerged at the same time and contributed to the movement's success. The experience of World War I galvanized efforts to prevent future wars. Peace activists promoted "world-thinking," determined to teach American youth about peoples around the globe in order to ensure a future of international harmony. A burst of educational programs established in the 1920s, part of what Akira Iriye has termed "cultural internationalism," aimed to improve world relations.[10] Many proponents of cultural gifts endorsed world citizenship as well and shared its pacifist orientation. Their analyses tied together international and domestic harmony, as they noted parallels between relations at home and abroad and targeted children as the best hope for new attitudes. Both racism and war, they argued, resulted from false assumptions of white superiority, which were used to justify the domination of other peoples. The solution was to develop respect for all nations and races: studying people in other lands would abolish war, just as learning about various groups within the country would resolve ethnoracial strife. As a culturally diverse nation, the United States could become a model for world democracy.

These advances gave rise to a new strand of liberalism that took shape along cultural lines. This liberalism had much in common with earlier Progressivism: both emphasized rational intervention and order, aiming to reconstruct society in the interest of democratic progress. Activists championed what Gary Gerstle terms the "civic nationalism" of twentieth-century America, as they promoted civil rights and democratic participation for all Americans, regardless of racial, ethnic, national, or religious background.[11] While many Progressives had emphasized Americanization and cultural conformity, the movement was capacious and variable; some left-leaning Progressives—including John Dewey, Jane Addams, and other settlement house workers—had advanced a notion of "immigrant gifts" that argued for the preservation of ethnic cultures as a way to strengthen American democracy. Post–World War I liberals built on this legacy as they directed their social engineering efforts at remedying the problems caused by urban diversity and racial prejudice.

What distinguished the liberalism of the 1920s was a new faith in social science as a vehicle of reform. Even as some liberals abandoned cultural reform in favor of economic reorganization, others found in science an inspiration for cultural renewal. A main thrust of Progressivism had been toward state regulation of corporate power; postwar activists, in contrast, crafted a campaign that involved little legislation or governmental control. Rather than thinking in explicitly political terms, they constructed a liberalism that looked to the scientific culture of the decade to correct the social order. The stunning new insights of social science offered a means to understand racial bigotry in rational terms. The maturation of such fields as psychology, sociology, and anthropology promised not only to analyze problems of ethnic diversity and prejudice but also to control them: the findings could inform educational programs, correct habits and attitudes, and guide people from bigotry to tolerance. Science, in other words, made prejudice an appropriate target for rational intervention. It was this scientific imprimatur that gave credibility and power to the cultural gifts vision and expanded it far beyond the settlement house world. Cultural gifts thus became instrumental to the reinvigoration of liberalism in the interwar years.[12]

In the mid-1920s, resistance to racial prejudice became an emblem of the modern mother or modern teacher, someone well informed on the theories of the day. Liberal members of the burgeoning middle class seized on pluralist ideas in order to be scientific and up to date. These were people who enjoyed prosperity and focused on personal development: professional educators and clergy, students who attended high school, and mothers who read child-rearing publications. The readers of *Parents' Magazine* or *Progressive Education* saw themselves as advanced, forward-thinking, cosmopolitan. Their acceptance of pluralism—like their embrace of Freudian theory, sex education, and new gender roles—came to symbolize the modern liberal spirit. As sociologist Ellsworth Faris, of the University of Chicago, said in 1929, "Freedom from prejudice is held to be the mark of a cultivated member of society."[13] Pluralism, in other words, came into fashion.

Education formed the heart of this work. Following John Dewey and the trend toward progressive education, activists expressed the liberal faith in the power of the schools to transform the social order. They understood prejudice as a problem of ignorance and misunderstanding that would be eradicated through information and proper conditioning. They were optimistic that they could foster appreciation by highlighting cultural achievements and contributions to American history. "What to do?" wrote R. B. Eleazar, a leader of the Commission on Interracial Cooperation, in a letter to southern teachers. "Just give folks the facts and trust them to draw right conclusions."[14]

Among the activists who served as conduits between academic and popular thought, Rachel Davis DuBois played a pivotal role. From 1924, when she initiated her assembly programs at Woodbury High School, until 1941, when she was pushed out of the Service Bureau for Intercultural Education, this indomitable figure was the visionary force behind the cultural gifts project, a tireless champion of pluralism who believed deeply in its promise for American life. A member of the Society of Friends, she brought passion and conviction to articulating a vision of an inclusive society that cherished cultural diversity and, simultaneously, to implementing that vision through pedagogical reforms. She explained her aim this way: "The fact that millions of Americans have their roots in varying cultures should promise a rich future. Rather than worry about the presence of people of Mexican background in the Southwest, of Oriental background on the Pacific Coast, or of Polish background in the Connecticut Valley, we should welcome and cherish the colorful diversity which the presence of such people makes possible."[15] DuBois devoted considerable skill and energy to establishing an institutional basis for antiprejudice education: she set up the first clearinghouse on the topic, developed curricular materials, published widely, and pioneered teacher training courses on intercultural relations. Her methodological and theoretical perspectives shaped this work to a large extent, and her career followed its arc.

While the cultural gifts arena was large, it did not encompass all progressive activists in the interwar period. It was distinct from the Chicago school, for instance, in its focus on educational programs for young people, although it did draw on the findings of Chicago social scientists. Nor was it allied with the Communist Party or the activists of the Cultural Front. It did not embrace the melting pot theory of assimilation, which some thinkers used to counter eugenic trends, nor did it refer explicitly to the work of the modernist writers and intellectuals of the period. Instead, the cultural gifts phenomenon drew liberal reformers who looked to science and education to rejuvenate American democratic institutions.

Immigrant and minority activists played an important role in shaping the course of antiprejudice campaigns, working alongside native-born liberals. These ethnic leaders had a strong stake in both integration and the maintenance of immigrant cultural traditions. Rachel Davis DuBois, who dated her ancestors' arrival in America to 1699, developed strong ties with such prominent immigrants as Louis Adamic, a journalist born in Slovenia, and educator Leonard Covello, who had spent his early years in Italy. She had close contact with Jews, including researcher Bruno Lasker and social worker Miriam Ephraim, who helped organize her school programs. Indeed, Jews played a particularly important role in cultural gifts work, especially members of the well-established German Jewish community, for example, Sidonie Gruenberg and her colleagues at the Child Study Association, the rabbis and lay leaders involved in the National Conference of Jews and Christians, and the philanthropists active in the American Jewish Committee. African American scholars and educators were other key figures: William Pickens, field secretary of the National Association for the Advancement of Colored People (NAACP), was a guest speaker in Rachel Davis DuBois's school programs; James Weldon Johnson served on her board; and W. E. B. Du Bois consulted with her for many years. Sociologist Charles S. Johnson, along with other black educators, participated in the Commission on Interracial Cooperation.

Many of these liberal thinkers were women; their traditional roles as teachers, mothers, and parent educators put them on the front lines of educational work with children and gave them vehicles to spread the cultural gifts perspective. Men dominated the ranks of social scientists but many of those who took the lead in implementing their ideas were women. Antiprejudice education provided a way for women to bring together their public and private roles, making political the work of raising and educating children. Rarely, however, did these activists directly call attention to gender as a factor in their work. And their analysis of cultural diversity did not consider women's particular contributions to the nation's history and to American life.

Why did white liberals care about dispelling prejudice? Their motivation emerged from genuine conviction and concern, as they were deeply disturbed by the tenor of nativist and racist rhetoric in the 1920s. Many had come of age in the Progressive movement and had absorbed its message of social responsibility. They were sympathetic to the peace movement that emerged in the aftermath of World War I. Some proponents, such as DuBois, were Quaker activists who drew on a tradition of concern for racial equality. Others, like Lasker, were immigrant Jews who had experienced prejudice and recognized their own stake in a pluralist society. For some native-born white Protestants, contact with members of minority groups had convinced them of the harm caused by bigotry.

These liberals were also concerned with the potential for disorder in a

heterogeneous nation. Like their more conservative counterparts, they feared a fracturing of American society; they, too, wanted to recreate a sense of community and shared values. Their fears increased in the context of the Great Depression, which heightened concern about social unrest and instability (particularly among middle-class white Americans), as it brought growing awareness of both economic deprivation and the influence of Marxist thought. It seemed critical to ameliorate the problems of racial prejudice in order to defuse the potential for disruption, violence, and crime.

In the interests of social cohesion, liberals preferred to channel— rather than suppress—ethnic difference. They embraced pluralism as a means to revitalization. In the midst of the economic crisis and the reinvigoration of political liberalism, the cultural gifts movement extended its institutional reach and deepened its analysis. Liberal activists increasingly made use of new forms of mass media, as they enlisted tactics of publicity and persuasion for the antiprejudice campaign. Popular magazines, radio programs, and motion pictures became vehicles for liberal intervention. The New Deal's spirit of experimentation, the progressive approach to solving social problems, and the recognition of ethnic minorities created a cultural environment in which antiprejudice education could flourish.[16]

At the same time, the rise of fascist regimes in Europe intensified the urgency of the antiprejudice cause. Observers feared that Nazism would find an entering wedge among white Americans convinced of their superiority over minorities and immigrants. This anxiety heightened the sense that the American political system depended on the inclusion of all its citizens. As the 1930s progressed, the stakes grew higher: in the context of the Nazi regime, racial prejudice and anti-Semitism appeared a threat to the American social order. The crusade for racial tolerance became a defense of American democracy itself.

The development of the cultural gifts movement demonstrates the continuities that linked the 1920s with the 1930s. The campaign against prejudice gained strength in the thirties, even as racist and nativist sentiment persisted in Father Charles Coughlin's anti-Semitic radio programs, antagonism toward Mexican immigrants, perpetuation of antiblack discrimination in New Deal programs, and the refusal to admit Jewish refugees from Europe. By the end of the 1930s, discussions of prejudice and tolerance had become well established in the public sphere, addressed with regularity in magazine articles, conferences, radio programs, and reports. Activists succeeded in gaining widespread support for cultural diversity. Their work was a significant contribution to the creation of an inclusive democracy and an expansive national culture.

Despite these accomplishments, the cultural gifts movement was plagued by important limitations. Even as liberal activists voiced allegiance to civic nationalism, they perpetuated a racialized way of thinking that ascribed particular qualities to certain groups and that included some more fully than others in the pluralist vision. These limitations help explain not only the movement's demise but also the broader course of twentieth-century American liberalism. For cultural gifts work, as for racial liberalism more generally, democratic universalism coexisted with racialist notions, forming a complex and sometimes contradictory understanding of American identity.[17]

Groups were encouraged to preserve and share only those traits deemed "socially valuable." Liberal educators highlighted the most cultured and successful members of each group: a black poet, a Japanese athlete, a foreign-born visitor who spoke beautiful English. They argued that the admirable qualities of these "ideal Americans" would inspire people to revise their acquired prejudices. Their notion of culture was limited to only those traits that appeared compatible with American values. This approach created stereotypes of its own, as it reinforced ethnic types and denied the complexity of cultural identity. It erased differences within groups and froze each culture in time. In a narrow reading of each group's traditions and beliefs, for example, Italians were emotional and musical; Jews excelled in science; Chinese were stoic, quiet, and patient. It was unclear how young people were to respond to individuals who did not match the nature assigned to each group—an impassive Italian, a Jew who struggled with math, or a volatile Chinese immigrant. Nor was it clear how they would approach ethnic Americans who did not boast such refined and cultured qualities. And where were they to place people of mixed ancestry or multiple affiliations?

The irony of the cultural gifts approach was that it perpetuated cultural stereotypes. To be sure, they were more positive than the ones they replaced. Even so, the pluralist model served to confine people to a particular cultural identity. Horace Kallen, the intellectual spokesperson for cultural pluralism, described America as a symphony orchestra in which each group played an instrument. It appeared that ancestry determined in which section a person would play. Kallen's imagined "federation" of cultural groups suggested the need to align with one of those groups in order to participate in civic life. In their quest to honor cultural contributions, interwar liberals overlooked the potential dangers of reinforcing ethnoracial categories and color lines.

A second significant limitation concerned the extent to which this movement focused on culture alone and failed to address fully the social and economic inequalities that also shaped race relations. Cultural liberalism was effective in regard to European immigrants, who were able to assume the identity of full Americans, but was ill equipped to address the circumstances of other groups. The particular blind spot was African Americans. Cultural gifts proponents downplayed the realities of segregation, political exclusion, economic oppression, and racial violence, and the kind of political activity that would be needed to correct these injustices.[18]

Links to international education facilitated the focus on culture. If internationalism helped animate the cultural gifts vision, it constrained it as well, for "world friendship" was easier to cultivate in the abstract than was interracial friendship in reality. Even as world-thinking bolstered the pluralist agenda, it diverted attention from structural problems closer to home. Proponents of world unity could cultivate international goodwill without having to confront pressing racial inequities in their own communities. To an extent, this orientation to international relations left unexamined the social order within the United States.

The avoidance of socioeconomic analysis and political activity reflected the anxiety about socialism and radicalism that emerged after World War I. The postwar Red Scare had raised suspicions about reforms that seemed "un-American." Fearful of being labeled radicals or communists, many liberals were careful not to discuss class divisions or to advocate collective action that would disrupt social relations. They phrased their goals in the language of American unity and democracy, speaking about cultural rather than social equality. This oversight suggests a distortion of social science findings. Throughout the interwar period, social scientists increasingly emphasized the institutional roots of prejudice. Many argued that children acquired racial attitudes from what they observed around them. Lasker, for instance, called attention to social exclusion, employment discrimination, residential and school segregation, and the denial of civil rights as important factors in shaping children's racial attitudes. The eradication of prejudice, he argued, required institutional reform.[19]

African American scholars, in particular, criticized the focus on individual attitudes. These thinkers situated the idea of cultural gifts in a larger socioeconomic framework that addressed the institutional roots of white racism and the unequal distribution of resources. They offered their own interpretations of the causes, effects, and remedies of prejudice. Charles Johnson at Fisk University argued that education should not only promote cultural appreciation but also teach children to recognize "the fact of an unequal economic struggle." His goals included awareness of both black contributions and "abstract considerations of social justice."[20] Johnson and his colleagues understood pluralism as a step on the path to integration and equality; their larger agenda encompassed political and economic parity and an end to racial segregation.

These weaknesses were not confined to the cultural gifts model; rather, they suggest shortcomings of American liberalism itself. In the interwar period, liberalism represented certain basic commitments: ideals of equal opportunity, freedom of expression, individualism, and social progress. Liberalism's approach was gradualist. Following John Dewey, it voiced faith in education and science, reason and debate as means to improve social conditions and solve social problems, and it emphasized the process of social planning, experimentation, cooperation, and agreement to bring about a more humane social order. In the urban industrial milieu, liberals looked to schools, voluntary organizations, and community agencies as the institutions best equipped to train citizens to exercise liberty, independence, and civil equality in a democratic society.

Racial prejudice and discrimination, which limited access to individual opportunity and social mobility, ran counter to these liberal principles, and so the promotion of racial tolerance and stable race relations became central to the liberal agenda in the twentieth century. Liberals embraced an ideology of common citizenship that advocated greater opportunity for minorities and the elimination of unjust discrimination. Their recognition of ethnic diversity as a mark of fairness created space for cultural pluralism. Their tremendous accomplishment was to extend the boundaries of citizenship as they incorporated diverse immigrants into American society, promoted religious tolerance, and fostered increased respect for the cultural achievements of African Americans.

But liberalism's confidence in the promise of equal opportunity did not fully address longstanding patterns of racism and discrimination. Although liberalism aimed to remove barriers to social mobility, its focus on individualism treated all groups on equal terms, failing to acknowledge that some faced more entrenched obstacles than others in their quest to join the common citizenry. It depicted America as a nation of immigrants who could succeed through individual effort. Liberalism assumed that once prejudicial attitudes were removed, all would enjoy ample opportunity, full access to American identity, and control of their own destinies. Class constraints appeared as temporary impediments; once the nation lived up to its promise of inclusiveness, inequalities would disappear. The promise of mobility and opportunity thus denied the very real limitations of material conditions. Because liberalism looked to the future rather than to the past, it neglected to take full account of the pernicious legacy of slavery and the failures of Reconstruction. Its emphasis on realistic objectives constrained more utopian or transformative goals. And in the era of Jim Crow, its refusal to challenge separate schools and public facilities implied that appreciation of racial diversity could be compatible with segregation.

These limitations ultimately led to the demise of the cultural gifts movement. The insistence on a narrow notion of group identity made the philosophy suspect by the eve of World War II, when developments overseas raised alarm over expressions of ethnic pride and national identity. In the late 1930s, as Americans worried about the possible incursion of Nazism into the United States, the attention to ethnic particularism came to seem dangerous and disruptive. It too closely mirrored developments in enemy countries and thus restricted the cultural gifts movement's appeal as a democratic alternative to fascism. Cultural gifts fell from favor among liberal thinkers, who now promoted "democratic citizenship" as a way to bolster American unity to fight the global war.

New interpretations of the origins of prejudice also challenged cultural gifts thinking. Social scientists came to argue that prejudice had deeper roots than simple ignorance or misinformation. They reconceptualized it as a problem of personality development rather than education—a psychological disease with complex origins. John Dollard, for example, described racial prejudice as an outlet for displaced aggression that took different forms in democracies and in authoritarian regimes. Scholars affiliated with the Institute for Social Research developed this theory more fully in the influential book *The Authoritarian Personality,* arguing that distinct personality types were drawn to intolerance and racial hostility.[21] Prejudice was thus transformed from ignorance to illness. This pathological interpretation suggested that new tactics were needed to address the psychological dynamics at work.

After the war, cultural gifts thinking seemed outdated, and ineffective at challenging the institutional problems of segregation and disfranchisement. Leaders in the burgeoning civil rights movement looked to new ways to address difference and inclusion in American life, new philosophies to meet the demands of black Americans as they sharpened their attack on state-sanctioned racism. The ethnic movements of the 1960s and 1970s—Black Power, Chicano activism, the American Indian Movement—also adopted more radical approaches to reconstructing society that looked beyond cultural appreciation and exchange. Cultural gifts faded from view, replaced by efforts to promote equality before the law, political franchise, and social mobility.

But the legacy of the cultural gifts movement has persisted through the years. Despite its failings, it had important effects on perceptions of ethnoracial difference. It shaped how Americans understood such essential matters as diversity, national allegiance, and democratic participation, while providing the rhetorical and institutional frameworks for later developments in American liberalism. Its central contention—that cultural difference could be a source of strength for the nation—reversed earlier assimilationist thinking and set the stage for inclusive notions of American identity. At its best, it insisted on unity as well as diversity, the particular and the universal, the pluralist and the cosmopolitan. As it brought together new ideas about social science, child development, and racial difference, the cultural gifts vision offered Americans a philosophy and a methodology for defending ethnoracial diversity. It represented a process of exchange in which groups would share traditions in order to create a larger, richer culture that would incorporate people from diverse backgrounds, encourage civic participation, and bring minorities into the democratic system. These innovations set the stage for what came to be called intercultural (and then multicultural) education. The focus on the child, as both the victim of prejudice and the hope for racial understanding, lasted throughout the century, emerging in the *Brown v. Board of Education* decision, the moral appeals of Martin Luther King Jr., and efforts to enlist support for work against racism through a focus on children's needs. Cultural gifts placed childhood at the heart of American racial liberalism—where it remains today.

The crusade against prejudice went under various names. By the end of the 1930s, it was known as "intercultural education" or "education for goodwill." In the 1940s, the field also was called "intergroup relations" or "human relations." I use the term "cultural gifts" to refer to the grassroots manifestations of racial liberalism in the interwar period. To describe the impulse in its broadest sense I employ the term "antiprejudice." Although this term defines the campaign by what it opposed rather than what it advanced, the implication seems appropriate: liberals were clear on what they were fighting *against,* but sometimes disagreed on what they were fighting *for.* Indeed, cultural gifts incorporated a range of ideologies. I call the campaign "antiprejudice" rather than "antiracist" to indicate that it was located in attitudes rather than institutions. Some liberals insisted on the need to dismantle the structural roots of white racism; this group included many social scientists, left-leaning activists, and African American thinkers. But their popularizers—the white liberals who disseminated pluralist ideas—tended to define the problem as racial prejudice itself.

My intention is neither to promote nor to refute multiculturalism as we know it today, but rather to uncover its history in all its complexity, ambiguity, and tension. Indeed, it is the contradictions—the profound insights mixed with the blind spots—that make this story so illuminating. By looking at the successes and failures of earlier educational programs, we can better analyze the strengths and limitations of our own efforts.

At the same time, this story illuminates larger and equally persistent themes in American intellectual and political life. Debates over the aims and methods of the cultural gifts movement—over difference and unity, individual and group identity, cultural persistence and integration—reflect enduring strains in liberal thought. Cultural gifts proponents of the interwar years engaged questions that lie at the heart of twentieth-century America: what it means to be an American; how to construct a unified identity from a diverse citizenry. They struggled to reconcile cultural differences with a common culture—a tension we still grapple with today.

1

Searching for the Origins of Prejudice

In 1925, a grandmother penned a letter to social researcher Bruno Lasker on the subject of children's racial attitudes. "I can just say one thing from experience," she wrote. "I do not think that race prejudice exists at all in children. It is wholly acquired." Her years as a parent, teacher, and missionary had convinced her that racial antipathy resulted not from instinct but from "training and environment." Under the auspices of a New York social research group called The Inquiry, Lasker had sent questionnaires to parents, teachers, social workers, and church leaders throughout the country, asking them to report incidents that illustrated the formation of racial attitudes. The aim was to investigate how those attitudes arose, developed, and might be changed. Lasker's findings, published in 1929 as *Race Attitudes in Children*, confirmed the grandmother's observations: children learned attitudes from their social environment, beginning with the home. Lasker detailed the development of racial attitudes at various ages and suggested ways to bring up children free from prejudice.[1]

Lasker's study emerged from a transformation in the 1920s in scientific ideas about the origins of racial prejudice. Two intellectual developments were critical to this process: the emergence of cultural relativism began to dismantle theories of scientific racism, and a new science of the child developed insights from behaviorist psychology. While earlier social science had understood prejudice as an instinctive—and immutable—reaction to difference, behaviorism explained that attitudes, like other habits, were subject to modification. Racial prejudices were learned in the first years of life and could be unlearned then as well, and replaced with sympathy and understanding. Children could be trained to practice tolerance, just as they could be trained to eat or sleep on schedule. By locating racial relations in the realm of attitudes, progressive social scientists provided an optimistic blueprint for change. Cultural relativism, with its insistence on the equal status of racial groups, provided the reason to instill tolerance; behaviorist psychology offered a method.

While social researchers provided the intellectual framework, liberal activists in the 1920s popularized the new research for a broad audience and used it to implement cultural gifts education. But they distorted some of the findings, frequently offering a simplified version that omitted important elements of the research. Lasker's work, for instance, emphasized the impact of racial segregation and social exclusion on the conditioning process. He insisted that since children's attitudes reflected the structure of race relations, social reform needed to accompany efforts to teach tolerance. The educators and activists who drew on his work tended to ignore this critique of social institutions, offering an incomplete reading of the new scientific consensus: the eradication of prejudices, they explained, simply required a shift in how children were trained.

This selective reading of social research minimized the legal, social, and economic barriers that Lasker and others identified as critical to the formation of prejudice. In the short term, it gained support for the cultural gifts approach, for it made tolerance seem easily attainable. In the long run, however, it obscured racial divisions. The interpretations voiced by liberal activists proved effective in altering attitudes toward European immigrant groups, but less successful at addressing the deeply rooted discrimination black Americans and other racial minorities experienced. As educational leaders interpreted social science research, they both advanced and limited the effectiveness of the cultural gifts campaign.

New Trends in Science

Cultural gifts had a history that reached back to the nineteenth century, when the theory of romantic racialism (historian George M. Frederickson's term) celebrated human diversity. This theory took inspiration from German philosopher Johann Gottfried von Herder, who had argued in the late eighteenth century that each cultural or national group manifested unique qualities. In antebellum America, some white antislavery activists insisted that differences between blacks and whites did not in-dicate inferiority, for elements of black character were praiseworthy, and some even suggested that blacks made up the superior race. While more benevolent than dominant racist theories, the affirmation of hereditary racial difference had dangerous implications: at best it fostered paternal-ism, and at worst it justified unequal treatment and slavery. A version of romantic racialism marked an 1887 study by Edward Blyden, a black scholar born in the West Indies, who asserted that white and African races were "distinct but equal," endowed through heredity with "pecu-liar gifts." Romantic racialism reappeared in the Harlem Renaissance of the 1920s, when white patrons celebrated the supposedly primitive and exotic temperament that made blacks "naturally" artistic and passion-ate.[2] The cultural gifts philosophy departed from this racialist thought, as it insisted that differences were due to environmental rather than hereditary factors. Cultural gifts advocates disputed the notion of fixed races and proposed instead that divisions were culturally determined, explaining that each group's characteristics emerged from its particular social and cultural heritage.

The cultural gifts approach had important antecedents in the Progres-sive Era as well, when reformers articulated the notion of cultural ap-preciation. In a speech to the National Education Association in 1902, John Dewey lamented the process through which children of immi-grants lost their native traditions in music, art, and literature. "They do not get complete initiation into the customs of their new country, and so are frequently left floating and unstable between the two," he worried. "They even learn to despise the dress, bearing, habits, language, and be-liefs of their parents—many of which have more substance and worth than the superficial putting on of newly adopted habits." Dewey hoped that the schools would introduce children to American institutions without depriving them of the culture of their parents. During the same period, the International Institute movement, an educational program for foreign-born adults, encouraged appreciation for immigrant cultures among children of the foreign-born.[3]

Settlement house leaders like Jane Addams advanced a theory of "im-migrant gifts" that praised cultural contributions to American life. At Hull House in Chicago, Addams became disturbed by indications that immigrant parents "so often lost their hold upon their Americanized children." Opposed to forced assimilation that stripped immigrants of their traditions, and concerned about the effects of too-rapid acculturation, she thought these trends could be counteracted by educational enterprises, which, she said, "should build a bridge between European and American experiences in such wise as to give them both more meaning and a sense of relation." Her Labor Museum invited parents to demonstrate their skills and folklore to their American-born children, showing "that immigrant colonies might yield to our American life something very valuable, if their resources were intelligently studied and developed." Addams and her colleagues hoped that such recognition would prevent family disintegration and ease adjustment to American society while reducing tensions among groups. At a summer school at Denison House in Boston, "the second primary pupils studied the art and home life of the Chinese and Japanese," its leaders reported in 1899. "The reason for this was the animosity which has at times been displayed in this neighborhood toward the Chinese. It is believed that a genuine kindliness of feeling was aroused."[4]

New developments in social science distinguished the cultural gifts model from its predecessors in the Progressive Era. While cultural gifts had much in common with the earlier impulse, its scientific basis gave it far greater reach than Addams and her cohort had achieved. The progressive thrust of anthropology, sociology, and psychology first became apparent around the turn of the century, but only gained visibility beyond academic circles after World War I. In the 1920s, liberal activists used the new science to explain how racial attitudes were acquired and modified. Working in venues far from the settlements, they promoted appreciation for immigrant cultures, among children not only of foreign-born but also of native-born parents—citing research findings to make a place for their work in homes, schools, and churches.

The new science of the child lent credibility to the crusade for tolerance in the 1920s. The twentieth century sharpened the view of childhood as a distinct time of life, giving rise to scientific study that emphasized children's special emotional and physical needs. Childhood was seen as a time to play rather than work, an extended period deserving of special protection. Children came to hold emotional value for parents, who lavished attention on them in the increasingly child-centered family. Not all children received such care, of course, but the new ideal of childhood captured the public imagination of the educated middle class. Reformers, who claimed that children suffered most from urban industrial conditions and offered the best hope for redemption, targeted young people as most likely to escape poverty and prejudice. In the first decades of the century, their efforts resulted in expanded state protection of children.[5]

Child science emerged alongside another new development in social science: a progressive orientation that stressed environmental over biological explanations of ethnoracial difference. In the years after World War I, researchers began to challenge assumptions about racial superiority, including the notion that whites possessed greater innate intelligence than blacks. This egalitarian perspective was indebted to the work of Franz Boas, the founder of American cultural anthropology. Beginning in the 1890s, Boas attacked the racial determinism that dominated social science and seemed to justify racial prejudice. In an era that favored rapid and forceful assimilation of immigrants, Boas opposed eugenics, nativism, and the use of intelligence tests to measure group capacities. While the nation tolerated segregation and antiblack violence, Boas

Children at the Bailly Branch of the Gary Public Library, Indiana. The Bailly Branch also housed the offices of the International Institute, an agency that assisted new immigrants. (Calumet Regional Archives, Indiana University Northwest)

argued forcefully against the concept of black inferiority, asserting that racial differences were culturally determined rather than hereditary and absolute. His notion of cultural relativism stressed the contributions that groups made to American life and undermined the perception that prejudices were innate. "According to Boas the fundamental reaction of two persons of different races upon meeting one another is friendly curiosity," one sociologist reported. "There is no such thing as a 'race instinct' among human beings."[6]

From posts at Columbia University and the American Museum of Natural History in New York, Boas exerted enormous influence over American social science. His ideas initially were confined to academic circles, but by the 1920s they shaped popular understandings of race and culture. Over the course of a long career, Boas trained such cultural commentators as Ruth Benedict and Margaret Mead, influenced the research agendas of varied disciplines, and reached the wider public through lectures and articles for popular publications. He also took action on behalf of black civil rights when he supported the NAACP and spoke publicly for equal opportunity. A German Jew who had immigrated to the United States in the 1880s, Boas encountered anti-Semitism both in Germany and in his new home, an experience that made him sensitive to antiblack prejudice. Like Boas, many progressive thinkers on race were Jews of German origin who realized that cultural relativism offered support for a pluralist society. Boasian theory did not go unchallenged, but its insights shaped understandings of race for a generation of progressive social scientists and reformers.[7]

Black scholars also played an important role in the emerging liberal consensus on race. W. E. B. Du Bois's historical and sociological studies of African American life, the first of which were published at the turn of the century, situated racial inequalities in the context of American slavery and its aftermath. Du Bois believed that the experience of black Americans offered insights for understanding race and culture. As an activist as well as intellectual, he became the preeminent spokesperson for black equality and helped found the NAACP. He advanced a romantic racialism that awarded blacks a special place in American life. In his 1897 essay "The Conservation of Races," Du Bois drew on Herder to assign particular qualities to certain races. He anticipated the cultural gifts idea when he argued that the black race made important contributions to world history and American civilization. He praised the "wonderful possibilities of culture" and the "stalwart originality" of black Americans. "We are that people whose subtle sense of song has given America its only American music, its only American fairy tales, its only touch of pathos and humor amid its mad money-getting plutocracy," he proclaimed. Black people "have a contribution to make to civilization and humanity, which no other race can make." Whites and blacks should "develop side by side in peace and mutual happiness, the peculiar contribution which each has to make to the culture of their common country." In *The Souls of Black Folk* (1903) he described black music as "the singular spiritual heritage of the nation and the greatest gift of the Negro people."[8]

Du Bois further developed his romantic pluralism in *The Gift of Black Folk*, published in 1924, in which he argued that "the American Negro is and has been a distinct asset to this country and has brought a contribution without which America could not have been." Chapters detailed black contributions to exploration, labor, military defense, music, art, literature, and democracy. To Du Bois, the most powerful gift was "the peculiar spiritual quality which the Negro has injected into American life and civilization." This characteristic appeared in "a sensuous, tropical love of life" and "intense sensitiveness to spiritual values." While Du Bois did not spell out to what extent he saw these qualities as inherited or culturally determined, he affirmed that "the fine sweet spirit of black folk" had been a central influence on America.[9] In the 1920s and 1930s, as increasing numbers of blacks entered the social science professions, they followed the lead of Du Bois in producing studies of black life and protesting the racial inequalities they documented. Such prominent figures as Charles S. Johnson and E. Franklin Frazier joined their northern white colleagues in shaping the new social science orientation toward black progress, integration, and pluralism.

The Rise of Behaviorism

Joseph C. Carroll, a professor at the historically black Wilberforce University and a former pastor, recalled that as a child he had played with white children in his New Jersey hometown, "and there was no thought of color, or racial discrimination, in our youthful minds." But when he returned as an adult, the same people treated him as a stranger. Even in southern cities, Carroll noted in 1927, "I see white and colored children playing in the streets together and all are happy." What happened, he asked, to make them part ways? Carroll rejected the notion of a "natural antipathy" toward those with different skin color. Instead, he explained antiblack prejudice as the result of systematic training on the part of white parents, for "the same white boy that plays in the streets with the colored boy by day may be taken on his mother's lap by night" and told falsehoods about his black neighbors.[10]

Carroll's conclusions repudiated earlier social scientific thought. In the first two decades of the century, social scientists had understood racial antipathies as an innate reaction to difference. G. Stanley Hall, the first promoter of the scientific study of the child, had advanced an "instinct psychology" that stressed the role of natural impulses.[11] Following Hall, most researchers agreed that such antipathies were inevitable and ineradicable. William I. Thomas of the University of Chicago explained in 1904, that race prejudice was an "instinctive reaction" to the appearance of unfamiliar people. "It cannot be reasoned with, because, like the other instincts, it originated before deliberative brain centers were developed, and is not to any great extent under their control." In 1908 another scholar, Alfred Holt Stone, delivered a paper to the American Sociological Society in which he described race prejudice as "a natural contrariety" that "involves an instinctive feeling of dislike, distaste, or repugnance." In his textbook *The Principles of Sociology*, Franklin Giddings of Columbia explained: "Our conduct toward those whom we feel to be most like ourselves is instinctively and rationally different from our conduct toward others, whom we believe to be less like ourselves."[12]

The rejection of the instinct theory was precipitated by the ascendance of behaviorist psychology. Behaviorism, the best-known child-rearing theory of the 1920s, was most closely associated with John Broadus Watson, its chief promoter. Watson began publishing in the 1910s while a professor at Johns Hopkins, offering a complex view of the interaction between heredity and environment in human behavior. In 1924, he reached a wide audience with *Behaviorism*, a book for general readers. By then an extreme environmentalist, Watson claimed that all human behavior resulted from conditioned responses to external stimuli. "Everything we have been in the habit of calling an 'instinct' today is a result largely of training—belongs to man's *learned behavior*," he insisted.[13]

Watson was interested in the process of conditioning, or habit formation, through which an individual learned response patterns. This process began in infancy, as traits that appeared to be instinctive were actually acquired in the first days of life. Character was thus fixed at a very early age. "In a way the whole of behaviorism is but an expression of the fact that infancy and childhood slant our adult personalities," he wrote. "These carry-overs are the most serious handicaps to a healthy personality." In experiments, he was able to condition a baby to fear a small animal and then to remove such fears. Verbal organization—reading stories about rabbits, playing with toy animals—did not mitigate the child's fears. What did was bringing the cage closer each day. "Our emotional life grows and develops like our other *sets of habits*," he concluded. While this emphasis on the first years of life had much in common with psychoanalysis, Watson took pains to distance himself from Freud. He dismissed the notion of the unconscious as unscientific and declared psychoanalysis "doubtful and passing."[14]

Watson's extreme environmentalism negated racial difference and eugenic thinking. Parents passed to children pigmentation of the skin, he wrote, but little else. "We have no sure evidence of inferiority in the negro race," Watson asserted, for differences were due to social conditions rather than genetic traits. He noted that "*racial* habit systems are bred into people" along with other family habits. In an often-quoted comment, he boasted: "Give me a dozen healthy infants, well-formed, and my own specified world to bring them up in and I'll guarantee to take any one at random and train him to become any type of specialist I might select—doctor, lawyer, artist, merchant-chief, and yes, even beggar-man and thief, regardless of his talents, penchants, tendencies, abilities, vocations, and race of his ancestors." A utopian at heart, Watson pictured a democratic world in which every newborn child would receive the same careful training, its emotional reactions scientifically controlled to meet the needs of society. He promised great progress. Would not each generation in turn, he asked, "bring up their children in a still more scientific way, until the world finally becomes a place fit for human habitation?"[15]

Watson applied the principles of behaviorism to the "science" of parenthood. He portrayed parents as engineers who could manipulate children like machines. In *Psychological Care of Infant and Child*, a best-selling manual published in 1928, he described the conclusions he had drawn from his experiments. "Children are made not born," he asserted. "There are no instincts. We build in at an early age everything that is later to appear." Given this tabula rasa, the task was to instill proper habits to make children self-controlled, independent, polite, and neat—ready for the adult world. Since a child's emotional life plan was set early, Watson prescribed strict schedules for eating, sleeping, and bathing, and recommended that toilet training begin when a baby was three to five weeks old. Lenient parents carried the blame for their children's failures. By the time a child turned three, "the parents have already determined for him whether he is to grow into a happy person, wholesome and good-natured, whether he is to be a whining, vindictive, over-bearing slave driver, or one whose every move in life is definitely controlled by fear." Poor parenting underlay social ills like poverty and delinquency.[16]

Mothers in particular often failed in their responsibilities. Watson's manual was in part a diatribe against motherhood and its pleasures, famously dedicated to "the first mother who brings up a happy child." In a chapter on "the dangers of too much mother love," Watson warned that affection made children dependent and demanding. He advised mothers not to pick up crying babies and to offer children handshakes rather than hugs and kisses. Excessive coddling was a dangerous instrument, "which may inflict a never healing wound, a wound which may make infancy unhappy, adolescence a nightmare, an instrument which may wreck your adult son or daughter's vocational future and their chances for marital happiness."[17]

Behaviorism formed the dominant theme in child-rearing literature in the twenties and thirties. Watson lectured widely and reached the general public through articles in popular magazines. Other psychologists and child development experts also disseminated behaviorist theory in less extreme form. Behaviorism influenced child study groups and the 1929 edition of *Infant Care,* the pamphlet distributed across the country by the federal Children's Bureau. The influence of behaviorism faded only with the emergence of more permissive ideas in the late 1930s and early 1940s, due in part to the association of authoritarian methods with fascist politics.[18]

Some child-rearing experts rejected behaviorism as overly mechanical and inflexible. Competing models of child development continued to flourish: Watson coexisted with Dewey, who encouraged children's curiosity and individuality, and with Freud, who criticized repression of children. Nor is it clear that most parents actually followed behaviorist advice. Historian Julia Grant has found that some parents, wanting to provide scientific and up-to-date care, followed Watson's guidelines as well as they could. But others disagreed with expert advice when it conflicted with their inclination or experience. They resisted ideas they found too extreme, or they combined behaviorist notions with other developmental theories. Mothers continued to pick up their crying babies, to kiss them when they fell, and to feed them when they were hungry.[19]

To historians, behaviorism has appeared as a rigid, overly authoritative, joyless philosophy of child rearing. Watson has received extensive criticism for having a mechanistic view of human nature that left little room for individuality, pleasure, or affection.[20] But behaviorism also carried more complicated implications, for its extreme environmentalism made it compatible with progressive ideas on race. Liberal thinkers drew on behaviorism to explain the origins of racial prejudice. They described attitudes as habits that were conditioned at an early age—and that could be unconditioned, as Watson had shown. If race prejudice developed in childhood, then it could be modified in the early years as well. Behaviorism was therefore repressive in its prescriptions but not in its epistemology. It added a scientific cast to the long-held image of children as the most redeemable members of American society. Cultural relativism provided the vision of a tolerant society, while habit training explained how to bring it about. Liberal thinkers, in other words, employed Watsonian means for Boasian ends.

In the 1920s, social scientists adapted Watson's analysis to the study of racial attitudes. "Is race prejudice innate or acquired?" asked Kelly Miller, a sociologist at Howard University, who made clear that a great deal was at stake: if racial antipathy were indeed instinctive, then it would call into question the claims of Christianity and democracy. But if it were acquired, "then we may reasonably hope that it will be ameliorated, mollified, modified, and finally removed." To answer his question, Miller turned to the theory of habit training. He rejected the idea of prejudice as "innate, inescapable, and everlasting"—a concept he associated with the Ku Klux Klan—and instead described it as "a stimulated passion," the outgrowth of particular circumstances: "any form of prejudice can easily be instilled in the minds of the young." Miller argued that white parents in the South taught their children to feel superior, an instruction "reinforced by social environment." Like Watson, Miller noted that this training took place so early that it was often mistaken for an innate characteristic: "Such insistent and persistent preaching is calculated to give the acquired prejudice the stubbornness and strength of instinct."[21]

In the second half of the 1920s, the growing fields of sociology and psychology produced a wave of studies promoting the new view of the acquisition of attitudes. At the University of Chicago, Robert Park argued that race prejudice was a reaction against a perceived threat to social status, and Ellsworth Faris called it "a social phenomenon with nothing in the organic or innate constitution of man that offers any explanation."[22] Researchers now agreed that children were born free from prejudice, that they acquired it at an early age, and that attitudes carried over to adult life. As evidence, they noted the absence of race consciousness in young children. Typical was a sociologist's assertion that "children of different colors play together and grow up together without any signs of race or color friction. When they do manifest unfriendly feelings toward each other such feelings can always be traced to the words and acts of older people." This example became a staple of the social science literature.[23]

Emory S. Bogardus, a sociologist at the University of Southern California, editor of the *Journal of Applied Sociology,* and a former student of Park, developed a "social distance scale" to measure a subject's attitudes toward various groups. Prejudices, Bogardus argued, originated from direct or derivative experiences, as with the child who "accepted uncritically the biases of parents and other elders" toward groups the child did not know. Family members "passed on" antipathies through racial insults, disapproval of playmates, or suggestions of superiority. In the nature-nurture debate over the origins of prejudice, social science now came down squarely on the side of nurture. In 1935, a literature review summed up the new consensus: "Observers agree that children learn social antagonisms at an early age, in fact, as soon as they are able to mirror back their social environment."[24]

Race Attitudes in Children

The most extensive analysis of the origins of prejudice came from Bruno Lasker. A German-born Jew like Boas, Lasker immigrated to the United States in 1914. In New York, he joined The Inquiry, the social problems organization, which had published a guide to the study of race relationsentitled *And Who Is My Neighbor?* By 1930, The Inquiry had sponsored fourteen publications that addressed differences in race, religion, class, or nationality. Lasker edited a collection that year entitled *Jewish Experiences in America: Suggestions for the Study of Jewish Relations with Non-Jews,* which included chapters by liberal thinkers Horace Kallen and Mordecai Kaplan, as well as sociologist Julius Drachsler, whose work on prejudices as "socially conditioned reactions" influenced Lasker's thinking.[25] Lasker also wrote widely on immigration and international relations. A racial liberal in the Boasian tradition, he valued the "distinctive folkways and ideals" of various groups and worried about a "cultural vandalism" that eroded "the rich soils of racial and national inheritance."[26]

Lasker's interest in children's attitudes emerged from *And Who Is My Neighbor?* Readers of that book requested solutions to counteract prejudices, which he found difficult to provide without understanding how attitudes came into being. Abby Rockefeller, an Inquiry funder, urged further study after observing that her sons picked up negative views even at the progressive Lincoln School in New York. "Such things they say!" she exclaimed at an Inquiry meeting, Lasker recalled. "Can't we do something about it?" In response, Lasker established in 1925 the Inquiry's Committee on Children and Race Prejudice, whose members included educational experts, social scientists, and progressive teachers, to plan a new study. He sent eight hundred questionnaires to mothers clubs, church groups, teachers, settlement houses, and social workers, asking them to respond to questions on the expression, origins, and effects of children's attitudes, to recount illustrative incidents, and to describe problems faced by parents and educators. By asking participants to comment on their own observations and experiences, the investigation would itself function as "an educational undertaking," a means to "open their minds to things they have never given attention to."[27]

Lasker's method challenged the faith in objective tests that many social scientists voiced. At the first meeting of the committee, he came into conflict with Daniel Kulp of Teachers College, who complained that gathering personal accounts would not be scientifically valuable. Several years later, Lasker affirmed "the cooperative nature of the study and its amateur character." Lasker was aware of recent social science work—he suggested that a graduate student draft an overview "of all that the newer psychology has to teach us about children's attitudes in general"— but he acknowledged "private doubts" about the validity of those findings. He advised a fellow researcher, Rose Zeligs, "to avoid all the usual errors of interpretation which make unreliable almost all material that has been collected by means of tests."[28]

In response to his queries, Lasker received reports from churchwomen in New Jersey, settlement workers in Kentucky, and teachers in California, among others, commenting on children of various backgrounds in many areas of the country. He analyzed these observations and began promoting his conclusions through magazine articles, addresses, and radio talks. In one speech, for instance, he declared that in many homes and churches, "children are quite unconsciously taught that their group, their race, their nationality, their religious denomination, is far superior to all others." He hoped that this work would reform race relations. He had come to believe "that you can't change attitudes in grown-up people. You must begin with children."[29]

Lasker employed the broad definition of "race" that was current at the time. He explained to the members of his committee, who were familiar with scientific debates over the term: "We never mean race; we put 'race' in quotation marks for we really mean race and national groups."[30] His examples, taken from around the country, discussed views of African Americans, European immigrants, and Jews, as well as Chinese, Japanese, and Mexican immigrants. Although Lasker expressed concern for minority children's experience, his focus was on the attitudes of white children. In his book *Jewish Experiences in America* he defended this emphasis, explaining that the dominant majority held greater power to determine relationships among social groups.[31]

Lasker's study resulted in *Race Attitudes in Children,* a nearly four-hundred-page volume published in 1929 which he described as a source book, a guide to class study and group discussion, and the first comprehensive survey of the topic. The book championed the theory that prejudice was learned, arguing that children were "born democrats." Although uncomfortable with Watson's prescriptions, Lasker accepted his general analysis. He cited Watson's claim in *Behaviorism,* that what people assumed to be innate "has really been acquired—and sometimes quite painfully—in the early years of life." Lasker noted that the erroneous belief in instinct still prevailed among parents and teachers (including many who responded to his questionnaire) and warned that it could lead to faulty educational practices. Lasker's correspondents reported recognition of racial differences in children as young as five. They detailed the development of attitudes, noting expressions of fear, ridicule, or rivalry in various age groups. In this process of reinforcement, "the grooves worn into the receptive mind" created habits of response. "What children feel and think about those of other national and racial groups represents for the most part what they have learned about them."[32]

To Lasker, the process of social conditioning was complex—far more so than in Watson's schema. Lasker had heard Julius Drachsler speculate that the traditions of a group influenced children's attitudes more than their own personal experience. Lasker agreed. Children absorbed racial attitudes from diverse sources—from home, school, church, neighborhood, from textbooks and sermons, from adults and other children. The cumulative pressure constituted a "staggering weight of prejudices" that burdened the rising generation. Even positive contact with members of other racial groups, he suspected, could not counteract the negative messages a child received from his or her environment. Some of Lasker's correspondents reported that early favorable experiences had fostered lifelong sympathy for other races. But in other cases, people discounted personal encounters in favor of prejudiced opinions. Early social conditioning was "likely to outlast all memories of personal experience to the contrary."[33]

Since it was the social environment that had the strongest effect, Lasker was skeptical of attempts to teach attitudes directly "as a technical problem for pedagogues." Early impressions carried emotional weight and could not be dislodged through mere reasoning, he warned in the *Woman's Press,* for interracial understanding "is not simply a matter of presenting information or arguments." More important was "indirect or 'attendant' learning." What children saw made a greater impression than what they were explicitly taught, and when words and actions conflicted, children gave greater credence to actions. Lasker believed that "children learn most of all through the observation of adult attitudes in circumstances when grown-ups are least conscious of being studied." Civics classes or Bible lessons were ineffective if what they taught was in obvious contrast to adult behavior, for children noticed the discrepancies. "With modern lack of respect, they call us older people hypocrites."[34]

Lasker thus saw danger in offering simple "action-solutions" that promised to resolve the problems he had identified. Instead he advocated a broad and humanistic education that would teach children to analyze conflicting messages and come to their own conclusions. He encouraged flexibility, open-mindedness, and ethical consideration. Even when adults differed from prevailing attitudes in the community, they should explain how and why those attitudes arose, Lasker wrote, moving far beyond Watsonian ideas about social conditioning. "Our object will be to make young people understand and evaluate, not off-hand accept or reject, existing attitudes toward classes, races and nationalities. Educationally, our whole effort will have failed if they merely endorse our own ideals and assume a priggish 'holier-than-thou' attitude toward those who do not happen to share them."[35]

The aim was not to control the child's mind, but to prevent "premature ruts of habit." Here Lasker challenged behaviorist thinking, as he argued that broad training would free the child "from that fetter of habit formation which, under the old, mistaken form of education, gave the child no real choice at all," and instead would give children skills to observe and think for themselves. Children taught to analyze conflicting attitudes would gain an "enlarged mental outlook" to appreciate other traditions without losing respect for their own. In fact, there would be little need to address race attitudes directly. "It is method, not subject matter, that counts." Lasker refused to offer concrete suggestions for plays, pageants, or exhibitions to instill race tolerance, an omission he recognized might disappoint some readers. "But where the foundation work in the earlier years has been good, no such props ought to be needed," he reassured readers. Rather than seek "cut and dried schemes," they should search for ways to "enlarge the horizon" of the young person. An example from a radio talk illustrated this approach: "It is more to be desired that little Bill shall learn to be cooperative in thought and deed while still in the kindergarten than that he should learn favorable facts about the Chinese." Lasker later explained that good elementary education "keeps open the natural curiosity of children," predisposing them to tolerance and cooperation.[36]

Lasker's analysis—which presaged what today we might call critical thinking—included a call for democratic inclusion, "a sincere desire to build up out of the varied ingredients of our national life an integrated commonwealth in which no smallest legitimate interest is overlooked." The aim was lofty: "we want to see our children sensitive to the demands of justice in all dealings between individuals and groups, irrespective of the place they occupy in our social life."[37] To seek this goal, Lasker looked beyond verbal training to consider the impact of exclusion and social ostracism. His questionnaire yielded illustrations of "how race segregation carries its own lesson for children of the dominant group," a lesson absorbed even without adult comment. The white child observed adult behavior: "He notices that people of dark skin are 'jim-crowed' or that they occupy a different part of the town," Lasker explained. "He becomes aware of the fact that immigrants do not belong to his church, that the clerks in his father's office all talk good English and wear good clothes, while the men in the mill speak broken English and wear dirty clothes." Segregation marked a family's social relations as well. The child "notices that at the summer hotel there are no Jews, that the well-dressed people who call on his mother do not include Mexicans (if he lives in the South-West) or Portuguese (if he lives in the North-East). He finds that the grown-up people in his set avoid calling certain kinds of people 'Mister' or avoid sitting next to them on the street car." Through these many subtle influences, the child learned that social status depended on race and nationality, and came to see that association as "permanent, inevitable," and divinely planned.[38]

These social messages were especially strong regarding African Americans. The white child learned from observation that African Americans did not "belong," that they were considered inferior. "He knows this from the simple fact that he does not meet colored people in the same circumstances in which he meets others," Lasker explained. "They do not call; they are not called upon. They do not teach at school, work in father's office or sell goods over the counter. They may serve food at a restaurant but are never seen sitting there consuming it. They do not live in any street where he plays or his mother visits. Of course, they must be different." If adults truly believed in equal citizenship, they would teach through example: "we would not exclude colored people from our churches; we should certainly not discriminate against race in public employment, and we should behave with equal courtesy to persons of every kind in every public or semi-public place, whether it be a streetcar, or a department store, or a public park."[39]

Segregation in the schools made a particularly powerful impression on young minds. "For the great majority of American children the fact that children of another color do not go to the same school as they do is a lesson which is ineradicable if it extends through the whole period of school attendance," Lasker wrote. Children were aware of the "inconsistency between profession and practice" that characterized segregated schools, as in the South's separation of black and white children or California's policy toward Japanese and Chinese students. Disparities in school funding reinforced the impression that children from certain groups were not worth educating. Lasker took pains to highlight the deep inequities in public school systems, detailing gaps in teacher training and salaries, school equipment, and educational provisions. He adamantly opposed permanent separation by race, citing alarms over "the danger of an American class stratification with the aid of the public schools." In a radio talk, he suggested the positive message that school reform would send. Even if a white child only encountered African Americans in his neighborhood in the role of servants, "the presence at school of colored children from better homes and, perhaps, even of a colored teacher, will correct his first erroneous—though perfectly natural—assumption that color and menial position *always* go together." To foster democratic ideals, the organization of the school was as important as the content of its lessons.[40]

Lasker's study inspired further research into the theory of the learned nature of prejudice. Rather than soliciting observations from adults, other social scientists attempted to measure attitudes in children themselves. When Ralph Minard of the University of Iowa gave questionnaires to 1,352 Iowa public school students in grades 7–12, most of whom were white and Protestant, he noted the "conditioning forces" of home and school. Minard found that as children grew older, their rational judgment became more tolerant but their personal feelings did not—a contradiction that reflected the development of both a higher thought process and an awareness of social standards. He found more prejudice in the cities, which he attributed to economic divisions and residential segregation, and speculated that prejudice would lessen under equalized social conditions. Minard stressed the early fixity of attitudes. Even in rural Iowa, racial attitudes "are already fairly well defined by the seventh grade." Antiprejudice efforts should be centered in the elementary and junior high schools, he concluded, since it was doubtful whether high school programs could free students from already-acquired prejudices.[41]

Rose Zeligs came to similar conclusions about the fixity of children's attitudes. A teacher and graduate student in education, Zeligs conducted studies with two hundred sixth-grade children at her school, located in a residential area of Cincinnati with a large Jewish population. She consulted with Lasker as she began her research.[42] She administered a questionnaire—a version of Bogardus's "social distance scale"—that asked the children to indicate whether they were willing to have a member of various races as "Cousin, Chum, Roommate, Playmate, Neighbor, Classmate, Schoolmate." She also interviewed fifteen students and gave an association test, reporting her findings in a series of articles in *Sociology and Social Research*. "Conditioning the child to the cultural patterns of his group begins with his birth and continues though life," she wrote in a Watsonian vein. "Racial prejudices, often the results of stereotypes communicated to the child through his social contacts, are built up before he finds out for himself what the facts are."[43]

Zeligs found results similar to Minard's: at age twelve, the children had already acquired definite racial sentiments that closely resembled those of adults. Children were most tolerant of those who appeared like them in color, language, or culture. Acceptance varied according to the intimacy of the relationships—that is, children were more likely to accept members of other groups as schoolmates than as cousins—but did not vary greatly among the children, indicating that racial attitudes were set for the school group as a whole. When Zeligs conducted follow-up studies, she found little difference from year to year, proof that racial attitudes were formed in early childhood and remained relatively unchanged. Zeligs was critical of existing training, which offered children little guidance in developing greater tolerance.[44]

The new understanding of prejudice had far-reaching implications: children could also be taught sympathy for other racial and ethnic groups. Antipathies that were learned in early life could also be unlearned, or prevented, then. To be effective, such habit training had to occur in the formative years. Lasker was optimistic that wrong attitudes might be modified "*in childhood*—and wherever possible at the very time of their first appearance or observation"—but would be more difficult to dispel after that. Later efforts could not make up for early prejudicial teachings, since it was difficult to smooth out "the ruts cut into habitual responses."[45]

The rejection of the instinct theory was widely reported in the popular press, as well as in academic journals, reaching a broad audience of middle-class, educated Americans. Lasker, for example, publicized his results in *Parents' Magazine, Child Study,* the *Woman's Press,* and *Opportunity* and was frequently cited by other authors. *Harper's, Survey, Crisis, Childhood Education,* and *Progressive Education* also promoted the new research beyond academic circles. James Weldon Johnson, secretary of the NAACP, declared in *American Mercury* that he had "long ago reached the conclusion that the so-called race problem is not based upon innate racial antipathies; indeed, the opposite is more nearly true." By the second half of the 1920s, the new doctrine on the origins of prejudice had come to widespread public attention.[46]

As liberal educators used new interpretations of prejudice to promote their antiprejudice campaign, they emphasized some aspects of the research findings above others. Thanks to such influential thinkers as Lasker, attitudes of hostility, previously regarded as innate reactions to difference, were now reinterpreted as the result of faulty training. Yet other aspects of social science analysis were lost on the activists who popularized the ideas. Lasker sought to remove barriers to active citizenship, to make possible the democratic participation of all groups in civic life on equal terms. He argued that direct teachings were insufficient to eradicate prejudice, for they did not address the "attendant learnings" children picked up from the segregation and exclusion they observed around them. He claimed that a teacher could not give a lesson on goodwill in a segregated church or school and expect it to be effective. Yet educators did just that. In a selective reading of Lasker's work, they drew on his findings to justify their pedagogical innovations, offering lessons and stories designed to instill favorable racial attitudes.

2

Parent Education and the Teaching of Tolerance

"Racial and religious prejudices are not instinctive," the new mass-circulation monthly *Parents' Magazine* proclaimed in 1926; "they have to be learned as we grow up, more's the pity. The natural mind, as seen in a child, is essentially honest, fair and tolerant." Under the headline "Tolerant Childhood," the magazine's inaugural issue celebrated a third-grade class that elected as president a Japanese girl and as secretary a Jewish boy. Its message to readers was clear: parents should learn about the acquisition of attitudes in order to foster their children's natural sympathy toward other peoples.[1]

This commentary from *Parents' Magazine* was part of a widespread effort to encourage American parents to teach tolerance to their children. The booming parent education movement of the 1920s and 1930s included frequent pleas to appreciate the "cultural gifts" brought by racial, ethnic, and religious minorities. Drawing on progressive currents in social science, parent educators explained the process of attitude formation and suggested ways to avoid passing on the taints of prejudice. "If any progress is to be made toward toleration, toward a sympathy and an understanding that will help to fuse the polyglot elements in this country, our children must be brought up without the bias of old antagonisms and beliefs," the liberal-minded magazine declared in 1929.[2] This anti-prejudice campaign reflected the defining characteristics of racial liberalism in the interwar years. Parent educators voiced faith in new scientific thinking, in the possibility of progress, and in equality of opportunity. Like other cultural gifts advocates, they followed progressive theories of race that attributed racial differences to environmental factors. They sought

39

ways to apply new ideas on the practical level, promising that child-rearing reforms would shore up democratic systems to benefit both the individual and the larger society.

Parent educators drew on behaviorist psychology to promise that racial tolerance would result from careful habit training. Their insistence on the malleability of young minds infused the antiprejudice campaign with great optimism. Yet as it located the genesis of attitudes in the home, habit training obscured the public forces that institutionalized racism, portraying prejudice as an individual matter to be remedied through the private realm of child rearing. This private approach limited the scope of antiprejudice work. Experts urged "sympathetic understanding" for other races and religions, but they did not ask parents to reconsider the exclusivity of their own social relations. Despite frequent pleas for tolerance, vehicles of parent education could reinforce rather than overturn certain racial stereotypes. The progressive vision of *Parents' Magazine* was especially conflicted. Even as it published articles on the teaching of racial tolerance, it included illustrations and advertisements that disseminated the very ideas it claimed to attack.

White leaders in parent education limited their portrayal of African Americans in particular. Like other proponents of the cultural gifts model, they were most comfortable when discussing the achievements of European immigrants to the United States and less at ease when considering groups who experienced more limited social and economic mobility. Despite their progressive slant, they found it difficult to overcome their own racial biases. In an era in which antiblack racism was deeply ingrained, these well-intentioned liberals were unable to extend the egalitarian vision to their black maids and gardeners or to imagine their children attending integrated schools. In the end, their ideal of cultural exchange left intact the structures of racial inequality.

Parents, Children, and Racial Attitudes

Of the many factors that social researchers identified as shaping children's racial attitudes, the home appeared most important. It was parents who guided a child's earliest and most formative experiences. In *Race Attitudes in Children*, Bruno Lasker recognized that parental influence took varied forms. He found evidence for "direct teaching," in which parents gave intentional instruction in racial thinking. But more significant were the "attendant learnings" through which children absorbed adult attitudes. To explain this process, Lasker drew on Freud as well as John B. Watson. He speculated that "probably most of the 'teaching' of race attitudes is totally unconscious and unintentional and therefore a process of influencing rather than of teaching in the narrow sense." This influence could vitiate educational efforts, since attitudes unconsciously transmitted were more powerful than those deliberately taught. Children learned of their own group's superiority from what parents did as much as what they said.[3]

Parents thus faced a challenge in cultivating a liberal outlook. Watson's instructions on habit formation had been practical and straightforward: he assigned very particular tasks. Here, however, conditioning suggested a more complicated venture that required efforts in many directions. There was no magic trick to help a child "to rise above the mists of prejudice that surround him," Lasker explained. It took careful attention to provide "anti-toxin" against the "poisoning influences from without." Parents needed to give positive instruction—and to watch their unconscious expressions; their interest had to be genuine, not superficial. They should not model racial segregation in their own social relationships, for such exclusion "makes protestations of absence of racial feeling ridiculous." Their task was not to indoctrinate with the "correct" outlook but to create "an inquisitive, alert, open mind." Lasker urged parents to teach adaptability, curiosity, desire for new experiences, and appreciation for worthwhile qualities wherever they appeared.[4]

Lasker was aware that most parents were unprepared to meet these challenges. Before they could instill favorable habits in their children, they had to shake off the prejudices they had learned when young. Parental education was critical because "it is pretty hopeless to try to give children the kind of attitudes which we would approve when their parents and the environment in which they live have attitudes of which we do not approve." But this created a quandary: parents—whose attitudes were supposedly set—were responsible for teaching a new outlook. One sociologist described the dilemma: "It would seem that the only sure way of eradicating this prejudice is by conditioning, with much care, the social reactions of the very young members of the group. But such conditioning presupposes an almost complete measure of social control by those who themselves are free from the prejudice; and such persons are rare in any group where race prejudice is a problem."

Lasker's thinking at times appeared circular: even when emphasizing the need for parental education, he suggested that "you can't change attitudes in grown-up people. You must begin with children," a situation he described as "the rising circles of a spiral." For him, the answer lay in the dissemination of scientific ideas to parents, whose education was inseparable from the education of their offspring. "No one can create tolerance in others who himself is engulfed in prejudice."[5]

To bring their findings to wide attention, Lasker and his fellow researchers turned to the parent education movement, which aimed to popularize scientific knowledge to help parents rear their children. In the 1920s, the Laura Spelman Rockefeller Memorial (LSRM), a foundation, donated heavily to parent education programs, creating the field's institutional structure. Lawrence K. Frank, the official in charge of child welfare programs at the LSRM, looked favorably on racial liberalism and progressive education, emphasizing "the influence of early childhood on later life" and "the plasticity of human nature." Frank believed in the practical application of scientific research to effect social change, hoping that parent education would lead to "wiser child-rearing" with long-lasting impact, for "the child is the bridge—biologically and socially—to the future."[6]

Parent education of the 1920s differed from the earlier child study movement in several ways. G. Stanley Hall, who had inspired the earlier movement, had asked mothers to submit observations about their own children's development, while progressive activists had advanced reforms in juvenile delinquency and vocational training, aimed to instruct poor mothers in parenting practices, and coordinated political activity on behalf of women and children. Parent education in the post–World War I years, in contrast, relied more heavily on the findings of trained scientists and social service providers. Due to behaviorism, parent educators paid increasing attention to the psychological growth of young children. And parent education claimed a new audience; it addressed millions of educated, middle-class parents who were convinced that scientific studies could help them raise their own children. In the 1920s, parent education burgeoned into an extensive movement, served by a variety of publications, conferences, academic programs, public agencies, and philanthropic foundations. While the center of activity was New York—home of the key funders, researchers, and popularizers—its message spread across the country.[7] A 1930 nationwide survey found

378 organizations and 5687 study groups engaged in parent education and estimated that half a million parents had participated in these during the year.[8]

Parent education offered a way for scientists to present progressive ideas on race to a popular audience. The Chicago Association for Child Study and Parent Education, for instance, invited academic researchers to address its 1932 conference entitled "Developing Attitudes in Children." Anthropologist Melville J. Herskovits, a student of Franz Boas, in a presentation entitled "Training for Racial Bigotry," explained to the assembled parents that young people learned prejudices "by the same unconscious conditioning that gives them their table manners, their manner of walking, or their concept of right and wrong." Harry Elmer Barnes, a sociologist and historian, complained that most children were "ruined" before they arrived at school and argued that the prevention of prejudice was "a matter for parents rather than the teacher." According to conference organizers, audience members realized "the imminent dangers of their own wrong attitudes" and the need to train themselves and their children. Adults had not learned to live together peacefully, "but the child is still a hope for us."[9]

As its name indicated, the parent education movement aimed to reach all parents. But the frequent alternation of the terms "parents" and "mothers" reflected a certain ambivalence over child-rearing roles. Men assumed some leadership positions in the movement and gave expert advice, while a few programs attempted to attract fathers to study groups or child-rearing literature. But in fact, most of the participants were mothers, and discussions in the literature largely focused on mothers rather than fathers. In the absence of biological explanations for behavior, mothers carried the credit or the blame for their children's development.

The Child Study Association

A central participant in the parent education movement was the Child Study Association of America (CSA). Begun in New York City with a membership that was largely educated, middle class, and German-Jewish, the CSA prided itself on high intellectual standards. With funds from the LSRM, it became a leader in parent education, influencing the intellectual trends of the larger movement, despite its small membership concentrated in the Northeast. The CSA sponsored child study clubs, conferences to educate mothers in scientific theories of child development, and a journal, *Child Study*.[10] Club members discussed expert advice on a wide range of topics, including behaviorism, through a question-and-answer format. *Child Study* gave a mixed response to Watson's theory; it published articles based on behaviorist principles, but also included pieces skeptical of this philosophy or influenced by other theories of child development, including Freudianism.[11]

Child Study endorsed the antiprejudice campaign. It assumed its readers were "liberal in their own sympathies," eager for their children to make contact with cultures not their own. Sidonie Matsner Gruenberg, the Jewish director of the CSA and editor of its journal, believed that children should learn "the racial or national sources of our cultural or spiritual enjoyments. Who gave us the music, the pictures, the poetry, the drama, the architecture, the science, the dance?" Yet she agreed with Lasker that "it is impossible to deal with race prejudice in children apart from the attitudes of parents." She served on Lasker's advisory committee for *Race Attitudes in Children,* and in an article in *Survey* in 1926 she previewed much of his book. "Since the earliest impressions and reactions find their place in the home, it is the home that is properly the source of prejudices," she wrote. To the readers of her own journal, Gruenberg voiced distress in Freudian terms that "parents allow their own infantile hostilities to manifest themselves before their children."[12] In 1929, she invited Lasker to address a conference entitled "Race Prejudices in Children," to broadcast a radio talk, and to contribute to *Child Study*. She published an approving review of his book and other articles on how parents taught by example. "Parents cannot hope to live in one way and instruct their children successfully in another," one writer explained. It would be ineffective to attempt "fascist methods of inculcation," for "we cannot graft social attitudes upon children as one splices an orange branch upon a lemon tree."[13]

Minority group parents also had to beware of the subconscious messages sent to children. Perhaps because the CSA included many Jewish members, *Child Study* asked such questions as "How can we help a child fortify himself against the prejudices and social disapproval of his group who are of a different faith?" The answer was to demonstrate the courage of holding to beliefs in the face of opposing public opinion. Another study question asked how to explain a school's quota policy "to a child of fourteen who is excluded on the quota basis?" When Lasker lectured to a CSA group, the audience wanted to discuss how to help children on the receiving end of prejudice. Lasker recommended that parents face the problem frankly and tell children the history of their nation or race, being sure not to encourage "a reciprocative racial antagonism." In a letter in reply to a Jewish mother whose sons demonstrated "a very bitter antagonism to their own race" and preferred Christian friends, Lasker recommended a "re-conditioning of attitudes and feelings" to replace unfavorable associations with favorable ones. This task involved more than introducing a different opinion of the Jewish people, for it was educationally wrong to substitute one set of judgments for another. To free children from one prejudice "means that we must free them from all prejudice—even those which perchance we ourselves are cherishing."[14]

The CSA pursued this topic in a 1936 handbook, discussing what to do for a boy who tried to conceal his Jewishness from his playmates. "How can I help him to accept the facts of a prejudiced world and make an adjustment to it?" Parents should consider inadvertent messages they might send: "Your own attitude and way of meeting the problem is likely to have more weight with him than anything you can say." Parents should not minimize the problem, for children needed preparation for the injustices of life. Gruenberg acknowledged that children of minority groups could exhibit unfavorable attitudes, telling in *Survey* of a black girl who refused to invite a Jewish classmate to her party and noting that "the chosen people themselves, perhaps as frequently victims of blind hostility as any group, are not altogether without prejudice." In their suggestions on how to improve attitudes, Gruenberg and her staff advised that a foreign-born girl, teased for her accent and unfamiliarity with school customs, share her traditions, songs, and games "to bridge the gap between her and her American classmates." To teachers, the journal suggested ways to promote "the worth and dignity of various races and their contributions to our national and cultural life" and to develop international understanding.[15]

Gruenberg struggled, however, to distinguish between evaluations based on racial prejudice—unacceptable to her ideal of tolerance—and those based on social class. She thought it possible to treat people fairly without regard to racial characteristics but still feel "repugnance to certain other classes of people," such as those who spat in public or delighted in shady stories. "Do not our very education and culture make us exclusive?" she wondered in *Survey*. She wanted to acquaint her own children with various religious, racial, and political ideals. "I may balk, however, at associations that make me fear a possible corruption of taste, or manners, or speech." Her magazine offered a similar distinction based on "desirability." In reply to a question about a boy teased for playing with the children of the neighborhood handyman, who were "foreigners," *Child Study* urged parents to assess the family's qualities. "If the children under question are reasonably unobjectionable, the boy should be encouraged to continue playing with them. If they are actually undesirable, the objection should be put clearly on the basis of specific qualities rather than nationality." The magazine did not elaborate on what would make the children either "unobjectionable" or "undesirable," but its readers must have understood what was included in the terms—perhaps such markers of socioeconomic class as health and hygiene, manners and diction, education and training, as Gruenberg had earlier suggested.[16]

Lasker had offered a similar distinction in a talk to the Yorkville Neighborhood Council, explaining that the problem lay in perceptions of racial or national groups "as a class." People assumed that German men were businessmen and Italian men were ill-paid laborers, yet in some neighborhoods in New York, there were "educated and refined Italians, lawyers, artists, editors, professors." The same was true of African Americans. Lasker reminded his affluent audience, "Harlem does not only furnish us with laundrywomen and elevator men, with maids and delivery boys, but it contains hundreds of high-class Negro physicians, chemists, manufacturers, writers, artists, even society women" whose business in life was to be "extremely well dressed." Blacks had their own aristocracy and proletariat, as did Jews, and Hungarians, and every other group. A first strike against prejudice was "to make sure that we do not confuse race and class," assuming things about neighbors that were untrue.[17]

Lasker recognized that parents wanted to protect their children from poor manners and "low ideas." The trick was not to pretend there were no differences, but rather to address them in keeping with democratic ideals. Lasker proposed a distinction between private and public behaviors. In their private lives, parents could choose associates whom they considered most congenial and who shared similar levels of cultivation. If those people happened to be all of one group, parents should recognize how few were their opportunities "to meet refined people of the other groups" who might become their friends. Democracy did not demand that we give up all preferences in selecting associates, he explained, but rather that "we should not cast unjust aspersions upon other people" because some members of their group seemed undesirable. Similarly, parents did not have to choose friends for their children who violated their standards of behavior. In response to a mother who posed a question along these lines—"Do you want us to have all sorts of ill-mannered foreigners and colored urchins to play with John just to prove to him our American democracy?"—Lasker allowed that parents might seek playmates who were their children's "equals in manners, intelligence, personal habits and correct use of language." If no such children of other nationalities and races were found, "it may be better to postpone personal contacts to a more mature age."[18]

In public life, however, no group should receive preferences, since the nation granted equal privileges of citizenship. Parents should teach through example: "if we really believed in this kind of Americanism, we would not exclude colored people from our churches, we should certainly not discriminate against any race in public employment, and we should behave with equal courtesy to every kind in every public or semi-public place." Cherish your own traditions and preferences as you like, Lasker urged. "Only don't let these private preferences affect your behavior in public or your sympathy for others as fellow-citizens and fellowmen. Above all, do not permit yourself or your children to mistake your prejudices for profound wisdom." Lasker admitted that particular social risks accompanied contacts across lines of class and race. A mother who defied community standards might find that her high ideals came at a cost: "if she persists, if her children actually associate with children who belong to one of the less approved groups in the community, her social position may become insecure, and her own children may later accuse her of having closed the 'best' homes to them," he acknowledged.[19]

As *Child Study* offered distinctions between racial prejudice and social standards, it skirted around a sticky question at the heart of cultural gifts liberalism. What role did socioeconomic factors play in shaping cultural traits? The journal did not consider whether the personal appearance of an immigrant child might reflect crowded living quarters, poor nutrition, or limited access to health care. It did not ask why some groups were more likely to achieve certain standards of "taste, or manners, or speech." Gruenberg wanted children and adults to learn of the accomplishments of people of various backgrounds. But she did not ask them to analyze why members of certain groups had been able to accomplish more than others, what barriers of class and race restricted access to the education, manners, and social graces she prized. Her suggestions left unaddressed the link between material conditions and cultural achievements.

This oversight may have resulted from the relative affluence of the CSA membership. *Child Study* assumed that readers came from positions of privilege, as when it promised: "The mother will find that the knowledge she gains in child study will help her in managing her servants, in dealing with tradespeople, and with her club associates," while the father would supervise his office force better. Gruenberg took for granted that her readers hired household help when she suggested that a mother's attitude toward "a Swedish cook" or "the Irish maid" might shape her child's prejudices. Class distinctions could appear immutable: a study outline from 1933 questioned a friendship between the sons of the leading banker and the furnace man. "Since their ways will eventually diverge should their intimacy be encouraged now?"[20]

Even as she assumed class distinctions, however, Gruenberg sought ways to inculcate "the element of justice." In the mid-1930s, although her materials rarely mentioned the Great Depression, they acknowledged economic inequalities. "My two little girls have been giving their outgrown clothing and surplus toys to the laundress' child," began one query in the 1936 handbook *Parents' Questions*. The parent was concerned that the children were growing "self-righteous and smug" and wanted to encourage "a more desirable spirit of giving." In reply, Gruenberg and her associates noted: "Any intelligent child realizes very early that there are marked differences in the economic status of the people who make up his world." Parents should not gloss over this fact, but rather "let our children know that we are aware of the unequal distribution of material things, and to help them develop a concept of social justice."[21]

Leaders of the CSA went further in another response in the handbook, reflecting the impact of the New Deal as they challenged economic inequities. The question concerned the lavishness of Christmas gifts: "How are our children to become aware of real poverty and want in the world, and to develop a conscience about social ills, if all they see is merriment and abundance?" In reply, CSA leaders suggested that children give gifts to "the much loved family cook," "the laundress in the country," "the family of the man who tends the furnace," although they admitted that such actions were limited by "a certain tinge of 'lady bountiful.'" Their analysis revealed their progressive, New Deal outlook: "As your children grow older, let us hope that they may develop the belief that both poverty and wealth in extreme forms are social ills, upon the cure of which our best intelligence must be brought to bear—that 'charity' as such is a mere makeshift."[22]

The CSA did reach poor and immigrant parents through child study clubs at settlement houses and work with African American parents in the Harlem schools. In 1929, with a grant from the LSRM, the CSA established its Inter-Community Child Study Committee, which sponsored study groups for black parents in New York, Washington, Baltimore, and several cities in New Jersey. A group in Brooklyn addressed the realities of prejudice in a discussion entitled "Teaching Children Race Pride"—a topic that suggests the concerns parents had for their offspring. According to Julia Grant, conflict emerged when white CSA leaders saw the black clubs as a way to pass on middle-class ideas. They failed to address the particular conditions confronting black families, such as discrimination in housing, education, and employment, but were forced to recognize both cultural differences and socioeconomic inequalities through the initiatives of African American parents, who used the study groups to discuss social and economic progress for their children.[23]

White CSA leaders had some contact with black parents through these activities. They invited a black social worker to CSA headquarters to discuss race relations, organized a series of meetings in Harlem, and maintained ties with Harlem professionals interested in parent education. Although CSA leaders went further than other white parent educators in cooperating with their black counterparts, their child study clubs remained segregated by race and class, and black groups were not integrated into the larger association. Harlem activities, for example, were not advertised in the organization's bulletin, and the journal published few pieces by minority parents.[24] This segregation belied the CSA's commitment to dismantling prejudice. *Child Study* reminded readers to "be sure that theirs is really a spirit of tolerance and not merely one of compassion and patronage," while Lasker explained that social segregation gave white children a sense of their own racial superiority. Yet white CSA leaders exhibited racial biases, unable to heed their own warnings about the importance of parental example. Children who saw their parents go off to all-white meetings absorbed the "indirect learnings" Lasker had identified.[25]

Indeed, despite the collaboration with black parent groups, CSA materials rarely mentioned antiblack prejudice or institutional discrimination, instead addressing personal difficulties faced by European immigrants or Jews. *Child Study* writers seemed more comfortable promoting tolerance toward minorities of European descent than toward African Americans. (Asian, Native, and Mexican Americans were mentioned even more rarely.) They seemed to assume that blacks would remain in subordinate roles and appeared unwilling to imagine the possibility of social mobility. A question in *Child Study* read: "Caste and class have al-ways played an important part in the life of a certain Southern family. What are the arguments in favor of preserving this attitude? How should it be done?"[26]

Gruenberg's distinction between racial prejudice and "undesirability" was especially problematic in regard to African Americans, who faced enormous barriers of segregation, violence, and disfranchisement in their quest for education and social status. In his article for *Child Study*, Lasker acknowledged obliquely that even the most progressive well-to-do white parents might object to the class background of most black children. "If parents desire their children to think well of the achievements of the American Negro and his capacity for progress, yet for practical reasons—such as differences in diction and in manners—cannot countenance the association of their children with the particular colored children who may be available, they can at least seek for suitable substitutions: for instance, books in which colored persons appear on the same cultural levels with white ones." Lasker was well aware of the "practical reasons" that led to differences in diction and manners; he understood what prevented more African Americans from reaching middle-class status. But when addressing affluent white parents, he was willing to acquiesce to their preference for cultural equals, and thus to suggest that images of educated blacks in books could replace actual encounters with real African Americans.[27]

Black Parents and Racial Prejudice

Unlike the CSA, publications aimed at black readers offered advice on raising black children in particular. These materials introduced social scientists' findings to African American parents, as when *Crisis* observed that small children played together without regard to racial distinctions. Educational methods provided a solution. Parents and teachers "interested in the abolition of intolerance should take advantage of these means to counteract the influence of bigotry upon the mind of the coming generation," the magazine declared. "Knowledge has the same power to banish ignorance that light has to dispel darkness."[28] Some African American parents also encountered the new child science through parent education programs in black colleges. Spelman College, the University of Cincinnati, and the city of Detroit received funds from the LSRM for child study work with black parents, while Alabama State Teachers College sponsored a nursery school and parents' club.[29]

African American parents had to undertake a different sort of habit training from their white counterparts. Behaviorism offered no easy answers for what to teach their children about racial attitudes. It was not enough simply to develop habits, for black children would need to navigate variable and potentially dangerous situations. Black parents therefore struggled to devise child-rearing strategies that prepared children for the prejudice they would face while also encouraging them to succeed. As they taught children to respect others, black parents with high aspirations also taught them to maintain dignity when others did not respect them. They aimed to instill self-esteem in the face of personal affronts, to build up self-confidence to prepare young people for the racism they would confront outside the home. They taught their children when to challenge and when to ignore the prejudices of others and insisted that youngsters not think that others were superior. "In the first place it is the Negro's duty to himself and his children to prevent this eternal semblance of an inferiority feeling from becoming a real inferiority complex," wrote William Pickens of the NAACP. "Colored children should be systematically taught the truth, and the whole truth—not 'protected' against it." He advised black parents to teach that there was no virtue in race or color itself, but that some people gained advantage from the environment. It was unwise to retaliate by teaching that blacks were superior to whites, for that "simply sets one folly or falsehood against another."[30]

These dilemmas were particularly painful for black families in the South who faced the indignities and terrors of Jim Crow on a daily basis—traumas white parents were able to ignore. "Truth or evasion for the Negro child?" asked an article in *Opportunity*. Eva Knox Evans, who had directed the kindergarten at Atlanta University, praised wise parents who "knew how devastating a condescending attitude can be to the personality development of young children." Black parents, she recognized, faced "subtle and delicate problems." They confronted such disturbing questions as "How can I tell my child his position in a white world without destroying his self-assurance?" A child who wondered why she had to sit in the back of the streetcar raised a difficult situation. "She cannot be given the impression that she is segregated because she is inferior. Neither can the questions be evaded." Children had to learn to observe the laws in order to protect them from unpleasant and dangerous experiences. While the truth was likely to inspire hostility against those who made such laws, early teaching of black children regarding their relationship with whites was "necessary and inevitable as long as there is such segregation," Evans wrote. Mary White Ovington of the NAACP recounted in the *Crisis* a conversation with a black mother in Jackson, Mississippi, who described the threats and violence her family had suffered. "So you can see sometimes I'm worried," the mother said. "I don't bring up my boy to hate the whites. I don't want to preach hatred to anyone, but I bring him up to avoid them."[31]

Parents adopted a range of strategies to negotiate the realities of racism. Evans recounted how one mother dealt with a child who asked why he could not buy ice cream in the downtown drugstore: "I always tried to distract his attention, because I didn't want to put prejudice in his little heart." Other parents kept their children away from public places "in order that the knowledge of their segregation might not become too evident to them," Evans reported. "Some of the parents did not want their children to find out that they were colored, living in a hostile white world. Some believe that it was best for them to learn the truth at once, while they were still young enough to minimize the forcefullness [sic] of its meaning." She quoted James Weldon Johnson: "The question of a child's future is a serious dilemma for Negro parents" aware of the obstacles that awaited, "and this dilemma approaches suffering in proportion to the parents' knowledge of and the child's innocence of these conditions." Some parents tried to spare their children the bitter knowledge as long as possible; others drove it home from infancy. "And no Negro parent can say definitely which is the wiser course, for either of them may lead to spiritual disaster for the child."[32]

Some African Americans questioned whether to become parents at all. Black women faced a cruel choice over whether to bring into the world children who would be victimized by the color of their skin, wrote Cecelia Eggleston, a social worker and teacher in Washington, D.C.

Since Eggleston faced restrictions in housing and health care, before her child left her arms, "he would begin to live a lie, to learn day by day in a hundred subtle but nonetheless definite ways that he was different—somehow inferior." Those messages would continue as the child grew. Because of these realities, she debated whether to have a baby: "*Will my child rise up to call me blessed or curse the day that he was born?*" A black child might be able to overcome poverty and ignorance, *Opportunity* stated, but would still have to confront "the spectre of despair which whispers again and again that 'this equality of opportunity which is the unique basis of American civilization' may never be his." Black parents understood that the elimination of prejudice would require social as well as personal transformation.[33]

Parents' Magazine: Research in the Service of Reform

No such difficulties apparently faced the white parents who read the literature of parent education. They aimed to instill tolerant attitudes toward others rather than confront prejudice themselves. Many of these parents encountered scientific ideas on child rearing in the pages of *Parents' Magazine,* the key vehicle for the new parent education. While the CSA was the intellectual vanguard of the movement, it reached only a limited audience. Through *Parents' Magazine,* founded in 1926 in New York City, the antiprejudice message reached into hundreds of thousands of homes. To explain the battle against prejudice, the magazine combined the tenets of behaviorism and cultural relativism in a recipe that included a little of Watson, a little of Boas, and a large dose of parental pep talk. It promulgated the findings of Lasker and his colleagues in often-repeated pleas to teach tolerance and consistently portrayed parents as the chief shapers of children's attitudes.

Parents' Magazine popularized social science findings for a wide audience. Experts in child health, psychology, and education translated scientific studies into popular terms and offered suggestions for practical application. Clara Savage Littledale, the editor of the magazine, later recalled the initial skepticism of professional researchers, who found it a "startling idea" that their findings "should not merely be stored away in theses, should not be confined to technical reports in professional journals, but should be passed on to those chiefly concerned—parents." The magazine was published with the official cooperation—and scientific imprimatur—of four universities and a distinguished board of advisory editors.[34]

Within a year of its founding, *Parents' Magazine* was selling one hundred thousand copies a month. After five years, steady growth resulted in two hundred thousand subscribers, many of whom shared copies with friends and neighbors. "Guides the rearing of more than a million children," the cover proclaimed. By 1932, a researcher noted that articles in the magazine were "consulted by progressive parents and cited to their friends." When conversations turned to problems of children's conduct, "as often as not the reply is '*Parents*' says.'" Circulation continued to grow even through the depression, reaching four hundred thousand paid subscribers at ten years and almost a million by the magazine's twentieth anniversary in 1946.[35] The regional balance of the subscribers was heavily weighted toward the Northeast, Midwest, and Pacific Coast states. Extensive advertising appealed to middle- and upper-middle-class tastes, promoting such items as ready-made baby food, preparatory schools, and summer camps. The magazine's motto, "On rearing children from crib to college," suggested the middle-class expectations readers held for their children. The majority of subscribers were probably white, native-born, and politically conservative.[36]

The magazine's leaders, more liberal than its readers, were committed to the social reform legacy of Progressivism. Historians of the parent education movement have argued that the 1920s saw a shift from reform to research, from a Progressive to a professional orientation. Parent education groups became more privatized and less political, more likely to discuss toilet training than to organize for child welfare.[37] But the reformist impulse shaped the new magazine. Its founder and publisher, George J. Hecht, came from a German-Jewish family active in welfare work. He had attended the progressive Ethical Culture School in New York City, where he met students from various backgrounds and absorbed a message of social responsibility. Hecht believed that *Parents' Magazine* should do more than help the individual parent. He promoted public policies on behalf of children and urged readers to assume responsibility for the well-being of all young people.[38]

Clara Savage Littledale served as editor of the magazine for thirty years, from its founding until her death in 1956. A graduate of Smith College and the mother of two children, she linked the private realm of child rearing with public concerns as she publicized social welfare causes. A Democrat who had come of age in the Progressive Era, she applauded New Deal initiatives and encouraged readers to lobby for progressive legislation on behalf of children and families. She worked to rouse parents to action on national concerns, asking them to "be a spokesman for children" by making their voices heard on social issues. Along with articles on child care, cooking, and fashion, she included impassioned editorials exhorting parents to take action to improve child welfare.[39] As a racial liberal influenced by Boasian theory, she championed cultural pluralism and published articles by anthropologists, including several by Margaret Mead. America derived strength from its many peoples, she asserted, and democracy demanded the inclusion of all citizens. In one editorial, she used the occasion of the Fourth of July to ask what children were learning about immigrants. "Do they remember that this nation is made up of peoples from many lands who have brought the gifts of their different heritage to enrich our national life?" Liberty and justice were not only for those who shared a common background but also for those "who have come bearing different gifts."[40]

From its inaugural issue, *Parents' Magazine* promoted social-scientific

Clara Savage Littledale. (The Schlesinger Library, Radcliffe Institute, Harvard University)

findings on the acquisition of prejudice. "Tolerant Childhood," about the third-graders who chose a Japanese girl and a Jewish boy as class officers, instructed readers on the learned nature of racial and religious bias. The repudiation of instinct psychology was in keeping with the magazine's general orientation toward behaviorism. While Littledale later came to reject extreme interpretations of Watson's work—calling it in retrospect "an overrigid, overconscientious, mechanistic approach to the rearing of children"—she maintained faith in a modified version of habit training.[41] She held out the promise of social progress through control of the home, in belief that children could be trained in tolerance as in other habits. Despite her progressive stance on social welfare issues, Littledale did not look to public policies to promote racial understanding. If prejudice had private origins, it would be remedied through the private methods of child rearing.

Lasker stressed the behaviorist perspective when he promoted his findings in *Parents' Magazine,* dismissing the notion of instinct as "a great deal of nonsense." In a review of Lasker's book, *Race Attitudes in Children,* sociologist Ernest Groves underscored that prejudices persisted "because they are built into the habit life of children." Readers regularly encountered such lessons over the next decades. In 1938, the magazine was still issuing reminders that race prejudice "is not congenital in children. It has to be taught to them." Children played together until "into their Eden enters the serpent, the injection by their elders of the artificial presumptions and superstitions of race or caste superiority."[42]

Parents' Magazine embraced both international and interracial understanding, with few distinctions between brotherhood abroad and at home. It appeared that domestic harmony would inspire a peaceful world order. Such typical titles as "World Friendship among Children" and "Mothers, Fathers, and World Peace" suggested that those taught tolerance from a young age would be reluctant to wage war overseas. Pleas for "world friendship" reflected the trend toward cultural internationalism that emerged after World War I. Littledale's own experience as a war correspondent in Europe, where she visited the front and witnessed the effects of fighting, shaped her opposition to militarism. "How teach peace?" she asked in a typical editorial. "Teach our children that the world is full of other children like themselves who can be their friends, whatever their race, color, or creed."[43] In fact, "world-thinking" could obscure the perplexing problems of American race relations. It was easier

WWI creates peaceful movement internationalism → respect others in some ways to advance international cooperation than to tackle racial tensions closer to home, as global harmony required tolerance for people far away with whom parents or children would likely have little contact.

Behaviorist doctrine informed these calls for tolerance. "It is as easy to train a developing child to be a citizen of the whole world of men as it is to train him to be a too prejudiced partisan of the nation on whose soil he happened to be born," psychologist Helen K. Champlin predicted. She declared that parents could proceed "methodically and with precision," like engineers with a blueprint, to build attitudes into the minds of their children. Readers could evaluate their child rearing with the help of a catechism: "Am I training them to realize the stupidity of race, class, or religious prejudice?"[44]

The scientific hue of habit training promised to shield children from the contagion of prejudice, just as scientific expertise protected their health. Prejudice often appeared in the metaphor of disease; young people could "catch" bad ideas. One writer ventured that children learned prejudice "just as they might get the measles or the chickenpox, in unaccountable, unpreventable times and ways." Another suggested that children's qualities "grow silently and slowly," acquired "through contagion rather than through planned learnings."[45] This image of prejudice-as-illness may have carried particular resonance with parents newly familiar with the germ theory of disease.

A parent who wanted to teach tolerance found an abundance of concrete suggestions in the pages of *Parents' Magazine*. With great frequency, the magazine encouraged readers to discuss current events with their children, to decorate their homes with art and handicrafts from around the world, to introduce posters, maps, and scrapbooks, to find pen pals in other places. Creative parents would organize costume pageants and plays and acquire toys, games, and dolls designed to encourage sympathy. "Felt-O-Gram Mishe," for example, was a cutout of a girl equipped with costume changes representing the national dress of seven countries. A common suggestion was for children to find the origins of things they wore, ate, or used and then mark those places on a map to underscore the interdependence of all people.[46] These activities created work for mothers (who were responsible for most child care), but the assumption was that they would eagerly embrace these extra tasks—and purchase these consumer goods—in order to instill a broad-minded outlook.

Travel and reading offered other means to build understanding. Parents should bring their children to immigrant neighborhoods, organize family vacations to other regions of the country, or take children abroad. Articles promoted the benefits of travel for exposing children to new viewpoints and ways of life (with the implication that readers could afford vacations to distant locales). In a radio talk, Littledale urged listeners "to broaden your children's horizons by introducing them to the children of other countries." While extensive travel was not possible for everyone, "through books our children can achieve an understanding and friendliness toward other peoples." Eleanor Roosevelt recommended that children read books from Europe "to appreciate the characteristics and the trend of thought of these nationalities which will help them to that international point of view so important to the world today." A monthly column highlighted books for children that promoted tolerance.[47]

Introducing children to other religions also held great promise. An article supposedly written by a twelve-year-old praised her mother, who had taught her that "though we are Protestants, any other religion is just as good to those that walk its path." "It does not damage their loyalty to the family church to teach children respect and appreciation for other denominations," another author explained. "It only broadens and deepens it. The home altar should be consecrated to the God of all nations and creeds, never aggressively sectarian." In this liberal view of religion, Presbyterian or Baptist children could learn to love such Catholic symbols as the crucifix and the rosary, or recite an "Our Father" on a "Mohammedan prayer rug" without harm. Attitudes in the home should reflect church teachings, for what good was it for a child to sing hymns about brotherhood "if he comes home and hears scornful remarks about other nationalities?"[48]

But despite their confident tone, most writers acknowledged the dilemma of the unreconstructed parent. Rose Zeligs, the teacher who studied the attitudes of sixth-graders, began her article with an optimistic title, "Teach Your Child Tolerance." But she quickly alerted readers to the covert power of attendant learning, through which children picked up on even the slightest, least conscious evidence of prejudice. She offered a test to assess "what attitude toward other races, religions, and nationalities are your children learning from you?" In addition to selecting proper toys and games, parents needed to monitor their own behavior with vigilance. Passing remarks, facial gestures, intonation, terms of insult, treatment of servants—all could instill unwanted prejudice. "We should habituate ourselves to ring a mental alarm whenever such remarks are about to pass our lips" and to watch glances and slips of the tongue, another author warned, since children sensed attitudes that parents were unaware of themselves. Studies indicated "that it is the expression of disgust, fear or hatred, the casual remark, the minor discourtesy" that built up unsympathetic attitudes in the child.[49]

To avoid inadvertent expressions of prejudice, parents had to rid

	Playmate	Neighbor	Schoolmate	TOTAL Yes No
American Indian				
Canadian				
Catholic				
Chinese				
Czecho-Slovak				
Dutch				
English				
French				
Filipino				
German				
Greek				
Hindu				
Hungarian				
Irish				
Italian				
Japanese				
Jew				
Mexican				
Mohammedan				
Negro				
Protestant				
Russian				
Scotch				
Spanish				
TOTAL SCORE	Yes No	Yes No	Yes No	

TOLERANCE TEST

Check up on your own and your children's racial, religious and national attitudes by means of this test. Answer quickly, giving your first reaction. In order to test yourself you must write "yes" in the column marked Playmate if you would be willing to permit your child to have as a playmate a person of the race, nationality or religion listed on the line opposite. Do the same for Neighbor and Schoolmate. If you are unwilling to allow the relationship write "no" in the place indicated. To score the test add the number of "yeses" for each relationship, writing your total at the foot of the column. In the same way add the number of "yeses" across, showing your attitude toward each group. Your score is the total number of "yeses" for all relationships and all races. Copy the blank test on another piece of paper and let your child fill that out.

Chart that accompanied an article entitled "Teach Your Child Tolerance" by Rose Zeligs, *Parents' Magazine* 9, August 1934, p. 15.

themselves of their own wrong ideas. Simple habit training was not sufficient: to instill tolerance was "not so much a matter of instruction and precept as of spirit." Parents should "unlearn the stupid platitudes which were foisted upon us as children by timid adults," a teacher admonished. But how were parents to rid themselves of fixed attitudes? One writer urged parents not to select their children's friends, for their old antagonisms might interfere. "We may dislike Chinamen, Jews, Catholics, Negroes and make our choice of a circle for our children excluding these, to us, undesirables." Another offered frank acknowledgment that attitudes might be too deeply ingrained to discard quickly. "If you cannot get over your prejudices," she instructed mothers, "then at least admit them to be liabilities and refuse to give them expression."[50]

To speed readers toward racial tolerance, *Parents' Magazine* published discussion guides for study clubs. Based on articles in each issue, these guides listed questions to discuss and situations to analyze, as well as recommendations for further readings, offering tacit acknowledgment that open-mindedness might require effort. One study guide asked readers to "give specific instances of the ways, conscious and unconscious, by which parents influence their children toward prejudices against people whose opinions and origins differ from their own. What are the main groups, racial, religious, and political against whom prejudice is directed in America?" Parents were invited to suggest concrete ways to cultivate social conscience. Another asked parents to list examples of intolerance in their communities and to consider their own attitudes. A "typical situation" concerned young Bill, who brought a "small colored boy" home to play. "What would you feel about this? Should Bill go to the colored boy's home?" were questions for the group.[51]

It is difficult to know how parents responded to these articles, study guides, and reading lists, for advice did not necessarily reflect actual practice or internalized attitudes. But there is evidence that parents did discuss this material. They participated in the popular study clubs and requested study guides, and they submitted suggestions on methods to foster tolerance.[52] Discussion does not indicate agreement, and the impact of these messages probably varied greatly. But it seems that at least some readers took these ideas to heart and tried to implement them in their own homes.

The extent of these efforts suggests that parent education provided an effective means for racial liberals to disseminate pluralist ideas to a wide audience. As a conduit for the antiprejudice campaign, parent education promoted scientific thinking to hundreds of thousands of parents. It popularized the vision of cultural relativism as well as the idea that child rearing could resolve the problems of prejudice and bring a racially harmonious future. Through parent education, Americans encountered an optimistic response to the country's ethnoracial diversity, alongside innovative techniques to teach tolerance to the next generation.

Yet the cultural gifts impulse in parent education was marked by significant limitations. Calls for teaching tolerance carried an undercurrent of blame. Underneath the upbeat tone lay Watson's suggestion that parents—implicitly mothers—were at fault for their children's shortcomings, guilty of passing on their own wrong ideas. This was the flip side of behaviorism: if children exhibited unfavorable habits, then parents had failed in their responsibilities. And a great deal was at risk: domestic harmony, cooperative citizenship, inclusive democracy, world peace. Helen Champlin, the psychologist who wanted to engineer children's attitudes, predicted a dark future for a four-year-old whose training was inadequate: "It is reasonable to expect that the man who Robert will become will be uncooperative, domineering, pugnacious, thoughtless of others and swayed by passions and personal desires," she warned. It was likely that he would "scarcely attempt to understand his fellow men" and would rush to arms. Like Watson, Champlin did not hesitate to blame parents for this terrible outcome. The training caregivers gave determined whether the future would bring conflict or understanding.[53]

Parents' Magazine's interpretation of habit training carried another important limitation. While the magazine offered an abundance of suggestions to eliminate prejudice, it mirrored the segregation of the larger society. Parents were to teach their children that people from all races could be their friends, but readers encountered few stories in which families hosted immigrant neighbors for dinner or socialized with members of minority groups. In this regard, the magazine's suggestions were at odds with Watson's findings. In experiments, Watson had found that telling stories and playing with toys had not overcome a child's fear of a rabbit. Yet the magazine promoted such methods of "verbal organization," hoping to end prejudice through books and games. Its translations of scientific research also ignored Lasker's conclusion about how social segregation sent powerful messages to children about racial status. Children should read about other people, the magazine implied, but they did not have to know them. Tolerance entailed respect from a distance rather than personal interaction. These omissions signaled a divide between social science researchers and the educators who interpreted their ideas.

Unlike the CSA, which addressed the concerns of Jewish parents and established African American study clubs, *Parents' Magazine* offered almost no advice to minority group parents on the racial dilemmas they might encounter in child rearing. The painful questions black parents confronted made little impact on the white parent education movement. When Littledale suggested visits to the "foreign quarter," for example, she offered no specific advice to families who lived in those immigrant neighborhoods or whose children may have been targets of prejudice. In its first fifteen years, the magazine printed no articles by prominent black writers and only a few by immigrant authors. It endorsed tolerance without depicting contact among people from different ethnoracial backgrounds.

The magazine's ambivalence toward personal interaction was apparent in its treatment of Native Americans. Frequent articles encouraged parents to introduce books, toys, and games that would develop appreciation for Indian customs. Even more than with other groups, these discussions were marked by romanticism and sentimentality, in which Indians were portrayed as timeless and unchanging, as bearers of remote and primitive traditions. Boys especially were encouraged to "play Indian"— to dress in costume, practice Native skills, chant Indian songs. One article advised mothers on how to organize an "Indian project" for summer vacation. An illustration depicted children dressed as cowboys and Indians, circling a tepee: "Indian costumes appear; tom-toms are heard; a rhythmic dance is performed to this primitive music." The mother should purchase a play teepee, which "can easily be folded and put away when primitive life must of necessity end and civilized occupations begin," and direct the children in Indian crafts, running and archery, and nature study.[54]

For white Americans, the ritual of "playing Indian" was a way to address concerns about the changing experience of childhood. Since the turn of the century, observers had worried about how to instill character and strength in the context of modern, industrial America, which provided few opportunities for children—boys in particular—to develop the hardy individualism of the early pioneers. One author listed the potential benefits of mimicking Indian life. "Familiarity with Indian lore teaches children to admire courage, unfailing hospitality, beauty in work-manship and good faith," promised Constance Lindsay Skinner, who said she had grown up among Northwest Indians. Echoing recapitula-tion theory, she observed that "the small white boy must and will become a small Indian boy off and on" between ages five and eight. "His small person 'gone native' is a symbol of the love of the wilderness" transmit-ted from Indians to white Americans. Skinner was intent on removing false perceptions of the Indian "as a treacherous and bloodthirsty ani-mal." While children could now learn the truth from sympathetic por-trayals, "their parents are still in the dark on the subject, their memories vaguely agitated by scalps and dripping tomahawks." Once they investi-gated, they would find "that the keynote of Indian life was not blood-thirstiness, but beauty." She recommended readings and visits to museums, through which readers would "discover that playing Indian comprises much more than getting Tommy an Indian suit."[55]

But despite Skinner's hopes for a more complete picture of Indian life, the magazine reinforced stereotypes that denied the complexity and va-riety of Indian experience. In its depictions, traditional ways of life re-mained untouched. A playset featured cutouts of tepees "hung with animal skins" and of "steely-faced Indians, seated before their wigwams engaged in their crafts, or standing, arms akimbo, motionless statues." One reader described with pride how her son had made a wigwam in his bed, while another explained how to fashion an Indian village from gun-nysacks. Books and discussions should accompany basket weaving, rug making, and bow and arrow contests, "and of course there must be a war dance."[56] In these portrayals, Indians belonged to a distant past, un-trammeled by violence, dispossession, or urban migration; indeed, there was little sense that Indians were still alive in post–World War I Amer-ica. Although the magazine trumpeted the benefits of learning Indian ways, there was no suggestion of personal contact between readers' chil-dren and the Native Americans they loved to imitate.

Similarly, depictions of African Americans offered sparse information to explain how particular prejudices emerged and what functions they served. A review of the film *Uncle Tom's Cabin* noted that the "long, brave struggle against oppression and tyranny stirs your imagination and com-pels your admiration." But further mention of slavery, disfranchisement, or political action was absent, as was reference to the economic dispari-ties behind racial prejudice. A few articles in the late 1930s referred to class divisions, as when a kindergarten teacher recounted how she had explained a strike picket to a child. Fears of radicalism restricted such discussion, the teacher noted: many adults "will think it dangerous to tell children of labor conditions; they will be afraid that such teaching will develop 'Reds.'" But she insisted that democracy required "economic as well as spiritual and political freedom." She stopped short, however, of linking economic conditions to racial discrimination.[57]

Despite frequent pleas for racial understanding, almost all of the photos, drawings, and articles in *Parents' Magazine* portrayed white children. Children from foreign lands were depicted occasionally, but ethnic and immigrant groups within the United States appeared only infrequently, and African Americans were almost entirely missing. On the rare occasions when black children did appear, they were portrayed in highly stereotypical terms, as in a photo essay that included a picture of three black children—smiling, barefoot, dressed in rags, on the doorstep of a rough shack. The caption implied that the magazine's focus on scientific child development did not apply to these children: "Way down south in the land of cotton days are long and sunny and pickaninnies follow the example of Topsy who 'just growed.'" This despite Lasker having warned that images of minority groups had to be carefully designed to create a positive impact. "There are dolls with swarthy features; but these dolls must be dressed in clothes as pretty as those of any blue-eyed Gretchen or the association between color and inferiority will merely have been strengthened," he cautioned. The magazine's first favorable image of a black youngster did not appear until 1940, when the magazine gave an award to the secretary of the Phyllis Wheatley YWCA in Washington, D.C. Even then, articles continued to perpetuate stereotypes as they promoted tolerance; for example, a 1942 piece on "democracy before five" described the gaiety of a small dark-skinned boy "who had the patterns of his race and knew more of the joy of dance and rhythm and music" than the white children who watched him play. "What a fine experience for the others to be exposed so directly to this African contribution to the way of life in America," the writer declared.[58]

African American adults who appeared in articles or stories in the magazine were usually described as servants or laundresses, not as neighbors, colleagues, or companions. They often spoke in an approximation of black dialect. Suggested activities for children reinforced patronizing images. Children could make a doll called "Door-Stop Dinah," covered with white cloth "or black, for a colored Mammy." A model for a toothbrush rack for children to build depicted a black servant, her exaggerated mouth painted white, "doing real service."[59] A subscriber might read an article that urged tolerance, but on turning the page encounter only familiar images of white children—or stereotypes of African Americans.

Advertisements similarly depicted white children almost exclusively, unless they were marketing consumer items designed to instill goodwill, such as dolls dressed in foreign costumes or books with characters from various racial groups. Images of blond babies and children were used to sell prepared foods, clothes, and household products. The materialist ethos of the post–World War I period existed side by side with the cultural gifts ideal, but the concurrent trends toward consumerism and plu-

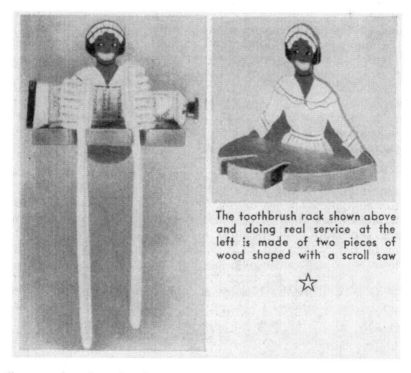

The toothbrush rack shown above and doing real service at the left is made of two pieces of wood shaped with a scroll saw

Illustration for "Things for Them to Do" by Edwin T. Hamilton, *Parents' Magazine* 10, January 1935, p. 65. Illustrations in the magazine could reinforce stereotypes even as articles urged racial tolerance.

ralism rarely overlapped. In a letter to Rose Zeligs, then a graduate student seeking advice on conducting research, Lasker suggested a class assignment "to have children study advertising cards and advertisements in the magazines they see and note racial references there."[60] Such an activity with *Parents' Magazine* might have turned up telling results.

The fact that advertisements did not match editorial content comes as no surprise, for the purpose of ads was to sell merchandise, not to reflect or reshape reality. Advertisers found little incentive to question social patterns or challenge popular thinking. While the editors of *Parents' Magazine* took the risk of promoting new ideas, its advertisers were more reluctant to challenge affluent readers' fundamental beliefs. As the editor and publisher of a for-profit enterprise, Littledale and Hecht depended on corporate advertisers, seeking to balance their reformist orientation with the practical exigencies of publishing. They were careful not to alienate white middle-class readers, some of whom employed black maids or gardeners or lived in highly segregated communities. They therefore advanced an ideal of tolerance that did not push too hard at their readers' own social relations. This strategy maintained the viability of the magazine, which continued to build its readership and advertising base even during the economic crisis of the 1930s. It is likely that readers did not view the magazine's messages as inconsistent, but rather took from them what they wanted to see, finding references that reaffirmed their own attitudes and beliefs.

These internal contradictions meant that parent education's most popular vehicle disseminated only part of the social science findings on prejudice. It reflected a divide between scientific researchers and the writers who popularized their findings. Lasker, the most perceptive observer of children's attitudes, had concluded that greater tolerance demanded both individual and institutional change. But, as noted earlier, parent educators adopted only the first part of his analysis. Despite Littledale's support for the New Deal state, she located racial attitudes in the private world of the home. Her readers learned about social conditioning and sympathetic understanding, but not about relations of power that underlay racial prejudice. In her many editorials about improving schools, she made no mention of ending segregation or equalizing funding. These omissions suggest the boundaries of racial liberalism in the interwar years, when promotion of tolerance did not seriously challenge the structures of white racism.

The literature of parent education thus fell prey to the very danger researchers had warned against. Lasker and other social scientists had noted the power of attendant learning, the unconscious messages that exerted even greater influence than direct teachings. They had warned that children distinguished between moral appeals and actual behavior. Yet parent education itself aimed to instruct through exhortation rather than example. Parent educators portrayed prejudice as a matter of habit, rather than social structure, whose solution lay in the attitudes of individual children. In this regard, parent education mirrored the conflict between precept and practice that its own practitioners had noted. The shift of emphasis in social science from instinct to habit offered parent educators a means to dispel racial prejudice, an important step toward an inclusive American society. But if their own analysis was correct, their indirect messages had more influence than any of their inducements to racial harmony.

3

Cultural Gifts in the Schools

While parent education provided one means to spread the antiprejudice message to children, liberal thinkers were aware of its limitations. Vehicles such as *Parents' Magazine* could not reach all parents or control how they behaved in the home, nor could they fully reform the attitudes of adults who had already absorbed racial prejudice. School programs promised a more expansive reach and a more carefully controlled message aimed directly at young people. The 1920s and 1930s saw the emergence of antiprejudice experiments in schools across the country. From kindergartens to high schools, teachers and school administrators fostered friendly attitudes toward all peoples: they sponsored school assembly programs, designed units on foreign cultures, assigned readings and reports on immigrant and minority groups. By the early 1930s, these efforts were a dynamic, widespread phenomenon.

These activities indicate that schools promoted pluralism as well as Americanization in this period. As some districts adopted textbooks endorsed by the American Legion or the Ku Klux Klan that upheld the superiority of Anglo Americans, others celebrated the nation's diversity. Liberal activists, like their more conservative counterparts, designated the schools as a place to assert their ideals for American society. They drew on a powerful tradition. Reformers had long portrayed the public school system as the great socializer, the mechanism for assimilating children of immigrants into American society.[1] In the interwar years, antiprejudice activists gave this strategy a new twist. Their efforts concerned curricula rather than school structure, for only a few challenged racial segregation or quota systems. In the 1920s, their efforts targeted chil-

dren from the dominant group—white, Protestant, and native-born—
under the theory that teaching these children about the achievements of
minority groups would eradicate prejudice at its source.

Antiprejudice education during the interwar years was innovative and
bold. Its proponents were genuinely committed to an inclusive American identity that would incorporate different peoples without demanding conformity. As pioneers, they struggled for financial support and
public acceptance. As they endeavored to balance diversity with unity,
cultural particularism with a shared national identity, they established
the ideological and methodological foundations for what later came to
be called multicultural education and ethnic studies.

Yet these educational programs had important shortcomings. Like the
theory of cultural pluralism from which they drew, their discussions of
ethnic harmony were marked by ambiguities. Although they relied on
new social science ideas, they offered a selective and sometimes contradictory reading of scientific findings. Their portrayal of ethnic groups
tended to be romantic and sentimental, reinforcing high culture (rather
than peasant traditions) and certain traits consistent with Anglo values.
The cultural gifts approach left unresolved critical questions regarding
individual and group identity. It offered a monolithic portrayal that
erased differences within groups, portrayed traditions as static and essential, and left little room for multiple affiliations or change over time.
The enthusiasm for cultural difference obscured economic and political
issues and avoided challenges to school segregation or institutional
racism.

The Beginnings of Antiprejudice Education

The originator and most prominent champion of antiprejudice efforts in
the schools was Rachel Davis DuBois. As first a teacher and then a doctoral student of educational sociology, DuBois was well situated to shape
both the theory and practice of this new field, and her work came to define cultural gifts education. She began her experiments in 1924 while a
teacher of history at the high school in Woodbury, New Jersey. A white
Quaker and recent college graduate who had been active in the peace
movement during the war, DuBois was troubled by the nativist under-
tones in the textbook provided for her students, who were mostly white
and native-born. When asked to take charge of the school's assembly

program, DuBois decided to promote sympathetic feelings for ethnic, racial, and religious minorities. With assistance from students and other teachers, she developed a series of assembly programs that highlighted the cultural achievements of various ethnoracial groups. This format, which she termed "the Woodbury Plan," served as the basis for the antiprejudice campaign she promoted with determination and vigor over the next fifteen years.

Through the Service Bureau for Education in Human Relations, the organization she founded in 1934, DuBois translated new ideas into practical suggestions for school use, introducing thousands of teachers and students to the insights of progressive social science. Her work drew on important intellectual developments of the post–World War I years: new scientific understandings of race, culture, and prejudice; the articulation of cultural pluralism; the emerging science of child development; theories of international cooperation; and the growth of progressive education. She offered the structure and materials for implementing new ideas in the classroom using teachers' manuals, curricular aids, lesson plans, and resource lists. She wrote extensively about her efforts, publishing dozens of articles in education journals, Quaker magazines, and the black press, and speaking at conferences and over the radio. Taking pride in the scientific basis of her work, she produced materials for classroom use, taught university courses, and corresponded with teachers around the country. Her initial experiments took place in the metropolitan areas of New York, Philadelphia, Boston, Washington, and San Francisco. Elite private schools, particularly Quaker schools and those based on progressive education, were also among the first to initiate antiprejudice activities. Experiments soon followed at public and private schools in other areas of the country.[2]

Through the antiprejudice campaign she promoted over the course of several decades, DuBois articulated the notion of "cultural gifts." She objected to the narrow patriotism and xenophobia that stripped immigrants of their ethnic heritages. Each ethnoracial group, she argued, made important contributions to American culture. She insisted on the appreciation, rather than eradication, of cultural differences, and on the preservation, rather than assimilation, of distinct cultural groups. To illustrate her objections to the melting pot approach, she frequently cited the story of a social worker who wrote on her family visitation card: "Not Americanized yet, still eating Italian food." To DuBois, ethnic food—along with ethnic art, music, literature, and other customs—was compatible with American identity. The celebration of cultural gifts would allow the country to benefit from the best each tradition had to offer. It would lead to what she termed an "American renaissance" in the arts and a more inclusive democratic system.

Born in 1892 to a Quaker family whose Welsh and English ancestors had come to America in 1699, Rachel Davis grew up on her grandfather's asparagus farm in southern New Jersey. In her 1984 autobiography, written at the age of ninety-two, she speculated that her childhood relationships with the black workers on the farm had provided "the beginning of my lifelong interest in race relations and intercultural education." She attended Bucknell University, where she studied the natural sciences and

Rachel Davis DuBois. (Records of the Women's International League for Peace and Freedom, U.S. Section, Swarthmore College Peace Collection)

learned to appreciate the scientific method—a technique she subsequently applied to understanding the causes of prejudice. She joined the dramatics club, fostering an interest she carried into her work. Although she became a student leader, she never felt fully accepted by the college social groups, an experience she later claimed helped her empathize with her minority group friends. After graduation in 1914, she returned to southern New Jersey to teach at Glassboro High School, where she began to dramatize historical events as a way to engage her students' interest. In 1915 she married Nathan DuBois, who told her to her disappointment that he could not have children. He agreed that his new wife should continue her career. The couple later lived apart before divorcing in 1942.[3]

World War I inspired DuBois's commitment to peaceful international relations. She refused to sell war savings stamps in her classroom. She took a leave from teaching from 1920 to 1924 and became a dedicated pacifist working with Quaker groups and the Women's International League for Peace and Freedom. In 1922 she attended the International Women's Conference at the Hague, chaired by Jane Addams, and on her return took part in a peace tour by automobile. She authored a discussion guide entitled *War and Its Consequences* for use in schools and spoke at school assemblies.[4] These activities reflected the post–World War I peace movement, which inspired widespread efforts to teach "world citizenship." Peace activists, who included many women, complained that education glorified military achievements, denigrated other countries, and instilled uncritical patriotism. They protested military drills and preparedness days, loyalty propaganda, and the content of school textbooks, all of which they claimed developed prejudices rather than international understanding. The schools were of critical importance: teachers, one activist explained, "hold the welfare of the world in their hands." Educational reforms attempted to instill world-mindedness through new curricula, textbook revisions, and extracurricular activities—such as international relations clubs, model League of Nations assemblies, exchange programs, and correspondence with students in other countries. Publishers introduced books about foreign lands, and school libraries developed international reading lists. In 1936, the federal Office of Education reported "unceasing effort in this direction, at every level from kindergarten to adult classes," over the previous fifteen years.[5]

DuBois came to link international and interracial harmony. When she attended the First International Conference of Friends, held in London in 1920, she was shocked by a report on the Chicago race riot of 1919 and conditions for blacks in the United States—and upset by her own ignorance, realizing that she had had to travel abroad to learn such facts about her own country. She later traveled to South Carolina on behalf of a Quaker committee, visiting black schools and meeting George Washington Carver. On the train back to Philadelphia, she read an article by W. E. B. Du Bois that impressed her deeply. What she recalled as the article's last line—that peace depended on overcoming racial injustice, "but the damn pacifists don't know it"—stayed with her for many years. She became convinced that "basic to the problem of peace and war is the problem of race." In Quaker terms, she had reached her "concern."[6]

Rachel Davis DuBois determined to dedicate her life to the improvement of race relations. In her analysis, both domestic racism and international conflict resulted from mistaken ideas about white superiority and ignorance about other peoples. To overcome divisions, people needed to understand other races and nations and affirm their common humanity. Egalitarian ideals would advance racial justice and world unity simultaneously by exposing the falsehoods that legitimized war and oppression. DuBois thus expanded her pacifist work in new directions: she organized Quaker committees and interracial conferences, built friendships across racial lines, and in the 1920s came to know African Americans and immigrants, many of whom became lifelong friends. At the 1924 summer conference of the League for Industrial Democracy, she met labor activist A. Philip Randolph, who awarded her an honorary membership card in the Brotherhood of Sleeping Car Porters, and William Pickens, then field secretary of the NAACP. At the suggestion of Pickens, she attended the NAACP annual conference in Denver the next year where she met W. E. B. Du Bois. In 1927 she attended the Pan-African Congress held in New York. Aware of her own ignorance about various groups, she sought out ethnic organizations as well. She became concerned over immigrant exclusion laws and on a visit to California learned about anti-Japanese agitation.[7]

As a Quaker, DuBois found colleagues who shared her concerns. Quaker schools were in the vanguard of international education in the interwar years. A 1933 survey of children's attitudes on peace and war found the greatest tolerance among children who attended Quaker schools. Since most of those children did not come from Quaker homes, their world-mindedness suggested the influence of the school and teacher, particularly the policy of the Friends to educate for world peace. Some Quakers urged the schools to extend internationalist concerns to racial problems at home. In an article in *Opportunity* in 1923, Anne Biddle Stirling of the Philadelphia Interracial Committee lamented that white northerners ignored racial problems and the achievements of their black neighbors. She wondered about "the chances of the rising generation of white children to escape from this stultifying prejudice." She was dismayed to find that even Quaker schools inadvertently reinforced old attitudes. Instead, schools should teach the "true history" of African Americans, their rapid rise and remarkable accomplishments, to foster sympathetic understanding and uplift the nation.[8]

DuBois answered Stirling's call. When she returned to teaching in 1924, as a social studies teacher at Woodbury High School, she looked for ways to promote interracial understanding. She rejected the civics textbook she was assigned because of its negative views of immigrants and asked the superintendent for permission to use instead the materials of Harold Rugg, an educator at Teachers College, Columbia. Rugg authored a set of pamphlets in the 1920s that later grew into a twenty-volume series of social studies textbooks for elementary and secondary schools. By the late 1930s, several million copies of his textbooks were in use in more than five thousand schools. Unlike other textbooks of the time, which he critiqued as conformist, dogmatic, and narrow-minded, Rugg's series introduced dissenting views and controversial issues to make the study of history relevant to contemporary society. He hoped his books would encourage open inquiry, analytical thinking, and "tolerant understanding." He pointed out social inequalities, for example, and in one section asked students to imagine the point of view of Native Americans. DuBois later recalled that these materials "highlighted the value of America's cultural diversity" and deeply influenced her teaching.[9]

Conservative groups, who accused Rugg of spreading anti-American sentiment and undermining patriotism, attacked his books as radical and subversive and worked to remove them from the schools. The campaign against Rugg was part of a larger repressive trend in school policy after World War I. Some cities and states instituted loyalty oaths for teachers, new intelligence tests to classify racial and national groups, and laws designed to minimize "foreign influence" and to force children to adopt Anglo-American ways. By 1923, thirty-four states had passed laws requiring English as the language of instruction in public elementary schools. Twenty-two states prohibited the teaching of foreign languages, particularly German, at the primary school level. Anti-Catholic efforts aimed to outlaw parochial schools; for example, an Oregon initiative passed in 1922, with backing from the Ku Klux Klan (and later overturned), required public school attendance for all children up to the eighth grade. In some communities, the Klan took over local school boards, fired Catholic principals and teachers, and campaigned for mandatory reading of the Protestant Bible. Patriotic societies such as the American Legion scrutinized curricula and textbooks for anti-American sentiment, promoted their own nationalistic textbook, and opposed teachers who promoted pacifism. In New Jersey, where DuBois taught, the state legislature considered a bill to bar supposedly treasonous history textbooks from the schools.[10]

DuBois came under fire as part of this repressive trend. Because of her involvement in the peace movement, she wrote, "I must have become a marked woman by the hunters of the 'reds.'" After she brought a World War I veteran to speak at Woodbury High School, helped students form a branch of the Fellowship of Youth for Peace, advocated on behalf of the few black students in the school, and spoke publicly about "the deep relation between the question of race and the abolishment of War," she became a target of rumors. In 1926 the local chapter of the Daughters of the American Revolution claimed that the Fellowship was part of a "red menace," and should be removed from the school. The local post of the American Legion accused her of Bolshevik leanings, refusal to salute the flag, and belief in interracial marriage and demanded her dismissal on the grounds that her work with the "radical" Women's International League for Peace and Freedom made her "a dangerous person in the community."[11]

DuBois's advocacy brought further censure the next spring, when the Woodbury Board of Education canceled her planned assembly program on black contributions and asked her to resign because of "rumors prejudicial to her patriotism." DuBois denied the charges, asked for a public hearing, and invoked the New Jersey tenure law to protect her position. The case received widespread publicity. "I have just learned from the papers that the one hundred percenters have been paying some attention to you," wrote W. E. B. Du Bois. "Won't you write and tell me all about it? I am sure this is an interesting story." She replied, "I am sorry to have brought our good name DuBois into disfavor with the American

Legion." She was convinced that her enemies objected to her ideas about racial equality as much as her advocacy for peace; while most did not mention race directly, "it is, as you may know, under the surface." She noted that one adversary on the school board was "opposed very strenuously to any attempt to have any colored students appear on the platform or to have any programs about the race." In the end, the Board of Education agreed to renew her contract but did not grant her the customary raise in salary. DuBois accepted the loss of money and reputation "as a part of the battle scars in the fight for Peace" and remained determined to carry on with her work. A. Philip Randolph later sent encouraging words: "You want to face problems that are entirely taboo among the powerful and respectable of modern society. That is why you spoke out of your turn for the cause of Civil Liberty, and got into trouble. You will have to learn not to be such a naughty girl as to fight for economic, civic and racial liberties, in an age of comfortable and complacent apathy and unconcern with the Cause of human justice."[12]

The Woodbury Plan

At Woodbury High School, DuBois pioneered what would become her trademark technique: assembly programs that dramatized the cultural contributions of various groups to American life. The insights and oversights of this technique would shape the cultural gifts model for many years. DuBois's "separate groups" approach considered ethnoracial groups one at a time, in distinct units of study, in order to confront stereotypes directly and replace them with positive images. The idea was to show the debt of gratitude Americans owed to various groups—"to the Italians for art and music; to the Germans for science; to the English for our system of government; to the Negro, our American folk music, and so on." At Woodbury, and in the schools where she later brought her programs, DuBois chose culture groups represented in the student body or about whom there seemed to be lack of understanding. She timed the programs carefully. She thought it most effective to save the groups who suffered the strongest prejudice—blacks in the East, Asians in the West—for late in the year, once students had already absorbed open-minded attitudes. The order was often tied to holidays, with discussion of Italians at Columbus Day, the British and the American Indians near

Thanksgiving, Germans at Christmastime, African Americans at Lincoln's birthday, the Irish in March for St. Patrick's Day, and the Orient during cherry blossom time in April. With characteristic optimism, DuBois suggested that racial prejudice "may be only the problem of utter ignorance about a group."[13]

In what DuBois termed the Woodbury Plan, each culture group was the focus of two assemblies that took place about a month apart. A planning committee of teachers and students surveyed the school and community, then met with representatives of the group to be studied to discuss common misperceptions, ideas for how to counteract them, and potential guest speakers and performers. The first assembly, designed to arouse student interest, featured community leaders who described the culture and history of their group. Assemblies might include a performance of English folk dancing, a talk on Chinese music, a dramatic interpretation of a Jewish story, a reading of black poets, or group singing of German songs. These presentations built friendly attitudes "by the indirect method of personal contact and dramatization" rather than by preaching against prejudice. An effective program, DuBois emphasized, appealed to students on three levels: emotional, intellectual, and situational. She thought educators should "start planning to develop the EQ [emotional quotient] with the same scientific analysis we now put on the IQ." Experiences should go beyond intellectual reasoning to "carry an emotional force that is strong and driving," she often explained, "because we act not according to what we know, but according to what we feel about what we know."[14]

The assembly programs struck a delicate balance between affirming cultural difference and assimilation. DuBois invited only the "most cultured" representatives of a minority group, individuals who would counteract students' stereotypes through their resemblance to Anglo-Americans—an educated black poet, an energetic and attractive young rabbi, a friendly Chinese dancer. "We choose for our speakers not the stereotype Jew, for example, but one who seems like the Y.M.C.A. Secretary whom they already like," she explained. Dissimilarities thus appeared slight; sameness was as salient as difference. DuBois drew on her personal contacts to invite prominent people: William Pickens, whom DuBois had met at a summer conference, spoke more than once at Woodbury High School. DuBois screened all the presenters to ensure that they would stress aspects of minority cultures that were in harmony with American ideals. In this way, she showcased only those cultural traits likely to gain approval with her audiences.[15]

After the guest assembly, students discussed their reactions with their homeroom teachers. DuBois found that "at this point there was special need for guidance to prevent the student from rationalizing himself back into his old attitude." These follow-up conversations pushed the program beyond pure sentiment, DuBois asserted, for "both students and teachers learned to face their prejudices and fears." The acquisition of sufficient facts would develop more stable and objective appreciation that could "withstand the counter pull of prejudiced social worlds outside the school." In later years, DuBois and her colleagues prepared outlines for homeroom discussion that included stories, questions to consider, activities, and readings.[16]

Classroom teachings furthered the intellectual approach. An English class might study Chinese theater and proverbs, while the drama class prepared a Chinese play and the art class designed the scenery. Science classes might teach that an African American performed the first successful operation on the human heart or that it was a Jew who made pasteurization practical. Information about culture groups could also be woven into extracurricular activities. Emotional training and factual material together created a cumulative effect, a multifaceted "method of attack" on prejudice.[17]

DuBois was particularly fond of materials that demonstrated a group's long residence in the United States. Students and teachers learned that many groups had participated in the central events of American history. "They found, for instance, that several Jews had come over with Columbus, that Italians had played an important part in the development of our country even before the Civil War, that the first man to lose his life in our Revolution, Crispus Attucks, was a Negro." DuBois made frequent reference to the story of Haym Solomon, "a Jew who gave his fortune to finance the American Revolution," and noted which of the revolutionary leaders were "of German, Polish, and French backgrounds." She thus added new groups to the familiar story of American freedom and democracy.[18]

One of DuBois's favorite examples of the dangers of narrow thinking about national heritage, repeated often in her articles and speeches, concerned a schoolboy in the Connecticut Valley named Borzelski who won a prize for the best essay on international relations. A leading club-woman in the town reportedly told his teacher, "Isn't it too bad the prize wasn't won by an American? You know what I mean—one whose ancestors came over on the Mayflower." Yet the Polish group to which this boy belonged, DuBois pointed out, first came to Jamestown in 1607 "and gave us Kosciusko and Pulaski, leaders in the American Revolution." In some versions, the boy was named Cohen and the first boatload of Jews had arrived in 1635, but the moral was the same: "We have been wrong in thinking that America was carved out of the wilderness and made into a nation by any single group." The composite American, DuBois liked to say, was "Indian-Scotch-Irish-French-Jewish-English-German-Negro-Oriental-Italian-Russian."[19]

At the second assembly, four to six weeks later, students wrote and performed dramatic presentations based on their own research. DuBois believed it was powerful for students to portray ethnic groups not their own. The assemblies "afforded opportunities of giving the students the kind of vicarious experiences that tended to modify their emotional attitudes," DuBois explained. Students who took the parts of Italian immigrants "actually lived, for a brief while, the lives of those immigrants," she wrote, while Gentile students who acted in a Jewish play long remembered their brief experiences as Jews.[20]

The situational approach, the third component of DuBois's program, encouraged students to act on their new ideas. A tea or reception followed each assembly, at which students met the honored guests in encounters that provided a rare opportunity for personal contact with members of minority groups. "Singing each other's folk songs, talking together, drinking tea together, are all experiences which tend to build sympathetic understanding," DuBois explained. One school planned a basketball game with Chinese students. A white school in Washington, D.C., organized a visit to the art department at Howard University. Parents or community leaders were sometimes invited as well. "In these intimate face-to-face contacts differences that once seemed important were forgotten."[21]

The assembly programs initially addressed white, native-born children. DuBois explained that her programs were appropriate for schools like Woodbury with few minority students, for "the real problem of attitude lies in the white group." Since these young people, as members of what she liked to refer to as "our older immigrant groups," would as-

sume dominant positions in American society, their attitudes were critical to upholding inclusive democracy. To illustrate this idea, DuBois recalled listening to Italian immigrant workers sing opera on the farm
where she grew up. As a Quaker, she had "a very narrow musical background" and would have benefited from learning those songs, but did
not because of her own sense of superiority, she lamented. She "lost a
rich opportunity," and without social recognition, these immigrants
"stopped singing their opera and folk-songs." As an adult, DuBois came
to appreciate others' musical traditions: "I therefore cherish the opportunity to be with my negro friends when they chant their spirituals, or
with my Ukrainian friends when they sing their marvelous songs."[22]

DuBois believed that the elimination of prejudice would contribute to
the emotional health of white children, which could be stunted by feelings of superiority. This rationale reflected cultural trends of the 1920s,
when psychologists, concerned over the adjustment of middle-class
children, established child guidance clinics to promote healthy personality development. DuBois frequently cited the poem "Incident" by the
black poet Countee Cullen to evoke the consequences of prejudice for
white children. The poem illustrated "that lack of sympathetic understanding affects not only the personalities of those who are its victims, but
also the personalities of many members of our older immigrant groups."
Children who felt themselves superior were egotistic, self-centered, domineering, and snobbish, "and thus their lack of sympathetic understanding prevents the development of the kind of individuals needed to preserve
our American democratic ideals." The effects were tragic: members of
the dominant group "cannot be creative citizens in a dynamic society, for
most of their energy goes into rationalizing themselves into thinking of
themselves as superior to whole groups of people."[23]

For DuBois, this work was deeply rooted in her Quaker faith. In a time
of growing intolerance, she remarked in 1927, Friends schools should
lead in helping students understand "the relationship between peace and
race relations. We can't stand on the backs of fifteen million or more of
our citizens and expect to have real peace." The assembly programs promoted this world-mindedness, even if they did not address peace and
war directly. To teach justice, fair play, and equal opportunity was part of
the Quaker imperative to put into practice "the kingdom of God on
earth."[24]

DuBois first publicized her work through a series of pamphlets. *A Pro-*

gram in Education for World-Mindedness, published by the Women's International League for Peace and Freedom, described the activities at Woodbury during 1926–1927, in which a different group took center stage each month and a final pageant celebrated "America and Her Immigrants." The second year program, which DuBois described in a pamphlet published by the American Friends Service Committee, explored world unity through such themes as science and invention, dance and games, literature, history, and government. She hoped that these pamphlets would encourage others to try similar experiments.[25]

A third program, which DuBois detailed in *Pioneers of the New World,* focused on "modern movements of social progress," including American women's struggle for equal rights. As a youth DuBois had heard the suffrage leader Alice Paul speak and "felt ready to join her at once," and later corresponded with her and supported her movement. As a teacher, DuBois wanted to help students realize that their freedom was "based on the courage and sacrifice of those who went before us," to create pride in women's accomplishments, and to motivate work for greater equality. In a dramatization of the 1848 Equal Rights Convention at Seneca Falls, students playing Lucretia Mott, Elizabeth Cady Stanton, and other delegates recited the Declaration of Sentiments. In a later program, a student dressed as Abigail Adams read her 1787 letter to her husband, followed by students impersonating such figures as Alice Paul, Madame Curie, Florence Kelley, Jane Addams, Jeannette Rankin, and Mary McLeod Bethune. The final sketch aimed to inspire students "to carry the torch of the pioneer into the future." DuBois quoted directly from such figures as Mott and Stanton: students heard Stanton protest against women's economic dependence and demand self-governance; they learned of limitations to the legal status of women and resolutions to resist unequal conditions.[26]

Yet as DuBois continued her educational work in later years, she rarely highlighted women's contributions to the nation's development or suggested that students study the work of female activists in particular. Although she herself felt strongly about women's rights, analysis of gender was almost entirely absent from the cultural gifts material she promoted in the next decade, which came to focus on racial, religious, and national differences exclusively. In her celebration of immigrant cultures, DuBois never explored how some of those cultures might reinforce patriarchal roles. While her later materials did include women leaders, and while she invited women to speak at the assemblies, she did not call attention to gender or to the particular barriers women had to overcome.

Nor did DuBois continue her early advocacy of black struggle. Another pamphlet from her time at Woodbury, *Some Racial Contributions to America* (published by the Philadelphia Yearly Meeting of Friends) asked students not only to examine the particular gifts of black Americans but also to ask "How is this racial group hampered in the giving of its gifts and what can each of us do to help matters?" DuBois explained that "America's biggest race problem concerns the relation of the white and Negro groups." Students were to analyze constitutional rights in light of lynchings, disfranchisement, inequalities in school funding, peonage in the southern states, segregation in the North, and migrations. They would explore "effects of injustice" and become acquainted with organizations working toward equal rights, including the NAACP, the Urban League, black colleges, and black newspapers.[27] DuBois's later assembly programs on African Americans, in contrast, celebrated contributions in art, music, and literature but no longer broached matters of violence or disfranchisement.

DuBois rarely returned to the kind of political and economic analyses she put forth in her early pamphlets. In her later writings she avoided discussion of rights or the political activism that would be necessary to bring legal equality, settling instead on the cultural approach that came to define her work. Her experience as a victim of red-baiting may have made her fearful of introducing students to social movements; the cultural contributions approach, divorced from political and economic concerns, carried less risk of alienating supporters, an increasingly important concern as she established her own organization and became dependent on external funding sources for economic survival. Her financial situation remained precarious. "I'm just sick of going around asking for help—to *do* the thing takes all my energy," she wrote in a typical comment to W. E. B. Du Bois in 1933. For funding, "I haven't the least idea what I'll do next year."[28]

By the end of the 1920s, DuBois had become part of a network of progressive thinkers, many based in New York, who were engaged in finding ways to combat prejudice. Prominent in this network was Bruno Lasker, whom DuBois first met when he spoke in Philadelphia about the material he was working on for his book. When DuBois told him of her assembly programs at Woodbury, he invited her to visit his office in New York City. "I did this three or four times a year and always came away with new ideas from his creative mind," she later recalled. She published a positive review of Lasker's *Race Attitudes in Children*, calling it "important, huge, unique," and made frequent reference to his work over the following decade.[29] In fact, however, DuBois tended to overlook aspects of Lasker's analysis. In her programs for students and teachers, she omitted his argument that institutional racism and segregation bolstered prejudice, and she sought instead to reform individual attitudes.

To Lasker, DuBois's efforts demonstrated how the school could promote healthy attitudes. The gradual enlargement of interests, knowledge, and sympathies signaled "the most promising use of the school as an instrument for better race relations." But Lasker acknowledged that such an approach was not clear-cut. No "process of magic" could undo the totality of community influences. Even as he cited examples of noteworthy projects—including DuBois's assemblies—he refused to offer a foolproof list of books or programs. "There are no easy tricks of teaching history, for example, which ensure that the pupil will not come out with a heightened contempt for peoples other than his own," he cautioned. The process had to be inherent in a school's management, programs of study, pedagogical principles, and selection of teachers. The broad outlook of the school should encourage children's mental development and allow them to come to their own conclusions. With a solid foundation, no "props" such as plays or pageants would be needed. He feared that "the very tools designed to create an appreciative or friendly attitude toward other races so often prove double-edged and unexpectedly produce snobbery and condescension."[30]

Lasker used his encounters with DuBois to clarify his own ideas. At times he criticized her methods, as when he warned that simple descriptions of her programs could bring "the danger that they will be thoughtlessly imitated as interesting and easy 'stunts,'" with potential for "disastrous results." He urged her to induce others "to apply the principles resourcefully and imaginatively for themselves." Writing to Daniel Kulp of Teachers College, Lasker explained his reservations about a manuscript DuBois had assembled: "Frankly, I am more impressed with the industry and resourcefulness that has gone into the collection of these extracts than I am with their availability in the present form for practical teaching purposes."[31] In later years, Lasker would voice a sharper critique of DuBois's reliance on pedagogical tools, which he came to see as ineffective and possibly harmful.

Yet Lasker's own ideas for classroom work remained vague. His research and ideology were clearer than their practical applications. As a researcher and writer, rather than a teacher or school administrator, he was better positioned to explain the pernicious effects of poor training than to detail the particulars of an antiprejudice program. The path from abstract theory to curricular reform was not well defined. Educators like DuBois were left with an urgent charge but few instructions for how to carry it out.

The Theory of Cultural Pluralism

The assembly programs were indebted to the theory of cultural pluralism, as advanced by Horace Kallen and other liberal intellectuals, which rejected attempts to erase cultural differences and enforce conformity to Anglo-Saxon standards. Pluralist thinkers took issue with the denial of ethnic identity, expressed in President Wilson's comments to new citizens in 1915: "You cannot become thorough Americans if you think of yourselves in groups. A man who thinks of himself as belonging to a particular national group in America has not yet become an American." In contrast, Kallen argued for the protection and persistence of ethnic groups as the path to national unity. In an influential 1915 article in the *Nation,* "Democracy versus the Melting Pot," Kallen referred to America as a symphony orchestra in which each national group played an instrument. In 1924, he used the phrase "cultural pluralism" to describe this inclusive ideal. While Kallen's vision was far-reaching, it overlooked the experiences of black Americans and immigrants from outside Europe. His orchestra metaphor, for example, described "the cooperative harmonies of European civilization" but made no mention of those with roots in Africa, Asia, or Latin America. Indeed, the symphony orchestra was itself a high-culture image with European origins. Nor did Kallen explore what role political identity might play in the process of cultural persistence. He remained vague about just how Americans might achieve both diversity and unity, which qualities they would share in common, and how they would balance individual and collective identity.[32]

Through her assembly programs, DuBois adapted the pluralist vision to the educational sphere. To her, as to Kallen, the heterogeneity of the country presented a problem of social adjustment but also "a great promise of cultural richness." While she recognized that some individuals and groups were eager "to lose completely their identity in American life," she offered a gentler form of Americanization that preserved distinctive cultural traditions. She was more of an integrationist than Kallen; while his pluralism depicted a "federation" of separate and autonomous cultural groups, her vision emphasized a shared national culture that would unite various groups into a broad American identity. And unlike Kallen, she incorporated African Americans into her vision, with school programs and teaching materials on the contributions of blacks to American history and culture.[33]

In DuBois's version of Americanization, the country as a whole would evolve through a process of mutual exchange. "Our American culture is not a finished and static thing," she explained; "it is still in the making, and we can each have a part in that making if all of us, no matter what our cultural background, will hold on to what is socially valuable, and share it with others." Racial prejudices wasted resources and made the country "culturally poor." As an example of the attitudes she hoped to instill, she cited the comments of one ninth-grader who participated in her assemblies: "I have learned to call all peoples my neighbors. I have learned to love their ways of living and to respect them for what they are."[34]

DuBois used the language of gifts to explain this approach. "Can we recognize and help preserve the great cultural gifts of the Jew?" she asked in a typical phrasing. "America needs tradition, cultural values, personalities. Will the Jew help supply that need?" She later explained: "Why ask Jews to be like the rest of us? We need the Jew; we need his deep and abiding spiritual aspiration as expressed in his concept of the *Torah*. We must ask, we must even insist, that he share his spiritual aspiration with us." Sadly, because of anti-Semitism, "we will not accept him or his gifts." As for other groups, "We must dramatize their cultural contributions in such a manner as to show our need of them and their need of us." Each group "has brought its gifts—music or scientific genius, spiritual endowment or technical training, arts-and-crafts or poetry, customs or dances—each eager to add its bit toward the building of a rich and great American civilization."[35]

Although DuBois first aimed to foster "tolerant" attitudes, she soon came to eschew the word "tolerant." Like other cultural pluralists, she preferred to speak of "sympathetic" or "appreciative" attitudes, "assuming that no one wants to be just tolerated." Tolerance was insufficient for a democracy, she explained. She wanted mutual exchange, not forbearance; celebration, not sufferance, of cultural difference. It was not enough to be "merely tolerant," she wrote during World War II; "because society is one organic whole it needs more than tolerance. It needs integration. It needs to make a creative use of difference." As she explained on several occasions, "by appreciative attitudes is meant not pity, not toleration, but *thinking, feeling, acting* together."[36]

DuBois's pluralist orientation was selective, for immigrants were only encouraged to preserve and to share those traits deemed "socially valuable." The implication was that other traits, less compatible with American values, were to be abandoned. But who would determine which traditions were socially valuable? Kallen provided little help with this question, neglecting to spell out which instrument each national group should play in the symphony orchestra that was America. It seemed that immigrants themselves were not to choose the "gifts" they would contribute. Rather, it was liberal thinkers like DuBois, many of them "old-stock" Americans, who made these distinctions. A Chinese professor of philosophy and education underscored these gaps when he questioned the liberal advice often given to minorities "to keep what is good in our own culture and to take on what is good from others." He found that such advice left two fundamental questions unanswered: first, "*What is the good?* That is, what is the criterion of judgment for the good and when do we *know* the good?" The second question was "What is the nature of the process of keeping and taking in cultural activities?"[37]

DuBois herself did not hesitate to pass judgment on cultural traits. Her assessment of which qualities were worthy reflected her faith in American ideals of liberty, democracy, and opportunity. They also echoed her own Quaker background, as she embraced folk traditions that reflected a cooperative outlook, peaceful relations, and artistic expression. Jews, through two thousand years of suffering and oppression, had developed "a passion for social justice," she explained. Italians offered "artistic inheritance and esthetic appreciation," while the Chinese expressed "deeply rooted worship of peace." These valuable qualities could be fused with the "mastery-through-discipline" characteristic of the New Englander. At the same time, less valuable differences should be "sloughed off." As an example of what traits to abandon, DuBois cited the Quaker tradition of using "thee" and "thy," which she considered less beneficial than the technique of coming to agreement in a meeting through common consent, a technique she thought Quakers might teach to others.[38]

DuBois thus offered a romanticized image that highlighted the qualities she deemed exemplary and promoted the rosiest image of each group. Her materials ignored divisive areas of cultural conflict—such as traditions that contradicted or offended the American values she cherished. Her school programs did not ask, for example, whether the Italian emphasis on family restricted the individual aspirations so important to American identity, whether Jewish patriarchal traditions limited women's civic participation, recently expanded in the United States through the Nineteenth Amendment, or whether the communal orientation of the Chinese ran counter to the capitalist orientation of American life. She assumed the role of deciding which traditions would benefit the larger national culture and which should be abandoned or ignored.

DuBois also created stereotypes of her own as she structured her assembly programs. Students may indeed have found themselves questioning their preconceptions when they encountered an African guest who spoke beautiful English or a third-generation Chinese American who was "a typical American college girl." But such idealized examples obscured the intricacies of cultural identity. The assemblies "disassembled" each culture and arrested it in time as they upheld supposedly authentic characteristics. DuBois depicted Italians, for example, as expressive and musical; Mexicans as mystic, courteous, enthusiastic, stoic, and courageous. She wrote that the Chinese demonstrated "instinctive happiness, quiet dignity, patience, pacific temper, dependence on justice rather than on force, and love of wisdom for its own sake."[39] Despite the best intentions, these depictions reinforced an essentialized and static view of culture that concealed individualized difference and minimized variations within groups. How were students to respond to ethnic Americans who did not possess the cultured appearance of the guest speakers? What were they to think of individuals who did not match the portrayal of each group, such as a phlegmatic Italian or a volatile Chinese? And what about people of mixed ancestry?

The separate groups approach meant that students only learned about a certain number of groups. It was unclear what would happen when they encountered someone from a minority group they had not studied. If their acceptance depended on having learned about a group's musical traditions or scientific discoveries, could they extend this attitude of respect to an unfamiliar culture? The cultural gifts approach also left unanswered the question of cultural persistence. In her celebration of minority cultures, DuBois never clarified how long she thought ethnic and racial traditions should endure in the American context—whether the third and fourth generation would continue to offer such cultural gifts, or whether these contributions would by then have become integrated into a composite "American" culture. "Anthropologists as you know assure us that there will be eventual merging of all our groups," she mentioned at one point, but her thinking remained vague as to when that merging would take place.[40] And for all the talk of cultural blending, she largely avoided the controversial question of intermarriage.

Nor did the cultural gifts approach analyze the social and political circumstances that gave rise to particular forms of expression. In keeping with new social science thinking, DuBois made clear that cultural characteristics emerged from social experience rather than biological inheritance, "for behavior is a result of the social situation."[41] But her programs did not explore just what those situations were. They did not consider culture as a form of resistance or group cohesion under oppression; most young people who participated in DuBois's programs did not learn that the black spirituals she prized arose from the terrors of slavery, for instance, or that European Jews came to emphasize education because they were barred from owning agricultural land. The cultural gifts approach did not acknowledge that culture itself could serve as a mechanism of domination; it avoided mention, for instance, of the process through which regional groups were assimilated into a national identity in many Old World countries. And cultural gifts advocates rarely confronted the prohibitions of class and gender that prevented some people from taking part in their own culture's achievements—the Italian peasants who could not afford to attend the great opera houses, the Chinese women unable to read the poetry written by their husbands. In her embrace of cultural pluralism, DuBois thus sidestepped a more explicit political program. She addressed difference and integration in purely cultural terms rather than as matters of power and privilege.

The narrow confines of this cultural approach were particularly apparent in regard to African Americans. DuBois's vision did go further than Kallen's in this area: her assemblies and teaching materials offered a positive view of the literature, music, and patriotic service of black Americans. But they made few distinctions between the status of blacks on the one hand and that of British, Polish, or Italian immigrants on the other, treating all groups in the same terms. She quoted a judge who asserted, "We Italians have to face the same kind of prejudice as the Negro,—it's only a difference of degree," but she did not explore just what caused that difference and how large was the degree. The mutual benefit she described remained exclusively cultural and often superficial, with little talk of African Americans achieving economic or social equality in exchange for their positive contributions. DuBois was dismissive of a school principal "who thinks that all Negroes are inferior because his particular Negro students happen to come from underprivileged homes," but her materials rarely encouraged educators to probe the causes and effects of socioeconomic discrepancies. In the end, DuBois's pluralist orientation failed to analyze accurately the position of African Americans and other racial minorities in U.S. society. It tended to minimize the harsh realities of the time—the Jim Crow laws, lynchings, disfranchisement, segregation, maldistribution of resources, and violent racism deeply embedded in America's legal and political systems—as well as the history of slavery, and instead presumed a universe of cultural equality in which all groups operated on the same level, giving and receiving without subordination or exploitation.[42]

These omissions were most likely intentional. DuBois encountered discussions of institutional racism: Bruno Lasker, for instance, sharply critiqued segregation in *Race Attitudes in Children,* a book she frequently cited. She counted W. E. B. Du Bois as an influence on her thinking and came to know him and other black leaders when she attended NAACP conferences and served on the national board. She read NAACP publications and was privy to discussions among prominent black activists. "Let me tell you how much I appreciate 'The Crisis,'" she wrote to W. E. B. Du Bois at the end of 1925. "Each time it comes out I must read it from cover to cover before putting it down." She later recalled that through her participation with the NAACP, "my own experience was widened and my sensitivity deepened." What she learned at the meetings "became valuable input for the factual material we were continually preparing for our schools," but in fact she bypassed the kind of political critique the NAACP advanced in favor of a softer approach to cultural difference. DuBois's early experience as a target of antiradical agitation may have influenced this choice. Throughout her career, she struggled for funding, appealing to various organizations and individuals each year in order to continue her work. The onset of the Great Depression made that struggle more difficult. In the face of financial pressures, DuBois may have avoided political advocacy so as not to alienate potential funders.[43]

Despite the ambiguities in her approach, DuBois's work provided a model for schools. By the end of the 1920s, cultural gifts experiments were underway around the country. *School and Society* and the *Survey* reported on a Cleveland public school that had experienced playground fights among Protestants, Catholics, and Jews. After seventh-graders took a class on religions of the world, the boys voiced new respect and engaged in fewer clashes. In a special issue entitled "Minority Groups and the American School," *Progressive Education* published an article by a teacher at a Philadelphia private school who designed an "appreciation unit" on China, in which her white eighth-graders visited Chinatown, experimented with musical instruments, read books and poetry, and prepared a tea. A teacher from Palo Alto, California, described how her students, most of whom were white and Protestant, immersed themselves in study so that "for some months, we lived in and with Mexico." She reported newly appreciative attitudes toward Mexican immigrants and visitors, "the representatives of a great and ancient race which we respect, admire, and hope to understand better as time goes by."[44] Official endorsement arrived from the Commission on the Social Studies in the Schools, sponsored by the American Historical Association and made up of prominent historians of the day. The commission's 1934 report said it deemed "possible and desirable the steady enlargement of sympathetic understanding and mutual toleration among the diverse races, religions, and cultural groups which compose the American nation."[45]

The pluralist approach received backing in Chicago, where in 1929 teachers in the public schools received a directive for the teaching of history. The directive followed a textbook controversy in which Mayor William Thompson and the Chicago school board, attentive to the power of ethnic voting blocks, agreed to remove certain texts and to distribute a pamphlet celebrating European immigrants' part in the American Revolution. Teachers were instructed: "Stress should be laid upon the fact that every race strain found in our citizenship has contributed much to the agricultural, artistic, commercial, industrial, material, moral, political, and scientific advancement of America." With a list that reflected the heterogeneity of Chicago's Old World immigrant population—but notably ignored its African American residents—the directive continued

"Our pupils should be led to realize how much of our progress in education we owe to Americans who were either born in Austria, Belgium, Bulgaria, Czecho-Slovakia, England, Esthonia [*sic*], France, Germany, Greece, Holland, Hungary, Italy, Ireland, Latvia, Lithuania, Poland, Portugal, Rumania, Russia, Scandinavia, Spain, Switzerland, Wales and Jugo-Slavia." The syllabus listed twenty-three prominent individuals from these groups whom teachers should introduce. The *Chicago Defender* urged that black figures be added to the list, while a black paper in New York asked Thompson to award the race "due credit for the heroes and patriots it has produced." Bruno Lasker warned that this "medley" of historical personages could lead to a distortion of history.[46]

Teachers of young children also endeavored to dispel prejudice. Since the foundations of character were laid by the seventh year, *Progressive Education* noted, it seemed possible that "seven years and one generation would be sufficient to alter the entire attitude of humanity."[47] To reach the very young, educators looked to the kindergarten, still fairly new in the 1920s. Schools for five-year-olds were not widely in place in the United States until the late 1910s, by which point most large public school systems had established kindergartens. Concerns about Americanization fueled this trend, as reformers sought to socialize children of immigrants at the most malleable stage. At first, some kindergarten leaders combined assimilationist goals with respect for cultural differences, incorporating songs and games from various countries into their curricula. Others advocated a stricter kind of Americanization. An editor argued in 1903 that the kindergarten provided the "earliest opportunity to catch the little Russian, the little Italian, the little German, Pole, Syrian, and the rest and begin to make good American citizens of them." Young children could breathe in the American spirit, another advocate explained a few years later, through song and flag drills and elementary patriotic exercises. Regional variations reflected these concerns: only 2 percent of young children in Alabama, Arkansas, Georgia, and Mississippi attended kindergarten in 1916–1917, while New York enrolled 29 percent of its four- to six-year-olds, the highest rate of any state. Public kindergartens expanded during the 1920s, reaching one-quarter of five-year-olds nationwide by 1930. Kindergartens enrolled children of all socioeconomic classes but included a smaller proportion of blacks than whites.[48]

Racial liberals came to see the kindergarten as a promising tool in the creation of a tolerant citizenry. A carefully designed program, led by a trained and enlightened teacher, would prevent the formation of prejudice. The early years were most important, according to *Childhood Education*, for "the gap between races and nationalities may be easily filled in when it is very shallow." In a 1926 article for the journal, Mary Chaplin Shute, an instructor at Teachers College in Boston, recognized that some might find it "absurd" to discuss "'the question of race relations with kindergarten babies.'" But the kindergarten teacher took responsibility for the "small beginnings of outlook and attitude" that would hold over to later years. Children arrived at kindergarten with racial prejudices already started by unwise parents; by age five, they had learned hateful names of race contempt. The teacher should undertake "small things with small people" to lay the foundation for cooperation. "Of course we cannot talk to kindergarten children of race relations, of international thinking, or of the abolition of war," Shute wrote, but she saw opportunities to instill ideals of justice, fair play, and tolerance. Racially integrated kindergartens offered the best chance for breaking down prejudices, while the teacher whose entire class was white and native-born had to employ creative methods, such as "a very pretty type of colored doll," as well as dolls dressed to represent Chinese, Japanese, and Indian children. Posters and stories could portray faraway children as "potential playfellows." This approach held great promise for the future: "the plays of children and youth may mold the spirit of the world!" The experience of the world war made clear the urgency of this mission. "We who desire peace must write it in the hearts of children," Shute proclaimed. Echoing John Dewey's comment that teachers would "usher in the kingdom of God," she wondered what would happen if every child could be taught tolerance and justice: "would not the world be made over?"[49]

To Teachers College

In 1929, after five years at Woodbury High School, Rachel Davis DuBois resigned her position and left classroom teaching. "I knew that I needed to seek further study in the psychology of how attitudes are formed and changed," she recalled. She was eager to spread her assembly plan to other schools. She enrolled at Teachers College at Columbia University to study for a doctorate in educational sociology, gaining academic training that helped her popularize progressive social science for a broad audience. As she became equally comfortable in university settings, ethnic organizations, and high school classrooms, she brought together the roles of social scientist, activist, and teacher. She came to serve as a conduit between academic and popular thought, between the theory and practice of cultural pluralism.

Teachers College in the interwar period was a center of liberal thought that boasted many of the leading lights in progressive education. In addition to Harold Rugg, the faculty included, among others, prominent scholars John Dewey, George S. Counts, William Kilpatrick, and Mabel Carney, who addressed problems posed by racial and ethnic diversity. Teachers College enrolled a number of African American students and hosted lectures by prominent black scholars. DuBois's advisor was Daniel Kulp II, an educational sociologist who wrote about the role of emotions in the formation of attitudes. When he left Teachers College before DuBois finished her degree, she worked with Frederic Thrasher at New York University, where she eventually earned her doctorate.[50]

DuBois reveled in the diversity of New York City and its lively ethnic communities, where she made friends with people from varied backgrounds, including artists and poets associated with the Harlem Renaissance. Her roommate was Harriet Rice, an African American woman who helped her prepare a pamphlet describing her work at Woodbury. Because the two could not find a place near the college that would allow them to share an apartment, they took a room at a YMCA house for professional women on the edge of Harlem. DuBois found that her dark coloring allowed her to "pass," often inadvertently, in black social circles; her friends at the house assumed she was black, as did a dance partner at an NAACP event.[51]

At Teachers College, DuBois was deeply influenced by John Dewey. Throughout his long and prolific career, Dewey argued that the school should reconstruct, rather than reproduce, the social order, developing democratic character in children by functioning as a cooperative community. A sharp critic of Americanization programs designed to rid immigrants of their culture, he portrayed ethnic and racial diversity as consistent with true democracy. At the same time, he awarded great importance to social harmony and insisted on communication among groups to enrich the common life. In a letter to Horace Kallen, Dewey endorsed the concept of cultural pluralism and the orchestra metaphor, "upon condition we really get a symphony and not a lot of instruments playing simultaneously." Dewey emphasized cooperation—"genuine assimilation *to one another*—not to Anglosaxondom."[52]

Dewey imagined a central role for the school in the promotion of cultural pluralism. He suggested that public schools "enlighten all as to the great past contributions of every strain in our composite make-up." Each group should contribute its special good "into a common fund of wisdom and experience." He described the school as a site where unity and diversity could coexist. In an often quoted phrase, he declared that "the point is to see to it that the hyphen connects instead of separates." In 1923, alarmed over instances of intolerance, he advocated "a curriculum in history, literature, and geography which will make the different racial elements in this country aware of what each has contributed." Such a curriculum would limit the spread of hatred and suspicion, "because when children's minds are in the formative period we shall have fixed in them, through the medium of the schools, feelings of respect and friendliness for the other nations and peoples of the world."[53]

DuBois embraced Dewey's educational philosophy, agreeing that the social mission of education was the development of good citizenship. To DuBois, as to Dewey, the school occupied a unique role in American culture as "the only institution, insofar as it is free and public, which is the common meeting ground day after day of all our varieties of cultures." It was imperative that schools take the initiative in solving racial problems. While DuBois embraced the separation of church and state as "one of America's gifts to the world," she thought it had one negative effect: "Because in our American public schools we dare not base our appeals on any one religion we have made the terrible mistake of making no appeal at all and thus have given our youth stones instead of bread," she worried. "If we cannot ask them to be religious, at least let us ask them not to be stupid." The development of sympathetic attitudes, she wrote at another point, was "a major *educational objective,* in fact an *obligation,* of our American communities and schools."[54]

DuBois's emphasis on the emotional impact of arts and culture reflected Dewey's influence. To Dewey, creativity provided a means to alleviate conflict and cultivate sympathy for others. In *Art as Experience,* Dewey argued for the power of imagination in bringing together viewer and artist. Through art, he wrote, "our own experience is re-oriented. Barriers are dissolved, limiting prejudices melt away, when we enter into the spirit of Negro or Polynesian art." Such a creative experience could have an impact "far more efficacious than the changes effected by reasoning, because it enters directly into attitude." DuBois hoped that students would experience this sense of identification. When they witnessed Japanese flower arrangement or heard the poetry of black authors, they had "a reaction that they cannot gain by mere reading or by other more or less purely intellectual experiences."[55]

During her years at Teachers College, DuBois came to a more sophisticated understanding of race and culture that reflected intellectual trends of the time. In the 1920s, while at Woodbury High School, she had portrayed immigrant groups in racial terms, asking students to make "a list of the various races represented in your class, such as Irish, Scotch, Dutch, Negro, French, etc., add to it any races which are of appreciable numbers in other parts of our country, such as the Japanese." By the 1930s, she was no longer describing European immigrants as distinct races, instead adopting an anthropological understanding of "culture groups" defined by nationality or religion. She also noted the presence of "black and yellow races," using terminology that implied that Europeans—of whatever background—belonged to a unitary white race. "Today, of our population of over 125 millions, about 30 millions are only one generation removed from Europe, and many additional millions are drawn from the black and yellow races," she explained. While DuBois's language reflected what scholars have recently called the "consolidation of whiteness" that was occurring at the time, her intention was not to dissolve European immigrant groups as distinct categories but rather to recognize and preserve European ethnic identities.[56]

DuBois's graduate training also introduced her to behaviorism. She recalled the pervasive influence of "this mechanistic psychological approach" at Teachers College: "At that time I heard that education is conditioning, and teachers were encouraged to apply conditioning principles developed largely from experimentation to their classroom plans." She adopted behaviorist ideas early in her career. Citing Lasker, she reiterated that attitudes were learned through family, school, and community: "This means of course that our emotions on race are being trained somehow all of the time." DuBois wanted teachers to "make social engineers of ourselves and realize that we can control human nature by the law of conditioned response."[57]

By the mid-1930s, however, DuBois came to view behaviorism more skeptically. Aspects of the theory countered the principles of progressive education, which stressed the development of the individual child and the unfolding of innate capacities and creative impulses. DuBois grew wary of Watson's extremism and, like other educators, combined theories to argue that the environment fostered the growth of the individual child. "We agree, but not completely, with the behaviorists that personalities can be conditioned toward ends democratically agreed upon," DuBois wrote in 1945, emphasizing the limits to that conditionability. Since researchers continued to debate personality development, "we are forced to be pragmatic and glean from the various schools of thought those concepts which seem to work best for our aim."[58]

As a graduate student, DuBois used social science techniques to analyze the effectiveness of the assembly method in reforming individual attitudes. She had first experimented with attitude tests after three years at Woodbury, finding that her students were more tolerant than those at a nearby school. For her dissertation research, she designed a more extensive experiment to evaluate the efficacy of different approaches in nine high schools in the Philadelphia area: three used the assembly program, three relied on a purely factual approach, and three served as controls. After DuBois tested four thousand students at the schools, she concluded that the assembly approach was more effective at changing attitudes than the factual approach alone and that the greatest results came from using both at the same time. These results lent support to her methodology, which centered on the emotional appeal of the assembly programs.[59]

DuBois's research made use of new attitude tests that social scientists devised in the 1920s. Some of the earliest came from Teachers College, where Goodwin Watson and George Neumann experimented with techniques.[60] When investigators used these new measurements to determine the impact of antiprejudice education, some reported success in altering outlook.[61] DuBois at first embraced the new tests, which appealed to her scientific bent. "Not only can attitudes be scientifically measured, but they can be scientifically modified or built," she declared. She recognized the tests' limitations but defended them as worthy experiments. In 1931, she reported that "it is now possible to test and measure attitudes with standardized tests which are reliable." When she employed tests, she "always found some change toward more liberal attitudes."[62]

Yet DuBois expressed increasing skepticism about attitude tests over the years. She recognized that results might be short-lived, for students could slip back into old patterns due to "the counter-pull of prejudiced social worlds outside the school." Other researchers pointed out possible discrepancies between test replies and actual behavior, between public and private attitudes. They voiced concern that students might have said what they thought teachers wanted to hear, or that other influences would counteract school teachings, and they noted variables that remained unclear, such as the role of education, personal contacts, region, sex, intelligence, religion, and political outlook.[63] Despite these misgivings, DuBois believed that testing encouraged teachers to adhere more closely to the scientific method. She maintained a sense of experimentation, repeatedly asserting that her methods were only a partial solution to racial problems. In 1934, she acknowledged, "we do not feel that we have arrived at the secret of how to do away with race prejudice. We offer only some of our observations up to this point." Ten years later, she still offered her reports "merely as a suggestion of one step which the schools might take," a step that, she said, "seems to be in the right direction."[64]

In fact, most of the evidence DuBois cited came from student comments and teacher anecdotes rather than objective measurements. After assembly programs at Englewood High School in New Jersey, for instance, students wrote such responses as "I discovered that Mexicans are much better than we learned at school," "I have changed my attitude toward the Chinese," "I learned that other people have contributed just as much as we have to the world." Teachers similarly reported new open-mindedness among the students. These evaluations were subjective, DuBois admitted, "but in the field of human relations we must as yet lean heavily on such judgments."[65]

DuBois's focus on older students overlooked certain research findings. By the early 1930s, social science investigations indicated that by the time students reached sixth grade, their attitudes were already formed. "Observers agree that children learn social antagonisms at an early age, in fact, as soon as they are able to mirror back their social environment," a review of the literature noted. But DuBois only occasionally acknowledged this insight and remained optimistic that teachers could counteract home influences. "If teachers were as intelligently conscious of prejudice, and as concerned about it as they are about ungrammatical language, we should know that we could rely on the prestige of the school to win over the home in the long run," she predicted. She considered ways to reach adults, authoring a discussion outline for church and community groups and later initiating the "group conversation" approach to bring together people from different backgrounds.[66]

Despite research findings on the early acquisition of prejudice, DuBois continued to promote assembly programs for high schools, which were expanding rapidly in the 1920s, and to a lesser extent for the new junior high schools emerging at the time. She had less contact with kindergarten and nursery school teachers who implemented antiprejudice activities. Although she counted both Lasker and Watson as intellectual influences, she largely disregarded their emphasis on early childhood. When she taught in-service courses for teachers, some instructors in the primary grades complained that the books and activities she offered were too advanced for the young children in their classes. As a former high school teacher, she may have felt more comfortable designing programs for older students. Or perhaps she was aware that secondary education carried greater visibility and prestige than did nursery schools and kindergartens.

DuBois's reliance on social science was therefore marked by contradiction. Even as she called for a scientific approach, she had little empirical evidence to evaluate the effectiveness of her programs, nor did she bring in outside researchers to conduct independent tests. She made selective use of social science findings that could challenge as well as justify her activities. Her instincts and anecdotes seemed to her sufficient to demonstrate the positive value of her work. A review of articles on intercultural education published in the *Harvard Educational Review* in 1944 noted the dearth of scientific assessments. The authors complained that "reliable demonstrations of worth are lacking and their usefulness in the reduction of objectionable phenomena are not demonstrated." Programs would be more helpful and more widely accepted "if they were first subjected to critical evaluation and improved in the light of the findings." DuBois defended her work against such criticism. Racial prejudice was just one phase of a very complex phenomenon, she wrote, but teachers and community leaders had a responsibility to do what they could. Experimental activities—a form of psychic "first aid"—could not wait for the conclusions of academic research. Inspired by a sense of urgency, she was reluctant to engage in constant evaluations: "Innumerable surveys have been made in the field of intercultural education. Can we not now follow those surveys with action?"[67]

The Establishment of the Service Bureau

In the first half of the 1930s, DuBois found a wider audience for the ideas she had developed at Woodbury. Her work gained attention through the pamphlets she wrote to distribute to schools. In 1930, the National Conference of Jews and Christians (NCJC) endorsed her efforts. Even as she pursued her graduate studies, she expanded her work to a larger scale, bringing assembly programs to schools in Englewood, Washington, D.C., Philadelphia, and suburban Boston. She received support from the American Association of University Women, the New Jersey Race Relations Survey Committee, and the Boston Chapter of the NCJC.[68]

By the time DuBois founded the Service Bureau for Education in Human Relations, in 1934, she had already been engaged in antiprejudice education for almost ten years. According to her reports, she had worked with thirty schools, two hundred teachers, and four thousand students. She designed the Service Bureau as a clearinghouse that would offer materials and guidance to schools interested in putting on assembly pro-

In 1935, Rachel Davis DuBois brought her Woodbury Plan to fifteen high schools. This student group in Fort Lee, New Jersey, presents information on black history. (From Rachel Davis DuBois with Corann Okorodudu, *All This and Something More*, p. 70. Photo courtesy of Edward and Carol Davis) ˎ

grams of their own. From its office near Teachers College, the Bureau assisted administrators and teachers, organized guest speakers, and produced classroom materials. DuBois enlisted prominent people to serve on the Bureau's national advisory committee, with a large representation from New York and Pennsylvania. The committee included faculty members at Teachers College, teachers and administrators, and activists in interracial and interfaith relations.[69]

DuBois's network reached beyond the Service Bureau committee. Over the years, she cultivated friendships with prominent black leaders, forging personal connections that influenced her thinking. She included among her mentors and friends the artist Aaron Douglas and his wife Alta, at whose home in Harlem home she socialized with sociologist E. Franklin Frazier and other black intellectuals and artists, sometimes as one of the only whites in the gathering. (She later recalled with delight the end of one party when Alta said to her, "Well, Rachel, now that the white folks have gone, let's have a good time!") William Pickens was present at the meeting that led to the formation of the Service Bureau and continued to speak to school groups. DuBois corresponded with sociologist Charles S. Johnson, poet Langston Hughes, and philosopher Alain Locke. She was proud that James Weldon Johnson of the NAACP and Crystal Bird Fauset of the Swarthmore Institute of Race Relations served on her advisory committee. "These face-to-face contacts gave richness to my life," she recalled. "They also gave me the courage to ask such persons to visit our school, to speak in the assembly, and to visit the classrooms."[70]

Rachel DuBois also developed a lasting friendship with W. E. B. Du Bois, whose writing had first inspired her interracial concerns. Several months after meeting him in 1925, she wrote for help with a school program at Woodbury, initiating a warm and lively correspondence that lasted many years. The two frequently laughed together over the predicament of sharing the same name and wondered if they might be related by marriage. (Soon after their meeting he wrote to a friend: "This will introduce Mrs. DuBois—not my Mrs DuBois but a very nice Mrs DuBois." He once took her arm at an interracial gathering and introduced her as "Mrs. Du Bois," enjoying the looks of surprise. She later joked that she was working for a doctorate so he could introduce her as "the other Dr. DuBois.") She wrote to him regularly to request material for her programs, advice on her outlines and speeches, letters of introduction, and assistance with fundraising. In her letters, DuBois expressed humor and irreverence, as well as the strain and exhaustion brought by the pace of her work. The editor nominated her for membership on the NAACP board, where she remained loyal to him when controversies flared. After he moved to Atlanta, they saw each other on his visits to New York, attending the theater together or meeting for supper. Observers sometimes assumed she was his daughter. In one sense, her work was an attempt to deal with the problem of "twoness," the "double self," that W. E. B. Du Bois had so passionately articulated. She saw the cultural gifts approach as a way to resolve the dilemma of dual identity, to make it possible to be both American and a member of a minority group.[71]

DuBois's professional network included Jewish leaders as well, and she came to count Jews among her chief supporters. She took a course with Mordecai Kaplan, the founder of Reconstructionist Judaism, and was deeply affected by his ideas. The Service Bureau drew on the work of Jewish intellectuals—including Bruno Lasker, Horace Kallen, and Franz Boas—employed Jewish workers, and received funding from Jewish groups and individuals. In May 1934, for example, DuBois told W.E.B. Du Bois that she had secured some money for the following year's budget from "most by Jewish sources." By June she had been promised additional funds "from another Jewish source." Over time, much of her funding came from the American Jewish Committee (AJC). "It is true that through the years this agency had been the only ethnic organization to contribute money enough to make a difference," DuBois later reflected of the AJC. "National organizations of other ethnic groups, as the Polish and Italian Americans, had been asked for funds for intercultural education but had refused." This support reflected Jews' recognition of their stake in a pluralist society. In interwar America, Jews understood that pluralism allowed them to retain their Jewish identities while participating fully in national life. In response to the Nazi threat, a topic of enormous concern to Jewish organizations in the 1930s, AJC leaders gave financial support to a number of institutions dedicated to upholding pluralist and democratic principles. Fearful that their own efforts to combat anti-Semitic propaganda might engender a backlash, they preferred to channel funds quietly through organizations like the Service Bureau that challenged prejudice more broadly.[72]

The Service Bureau developed materials to bring the insights of progressive social science to teachers and students. Since her time at Wood-bury, DuBois had been dismayed by the presentation of ethnic and racial groups in school materials. Her surveys uncovered numerous examples of misinformation, bias, and omission in American history books. She determined to produce a series of mimeographed pamphlets, each devoted to the history of a particular group and its contributions to American life. She solicited help from ethnic organizations in New York, including Casa Italiana, the Jewish Publication Society, the China Institute, the Japan Institute, the NAACP, and the Urban League. The New York Foundation awarded $500 for DuBois and two assistants to conduct research at the New York Public Library. DuBois received funds from two New Deal agencies, the Works Progress Administration and the Civil Works Administration, to hire workers to gather information

A group of students from Benjamin Franklin High School in New York exhibiting Jewish ceremonial objects, 1935. (From Rachel Davis DuBois with Corann Okorodudu, *All This and Something More,* p. 70. Photo courtesy of Edward and Carol Davis)

about America's ethnic groups. By the end of 1934, these researchers had developed seventy-four pieces of classroom material, which the Service Bureau used in its New York schools project and made available through its "guidance by mail" department. It distributed articles on antiprejudice education to nine hundred secondary school principals across the country. DuBois also reproduced the best of the papers produced by the teachers enrolled in her courses and completed a pamphlet on her project in the Englewood schools, entitled *Changing Attitudes toward Other Races and Nations.* In 1936, the Service Bureau had available ninety-five pieces of classroom material.[73]

Following the philosophy of cultural gifts, each piece of the curriculum described some aspect of the culture or history of one ethnoracial or religious group. The materials were upbeat and celebratory, focused on noteworthy individuals or contributions to American life. Titles included "The Arts and Crafts of the Pennsylvania Germans," "The Negro in Literature," "Orientals in Science and Invention," and "Jewish Orchestra Conductors in American Life." Other lessons considered "Italian Cookery and Home Customs," "Carver of Tuskegee Institute," "Japanese Flower Arrangement." DuBois also coedited, with her research secretary Emma Schweppe, two volumes of what she planned as a series of ten: *The Jews in American Life* and *The Germans in American Life,* published in 1935 and 1936, just as these groups came under increased scrutiny. Chapters covered such topics as "Germans in Eighteenth-Century America" and "The Jew in Philanthropy." "We do not want all people to enter a melting pot and come out exactly duplicating each other," DuBois and Schweppe wrote to students. "We want differences so that we may share our strengths." Through knowing each other, people would attain "a sympathetic understanding, open-mindedness, and tolerance to other peoples of diverse cultures," building a better world "in which the peculiar talents of each group will enrich the life of the whole."[74]

DuBois became concerned as well with the impact of visual materials on attitude formation. Her analysis echoed researchers who recognized that films built stereotypes through the emotional appeal of sight and sound. Sociologist Emory Bogardus identified motion pictures as a source of racial antipathy, noting that a movie such as *The Clansman* could create dislike of an entire race, arousing "repulsive effects" in viewers' minds. He urged producers to stop portraying members of minority races as villains and suggested that ethnologists assist movie makers in the correct depiction of cultural roles. A professor at Ohio State University concluded that "some pictures are extremely potent in influencing attitudes." Students who viewed *The Birth of a Nation* exhibited an adverse change in attitude toward blacks, while *The Sons of the Gods* produced positive impressions of the Chinese. Results indicated that exposure to the right films could produce desirable results, but other pictures might "cumulatively break down favorable attitudes toward mores which teachers and parents have built up with thoughtful care."[75]

DuBois believed that teachers could undercut this negative outcome by interpreting movies with their students, as well as by analyzing stereotypes found in comics, vaudeville, plays, and newspapers. While the school could not eliminate propaganda, teachers could "train ourselves to counteract it intelligently, consciously, and scientifically." She also urged the creation of films that would show a "cosmopolitan" America. She encouraged aspiring filmmakers to portray such scenes as "the artistic homemade cart of the Greek flower vender; the hurdy-gurdy of the Italian playing a bit of opera; the onion fields of the Connecticut Valley Polish farmer; the Negro orange pickers of Florida." Motion pictures could show the waves of immigration "and how all became adjusted and assimilated" and could shine the spotlight on such historical figures as Crispus Attucks and Haym Solomon. This new medium would bring to life the poetry and music, art and architecture, of America's culture groups.[76]

DuBois eagerly disseminated her teachers' plans, classroom units, assembly programs, plays, and bibliographies. In one six-month period, the Service Bureau received 207 requests for teaching materials from teachers, principals, religious education groups, PTAs, and youth clubs. Requests came from thirty-three states and the District of Columbia, with the bulk from the Northeast. This eager reception, DuBois believed, "shows how widely the need is felt." In 1938 she produced a manual for secondary school teachers, *Adventures in Intercultural Education,* based on her work in fifty public schools.[77]

DuBois devoted significant energy to teacher training as well. While she aimed to be scientific in method and to introduce teachers to recent research findings, she faced challenges in implementing new ideas. Even after training, teachers sometimes held fast to their own prejudices and stereotypes. Some voiced ideas that contradicted DuBois's notion of cultural exchange, while others questioned the omissions and unresolved elements in her approach. Educators could embrace pluralist thinking in the abstract without agreeing to give up social power and privilege. For some, there was little contradiction between the cultural gifts perspective and the perpetuation of social segregation and exclusion.

DuBois recognized that for teachers to be "social scientists in the field" they would need special education. Like Dewey, she saw teachers as guides to social progress, social engineers who "have it in their power to determine the cultural future of American life." Their attitudes represented a potential solution to racial problems. To a teacher who was concerned that studying black Americans would lead to intermarriage, DuBois replied, "We as teachers can not be held responsible for what may or may not happen 500 or a thousand years from now, but as leaders of youth in a free public school system in a Democracy we certainly are responsible for giving facts to young people about other young people with whom they must live in our social body."[78]

Through the Service Bureau, DuBois hoped to promote the ideas she had encountered at Teachers College, "to assist teachers in the practical application of some of the techniques of social control as developed by social psychologists." As she explained, "nothing is done in the field of education until the classroom teacher starts doing it." She disseminated new ideas on race and culture, particularly the insights of cultural anthropology, regularly citing Boas, and later Ruth Benedict and Margaret Mead. In her writings for popular audiences, to counter eugenic assumptions, DuBois endorsed historical and scientific studies on the origins of cultural traits and the process of immigrant adjustment. "No one race is any better than any other race, so far as anybody has ever been able to prove," she told teachers, echoing Boas. "Most people in every race are about average in intelligence and morals, while each race has a few great men and a few criminals." She stressed essential similarities: "If we were to select the most intelligent, imaginative, energetic, and emotionally stable third of all mankind, all races would be represented."[79]

DuBois lamented that most teachers were not up to date on these social science findings and that "the average citizen has not had an opportunity in school or out to learn what the science of cultural anthropology has to offer. He has thus become the victim of the propaganda of race superiority and race hatred." Scientists had begun to write books for the lay reader, but most people remained ignorant of anthropological discoveries. DuBois wanted social scientists to bring their findings to public attention, writing on the level that high school teachers and students could understand, and urged them to attend to the practical implications of their work. She implored "the best of our philosophic and scientific minds to lead the rest of us into this uncharted field of human relations." Abstract theories, she suggested, were of little value if divorced from real-life applications. Busy public school teachers were already overburdened by crowded classrooms and heavy schedules; they needed guidance in ways to fulfill new educational objectives.[80]

The danger was that teachers might implant their personal prejudices in children's minds. Lasker wanted teachers to know more about the groups in their schools and to engage in "continuous self-criticism and self-education." This would require a dramatic shift in teachers' preparation: "their whole training will practically have to be reconstructed." In the 1930s, several studies highlighted the importance of teachers' attitudes in shaping students' outlook. Reports from the field corroborated these findings. Ruth Wanger, principal of a Philadelphia high school, recalled that she did not at first recognize her own prejudices. But as long as she made comparisons detrimental to her black students, "I could teach no lesson on the brotherhood of man that would ever ring anything but false and artificial." She finally broke through her own "wall of prejudice," gained black friends, and gave up feelings of superiority. Wanger concluded "that the most important point in the preparation of the teacher who would undertake to improve Negro-White relations is completely to overcome his own prejudices." Otherwise, work with young people was of little avail.[81]

Child Study sent a similar message, in reply to a teacher who wanted to improve her fifth-graders' attitudes toward classmates from minority groups. The magazine advised the teacher to "steep yourself in background material about the cultures and heritages of the races and nationalities which make up your group" and then bring this information into classroom work and field trips and encourage parents and other teachers to study it. Mary Chaplin Shute, who trained kindergarten teachers, advocated "the mixture of races in the training class itself, where the give and take of classroom contact teaches better than any books can do," and recommended that student teachers undertake welfare work in immigrant neighborhoods in order to understand the contributions of each group to America.[82]

DuBois was aware that most educators were unprepared for the role she was asking them to assume: "most of those who build our curricula do not *know* the facts," she lamented. "These dominant-group teachers have not identified themselves with the various culture groups which they are serving." She encouraged educators to meet representatives of minority groups, particularly individuals of their own professional or social standing, to dispel their stereotypes. DuBois encountered some resistance from teachers, even those outwardly sympathetic to her goals. Some were friendly but ignorant, denying racial antagonism at their schools and unaware of the ostracism minority children suffered. Others gave false information to their students or asserted that white children had no need to learn about other cultures. She reported in 1936 that her work with four hundred teachers had revealed a wide spectrum of attitudes, "ranging all the way from enthusiastic acceptance to indifference, ignorance, and antagonism. The hopeful thing is that even teachers' attitudes are subject to change."[83]

DuBois began to offer in-service courses for teachers in the schools where she worked. She also developed university courses for teachers and teachers-in-training that aimed to make social science findings accessible and relevant. In 1933 she taught her first course at the Harvard-Boston University extension school to a class of twenty-five white teachers, becoming the first person to teach a course on intercultural education. She soon began teaching at New York University as well, a position she held throughout the 1930s. Over the course of her career, she taught at Temple University, Brooklyn College, San Francisco State Teachers College, Columbia University, the New School, and the state teachers colleges in Newark and Paterson, New Jersey. In the fall of 1934, she noted that she was lecturing five days a week. She also reached teachers at conferences and through articles in education journals. She considered this work critical, because "I knew that no school project can be successful unless the classroom teacher understands and cooperates."[84]

In the courses, DuBois combined factual information and introspection. She discussed the philosophy that underlay her work, reviewed the history of immigration and Americanization, described cultural contributions, and introduced the latest findings in anthropology and social psychology. She provided material on various groups that teachers could integrate into their classes and club activities. She also asked teachers to conduct school projects and submit reports and arranged for them to meet people of different cultural groups. She invited guest speakers, encouraged teachers to visit their pupils' homes, and organized interracial gatherings hosted by students or friends.[85]

For the most part, teachers responded well to the courses. DuBois typed up a sheet of positive comments she had received from class participants, perhaps to distribute to interested educators and school districts. The comments highlighted the "wider range of understanding and sympathy" teachers gained. Participants appreciated the positive convictions of the instructor and the extensive material she offered. Any teacher "would profit by this course in a richer understanding of the worth of integrated cultures," one comment read. Decades later, an Italian American who in 1937 had participated in the class at New York University recalled how her association with DuBois had changed her outlook. "I learned to be understanding of other people, and not to accept prejudice," she remembered. She noted that she had acquired many Jewish friends and described one occasion when she felt "proud of walking next to a colored girl," something that would have previously made her uncomfortable.[86]

The individual evaluation forms DuBois received, however, tell a more complicated story about teacher responses. After an in-service course in Englewood, New Jersey, in 1934, DuBois asked teachers to assess which aspects of the course were most helpful and how practical they found the material. She also asked participants to write a brief description of their attitudes toward each group studied before and after taking the course. The comments revealed a range of perspectives. Many teachers found the materials useful for their classes. "I can only say that I am more aware, more sensitive to the problem than I was before taking this course," one teacher reflected. "And I shall take advantage of any opportunity to use any of the material brought up in our discussions. I am more sympathetic toward these groups than I have been." Other comments echoed DuBois's philosophy. "I think the schools should be the best place to start the assimilation of the races," one read. "It is the duty of the teacher to acquaint herself with the various cultural backgrounds" of her students to overcome racial prejudices. Teachers used such terms as "enjoyable," "helpful," and "splendid" to describe the course and suggested that it be extended across a full year.[87]

For some teachers, it was a revelation to meet educated members of minority groups. African American guests made a particular impression, as DuBois recognized. In 1933, she commented to W. E. B. Du Bois on how enthusiastically white teachers in Washington, D.C. had responded to the program on African Americans: "I'm wondering why they were so keyed up about it when they have done similar things on the Jew, German, Italian, etc.," she mused. "But I suppose there is greater tension on this subject so that *successfully* to have passed thru the crisis gives them more emotion and then too—whether they admit it or not the Negro is more attractive to *them*." After hearing Crystal Bird Fauset sing, the teachers "*raved* about her—'Didn't dream anyone of that group could be so charming.'"[88]

In Englewood, DuBois had invited, among other speakers, Jessie Fauset, the novelist, and had arranged for the class to hear a poetry reading and meet for tea in Harlem. "New to me—I have always known only the other extreme of the social ladder," a participant explained. One teacher wrote, "Before taking this course I did not realize the number of educated Negroes there are in the world. I simply thought of them as no account and as being for the most part very low, morally and intellectually. I now realize that there are many educated, cultured and refined Negroes." Another reported, "I now see that they have a definite place among us and are deserving of great praise, to have contributed so much to our civilization, in proportion to the privileges they have enjoyed." For a third, "feeling for Negro has been raised greatly from relation of mistress and maid to tolerance and appreciation." One participant looked beyond DuBois's cultural focus to other forms of inequality: "Since taking the course I think the Negro does not want our sympathy and pity but they do want to be on our own social level in Education, etc. and to have the rights of citizens."[89]

But the Englewood teachers were aware as well of the tensions inherent in DuBois's presentation of culture groups. Several noted the importance of the socioeconomic distinctions her materials left out. One teacher wondered if the guest speakers "are not as far removed from the negroes we cope with as we are ourselves." The economic divide among blacks was as stark as it was among whites, the teacher realized. "How can we expect these educated, cultured, refined people to be able to tell us what causes the ignorant, vicious negro we deal with as problems to display the type of conduct they do," she asked in her evaluation. Another participant critiqued the practicality of the course: "you talked so much about tolerance and I think the educated people whom you introduced us to were rather intolerant of the lower classes themselves. I think you might have more application to the lower type as we never come in contact with the cultured type in the teaching field." To make the course relevant to real circumstances, the teacher suggested concentrating on "the types we come in daily contact with" but found difficult to understand. "How to help that class more would be a greater aid than too much concentration on the higher groups." DuBois scribbled a response in the margins of the form that made clear the boundaries of her own aims: "This is a human, *social* problem not cultural or racial," she retorted. Problems of social class or economic oppression, in other words, lay outside her focus on cultural and racial diversity.[90]

Not all of the teachers were able to overcome their prejudices. Some seemed even to have found scientific justification for long-held biases. One participant reported that previously she had known only "lower level" Italians. "These people were very displeasing to me because of their uncleanliness and thievery, and dishonestness" [sic]. She gained greater respect for them—not because those stereotypes were inaccurate, but rather "knowing that environment is the chief cause for attitude and personality." Cultural relativism, it appeared, could support biased perceptions.[91]

For several teachers, the course reinforced stereotypes of Jews even as it explained the origins of their behavior. One participant wrote of "the Jew": "Before taking this course I could not understand why he was so aggressive—after hearing the history of the Jew as given by Dr. Weinstein, I understand the reason." Another admitted to having strong animosity toward the "aggressiveness" of Jews: "My first trip to the city made me dislike them so much and each year the dislike grew so if possible I would go out of my way to avoid them." Through the course, the teacher found to her surprise that "suppression has made them turn to their own." After learning about their contributions, "I think they are much under rated and deserve a more gracious assimilation into American and European social groups." A teacher who had been "impatient and annoyed with their offensive manners and aggressiveness" came to understand the reason for this negative conduct in the history of persecutions they had endured. This teacher was impressed by Jews' "beautiful and devoted religious home-life" for which "they are deserving of more credit than they receive." It seemed that appreciation could coexist with disdain. One teacher demonstrated the complications of "sympathetic understanding" in a comment that expressed just the kind of forbearance and sufferance DuBois opposed: "The work on the Jews helped me to understand their problem better. I cannot say I like them better but I think I am more tolerant."[92]

Other teachers were even more explicit about the perdurability of old attitudes. One wrote: "Lived at college with a Jewish girl. Experience rather tiresome. As yet have not been able to acquire toleration." The rabbi who spoke to the class was "not convincing. Felt an unAmerican spirit." Another concluded, "The Jews are also on the defensive even some of their leaders. They resent us even though they do not care to assimilate with us." Nor had this teacher managed to dispel her anti-Asian prejudices: of a guest speaker, she wrote, "She clarified some of my personal experiences and dislikes for the Oriental." Another was blunt about the limits to her change in attitude: "Can't thoroughly accept idea of complete integration among peoples' [sic] whose philosophy and religion is totally different but certainly have a greater understanding and appreciation for them." These comments suggest the limits to DuBois's success. Exposure to new scientific thinking on cultural difference may have fostered greater sympathy for minority groups, but it did not necessarily translate into the kind of active appreciation and mutual exchange DuBois desired. For some participants in her programs, cultural gifts work was compatible with cultural stereotypes. And as some of the teachers recognized, it did little to challenge patterns of economic status and social exclusion.[93]

Despite this evidence for the persistence of old attitudes, the scientific slant of DuBois's teacher training represented the modern outlook of the era. She enlisted the booming fields of cultural anthropology, sociology, and psychology for use in the schools, urging teachers to discard old-fashioned ideas in favor of up to date, scientifically demonstrated findings. Rather than passing on misconceptions and biases, she said, "teachers will have to make social scientists of ourselves," applying the scientific method to the study of racial differences and attitude modification. Teachers were key figures in the creation of a pluralist democracy: it was up to them to transmit the newest ideas to the next generation. "Thus by approaching the subject in as scientific way as possible," she explained, "we will be able to hand on to those who come after us a body of observed facts which may help to bring some order out of our present social chaos." Antiprejudice work signaled a rejection of narrow provincialism and conformity, an advance over the timidity and speciousness that had marked earlier understandings of race. For the teachers who accepted its tenets, the cultural gifts vision seemed forward-looking and bold, the mark of a modern spirit.[94]

Through the assembly programs, DuBois introduced students and teachers to the cultures of America's racial, ethnic, and religious groups. In the midst of an era usually described as repressive and anti-immigrant, she advanced a liberal agenda, demonstrating the role that the school could play in dispelling racial prejudice. At her best, she managed to advance both diversity and unity, both cultural difference and common culture through a process of mutual exchange. As a result of her efforts, cultural pluralism extended far beyond the intellectual and scholarly elite, gaining public acceptance as it found its way into classrooms, school assemblies, textbooks, and teacher training courses. DuBois's celebration of cultural differences pointed the way toward a more inclusive American identity. Yet the tensions in her approach limited its effectiveness and would reappear as the cultural gifts agenda found its way into the interfaith movement and as it extended across the American South. They would continue to shape DuBois's work as it evolved in the 1930s, when she came to see cultural gifts education as a way to bolster self-esteem among the children of immigrants, and as Americans confronted the economic crisis and expressed alarm over rising nationalism overseas.

4

Religious Education and the Teaching of Goodwill

"Has the church school any part in causing children to become prejudiced against other religious groups?" asked a roundtable at the 1932 seminar of the National Conference of Jews and Christians (NCJC). Representatives of Protestant, Catholic, and Jewish groups acknowledged that religious instruction could exacerbate hostilities among children of different faiths. They proposed that the church and synagogue instill respect for other religious traditions.[1] In the interwar period, liberal Protestants took the lead in promoting this view, asserting that the majority group had a particular responsibility to advance religious tolerance. Through conferences, speaking tours, textbook revisions, and Sunday school reforms, they reached out to Jews and Catholics for dialogue and exchange. Jews were particularly responsive to these overtures, offering institutional and financial support.

The New York–based NCJC, organized in 1927, stood at the center of this goodwill movement. Its leaders adapted the cultural gifts approach to describe America as a country shaped by three major religions. Linking cultural pluralism with the social message of Protestant liberalism, they claimed that Judaism, Catholicism, and Protestantism had all made—and would continue to make—important contributions to American life, an interpretation that predated by several decades the "triple melting pot" concept that Will Herberg's book *Protestant-Catholic-Jew* popularized in 1955.[2] Since the nation was heterogeneous in religion, NCJC leaders maintained, Protestantism did not have exclusive claim to American culture and identity. This initiative "sowed the seeds of goodwill," as an NCJC publication put it, for the interfaith efforts that blossomed after World War II.

Like their counterparts in parent education and the schools, leaders in religious goodwill relied on progressive intellectual trends to explain the origins of prejudice. Following behaviorist principles, they scrutinized Sunday school materials, youth group activities, and teacher training to evaluate what children learned about other religions. They approached the education of young children with caution, however. This reluctance reflected two recurrent tensions within the goodwill movement. The first concerned what appeared to be an inherent contradiction between pluralist ideals and religious belief. Pluralism depended on diversity, on appreciation, on dynamic mixing and exchange. Institutional religions, in contrast, were based on exclusions, on the indoctrination of children into the beliefs of a particular faith. Goodwill participants struggled to reconcile the distinctive and divisive nature of religious faith with the pluralist vision of equality and interaction. A second, related tension concerned Protestant missionary aims. Suspicions of proselytism shaped the early interfaith movement and remained a point of mistrust in later years. Jewish leaders in particular feared that Christians retained an unspoken goal to convert Jewish children. Aware of Jewish sensitivity on this matter, liberal Protestants proceeded carefully in designing programs for young people. They found that adolescent and adult education offered a less threatening means to disseminate the interfaith message.

While liberal clergy and laypeople mobilized to advance religious tolerance, they were less attentive to prejudice aimed at blacks or other racial minorities. Their focus on the "three cultures" of Protestants, Catholics, and Jews obscured differences among those groups while marginalizing other religious traditions. They occasionally identified racial discrimination as an area for fruitful cooperation and acknowledged that the most blatant bigotry occurred in the most solidly Protestant region of the country. However, as with other cultural gifts liberals, their reluctance to address racial segregation limited their ability to promote true pluralism. Their particular task, as they understood it, was to dispel religious bigotry against Jews and Catholics, particularly those with origins in Europe. They instructed children in a definition of American identity that included three faiths but largely excluded other minority groups from the national story.

The Origins of the Goodwill Movement

A number of factors contributed to the trend toward religious goodwill in the 1920s. World War I brought increased contact between Christians and Jews, including among chaplains who worked together in military units. The postwar peace movement stirred church leaders to argue that international harmony required domestic harmony and that religious groups had a moral obligation to work for peace. The Federal Council of the Churches of Christ in America (FCC; later the National Council of Churches), which comprised twenty-five Protestant denominations representing twenty million congregants, was deeply involved in peace efforts; its Committee on World Friendship among Children arranged for the exchange of letters and gifts between American children and children overseas. The FCC sponsored an annual "Race Relations Sunday," on which ministers from black and white churches exchanged pulpits, and began to study how religious agencies affected children's attitudes toward other nations and races. The "social gospel" movement, centered at Union Theological Seminary in New York, also inspired religious goodwill as it promoted social equality and democracy as fundamental to Christian teachings.[3]

The goodwill movement emerged as well in response to repressive trends of the time, which looked to conservative Protestantism to reassert traditional values. The revival of the Ku Klux Klan—with its virulent anti-Catholic, anti-Jewish, and antiblack rhetoric—distressed many liberal Protestants, as did discussions of immigration restriction, which targeted Jews and Catholics, and anti-Semitic literature, especially Henry Ford's promotion of the *Protocols of the Elders of Zion,* an anti-Semitic tract. Liberals worried about Protestant anxiety over the growing Jewish population (over four million Jews lived in America by 1927, mostly concentrated in ten major cities). This apprehension emerged in a blood libel incident in Massena, New York, in which the mayor accused a rabbi of sacrificing a Christian child for ritual purposes, highlighting in 1928 the depths of ignorance and fear that existed regarding Jewish customs and beliefs. Liberal Protestants were also distressed by the anti-Catholic sentiment that emerged during Al Smith's 1928 presidential campaign. Some objected to restrictions against Jews in employment, social clubs, housing, hotels and resorts, and universities and to the association of Jews with radicalism. In the 1930s, the threat of Nazi agitation in the country heightened these concerns. American ideals, these liberals argued, had no room for anti-Jewish and anti-Catholic bigotry.[4]

Jewish responses to the missionizing activities of Protestant churches were also important to the establishment of interreligious organizations. After World War I, home mission boards attempted to influence new immigrants, directing them to church groups and Christian settlement houses and preaching in immigrant neighborhoods. Some of these missions were aimed at Jews in particular, as Protestant leaders of the postwar evangelical revival equated Americanization with Christianization. According to historian Benny Kraut, the angry response of Jews to these conversion efforts encouraged some FCC leaders to form in 1923 a Committee on Goodwill Between Jews and Christians and to approach the Central Conference of American Rabbis (CCAR), an organization of Reform Judaism, to propose collaborative efforts. Members of the CCAR had initially been suspicious of overtures from the FCC, fearful that protestations of goodwill masked underlying missionary aims. Indeed, while some FCC leaders abandoned proselytizing in favor of goodwill efforts, more fundamentalist colleagues appeared less willing to cease their efforts to convert Jews, as their missionary backgrounds inspired commitment to evangelism as the true expression of Christianity. This tension over conversionist aims would reappear throughout the goodwill movement.[5]

Despite some of its members' hesitation, the CCAR agreed to cooperate with the FCC, establishing its own Committee on Goodwill. At the end of 1924, the two committees approved a declaration of principles that agreed to respect the integrity of each religion, supported full opportunity for each faith's development, and disclaimed any proselytizing aims. Practical cooperation in common tasks, the declaration stated, would demonstrate fellowship. The Anti-Defamation League of B'nai B'rith, a Jewish defense agency, enthusiastically endorsed the joint statement, finding it "exceedingly gratifying" that a Christian organization was proposing to work for understanding between Jews and non-Jews.[6]

While the FCC's Goodwill Committee gained the support of Jewish leaders, it was less popular within the FCC, some of whose members continued to advocate conversion of Jews to Christianity. Jewish anger flared in 1927 over an international missionary conference, in which the FCC-affiliated Home Missions Council participated, that included sessions on converting Jews. Leaders of the CCAR complained to leaders of the FCC's Goodwill Committee, who reaffirmed their own—but not the larger FCC's—repudiation of proselytism. Recognizing the limitations of a Protestant-led effort for interreligious understanding, FCC leaders, in conjunction with industrialist Roger W. Straus of the Union of American Hebrew Congregations, proposed the formation of a new interfaith group that would be nonecclesiastical and independent of the FCC. They hoped to assuage Jewish fears by remaining unaffiliated with Protestant institutions.[7]

The new organization adopted the name National Conference of Jews and Christians. (In 1938 the name changed to the National Conference of Christians and Jews [NCCJ].) What had started as a Protestant-led effort now included an advisory board of prominent Jews, Protestants, and Catholics and three cochairs, one from each faith. Straus, who had worked with the FCC's Committee on Good Will, was the Jewish chair. The Protestant chair was Newton D. Baker, an Episcopalian, who had been secretary of war under Woodrow Wilson. The organization had no Catholic chair until 1930, when Carlton J. H. Hayes, a prominent historian at Columbia, agreed to serve. Catholics played a smaller role in the early leadership and offered less enthusiastic support. Their hesitation resulted from papal opposition to interfaith interaction, theological doctrine that denied the equality of religions, and suspicions about the genuineness of Protestant sympathy for Catholic concerns.[8]

The new organization won greater acceptance from Jews, who hoped that a nonsectarian group would be effective in fighting anti-Semitism. Protestant response to Jewish concerns was of tremendous importance to Jews, who were still struggling to gain recognition of their rightful place in American society. Nine of the ten organizations that immediately affiliated with the NCJC were Jewish, and much of the group's initial small budget came from Jewish sources. B'nai B'rith was an important financial sponsor, while the AJC offered support both directly and via members who followed funding recommendations—involvement that allowed the AJC to influence the new organization's policies.[9]

In 1928 Everett Ross Clinchy became secretary of the new NCJC, a position he would hold for decades. A young, creative, and energetic Presbyterian minister, Clinchy had come to know men from various religious backgrounds while serving in the army. After the war he earned a master's degree at Union Theological Seminary and a doctorate in education from Drew University, and then he became minister of College

Church at Wesleyan University, where he arranged interreligious gatherings. He visited the Near East to study how Christian colleges developed religious cooperation and explored relations among Christians, Jews, and Muslims in Palestine.[10]

The NCJC soon took up educational projects. In 1929, Clinchy organized a seminar with leading Catholics, Protestants, and Jews, held at Columbia University. Despite threats from some Jewish groups to denounce the event as an attempt at proselytizing, the representatives openly discussed their convictions and agreed on "freedom of conscience" as a basic principle for working together. The impetus for the seminar came in part from Claris E. Silcox, a Protestant clergyman from Canada who had worked with The Inquiry organizing interfaith conferences for Catholics and Protestants, experiments that provided the pattern for the NCJC seminars. The connection was reinforced when Clinchy asked Silcox to organize the Columbia seminar and later to direct the study that resulted in *Catholics, Jews and Protestants,* a 1934 volume he coauthored with social researcher Galen M. Fisher. The Inquiry sponsored other early ventures in intercultural education, including Bruno Lasker's influential study *Race Attitudes in Children,* a series of books on race relations, and an educational pamphlet entitled *How Catholics See Protestants.*[11]

Everett Clinchy. (National Conference of Christians and Jews Records, Social Welfare History Archives, University of Minnesota Libraries)

In 1933, Clinchy initiated goodwill tours, in which a rabbi, priest, and minister toured the country together—a novel idea that brought national attention to the NCJC. In 1933, Clinchy, Father John Elliot Ross of Charlottesville, Virginia, and Rabbi Morris S. Lazaron of Baltimore traveled the country for seven weeks, visiting colleges, high schools, and community groups in twenty-one states and conducting radio broadcasts. On stage, the three clergymen engaged in a public dialogue about their religions: following a script, they asked questions of each other and told stories and jokes. This was the first time many audience members had seen representatives of the three groups talking in a friendly way about their similarities and differences. The "tolerance trio" generated extensive publicity and led to the formation of local NCJC chapters. The NCJC employed this technique many times over the next decade. In 1936, for instance, twenty-five teams toured the country. During World War II, trio presentations at military bases reached seven million members of the armed forces.[12]

From the late 1920s through the 1930s, the NCJC sponsored hundreds of local conferences, roundtables, and institutes. Its first national seminar in 1932 drew 475 participants. In 1934 the organization reported a membership of several thousand and communication with people in two hundred cities and towns. By 1942 there were ten regional offices. Brotherhood Day, established in 1934 and expanded to Brotherhood Week in 1939, encouraged churches to emphasize interfaith understanding. The Religious News Service sent weekly news coverage to hundreds of religious and secular newspapers around the country. The NCJC published articles and pamphlets and made use of new mass media to promote goodwill and interfaith collaboration on common civic problems such as labor relations, social welfare programs, and militarism and peace.[13]

Cultural Pluralism, Behaviorist Psychology, and Religious Attitudes

The NCJC looked to scientific expertise from its inception. In 1928 it invited prominent social scientists and intellectuals to join a committee to study relations between Jew and non-Jew. The thirty-member committee included, among others, notable thinkers Horace Kallen, Franz Boas, Melville Herskovits, James Weldon Johnson, Howard Odum, and Goodwin

Watson. The findings of progressive social scientists were regularly disseminated at NCJC events. When religious groups saw themselves as superior to others, a minister said at one gathering, it was "not only intolerant spiritually but, worse than that, it is untrue scientifically." For the national seminar, social scientists prepared a sourcebook and spoke at sessions along with representatives of the three faiths.[14]

Clinchy himself drew on the insights of progressive social science. He straddled the lines between minister and educator, comfortable in both the spiritual and academic realms. He read widely in sociology, anthropology, and education, was well versed in the literature on race and prejudice, and sprinkled references to Franz Boas, John Dewey, and other theorists throughout his writings. To explain cultural behavior, he made frequent reference to anthropologist and psychologist Clark Wissler, author of the 1923 book *Man and Culture*. Following Wissler, Clinchy saw religions as culture groups into which individuals were bred and in whose superiority they came to believe. He rejected the melting pot theory of Americanization in favor of a religiously based version of the cultural gifts vision. Literature put out by his organization traced the history of religious groups and the doctrine of religious liberty in America, implying that roots in early America lent legitimacy to the goodwill agenda.[15]

Clinchy's own commitment to cultural pluralism followed directly from the work of Horace Kallen. Drawing on Kallen's metaphor, Clinchy asserted that national life was enriched by differences just as "the *ensemble* of a symphony orchestra is more colorful than the single note of a shepherd's flute." The virtues of America "have been achieved because of cultural diversity, not in spite of it." Clinchy set this vision against the recurrent trend toward "cultural monism," in which the majority sought to dominate national life. He imagined a society "in which can be maintained a parity of the different, a democracy of cultures, a kind of *cultural pluralism*." He articulated these ideas with care, repeatedly detailing what he did *not* believe. Parity did not mean that each religion was as good as another, or that religions were interchangeable or all the same. He also denied that each had to dilute its theology or that people should give up their beliefs. Interfaith dialogue did not aim to create hybrid religion or to seek the merger of religious bodies, for the philosophies of each faith could not be reconciled or fused. "The Conference does not underestimate the differences that distinguish Protestants, Catholics, and Jews, nor minimize them," stated its literature. "It seeks no common denominator of belief. Its purpose is not served by any watering down of religious conviction or lessening of loyalty to one's own household of faith." Trio tours did not engage in theological debate over matters of salvation and damnation. As one participant at the national seminar put it, goodwill implied "a courageous attitude of study and reverence toward the reverences of other faiths" but not a compromise of doctrines to make them acceptable to all.[16]

Clinchy argued that this pluralist viewpoint would not weaken each religion. On the contrary, it would strengthen each through lively exchange. Pluralism would not encourage proselytism, for it affirmed the integrity of each faith: "every individual must be taught to reverence the right of others to their reverences." Interreligious cooperation would make Christians better Christians and Jews better Jews—in other words, it would elevate the importance of organized religion, bringing people into closer allegiance with their own religious institutions. It was the responsibility of the majority group to protect religious pluralism, to "make America safe for differences." Evoking cultural gifts language, he asked, "How can we be sure that each minority will have an opportunity to contribute fully and heroically the unique contribution it has for American life?" While minority groups needed to do their part, "it is up to us Protestants to see that minority groups are treated respectfully in the 20th century," he told readers of the *Christian Century*.[17]

The pluralist framework extended the goodwill message beyond simple tolerance. Like Rachel Davis DuBois, goodwill leaders eschewed the term as inadequate to describe the extent of their vision. As early as 1926, the president of the FCC explained: "Tolerance is a cheap word of political origin. We do not seek tolerance. We seek brotherhood, understanding, co-operation." Clinchy rejected the notion of "Live and let live" in favor of "Live and help live." Participants at the national seminar acknowledged that well-meaning efforts to combat prejudice could instill "a mere toleration of something one does not approve of" instead of open-minded curiosity and desire to find shared ideals. At best, tolerance appeared condescending, "too negative, too passive a state of mind."[18]

Interfaith advocates preferred to speak instead of fostering "good will," a term that implied mutual respect, Roger Straus explained, "a positive acknowledgment of the *value* of differences." Other leaders invoked "cultural variety in unity," a principle that suggested "positive appreciation of religious and other cultural variations." One roundtable centered on "the desirability of developing unity without uniformity in the cultural life of America." Participants ventured that "there is positive value in diversity of cultures. It may be that in the United States we should educate more specifically in terms of 'cultural pluralism.'"[19]

Religious pluralism offered a countervailing trend to the secularization of the 1920s and 1930s. In the interwar period, scientific developments challenged the religious worldview, making religious practices seem outdated and unsuited to the modern world. Some observers worried that new awareness of the history and sociology of world religions would also undermine faith by demonstrating that beliefs were socially rather than divinely determined. Speakers at the NCJC national seminar, for instance, "drew attention to the difficulty of teaching comparative religion to adolescents without weakening that loyalty which was felt to be so essential." But for liberal ministers like Clinchy, pluralism reinforced allegiance to religious institutions and revitalized Protestantism by giving it new meaning and purpose. The forums of the NCJC reasserted both shared values and each group's distinct religious identity as they promised that religion could help solve social problems. In this way, Clinchy believed, religious pluralism helped update the message of Christianity to make it more relevant to the modern world.[20]

In addition to cultural pluralism, behaviorist psychology set the intellectual agenda for the goodwill movement. Like other progressive thinkers of the time, Clinchy was persuaded that children acquired attitudes in the early years. He cited Watson's analysis of habitual responses and the work of F. H. Allport, another behaviorist psychologist, and echoed Lasker's *Race Attitudes in Children.* "Born without prejudices we rapidly learn them from our environment," Clinchy wrote. He explained that Christians "become 'conditioned' in regard to Jews." The family, school, church, and community determined children's attitudes to their neighbors. A child who grew up with positive associations with other religions and races would come to value cultural differences. To spread these ideas, Clinchy included an article by Lasker entitled "How Children Acquire Race Prejudices" in the NCJC's first information bulletin in 1928.[21]

Other goodwill advocates adopted the theory of social conditioning to explain the genesis of religious prejudice. By 1927, readers of *World Tomorrow* and *Religious Education,* liberal Christian magazines, had learned that modern psychology rejected the old idea of fixed instincts and now understood human nature to be plastic. *Literary Digest* reported on a study by Adelaide T. Case, a professor at Columbia University, who surveyed a thousand children in New York and found religious ignorance and misunderstanding between Catholic and Protestant children as well as between Jewish and Christian children. In another study, Albert Murphy of Columbia gave attitude tests to four hundred Protestant young people in Philadelphia. He found ignorance and provincialism regarding Buddhists, Muslims, Hindus, Jews, and African Americans. "Our religious education has been antiquarian," Murphy concluded. "It smacks of tribalism. It worships the God of tradition rather than the God of social improvement."[22]

If prejudices against other religions were socially conditioned, could they be replaced by attitudes of appreciation? To goodwill advocates, the answer was yes. Clinchy asserted that through conversation and companionship, Jews could learn that fears of Christians were unfounded, while Christians could "slough off the distorted, exaggerated mental images of what they thought all Jews were like." Such a "reconditioning experience" had to follow up-to-date methods. "The problems of intergroup relationships must be approached in a scientific spirit. We must uncover the roots from which bigotries grow before they can be extirpated," Clinchy wrote. An optimistic slant characterized these discussions. John Haynes Holmes, a New York minister, explained that the task was "to purify the atmosphere in which our boys and girls are reared, and we will find that prejudice and dislike and fear will disappear." A master's thesis produced at the Pacific School of Religion described the spirit of unity and fellowship that followed an interracial worship service with white, black, Japanese, Chinese, and Filipino students.[23]

Yet the implications of behaviorism were complex for religious liberals, who wanted to avoid prejudice without diminishing allegiance to faith. More than ethnoracial communities of descent, into which people were affiliated by birth, the perpetuation of religious belief required conscious indoctrination of children. The dilemma was that religious tenets, with their claims to sole truth, could cultivate a sense of superiority and separateness, sentiments contrary to the goodwill impulse. At the NCJC national seminar in 1932, one participant ventured that if adults would "leave the young alone" there would be no need for special education to overcome prejudice. But others recognized that the problem was more complicated. Since prejudice functioned as a means to defend the in-group and create group cohesion, there was "an actual desire to hand on from generation to generation traditional attitudes of loyalty with their full concomitant of hatreds." Conditioning for intolerance was therefore not accidental, but part of a deliberate attempt to reinforce cultural loyalties.[24]

The challenge for progressive educators was therefore to find ways to imbue children with the ideals of their own religious groups without sacrificing open-mindedness. Participants in the roundtable on church schools thought that teachers of each faith should encourage reverence, sensitiveness, and appreciation for the rights and spiritual values of others, but warned that such ideals should not be cultivated too soon, for they might break down the inner cohesion that sustained group habits. A firm grounding in one's own faith should come first. The participants concluded that the adolescent years were a promising time to introduce comparative religious ideas without weakening youngsters' loyalty to their own churches. Clinchy voiced similar concerns about balancing group allegiance with open-minded attitudes. "Each group goes to great pains with its youth that they may consciously identify themselves with the 'we-group' against all 'other-group' people," he explained. "It is the difficult task of education to nurture enough ethnocentrism to insure satisfactory group loyalties and, at the same time, to safeguard satisfactory relationships with neighbors of other groups in a culturally pluralistic society." Pluralism could flourish only once religious belief was firmly established.[25]

Behaviorist findings on the early acquisition of prejudice focused attention on parents, mothers in particular. Parents inherited attitudes from *their* parents, and so prejudices were handed down from generation to generation. According to one rabbi, the challenge was to break this chain; religious antipathy could then be dispelled in one complete generation, "the duration of a parent-child cycle of existence." As custodians of children's environment, mothers were responsible for "patterns of intolerance," concluded an NCJC roundtable, and urged women to cultivate desirable attitudes. For the most part, however, women played an uncertain role in the NCJC, whose member religious institutions rested on structures of hierarchy and authority that excluded women. Although women were among the first contributors to the organization and took part in many activities, including a tour to meet with women's groups and a women's national advisory committee organized in 1937,

Silcox and Fisher acknowledged the failure of interfaith movements "to enlist the energies of either women or youth."[26] Because women were excluded from religious leadership in all three faiths, they could not participate in the tolerance trios or sign the public statements issued by ministers, priests, and rabbis.

Education for Religious Goodwill

Clinchy's faith in education mirrored the work of Rachel Davis DuBois. His board voted to assist DuBois's Service Bureau for Education in Human Relations, while the staff helped type and copy DuBois's teaching materials and at one point publicized the Service Bureau as part of its own program. In addition, readers of the NCJC *Information Bulletin* learned of DuBois's work to combat anti-Semitism: at some New York public schools in 1931, she introduced books on Jewish themes, invited prominent Jews as guest speakers, arranged for personal contact with synagogue youth, and staged a dramatic representation of a dinner given in honor of Albert Einstein at which students impersonated famous Jewish scientists.[27]

Over the course of the 1930s, Clinchy offered DuBois encouragement and financial support. In October 1932 he passed on the advice of Daniel Kulp II, DuBois's advisor at Teachers College, who suggested that she accept no subsidies from a "propaganda organization," perhaps because affiliation with Jewish funders might discredit her motives, and instead work as a freelance educator. Kulp was "sure that there are a sufficient number of communities ready for your idea to keep you going financially," to which Clinchy added his own reassurance: "I have no doubt but that we shall be able to uncover a number of such cities this fall and winter." Clinchy followed through on his promise, arranging for DuBois to bring her programs to the Boston-area schools of Newton, Melrose, and Watertown in the spring of 1933, with funding from the NCJC, and to teach her first course on intercultural education at Boston University.[28]

Clinchy also helped DuBois secure foundation funds and invited her to speak at conferences. Some of these connections were critical to her success. It was at a NCJC conference in 1933 that DuBois met Theresa Meyer Durlach, a philanthropist who funded DuBois's work. DuBois met Louis Posner of the New York City Board of Education when Clinchy invited her to speak at a luncheon. DuBois later recalled a close connection with the NCJC leader. "Dr. Clinchy and I felt that an organization should be formed to work through the schools," she wrote in a draft of her memoir. The work should relate to general education "so that it would not run into the danger of being considered propaganda." She portrayed Clinchy as central to the establishment of the Service Bureau: "We therefore agreed not to join forces in one organization, but to start another and work closely together, one in the churches, the other in the schools."[29]

Throughout the thirties, the contact between DuBois and Clinchy helped spur the cultural gifts crusade. Clinchy endorsed the assembly programs as an ideal vehicle for its message and served as an advisor to DuBois's Service Bureau. In return, DuBois offered support to the NCJC. She was a prominent participant in a conference on intercultural education organized under the auspices of the NCJC and the Progressive Education Association. Recognizing the churches' potential for reform, she prepared a discussion outline for church groups to "think through the problem of justice in race relationships and the contribution which the Christian churches of today can make," and in an article in the *Church Woman* she urged that school, community, and church organizations work together for cultural understanding.[30]

Bruno Lasker also helped to bridge various manifestations of the anti-prejudice campaign. An early supporter of the NCJC, he was present at many events and played a significant role in the organization. When analyzing denominational literature for *Race Attitudes in Children*, Lasker had found attitudes of supremacy and patronage. His research made him skeptical of "the unending texts on 'neighborliness,' 'world-friendship,' 'adventures in brotherhood,'" which he considered ineffective. One book designed to instill world friendship, he complained, "has the net effect of strengthening rather than reducing a sense of racial superiority." It reflected "a spirit of kindly condescension and not of brotherhood." Christian literature revealed empty sentiment, benevolent paternalism, and self-satisfaction; it pictured non-Christian peoples in tragic terms and implied "a superiority and a consequent handing out of benefits to the 'poor' or the 'heathen' of other lands." In a 1926 talk, he complained that Sunday schools were "making snobs of the little children." He described a pageant staged at a church conference supposedly devoted to racial tolerance and international understanding. The pageant depicted foreign groups—Chinese, African, Indian—in misery and superstition, "and at the end of each scene an American missionary lady turned up just in the nick of time to save the dying baby or rescue whoever there was to be rescued, putting everything right that had been wrong." The effect on young people "was to confirm them in the belief that the white race is far superior to all others." Lasker wondered how children who received this teaching would behave toward other peoples in their own neighborhood. "Will they accept them as equals," respect their leadership, and share their privileges?[31]

Like Lasker, Clinchy drew on behaviorist thinking to explain the effects of religious school teaching. When he surveyed Protestant Sunday school teachers on their understanding of Jews and Judaism, he found great ignorance. Teachers did not realize that many so-called Christian teachings about peace and forgiveness were Jewish in origin and revealed "widespread lack of acquaintance about the aspirations of present-day Judaism." Clinchy observed that such ignorance had a profound effect on Jewish as well as Christian children. As Christian schoolchildren made fun of Jews, they instilled a feeling of inferiority and drove them to deny their heritage. "The fact is that we Christian educators are doing too little to make Christians respect Jews," he lamented.[32]

The teaching of the crucifixion story drew a great deal of discussion. Jews complained that generations of Christian children had been taught that Jews were responsible for the death of Christ. Lasker noted the effects of this teaching in *Race Attitudes in Children,* recounting stories of small children who came to fear Jews. He commented, "Frequent repetitions of historical associations between two terms may so firmly knot them together in the child's mind that one will always tend to suggest the other. For example, for many the often-heard phrase, 'The Jews killed Christ,' continually gets into the way of an objective observation of the Jews as an ethnic group." Rabbi Abram Simon noted that other groups were not similarly blamed for the outrages of their ancestors. "An average Christian child can not take his eyes from the trickling blood of nailed hands without resting them in resentment upon the Jewish child as Christ-killer," he lamented.[33]

Liberal Christians, responsive to these complaints, denounced the charge that Jews were to blame for the death of Jesus. A theology professor proclaimed in the *Federal Council Bulletin:* "It is up to Christians to speak out openly, entirely to disassociate themselves from the mood and temper which, having once crucified Jesus the Jew, has assisted down through the centuries in the daily crucifixion—by more subtle and less forthright methods—of his brethren after the flesh."[34] Everett Clinchy recounted that during one discussion, a rabbi displayed a lesson card used in Sunday schools that asked "Who killed Jesus?" and answered "The Jews." In response, Clinchy surveyed the Sunday school materials of nine Protestant denominations and found many negative references to Jews and Judaism as "the first enemy of the church." Clinchy objected that these references were inaccurate and incomplete, flawed by generalizations. He objected to depictions of Judaism as a dead religion and to accounts of the perfect love and kindness of Christianity that ignored such events as pogroms in Europe and discrimination against blacks in the United States. He complained that few lessons suggested that Judaism had something that could be of worth to modern Christianity.[35]

Under Clinchy's leadership, the NCJC recommended modifying the teaching of the crucifixion. At the national seminar in 1932, participants urged religious leaders to stress that the crucifixion was an ancient event, that some Jews loved Jesus and accompanied him to his death, that Jews were among his followers and were the first Christians, and that ancient differences should not lead to modern antipathies. One success followed a NCJC gathering in Syracuse, New York, when a local pastor canceled a presentation of the Passion Play. "He would not have the little children taught that the Jews as a people crucified Christ centuries ago," reported a Jewish attorney who had attended the conference. "He would not bear the burden of having Christian children call their Jewish playmates, little children like themselves—'Christ-killers.'" Clinchy brought his critique to the attention of textbook editors, publishers, and lesson writers. He asked writers to avoid negative references to Jews, to treat anti-Semitism frankly, and to include material to cultivate correct notions. One syndicate of religious school papers for children agreed to secure stories that pictured Jews "in a true light."[36]

While liberal Christians were alert to concerns about the crucifixion story, some suggested that Jews exaggerated its importance. Silcox and Fisher complained that Jews "tirelessly reiterate, even against the judgment of their Gentile friends, that they are hated because the Christians regard them as Christ-killers" and concluded that "this insistence is ill-founded and only alienates the philo-Semites among Christians." In their discussions with Christians on the Jewish question, few mentioned the charge of Christ-killing, and most "vehemently denied" it when the researchers introduced the topic. "Most of the Protestants interviewed said that they had heard the phrase 'Christ-killers' first from Jewish rabbis and had never heard it used in Christian circles." Representatives of the NCJC similarly remarked that the extent of the teaching had been overemphasized.[37]

Even Clinchy thought that Jews could make too much of theological anti-Semitism. He wrote that "if one listened to the garden variety of Jews he would conclude that the only thing about Jews that Protestant Sunday schools impress upon children is that Jews are Christ-killers." This criticism was "a distorted exaggeration of the truth." Clinchy considered it an oversimplification to think that Christian-Jewish relations would be solved if the anti-Semitic version of the crucifixion story were not told. Other non-Jews noted that Jewish teachings could inspire anti-Christian feeling in Jewish children, just as Christian feelings inspired anti-Semitism. Jewish ideas of "chosenness" seemed to challenge pluralist ideals, reinforce stereotypes of Jews as clannish—and prejudice Jews against all others. In response to these criticisms, some Jewish leaders noted that they no longer emphasized chosenness or claimed special protection. They were willing to forgo this divisive concept in the interest of pluralist cooperation.[38]

Clinchy endorsed a cultural gifts approach to religious education. When children learned that each group contributed to American life, "the sense of mutual interdependence and indebtedness becomes a dynamic for sincere brotherhood!" He wanted church schools to teach about Jewish contributions to science, arts, music, literature, and philosophy. He praised one textbook that described the beautiful traditions that immigrants brought to America and another that called Jews "our teachers." He suggested that instructors arrange meetings between children of different faiths or take Sunday school classes to visit a Catholic church or a Jewish synagogue. At the NCJC's national seminar, a rabbi reported on his experience as a guest speaker at a Protestant religious class, where he had "watched the children's expressions change from fear to curiosity, and from curiosity to friendliness" as he described Jewish belief and practice.[39]

Other progressive religious leaders adopted this approach. Albert Murphy, who had given attitude tests to Protestant youth, urged churches to teach "that the Jews gave us our Bible and religion, and that Jesus whom Christians worship was a Jew." The *Pilgrim Elementary Teacher,* a publication of the Congregational Church, praised a teacher who intervened when her students called Jewish children "Christ-killer" and encouraged implementation of DuBois's methods, since "the building up of sympathetic attitudes toward all people is the obligation of both the school and the church." Religious school offered the teaching of brotherhood, the emotional tone of worship, and "the interpretation of our experiences in thinking, feeling, and acting together."[40]

In 1932, Clinchy commissioned an in-depth study of anti-Jewish prejudice in Protestant pedagogical literature. He proposed to identify ways Sunday school textbooks created undesirable or appreciative attitudes toward contemporary Jews. He received a grant of $5,000 from the New York Foundation, funds that may have originated with the AJC, which was also involved in the project and whose leaders may have feared that their sponsorship would discredit the study. Clinchy also secured the cooperation of the FCC, the International Council of Christian Education, and six prominent Protestant denominations. James V. Thompson of Drew Theological Seminary agreed to direct the project. In a letter to Morris D. Waldman of the AJC, Clinchy noted that this arrangement would provide qualified staff, scientific objectivity, and the prestige of a school affiliated with the Methodist Episcopal Church, the largest Protestant denomination.[41]

Thompson's findings, submitted in 1934, confirmed Jewish fears. He found in official Protestant literature many disparaging or hostile references to Jews and Judaism, especially to the Jews of the New Testament, who were depicted as Pharisees who rejected Jesus and caused the crucifixion. The textbooks did not explain that early Hebrews were ancestors of present-day Jews, so that a Protestant child might think that Jews had disappeared. Thompson also found that juvenile periodicals included more information about groups in other lands—Chinese, Africans, or Muslims—than about minority groups in the United States, for example, Jews, Catholics, blacks, or American Indians. Although he noted increased awareness of interfaith and intercultural relations, the underlying assumption remained that white Christians were superior, that their thoughts and behaviors established the criteria for others, that they were saviors of heathens in the rest of the world who were unable to handle their own affairs. "In many of the stories the reward for courageous action on the part of a non-Protestant person is to be permitted to become a Christian," explained a report on the study. Some religious school material was "of a nature likely to inflame prejudices in the minds of the pupils." Thompson emphasized that adult attitudes shaped children's outlooks. A survey of five hundred Protestant religious school instructors showed that 12 percent held the Jews responsible for the death of Jesus, while 68 percent believed Jews were "underdeveloped" but had the same potential as "whites." Seventy percent reported that they had become aware of racial or cultural differences between ages nine and twelve, a finding that highlighted the importance of childhood education.[42]

The results of Thompson's study were not published, but were made available to publishers and church leaders and led to some textbook revisions. Silcox and Fisher reported that mistaken points were called to the attention of editors, "most of whom are eager to make corrections and to add material calculated to foster appreciation of the Jews." If a similar policy were applied to the textbooks of all three faiths and the public schools, "there surely ought to be much less prejudice and lack of cooperation among the faiths in the next generation than in the present." By 1944, the NCJC could report that writers, publishers, and religious educators had cooperated on the research recommendations.[43]

Jewish leaders volunteered to survey their religious school textbooks as well. Rabbi Philip Bernstein, who observed that Jewish attitudes toward Gentiles were often learned in the synagogue school, urged both groups to monitor teachers' attitudes and textbook materials. In the late 1930s the AJC funded a study of Jewish religious education literature, undertaken by the Synagogue Council of America, that resulted in the elimination of passages offensive to Christians. "It may interest Christians to know that in many Jewish Sunday Schools the story of the Nazarene is taught with reverence and understanding," Rabbi Morris Lazaron wrote. According to the NCJC, the study encouraged "a proper understanding of Christianity and wholesome relations with Christians." The organization continued to monitor religious school texts in later decades.[44]

The new aim of religious education, according to Estelle Sternberger of the National Council of Jewish Women, was to raise a generation who would seek understanding and cooperation, "however different their religious faiths, without the hindrance of prejudice inherited from the past," she wrote. "Our children will bring the refreshing winds of truth into our communities if we will not insist upon poisoning their minds with the hatreds which we developed and which we, for some reason or other, found necessary in our service of God." Even Lasker found cause for optimism: he commented in 1932 that texts for church schools were increasingly successful at awakening a sense of friendship with children of other races and nations. He was pleased to note "the emergence of a liberalism in the appraisal of non-Christian faiths."[45]

Religious Education and the Missionary Threat

Even as goodwill advocates scrutinized Sunday school materials, however, they approached childhood education gingerly. To be sure, they recognized the importance of early training, agreeing on the process of social conditioning and the malleability of children's attitudes. They were familiar with the findings of the behaviorists, with Lasker's analysis of the acquisition of prejudice, and with cultural gifts programs in the public schools. At NCJC events, religious leaders analyzed educational influences on young people and discussed methods to instill religious tolerance. But despite this recognition of early influence, goodwill advocates initiated few educational activities for children, directing the bulk of their seminars and roundtables at adults. They critiqued existing curricula rather than designing new programs for Sunday schools, as Rachel Davis DuBois was doing for secondary schools.

Why did goodwill leaders not direct more of their resources to childhood education? In part, their hesitation reflected the institutional structures of religious education, which were rooted in the denominations rather than in interfaith organizations. The focus on adult education also emerged from recognition that it was teachers and parents who shaped the attitudes of children. Lasker thought it important to work with ministers, Sunday school teachers, and church workers, whose ignorance and prejudice created the Sunday school pupil's "attendant learnings." He pointed out that churches depended on volunteer religious teachers who had little training and few qualifications. In this situation, good texts did not ensure good teaching. "To some extent, reeducation of adults must precede the education of children." Clinchy agreed, suggesting that adult education could reform the image of Jews "which Christians harbor and pass to the oncoming generation." An NCJC roundtable noted that children in religious schools were educated according to the conditions of the community, which was organized by and centered on adults. "This raised the question of the Why and the How of adult religious education" to emancipate people from their prejudices.[46]

Yet the interest in adult education does not fully explain the NCJC's reluctance to design programs for children. More important were recurrent anxieties over proselytism. From the start of the interreligious movement, Jewish leaders had feared that goodwill gestures masked missionary aims. The long history of forced conversion made Jews sensitive to the issue, while more recent evangelical efforts put Jews on the alert. Suspicions of proselytism called into question the entire foundation of the goodwill movement. Although missionary activities resulted in only small numbers of converts each year, their implications troubled Jewish leaders. Conversion drives suggested that Judaism was not in fact equal to Christianity, that Jews could not be full Americans, and that Protestants continued to exert cultural authority. Because this issue continued to raise the ire of Jewish spokespersons and made them suspicious of goodwill overtures, leaders in the NCJC were eager to avoid any activity that might suggest missionary intent. They understood that interreligious youth education might threaten the fragile alliance if it appeared in any way to be directed toward conversion. Aware of Jewish concerns, these leaders directed their messages to adults because they did not want to be seen as proselytizing children.

Jews particularly objected to Christian efforts to evangelize children. "Much of the opposition to Jewish missions on the part of the Jews is due to alleged cradle-snatching and the bribery of small children by 'confectionary' and ice-cream to persuade them to attend the various classes and clubs," Silcox and Fisher explained. They dismissed these concerns, noting that it was "easy to interpret any social gathering at which refreshments are served as bribery, and to read sinister motives into what is really a normal mode of social intercourse." Yet their own investigation showed that Jewish fears were not unfounded. When the researchers surveyed missionary centers on how they reached children, they received a range of answers. One center stated that its policy was not to appeal to children at all, but others had fewer qualms. A center that preferred to reach children through their parents commented, "We do not feel ironbound by this rule," and admitted that its display window attracted young people. Another acknowledged that it offered a "button to the one who brings a new child." Missionary centers offered playgrounds, clubs, and vacation schools that attracted children. Some required parental consent for children to attend, but at other centers children came without parental knowledge. Christian missionaries often claimed they were looking not for practicing Jews but for people who had drifted away from religion entirely. One acknowledged that "we ought to accord Jewish religious leaders first opportunity to win their own people, both children and adults, to practical religious living and we ought to cooperate with them to that end." But if Jews were estranged from the synagogue, he thought them fair game for conversion. This approach embarrassed Jewish leaders, who were well aware of the numbers of unaffiliated Jews.[47]

The question of missionary activities aimed at children was a topic of heated debate at NCJC events. This was the most important issue raised at a 1930 seminar in St. Louis, according to Samuel Cohon, a professor at Hebrew Union College. Jewish participants at the seminar expressed indignation over evangelical methods, the "activities of missionaries who literally bribe the children of the poor." Cohon noted "the tension of the atmosphere" during the discussion. Protestants at the meeting did not disavow missionary work in general but did condemn "any methods that are unworthy, tawdry, and cheap." At the national seminar two years later, participants were alert to the potential dangers of interreligious work with young people. They voiced distress over proselytism, which they defined as "the use of unfair methods to lure, coerce, deceive, largely directed against children; to cause them to forsake the faith to which they belong and to embrace a new faith." They complained that Protestant missions in Catholic and Jewish neighborhoods showed disrespect for other faiths.[48]

Clinchy insisted on the benign intentions of the goodwill movement. In an article in *B'nai B'rith* magazine, he addressed Jewish concerns over statements made by a Protestant goodwill advocate who had asserted that Christians must missionize Jews. Clinchy explained the missionary impulse in anthropological terms, referring to the theory that each group wanted to spread its ideas to others. He reassured readers that no responsible church representative would defend "socially baiting Jewish children, in return for their acceptance of Christianity." Missions posed no real threat to Judaism, he argued, because of the anthropological law of group integrity, the vitality of Judaism, and their past ineffectiveness. He described the goodwill movement as "an antidote for proselyting." Interreligious cooperation made conversion efforts less likely, he promised, for it taught young people to value differences. "These children will grow up a generation which will want Jews to be proudly Jewish, and these Christians will respect Jews *as Jews*." Despite these reassurances, Jews received scant comfort from a 1932 statement of goodwill prepared by the Home Missions Council and the International Missionary Council and signed by thirty Protestant leaders. The statement renounced anti-Semitism, called for understanding of Jews, and professed "friendly fellowship and cooperation"—however, it did not explicitly disavow conversion.[49]

Because of this background, Jews were reluctant to engage in education that hinted of proselytism. For example, while Silcox and Fisher found Protestant ministers in several cities who had invited liberal rabbis to explain Judaism to their congregations and young people's societies, they found no rabbi who had invited a Christian minister to expound Christianity to his people. Silcox and Fisher explained: "it was too soon to expect people who inherited an ancestral tradition of Christian persecution to wish to know any more than they must about Christianity." Some Protestant NCJC members imagined a cooperative interdenominational program for religious education, but Jewish representatives, along with their Catholic counterparts, objected. Children appeared susceptible to the emotional pull of religion. The Catholic Church, the Jewish cochair Roger Straus commented, had long said that if it reached a child in the first five years he would be Catholic forever. "This observation has been approved by modern psychology which says that a child's character is largely formed in its earliest years." Such a finding suggested to Jews the importance of giving a child a Jewish education—and of shielding the child from competing religious beliefs.[50]

Fears of proselytism also emerged in discussions of religion in the public schools, where frequent expressions of Christianity challenged the pluralist ideal. Lasker noted that although the public school was extolled as a unifying institution that taught respect for the rights of all, this role had not been fulfilled. Controversy over Bible instruction was only part of the problem. Discussion at the NCJC national seminar revealed that even when there was little open hostility to Jews or Catholics, there was suspicion and mistrust. In some places the school system was essentially Protestant: Christian holidays were celebrated; teachers were expected to demonstrate good character through membership in a Protestant church; textbooks and activities expressed the outlook of the Protestant majority; and teaching was imbued with exclusive nativism. As attitude tests confirmed, children in such schools would easily believe that

Jews were unpatriotic or that Catholics aimed to set up a papal government in the United States.[51]

Interfaith leaders complained about the imposition of Christian customs on non-Christian children. They objected to the inclusion of Bible-reading, prayers, or hymns in the curriculum. The celebration of Christmas was a troubling example. Public schools held Christmas exercises "in which Jewish children can hardly avoid participating," complained Estelle Sternberger of the National Council of Jewish Women. A Protestant minister at the St. Louis seminar noted "that Jewish children are imposed upon during the Christmas and Easter sessions by making them join in Christian exercises." In some places, Jews were vigilant in eliminating Christian teaching in the schools. Silcox and Fisher told of a rabbi who visited the local school before Christmas to see that no carols were sung and no references to Christmas made. In their assessment, the rabbi did more harm than good: "He succeeded in making a nuisance of himself and in helping on the cause of anti-Semitism in that community."[52]

Lasker noted that even those teachers who took part in interfaith groups did not understand the perspective of religious minorities. While teachers recognized that readings of the New Testament or recitals of the Lord's Prayer constituted a legitimate grievance, they thought that Jewish parents exaggerated the public school's sectarian approach at Christmas and Easter. One principal who attended the national seminar considered it acceptable for the school to teach Christmas carols, while a teacher defended school Christmas trees. "That Jewish parents object to having their children interested in Christianity in this indirect way, they did not, apparently, appreciate; nor that the school as a public institution, by celebrating these holidays, does practically acknowledge a state religion," Lasker commented. Rachel Davis DuBois found similar resistance when she asserted that schools should teach about the contributions of Jews and explain that the United States was not a Christian nation. "Yet when a group of teachers was recently challenged with the idea that perhaps too much emphasis is laid on the Protestant Christian religion in our public school exercises one teacher said, 'Why should *we* give up our religion for the Jews?'"[53]

The cultural gifts approach offered a means for the schools to reduce religious intolerance. According to Rabbi Abram Simon, "course books on the contribution to civilization of different religions and races will tend to remove the customary arrogance of superiority of one religion over another." Yet teachers needed training for this work. Journalist Heywood Broun, who termed the school "a fertile breeding ground for discrimination," remarked that if the teacher exhibited prejudice toward a single Jew in the class, "the gentile child will be reassured in his own passion to haze and tease." Yet as Lasker reported, most instructors were unprepared to address intergroup relations. "You must educate the teachers before you can educate the children," a seminar participant suggested.[54]

The selection of public school teachers reinforced religious prejudice. At the Oakland-Berkeley Seminar on Human Relations, held in 1931 under the auspices of the East Bay Religious Fellowship and the NCJC, participants denounced the common practice of appointing only Christian teachers. Most believed either that religious affiliation should not be a factor in appointments, or that in order to broaden experience "a teacher from a religious background other than that of the community might be appointed." Attendees at the national seminar the next year echoed this concern. Silcox and Fisher reported widespread discrimination against Catholic and Jewish teachers in the public schools. The exceptions were in cities like Chicago and New York. "On Jewish holidays some classrooms are almost emptied" in certain American cities with large Jewish populations, a fact the authors thought created "some embarrassing situations."[55]

Fears of missionary activity eventually diminished. Writing to Clinchy in 1952, at the twenty-fifth anniversary of the NCJC, Rabbi Israel Goldstein recalled that in the early days "some of us were troubled lest it be used by some as a vehicle of a subtle attempt to win Jews to Christianity." Goldstein reported that misgivings over missionary attempts had dissipated "and there today are no such mental reservations in any responsible quarters of Jewish leadership." He and his colleagues had finally put aside their concerns. "It is quite an achievement that the NCCJ has won the confidence of the community on that score."[56]

Debating Jewish and Catholic Identity

Not all goodwill advocates were willing to go as far as Clinchy in embracing pluralism. Silcox and Fisher, authors of *Catholics, Jews, and Protestants*, valued cultural pluralism only to the degree that it would not divide society at large. On the one hand, they agreed that instead of the melting pot model "we should encourage the perpetuation of unlikeness and seek a society in which the rights of each cultural variety, however small, to growth and perpetuity, should be frankly recognized." They described Jews as champions of this philosophy, who "deem it to be the 'mission of Israel' to stand for the rights of minorities the world over." Historical factors explained this perspective. "If any group is historically justified in propounding cultural pluralism, then it seems reasonably clear that the Jews have that right." Indeed, as Silcox and Fisher recognized, Jews supported the interreligious movement precisely because of its pluralist perspective. In America, as in Europe, they eagerly embraced pluralism as a way to maintain both Jewish and national identities, to participate as full members of society without sacrificing their distinct heritage. In the interwar period, anti-Semitic expression threatened Jews' sense of security in America and made them particularly receptive to public recognition of the rights of minority religions.[57]

On the other hand, Silcox and Fisher warned that Jews could go too far with this pluralism. Minorities should accept their responsibilities as well as their rights and understand that they complicated the life of the majority, these authors insisted. They worried that pluralism would perpetuate difference at the expense of national unity and political organization. Their fears called up the common stereotype of Jews as clannish and self-segregating, opposed to intermarriage, set apart by their sense of chosenness. If Jews wanted to ensure their own separation, then other groups would demand that privilege, too, "and out of it comes something that can only be deemed a nation by wishful thinking." Separation was acceptable as a transitional stage, but the majority "deeply resents a philosophy which postulates the permanence and perpetuation of cultural pluralism." Would it be best, they wondered, to seek unity through "the creation of a new and hybrid culture in which the best strains of each will be diligently retained?" If realized, this ideal would prevent too extreme a cultural pluralism.[58]

Such misgivings reflected a persistent question within the goodwill movement: were Jews a religion, a culture, a nationality, or a race? Some observers suggested that anti-Semitism resulted from social and cultural traits common to Jews—economic mobility, occupational niches, refusal to intermarry, internal cohesion—and not from hostility to the Jewish religion itself. In 1932, the Protestant cochair, Newton Baker, suggested that the NCJC investigate the "racial" as well as the religious causes of prejudice against Jews. In reply, Carlton Hayes asserted that it was im-

possible to distinguish Jewish religion from other factors and that in regard to Catholics, prejudice did reflect ignorance and dislike of the Catholic religion itself.[59]

Silcox and Fisher suggested that economic and social factors were as
important as religious ones in causing anti-Jewish prejudice. Uncertainty over Jews' classification made them an "international irritant" in
the Gentiles' minds. The majority of Gentiles, the researchers reported,
considered Jews to be a racial unit sustained by religious practices. Gentiles who denied having religious prejudice against Jews admitted to
racial aversion. Silcox and Fisher concluded that Jews were to blame for
this ill-defined position. "In short, the whole situation is a frightful mess,
and by his strange dexterity in playing the triple role of a racial, religious
and national group, the modern Jew brings down upon his head a triple
type of antipathy." In a review of Silcox and Fisher's study, sociologist
Ellsworth Faris described the conflict between Jews and others as a
racial conflict in sociological if not biological terms, because "they are
regarded as a separate race, are treated as a separate race, and hold themselves together as if they were a separate race."[60]

Jews involved in the NCJC insisted that Jews be seen as a religious
rather than an ethnic, racial, or national group. As historian Nicholas
Montalto has noted, most of the rabbis who participated in the trio tours
represented Reform Judaism, at the time the most integrationist wing of
American Judaism and the one least interested in Jewish ethnic identity.
Reform Judaism attracted established Jews of German descent rather
than more recent arrivals from eastern Europe. Morris Lazaron, a Reform
rabbi who took part in the first goodwill tours, was an anti-Zionist and
integrationist. Roger Straus's integrationist perspective was shaped by
having grown up in rural Georgia far from the centers of Jewish population. Members of the AJC, one of the NCJC's chief funders, also tended
to be from Reform backgrounds. Many were prominent bankers and
merchants, aligned with the Republican Party, who believed that Jews
should Americanize, drop Yiddish and eastern European customs, and
oppose Jewish nationalism. Their financial support allowed the AJC to
influence NCJC policy.[61]

In their reliance on the perspective of Reform Judaism, leaders of the
NCJC obscured cultural conflicts within the Jewish community that di-
vided Jewish factory owners and workers, Republicans and radicals,
Zionists and anti-Zionists. While Reform leaders affiliated with the AJC

were hostile to immigrant culture, other Jewish agencies resisted the drive toward cultural conformity. The American Jewish Congress, for example, made up mostly of eastern European Jews, adopted a more overtly political stance that attracted American Zionists who saw Judaism in national terms. Yet the leaders of the NCJC, who dealt almost exclusively with Reform rabbis and lay leaders, portrayed Jews as a single entity defined by religion, a portrayal that left little room for ethnic or political variance. Similarly, the goodwill movement portrayed Catholics in monolithic terms that ignored internal rivalries and divisions.[62]

This portrayal of Jews was at odds with that of Rachel Davis DuBois, who depicted Jews as a cultural group, treating them much as she treated Italians, African Americans, Germans, or Japanese. DuBois was influenced by her contacts with Mordecai Kaplan, the founder of Reconstructionist Judaism, who defined Judaism as a civilization and a way of life. For DuBois, tension over the status of Jews brought serious repercussions when the AJC threatened to stop giving funds to the Service Bureau if it continued to present Jews as an ethnic rather than a denominational group. Why a program on the Jews, asked AJC leaders, but not the Baptists? In the late 1930s, the AJC reduced and then withdrew support from DuBois's work because it disagreed with her portrayal of Jews.

Clinchy himself, as a supporter of Rachel Davis DuBois, may have been sympathetic to the notion of Jews as a cultural as well as religious group. However, he remained responsive to his funders and to his vision for a religiously based pluralism. Following the lead of his Jewish colleagues, he tended to view intergroup tension in religious rather than ethnic or cultural terms and to portray Judaism as a purely religious affiliation, much like Methodism or Presbyterianism. This sectarian approach had mixed implications, as Montalto has pointed out. Even as the NCJC granted Judaism equal status with Protestantism and Catholicism as a major religion, it minimized ethnic identity within each religious group. Judaism gained equality as a central element in American life—but at the expense of its ethnic character.[63]

Even as they debated whether Jews made up a religion or a culture, most goodwill advocates agreed with progressive social scientists that Jews were not a race. Scientific rejection of racial theories took on particular urgency in the 1930s in the context of rising Nazism overseas. At an NCJC institute in 1935, anthropologist Edward Sapir of Yale reminded participants of the fallibility of racial divisions. "All the tangible groups with which we have to deal are social groups. There is no such thing as a French, German, Russian, Anglo-Saxon or Jewish race," Sapir insisted. Donald Young, a sociologist at the University of Pennsylvania, similarly attacked "pseudo-scientific theories of racial inequality." He asserted that neither the Jews nor other people or nations could qualify as a race. Yet he recognized the use of such claims by groups such as the Nazis, who asserted the right of domination because of superiority of stock—a claim too common and too powerful "to be killed with a scientific sneer." A concluding report summarized these findings: "Neither ethnology nor psychology lend countenance to many of the loose race theories now being popularized. The Aryan is a myth. The Jews do not constitute a race."[64]

Catholic beliefs also generated debate within goodwill circles. Some liberal Catholics proposed that their schools mobilize to fight prejudice. The Catholic Association for International Peace, with which Carlton Hayes was affiliated, conducted a study of children's racial and national attitudes whose results, reported in 1932 in the *Commonweal,* a liberal Catholic publication, tallied with earlier observations: children as young as six reflected adult prejudices. The committee recommended textbook revisions for Catholic schools, programs for international goodwill, teaching units to improve attitudes, and "an active effort through seminaries, lay organizations and parishes to mobilize Christian thinking against the un-christian state of mind that underlies false nationalism."[65]

But for the most part, Catholic insistence on parochial schooling brought an additional challenge to the goodwill movement's pluralist hopes. Good citizenship, Catholic leaders claimed, depended on sound religious training, which could not be accomplished by public schools or by part-time religious instruction. In the United States in 1932–1933, ten thousand Catholic primary and secondary schools enrolled two and a half million students, half of all Catholic children. Jews, in contrast, supported very few parochial schools: Silcox and Fisher reported that in 1927 there were only twelve Jewish day schools located in three communities. Almost all Jewish children attended public schools, in keeping with American Jewry's reliance on public education as a vehicle for acculturation, social mobility, and pluralism.[66]

Indeed, Catholics' relation to cultural pluralism took a distinct form. Despite their minority status in American society, Catholics could depict their religion in triumphalist terms, as a superior force destined to achieve supremacy in America. Protestant leaders objected to this assumption of authority. Silcox and Fisher, for example, recorded Protestant suspicions of the Catholic Church as a "super-state," "a dictatorship" in "a bid for universal power." They evoked popular conceptions of Catholics as hierarchical, antidemocratic, and un-American in their allegiance to a foreign pope, warning of the danger of extending religious liberty to Catholics when it was unclear whether Catholics, if they were in the majority, would extend the same liberty to Protestants. "Can democracy really endure if one group is educating its children for freedom while an influential minority in its midst continues to educate its children for authority?" they asked.[67]

In the 1920s, attacks on parochial schools revealed animosity toward Catholicism in American life. In the instance of the Oregon law (later struck down) that required all children to attend public schools, the AJC came to the defense of the Oregon Catholics, filing a brief with the Supreme Court asserting the right to Catholic parochial schools. At other times, however, Jews as well as Protestants expressed consternation over Catholic parochial schools. While non-Catholics recognized (sometimes grudgingly) that Catholics were entitled to set up their own school systems, they grew uncomfortable at attempts to secure public funds. Parochial schools seemed to challenge principles of the goodwill movement: separation of church and state, unity in the midst of pluralism, friendly contact that would inspire understanding. They appeared undemocratic, hierarchical, contrary to American values. Because they enrolled children in the formative early years, parochial schools seemed to play an important role in shaping religious attitudes.[68]

The maintenance of parochial schools was a point of disagreement at NCJC events. In St. Louis, Catholics criticized public schools as "godless," while Jews and Protestants affirmed the importance of the public school system. The Oakland-Berkeley seminar produced "sharp division" when non-Catholic participants questioned how parochial schools prepared students for citizenship. Protestants and Jews at the national seminar in 1932 suggested that parochial schools might be a cause of religious prejudice, since they marked children off from those in the public schools and emphasized a sense of difference.[69]

A questionnaire distributed after a 1935 institute found that non-Catholics believed parochial schools to be "divisive and un-American in their influence." Donald Young worried that with parochial schools, "it is difficult to see how a conflict of cultures and strained race relations can be avoided." According to Silcox and Fisher, religious segregation appeared to foster undesirable attitudes in both public and parochial schoolchildren. National unity demanded that all children be trained in one system. "Playing and studying together, it is urged, will break through the superiority complexes, prejudices and bigotries which, if allowed to develop, lay their devastating hand upon adult attitudes in later life." As Silcox and Fisher pointed out, such complaints about the harmful effects of religious segregation through Catholic schools had a hypocritical air, since segregation of the races was carried out most rigidly in the public school system in the region of the country that was most overwhelmingly Protestant.[70]

In the context of these debates over religious particularism and integration, the NCJC came to focus the bulk of its educational activities on the adolescent years, when loyalty to religion was already well established. In 1934 the NCJC began to expand its programs for young people. Teams of minister, priest, and rabbi appeared before high school assemblies; in Detroit, for instance, more than eighteen thousand students in sixteen high schools heard representatives of the three faiths discuss the American tradition of religious freedom. A booklet for Protestant young people, entitled "New Relationships with Jews and Catholics," included discussion outlines and resource materials, drawn in part from Rachel Davis DuBois's work. Community YMCAs received copies, and in Baltimore the Federation of Church and Synagogue Youth, which brought together young people from two Jewish and fifteen Protestant groups, used suggestions from the booklet to survey attitudes and to organize forums, visits, and religious services that stressed points held in common.[71] It seemed that young people were eager to engage in interfaith dialogue. At the University of California at Berkeley, Clinchy noted with pleasure, "students of different faiths have found it easy to cooperate and are ready to go much further along the road of cooperation than many of their elders." Cornell University organized a central council with Catholic, Jewish, and Protestant representatives; the University of California at Los Angeles experimented with a plan to house students from different faiths in the same building; and the University of Iowa offered courses on the three major faiths.[72]

Youth activities became central to the NCJC agenda. As the organization proved its nonconversionist principles, Jewish fears of missionizing children took a back seat—especially as events in Europe heightened the urgency of combating anti-Semitism at home. Jewish leaders submerged their suspicions and embraced adolescent education as a means to promote religious pluralism and prevent the spread of Nazi propaganda to the United States. The NCJC sponsored discussion programs in high schools, sent staff members to visit colleges and schools of education, organized a national tour for educators from the three faiths, established a committee on educational policies, and sponsored a conference on teaching. Leaders of the NCJC assessed the influence of new media on young people's perceptions, discussing the educational impact of motion pictures and making use of print advertising, radio programs, popular magazines, and movies in Brotherhood Week events. At the end of the decade, the NCJC sponsored a study of methods used by the school to inculcate religious tolerance. "Only when the schools weave into their materials appreciation of all the cultures which constitute the diverse American society," read Clinchy's 1939 report, "and teach ways in which each group can maintain its distinctive tone, color, and essence even while it lends itself to the whole national design, can the real job of educating for better human relations be done."[73]

But adolescence brought its own dilemmas. Goodwill advocates understood that young children's malleability made them vulnerable targets who could be seduced away from their parents' religion if they encountered too much difference early on. With older children, the potential dangers were less clearly articulated but equally serious. Unspoken in these discussions were the perils inherent in too much social contact among adolescents, contact that might lead to interfaith relationships—a possibility increasingly imaginable in the interwar years, thanks in part to heightened secularization and to such symbols of popular culture as *The Jazz Singer*. After all, if young Christians and Jews came to know each other and to appreciate each other's faiths, perhaps they might want to date, or even marry—a form of assimilation particularly threatening to second-generation Jews. As Clinchy had explained, it was important to "nurture enough ethnocentrism to insure satisfactory group loyalties."[74] In other words, it was necessary to police the boundaries of assimilation. Goodwill advocates thus promoted interactions between young people of different religions in a public, civic kind of exchange; they wanted to foster coexistence on a cultural or commercial level that acknowledged members of minority religions as fair players in the larger national culture.

But they guarded against a private kind of contact and exchange that might lead to excessive intimacy, seeking a careful balance between particularism and universalism. As with other cultural gifts activities, new forms of religious education asked young people to remain loyal to family identity while embracing the pluralist vision.

"New York—A minister, a priest and a rabbi unite against intolerance! Goodwill trio to preach gospel of amity and fellowship throughout the United States."
Paramount Newsreel Magazine

The first goodwill tour, 1933. From left to right, the Rev. Everett R. Clinchy, Father John Elliott Ross, Rabbi Morris S. Lazaron. (National Conference of Christians and Jews Records, Social Welfare History Archives, University of Minnesota Libraries)

Religious Goodwill and Antiblack Prejudice

Rabbi Philip S. Bernstein of Rochester, New York, who participated in a trio tour through the South in 1934, later recalled a "disturbing problem" that came to his attention through the reactions of black audiences. "In South Carolina our itinerary brought us to a Negro college," he remembered two decades later. "We gave them a typical program. After we finished, a man stood up and said, 'Why talk good will to us?'" Bernstein understood the limitations of his approach. "Our answer had to be lame. The problem of prejudice against the Negro haunted, and I believe still haunts, every effort for religious good will, including that of the National Conference." Attempts to foster interreligious understanding, he suggested, could go only so far if they did not also address prejudice and discrimination against black Americans.[75]

Some liberal churches did make attempts to dispel bigotry against African Americans. The FCC's Commission on Race Relations distributed information about black achievements; sponsored conferences, educational publications, and worship services that addressed racial discrimination; and campaigned against lynching and for support of black education, health, and welfare work. On Race Relations Sunday, which took place each year near Lincoln's birthday, white and black ministers exchanged pulpits and arranged for visits between churches. In the 1930s the FCC, the Fellowship of Reconciliation, and the Society of Friends cooperated to publish the monthly *Interracial News Letter*, edited by Rachel Davis DuBois. The Catholic Interracial Council movement, established in 1934, worked to eliminate racial inequality in the Catholic Church and in American society. The liberal journal *Religious Education* suggested ways for teachers in religious schools to demonstrate that Indians, blacks, Japanese, Chinese, and Mexicans all made their home in the United States and contributed to its civilization.[76]

But observers commented that the brief and impersonal contacts arranged by the FCC were unlikely to have lasting effect and complained that the churches were doing far too little to counter racial discrimination. In most of the South, observed Paul Baker, a white minister who surveyed interracial organizations, "many teachers get their pupils very much concerned about the underprivileged and suppressed peoples abroad and remain seemingly unconscious of the identical evils which surround the Negroes in their own communities." Other agencies—

schools, colleges, clubs, social organizations—had responded more fully to the problem of racism than had the churches. Church teachings would suggest that the church be in the front on race matters, Baker remarked, "yet indications suggest that the Church is inclined to hold theoretically to the principles of Jesus but is guided practically by the *mores* of the community in which it is located." While the FCC included black churches as members and worked with Mexican immigrants and American Indians, many churches remained segregated. The message this segregation could send was revealed in a comment from a fifteen-year-old at a church school. Francis Brown, professor of education at New York University, recounted that the girl's class had studied the contributions of blacks to American life. When the teacher asked her to lead a prayer, the girl "thanked God for the contributions of the Negro, enumerating them in some detail, and then concluded, 'Teach us to be tolerant and to keep the Negro in his place.'"[77]

Black leaders were outspoken in their criticism of the churches' inaction on racial matters. W. E. B. Du Bois lamented that the record of the church "has been almost complete acquiescence in caste, until today there is in the United States no organization that is so completely split along the color line as the Christian church." The church was a social organization, "pathetically timid and human; it is going to stand on the side of wealth and power; it is going to espouse any cause which is sufficiently popular, with eagerness; it is, on the other hand, often going to transgress its own fine ethical statements and be deaf to its own Christ in unpopular and weak causes." *Opportunity* pointed out that white churches had done little to combat discrimination or end lynchings. "Has the voice of organized religion in America ever been lifted against peonage? Against discrimination because of race? Against segregation? We would ask in all humility that the great religious leaders of America think on these things."[78]

Lasker also came to think that racial segregation in the church had a profound influence on young people. In a pair of articles in the *Woman's Press* in 1926, he explained these effects. "You can teach the youngsters every morning that it is right to love one's neighbors," he wrote, "but you might as well save your breath if they observe you building a spite wall of non-recognition, if not of actual hostility, between your home and that of the people next door." Bible lessons in Sunday school, like other educational activities, were made ineffective by adult behavior. Young people grappled with the discrepancy between the exclusiveness of their environment and the idealistic lessons of their religious faith. Lasker criticized one church program designed to foster "a Christian attitude of interracial friendship" with talks on "How the Negro Is Responding to Efforts for His Betterment" and "How American Ideals Are Taking Root among the Mexicans in the United States," warning that this presentation evinced ideas of "superiority and condescension" and encouraged "children to think of racial minorities as afflicted by some sort of disease until they have undergone the mysterious process of 'Americanization.'" Most Sunday schools and Christian associations, he explained, were unable to teach true world friendship, for "the institution itself is the creation of the spirit prevailing in the community."[79]

In *Race Attitudes in Children*, Lasker further developed his belief that religious teachings were "riddled with inconsistencies." Like W. E. B. Du Bois, he noted that the church faced a dilemma in regard to racial problems: the contrast between the values professed by the faith and the cultural traditions of its members. While the larger church believed in the universality of humanity, the local church reflected the racial thinking of its community. Its restricted membership gave a social arrangement "the authority of religious sanction." More than other institutions, the churches "impress upon children the lessons to be learned from segregation," such as aloofness and superiority. Its exclusiveness "provides an 'attendant learning' that often leaves a far deeper impress than anything that may be printed in the hymn-book or lesson sheet." Lasker saw hypocrisy in Sunday schools that worked to uplift Africans in Africa but ignored racism at home, or that sang hymns of fellowship but ostracized immigrant children.[80]

Lasker lauded one unusual church school that enrolled children from various backgrounds and, in a radio talk, commended white Sunday schools that arranged exchanges with black and immigrant churches, rare occasions for children to meet on equal terms. Yet he questioned churches as agents of reform. If churchgoers truly adopted the values of universal brotherhood that churches professed, "we should have nothing less than a social revolution," he exclaimed. This stance may help explain Lasker's later criticism of the NCJC. In a 1956 interview, he complained that the interfaith movement had become "shallow." Clinchy, he commented, "never was an intellectual giant." Lasker disparaged the NCJC as "too popular and too well financed" and therefore "afraid of real controversy." He no longer regarded the movement with favor: "It is just a rabbi and a priest and a clergyman standing together on a platform and throwing their arms around each other, or patting each other on the back." More important was to get "into the very heart of the thing," which to Lasker meant asking in a deeper way than NCJC leaders had done, "what are our real differences, and how can we cooperate in spite of those differences? What are the kinds of things we can cooperate about?"[81]

Goodwill leaders, however, initiated few attempts to create interracial Sunday schools or churches. In the 1920s and 1930s, they appeared unwilling to confront the essential contradiction Lasker identified between church teaching and social custom. Some sponsored interracial worship services, but on an occasional rather than ongoing basis. While black leaders called on the church to end racial segregation, white liberals urged it to dispel prejudice against Jews and Catholics through interfaith work that focused exclusively on white congregants from the three religions. By overlooking racial discrimination, NCJC leaders implicitly categorized black Protestants as members of the dominant group, an ambiguity they preferred not to address. They avoided the difficult question of segregation, made little mention of black churches, denominations, or clergy, and included almost no black leaders in their goodwill programs. A participant who attended an NCJC event or read its literature could have come away with the impression that all American Protestants were white.

College students, more than older leaders in the goodwill movement, took steps to challenge antiblack prejudice. They began "to wonder at the fearful inconsistency between 'the reading and the prayers' and this thing, race prejudice," noted a professor of Biblical literature. The YMCA and YWCA, as well as their Jewish counterparts, sponsored antiprejudice efforts, including the interracial Conference of Youth Organizations in 1924, which deplored racial and religious prejudices and endorsed cooperation and equal rights. Youth conferences brought together students from various backgrounds, showing that "they are able to teach many of their elders a lesson," *Opportunity* opined. The *Christian Century* carried frequent articles on youth activism regarding race, such as a student gathering that advocated equal opportunity and intermingling of the races. Although churches had not done much regarding racial problems, the journal commented, the student movement "has again and again revealed the resources of a religiously inspired social idealism" in addressing racial matters. The Catholic Inter-racial Conference at Fordham University drew three hundred delegates, who called for interracial organizations at every Catholic college and pledged to uphold civil rights and justice.[82]

Clinchy, despite Lasker's criticism, suggested that opposition to racial discrimination was an area for fruitful cooperation among Protestants, Catholics, and Jews. Carlton Hayes, the NCJC's Catholic cochair, also urged interfaith activists "to deal with the race problem in the United States and to prove that under the American democracy Whites and Negroes can live side by side in relations of mutual justice and esteem." He suggested collaboration on poverty, social justice, good government, and the prevention of crime. He noted that some members of the NCJC thought "that we should include within our purview all the problems of all group relationships in the United States and perhaps in the world." But he argued that the group should not become a general defense agency. Interfaith efforts were enough: "we are sufficiently bold and adventurous to concentrate our attention right at home and among ourselves." Once better relations were achieved among Jews, Catholics and Protestants, "we can then pass on to other undertakings. With limited objectives we have a better chance than with unlimited objectives, of doing something besides talk." The NCJC maintained its focus on religious prejudice and, despite occasional calls from Clinchy and Hayes, appeared hesitant to speak out against racial segregation and discrimination.[83]

As it granted recognition to the three "major" faiths, the NCJC solidified a definition of whiteness that included Jews and Catholics, even as it marginalized other religions and reinforced racial divisions between white and nonwhite peoples. In the NCJC's literature, the rare references to non-Western religions assumed that their adherents were overseas, rather than being fellow citizens or potential citizens of the United States. Attention to the three religions crystallized into what came to be called the "Judeo-Christian heritage"—a phrase that elevated Judaism as truly American while, by implication, dismissing the role of other religions in the national story. By 1942, in the midst of war, the NCJC asserted that American institutions rested on religious principles shared by the three faiths: "Victory for our American way of life demands that we preserve intact the Judeo-Christian religious tradition."[84]

5

A New Generation in the South

The cultural gifts movement reached the South as well as the North. In the 1920s and 1930s, the Commission on Interracial Cooperation (CIC), a liberal southern group based in Atlanta, worked to educate youth for racial cooperation, targeting white children as the most promising agents of change. Educators affiliated with the CIC taught young whites about black participation in American history and introduced them to black contributions in music, literature, and science, hoping to instill sympathy and goodwill. When the CIC began after World War I, few white schools in the South addressed racial problems in their curricula. By the time the organization dissolved in 1943, hundreds of thousands of white students, teachers, and school administrators had learned about the cultural achievements of black Americans. In cities and small towns from Arkansas to Mississippi to Virginia, they studied pamphlets on black history, enrolled in courses on race relations, took part in essay contests on black contributions to American life, and attended summer conferences. For the CIC, this expansion represented a tremendous achievement, the triumph of tolerance over racial prejudice.

The widespread appeal of these projects ran counter to the dominant trends of the American South of the 1920s and 1930s, when antiblack hostilities brought persistent violence, political disfranchisement, segregation, and economic inequalities. The story of the CIC's work in the schools presents a paradox: the simultaneous expression of both virulent racism and education for racial cooperation. How did the CIC's efforts to promote racial understanding gain such wide appeal among white southerners? The work of the CIC indicates that the grip of racial hostility may have been less solid than we have come to think. While the CIC did not represent the views of the majority of white southerners or prevail in the interwar years, its attempts signaled the beginnings of new racial ideals and laid the groundwork for later efforts to change the politics of citizenship.

Yet the widespread acceptance of the CIC was a sign of its limitations as well as its successes. At the CIC headquarters in Atlanta, racial idealists did not talk—as did northern liberals—in terms of mutual exchange, common values, or unity. They did not describe a dynamic process of sharing traditions to create a richer American culture. Their liberalism instead promoted acceptance from a distance in a tone more respectful than celebratory. The CIC's programs trumpeted the achievements of black Americans as a means to peaceful interactions and better social conditions. But CIC leaders did not ask white students to incorporate the best of black culture into their own American identity. They did not suggest that white students would adopt, or even learn from, black traditions. In the context of black disfranchisement, they made fewer references to democracy than did cultural gifts proponents in the North. The CIC promoted adjustment, cooperation, and tolerance—the last a term northern liberals eschewed as inadequate.

Just as CIC leaders interpreted pluralism differently from the way their northern counterparts did, southern educators understood it differently from the way the CIC leaders did. The cultural gifts movement traversed complicated paths to schools and colleges across the South, diverging from its intellectual antecedents along the way. The process of disseminating ideas revealed important discrepancies between theory and practice. Leaders of the CIC could not control how their materials were received and used by teachers and students, some of whom offered an imperfect understanding of the organization's aims or adapted its projects for their own purposes.

Indeed, it was these varied interpretations that made possible the widespread acceptance of the antiprejudice campaign. The CIC's approach was limited in ideology and scope, most particularly in its refusal to challenge the Jim Crow system or to acknowledge the socioeconomic basis of race relations. In an era in which racial hierarchies were so entrenched that merely to suggest that whites treat blacks with respect was notably progressive, the organization's leaders determined not to challenge deeply rooted systems of domination. Instead, their gradualist ap-

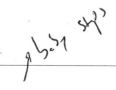

proach implied that change could result from individual adjustment rather than social reform, that tolerance could proceed without integration. Their educational programs gained support among white southerners because they failed to confront the institutional forces at the heart of southern race relations or to contest the foundations of white supremacy.

These limitations to the cultural gifts agenda appeared in particularly stark relief in the South, where racial segregation was so salient in everyday life. In working to mitigate racial prejudice, cultural gifts liberals did not necessarily advocate equality or aim to remove structural barriers that prevented blacks from achieving opportunity, mobility, and full citizenship. While such caution made these efforts palatable to southern white audiences, it suggested that in both creation and reception, cultural gifts thinking could be congruent with racial segregation and economic injustice. This limitation overshadowed the successes of the cultural gifts movement and planted the seeds for its demise in the years after World War II.

The Commission on Interracial Cooperation

The CIC, the primary organization devoted to interracial reform in the South in the 1920s and 1930s, was founded in Atlanta in 1919 by a group of white southerners concerned with the postwar race riots and the migration of blacks to the North. The director of the new organization was Will W. Alexander, a Methodist minister who had worked with black and white soldiers during the war and who remained director throughout the organization's twenty-five-year existence. The CIC sponsored interracial committees, active in thirteen southern states and hundreds of counties, to reduce racial tensions and promote black welfare. Willis D. Weatherford, one of the organization's founders, explained its strategy: "It has tried to bring together white and colored people in each local community, to think cooperatively about their particular problems." Friction would diminish "if only the leaders of the two races can come to know each other and associate their efforts around a common task."[1]

In many ways, the Commission signaled a dramatic shift in thought for white Southerners who took part, because before 1919 southern reform organizations had not included both white and black members. For whites who had grown up in a system of rigid segregation and white supremacy, it was a significant step to imagine a cooperative relationship with black neighbors, one that signaled a genuine commitment to improve racial understanding and social conditions. In other ways, however, the CIC followed the status quo. Its leaders took pains to reassure white southerners that the CIC sought a moderate approach. According to Robert B. Eleazar Jr., the CIC's director of education, "The philosophy of the movement is not that of 'seeking to solve the race question,' but simply that of taking the next step in the direction of interracial justice and goodwill." One leader explained: "Let us not go too fast. We are likely to antagonize. It is better to go slow and carry the people along than to go too fast and lose the crowd." This gradualist approach has led some historians to portray the organization as paternalistic and accommodationist and to label white participants as self-interested, intent on preserving southern society.[2]

Black affiliates were willing to accept the CIC's moderate position. Although the CIC was designed as an interracial organization, it took a year before it admitted its first black members. Prominent blacks active in the early years included Robert R. Moton, president of Tuskegee Institute, Isaac Fisher of Fisk University, John Hope, president of Morehouse College, Bishop R. E. Jones of New Orleans, and Robert E. Jones, a Methodist minister. By the mid-1920s, the CIC membership included two dozen black men, representatives of an emerging black middle class. But few blacks set policy, even as the CIC membership expanded. In 1934 there were no black workers in the agency's head office in Atlanta; the one black member of the national staff had his office in a black neighborhood and only visited the central office for conferences.[3]

The new CIC identified its aims as twofold: to improve conditions for blacks in the South and to change the attitudes "out of which unfavorable conditions grow." Research and publicity constituted an important part of this work. The staff included several social scientists: Thomas Woofter Jr., a native of Georgia who had received a doctorate in sociology from Columbia, was research director until 1926. His successor was Arthur F. Raper, who had studied sociology with Howard Odum at the University of North Carolina. Robert Eleazar served as director of education and publicity for over twenty years, beginning in 1922. The staff conducted surveys of black life and disseminated findings through a public relations campaign. They maintained contact with the southern press and issued a steady stream of pamphlets, press releases, reports, articles, and books. They advocated better funding for black schools and health facilities, equal education opportunities, improved housing, fair treatment under the law, justice in the courts, and economic betterment. The CIC published a major report on racial violence and sponsored the Association of Southern Women for the Prevention of Lynching.[4]

Over time, CIC leaders came to see the second of their aims—the improvement of racial attitudes—as their most critical task. This appeared even more fundamental than improving social conditions, for once attitudes changed, they believed, social reform would follow. The CIC's department of education, established in 1922, became the heart of the organization's work. "It is believed that nothing the Commission is doing is more potential of good than its efforts in this field," a 1924 report noted.[5]

Southern Colleges

The CIC brought its message to young white southerners through speaking tours that showcased educated African Americans in order to challenge stereotypes. In 1922–1923, prominent blacks spoke in white colleges in Tennessee, Kentucky, and elsewhere in the South.[6] George Washington Carver, the Tuskegee scientist, spoke to three thousand white students at South Carolina colleges in 1924. "He was heard everywhere with the deepest interest, respect and appreciation, and made a profound impression," the CIC reported. Several years later Carver traveled to a dozen institutions in Virginia and Tennessee, where he addressed several thousand young people. Mary White Ovington, a white activist with the NAACP, reported to the *Crisis* that Carver impressed the white students. "They have seen a great scientist and he is black," she wrote. "Without saying a word on the subject of race, Professor Carver is the best propagandist for the doctrine of good fellowship that the Interracial Commission knows."[7]

The content of these addresses followed the CIC's moderate approach. When James Weldon Johnson spoke at the University of North Carolina, he declared that "Negroes want full participation in American life and they expect to secure it." More often, however, black speakers emphasized cooperation and friendly feeling, choosing their words carefully to enlist the support of white audiences. The editor of the *Fisk University News,* who visited ten white schools in Tennessee on a trip financed by the CIC, explained that his mission "was to go alone into certain schools in a Southern State where no colored speakers had ever before been permitted to go, and address white students, many of whom had never before listened to a colored man making a public address." He aimed to foster "a regime of kindliness and peace between the races here in the South" as he pleaded for "good will and mutual helpfulness."[8]

Officials of the CIC held great hopes for these tours. "A most convincing exposure for white students is the appearance on the campus, usually at chapel, of an accomplished Negro," Arthur Raper explained in 1937. When R. R. Moton spoke at the University of North Carolina in the early twenties, "his big, black face demonstrated strength, understanding, dignity. The students got new ideas about the capabilities of the American Negro." Raper noted that a score of "outstanding Negroes" had since visited white campuses. Each one, "whose very life gives the lie to the racial dogmas which support the prejudice and antagonisms which have so severely handicapped both races," could alter students' attitudes. Staff members of the CIC, both white and black, also spoke at colleges, student conferences, and YMCA meetings. They emphasized cultural achievements in music, art, and literature as they drew attention to such figures as Phillis Wheatley, Benjamin Banneker, George Carver, Booker T. Washington, and Paul Laurence Dunbar and as they introduced students to black history and contributions to economic development. They also encouraged white institutions to invite singers and artists from local black schools to perform for their students. The CIC endorsed interracial forums at the colleges, hoping that personal contact would shift attitudes. These activities were "beginning to span the chasm between white and colored communities," a CIC report noted. Ovington promised: "If the young white men and women of education in the South learn to work with the educated Negro youth, they will outrival the progress of the last twenty-one years."[9]

To advance its educational agenda, the CIC looked to the curricula at southern colleges. After the research director, Thomas Woofter, conducted an initial survey that found only one or two schools that gave a course on race, the CIC contacted instructors and deans and was pleased to see such courses multiply rapidly. The CIC also encouraged colleges to incorporate information on race into sociology, anthropology, economics, and history courses. In 1933 Alexander counted more than one hundred colleges that now included study of race in the curriculum. Some southern students went on to pursue graduate work on racial problems, including a number who attended northern universities on fellowships administered by the CIC.[10]

College courses treated white prejudice as a product of ignorance and misinformation, of "tradition, false assumptions, mistaken opinion and groundless fear" rather than deliberate malice. Eleazar explained that while interracial distrust was usually considered a political or social problem, "only through educational processes—the search for facts and intelligent reasoning about them—is there any hope of a solution," although he complained that most schools were doing little to resolve the problem. "It may even be questioned whether they do not sometimes complicate it." The extension of social science education promised to uncover the facts and thus reform attitudes. According to Woofter, "Prejudice in the past has rested in part on popular misconceptions as to the health, morality and mentality of the Negro, and the discovery and dissemination of the truth has ameliorated prejudice among well read people."[11]

Staffers of the CIC were dissatisfied with the educational materials available to answer the many inquiries they received each year from teachers and students. Woofter recalled that "college faculties and students were increasingly open-minded on race questions but had little ammunition in the way of systematically compiled facts." To fill this need, he authored a textbook in 1928, *The Basis of Racial Adjustment,* in which he reviewed new research on racial difference and black advancement. Teachers should translate this knowledge "into the practical application of morality and democracy to interracial affairs." Drawing on the cultural gifts approach, the textbook asserted "that the colored man has some special contribution to make to American life." But unlike his northern counterparts, who emphasized contributions already made, Woofter thought such contributions possible "if [the black man] only bestirs himself to develop his own peculiar strong points and is aided by the white man to develop these capabilities and find places where they fit into the scheme of American progress."[12]

To bring attention to its activities, the CIC sponsored an annual essay competition that awarded cash prizes (of up to one hundred dollars) for the best essays by southern college students on how to improve race relations. In 1928, eighty-two students from forty-nine colleges entered the CIC contest. The judges favored essays that described the process through which white students reformed their attitudes. In the prize-winning essay from 1932, for example, Charles H. Brown, a student at the University of Oklahoma, echoed social scientists in his account of how he acquired—and discarded—his own racial prejudice. "As a child, I often heard derogatory remarks spoken about the Negro," he wrote. Learning facts broke down his prejudices—as CIC leaders claimed it would—and inspired him "to want to do something to improve conditions." New knowledge helped him to see "that the Negro is a gift-bearer rather than a gift-receiver, as we have too long considered him." Brown emphasized that education would "gradually change the thought of the whole nation." A prize-winner in 1934 faulted educators for ignoring matters of race: "the burden rests principally on the shoulders of public school teachers and curricula," she argued. "I am only one of millions who should be instructed and made to realize the importance of this interracial problem."[13]

Despite the emphasis on scientific thinking, however, there was little data about the results of these college programs. Leaders of the CIC relied on the comments of instructors and students as evidence for their effectiveness. Alexander boasted that "an exhaustive examination of these papers from all parts of the South reveals that they are thoughtful, honest and liberal." When the CIC surveyed forty instructors in 1939, the majority reported that their courses modified students' attitudes. "The course leads students to look for scientific evidence before forming opinions and attitudes," one instructor wrote. Another commented, "Prejudices largely disappear when replaced by facts." Anecdotal evidence seemed to bear out positive reports: Alexander told of a young man in Mississippi who refused to attend a lynching because of what he had learned in his sociology class. Only one teacher confessed defeat: "I'll have to admit that student attitudes against the Negro are stronger than my ability to change them." He had determined to give up the course.[14]

In its promotion of new research findings, the CIC portrayed itself as forward thinking and modern, an approach that may have appealed to young people. Woofter observed that the organization "has helped to create a new atmosphere in which it is no longer unfashionable to be an outspoken friend of the Negro." According to Eleazar, "the South's most liberal leadership in the matter of race relations in the next twenty years will come from the young men and women who today are having their minds opened and their attitudes transformed as a result of these college courses in race relations." Indeed, the CIC programs seem to have inspired further study. The college essay contest in 1928 included an entry by an Emory College student named C. Vann Woodward who would go on to become the preeminent historian of race in the South.[15]

The CIC's focus on social science reflected its ties to northern liberals and to the national social science network. As early as 1923, Will Alexander met with Bruno Lasker to discuss reforming race relations. Members of the CIC included prominent southern sociologists, for example, Howard Odum, a white southerner who had done graduate work with Franz Boas at Columbia before heading the sociology department at the University of North Carolina. In the 1930s, Odum helped coordinate college courses on race and enlisted support for CIC activities in North Carolina. Charles S. Johnson, a black sociologist at Fisk University, was also an active member who coauthored a college textbook with Weatherford.[16]

Although Alexander depicted the CIC organization as a southern solution to a southern problem, the bulk of his funding came from outside the South. He saw advantages to this arrangement. He recognized that raising funds in the South "would result in our having to change and adapt the present program so as to meet the prejudices and special interests of those who would furnish the finances." He traveled regularly to New York and other northern cities, where he received money from the Phelps-Stokes Fund and maintained close connections with the Rockefeller foundations, including the LSRM. With the closure of the LSRM in 1929, the CIC turned to the Julius Rosenwald Fund, where Alexander became a trustee and later a vice president. The CIC remained dependent on the Rosenwald Fund for the last fourteen years of its existence. It also received a grant from the Carnegie Foundation for work with teachers colleges and school superintendents. Between 1919 and 1944, the CIC received and spent over two and a half million dollars.[17]

The CIC's social science perspective was shaped in part by these northern donors. In 1927, Alexander and others affiliated with the Commission attended an interracial conference in New Haven organized by Leonard Outhwaite of the LSRM. A trained anthropologist, Outhwaite voiced the progressive view of racial difference, asserting that it was not blacks who suffered an "inferiority complex," a notion much discussed at the time, "but it is the white folks that use colored prejudice as a method of compensating for their own feeling of inferiority." He wanted to understand sources of violent prejudice among whites. "We have got to know what it is that makes these people so cussed." At the conference, James Weldon Johnson of the NAACP pointed out that little thought had been given to the education that whites received about race. Johnson hoped "that we will try to bring about as much concerning the importance of education about the negro, learning something about him, as the education of the negro himself. Both phases of it are very important."[18]

Alexander did not see his work as merely derivative of northern thinkers, but rather as a model for the North to emulate. While his northern colleagues may have seen the South as backward, Alexander insisted that his experiences would benefit northern universities, which were enrolling increasing numbers of black students. In a letter to the LSRM, he ventured that "the great masses of college students in the North are either antagonistic or utterly indifferent to the whole situa-

Will Alexander. (Atlanta University Photographs, Robert W. Woodruff Library of the Atlanta University Center)

tion" regarding race relations, while college administrations appeared "confused and ineffective in dealing with the question." He invited Leonard Outhwaite to come to the South to observe the CIC's work.[19]

Alexander maintained contact with colleagues in the northern states. He published articles in the *Bulletin* of the FCC and served on the national committee of the Service Bureau for Education in Human Relations, the organization founded by Rachel Davis DuBois. In 1935, DuBois asked Alexander to support her funding request to the Rosenwald Fund. Discouraged when her appeal was rejected, she told Alexander: "I had hoped that this work in the schools would gradually do for the North something of what your Interracial Commission is doing so well for schools in the South." (In fact, her Service Bureau served southern as well as northern teachers; nearly a quarter of her requests for materials came from southern states and the District of Columbia.) Leaders of the CIC also strove to reach teacher education centers at Columbia University and the University of Chicago, which "have an important part in the training of Southern teachers and administrators."[20]

Despite close ties with northern colleagues, the CIC programs differed from their northern counterparts in important ways. Northern programs were inspired by the ethnic diversity brought by immigration, while southern programs focused almost exclusively on white-black relations and made little mention of white ethnicity, European nationalities, religious diversity, internationalism, or Asian and Mexican immigrants. The CIC also differed from its northern counterparts in its explicit reference to liberal Protestantism. While Rachel Davis DuBois relied on Jewish donors, the CIC derived its funding and prestige from church affiliations. An undercurrent of religious conviction ran through its work. Alexander and Weatherford were both ministers, as were more than a quarter of CIC members at one point, while Eleazar had been active in the Methodist church and editor of the *Missionary Voice*. These activists believed in the social messages of religion, hoping to shape public opinion through church workshops and conferences, moral appeals, and sermons on interracial cooperation. They called on social science to promote their understanding of Christian ideals.[21]

Liberal white college students in the South also attributed their friendly interracial attitudes to their involvement with Christian youth associations. The YMCA and YWCA provided initial funding for the CIC, which in exchange offered speakers and literature on race relations.

The CIC reported that some Sunday schools studied interracial topics and that theological schools in the South prepared graduates to work on race relations. Staff members created a discussion course for youth groups entitled "Christian Principles and Race Relations" and responded to a request from the Southern Baptist Church for youth education materials. In an article in *Religious Education,* Eleazar described these efforts to put race relations in the South "upon a sound Christian basis." The CIC maintained contact with churches through their representatives who were CIC members, presentations at conventions, and the church press.[22]

Alexander himself defined his work in the language of Protestant liberalism, offering a mix of religious and scientific language that appealed both to research findings and to Christian morality. To him, religion could be modern and progressive, enlisted in the interest of social reform. Yet he lost faith that the institution of the church would change racial attitudes. In 1923 he faulted white churches for their silence about racial discrimination: "We have not found that ministers are better informed or more interested in this question than other leaders." In a conversation with Lasker, Alexander complained that "church people do not like to think or discuss" and were less engaged in social questions than were physicians, teachers, or editors. Several years later, Alexander was gratified to see some southern denominations develop liberal programs for their young people's societies and Sunday schools: "Although somewhat limited, it marks a radical step for these denominations." But he remained skeptical about the church's commitment to restructure race relations. He informed teachers in 1932 that they were "about the only people in America that have any influence left." Church leaders had lost prestige, as had businessmen, due to the depression. "The teacher's place of leadership, however, remains secure," he asserted. "Your place is unshaken. The future is yours to mold. If our civilization is to be reconstructed, it has got to be done at that level; teachers are the men that are to do it."[23]

The "Tenth Man" Project

To reach students earlier, in 1928 the CIC began to invest more energy in the high schools of the South. Robert Eleazar instructed teachers that interracial antagonism resulted from misunderstanding and would dissipate with greater knowledge. He complained, however, that school publications failed to provide accurate information. Textbooks used in the South described slavery as benign and blacks as inferior citizens. According to Eleazar, schoolbooks "represent the Negro only as a disturbing factor in American life, a semi-savage slave, an illiterate, dangerous freedman, the source and center of constant internal conflict, and the cause of our greatest national tragedy—always, whether slave or free, a liability rather than an asset." A writer for the *Crisis* made a similar complaint: in no textbook did blacks appear as a people "with a past and authenticated history of their own in Africa." No textbook explained that most peoples had been enslaved at some point and that "slavery is a condition imposed, endured, not necessarily merited." Nor did the books present the "rights and attributes" of blacks or their contributions to the economic development of America.[24]

To counter these misrepresentations, over the course of the 1920s and 1930s, the CIC produced publications of its own. Most popular was *America's Tenth Man,* a booklet distributed free for high school study. (The title referred to the percentage of blacks in the population.) *America's Tenth Man* emphasized the long history of blacks in the United States, including black revolutionary heroes, the achievements of notable individuals, contributions in literature and music, and economic progress since emancipation. Eleazar asserted that recognition of this "astonishing record" would lead to better relations. The booklet was in great demand. By 1932, teachers had ordered more than fifty thousand copies. By 1943, it had gone through twenty-one editions, with 230,000 copies sent to schools across the South.[25]

The CIC expanded its essay contest to include high school students, a move that proved popular: by 1933, almost fifteen hundred students competed for the cash prizes. The CIC pointed out that since teachers sent only the best examples, even more students wrote papers. Essays tended to echo *America's Tenth Man.* In a prize-winning entry from 1932, Virginia Davidson of Fayetteville, Arkansas, explained that "the white man" was blinded by prejudice and so "permits himself injustice and takes no cognizance of the Negro's important contributions to the making of American history." She was convinced that "the era of prejudice is passing."[26]

The CIC's competition for the best school projects brought participation from cities and small towns all over the South. In 1930, Eleazar received nearly five hundred reports, evidence that *America's Tenth Man* was widely used. In total, more than a thousand schools took part. White students read black poetry; sang spirituals; visited libraries; sponsored literary or oratorical contests; examined newspapers and magazines; provided books and equipment to black schools; wrote and performed plays; produced posters; presented programs to local business, civic, and religious groups; and published articles in local and school newspapers. Some schools used the new technology of the radio: in Prattville, Alabama, white students listened to a broadcast of the anniversary program of the Tuskegee Institute, while in Biloxi, Mississippi, radio talks on black achievements reached listeners along the coast.[27]

"My viewpoint on race relations has been broadened through this study," came a typical comment from Clinton, Mississippi. "I think every student should study race relations and know the conditions that exist because the children of today are the men of tomorrow and then it will be our problem." A student from the R. J. Reynolds High School in Winston-Salem, North Carolina, a school that won the CIC's contest several years in a row, explained the value of the project. "Most of us have knowledge of the servant class only, and many of us are unjustly prejudiced against the Negro, since we know nothing whatever about his other side." Through study, "we may abolish some of that prejudice and give people a clearer view of the Negro."[28]

High school teachers also reported success in altering attitudes. A teacher from Swainsboro, Georgia, thanked Eleazar "for affording us an opportunity for studying our friends. Besides having gained a great deal of information of them, we feel that a kinder and more sympathetic feeling exists now than it did in our town before." The project in St. Joseph, Missouri, convinced students "that the 'Tenth Man' has been as essential as any other race in building up a great nation. In most instances prejudices were removed."[29]

Many of the high school teachers who implemented these educational programs were women, as were many of the students who submitted essays and won awards. At the CIC, women played an active role through a women's committee and the antilynching association, although the Atlanta staff and state chairs were mostly men. The CIC's educational strategy made women central to the dissemination of liberal ideas on race. Alexander recognized this when he wrote: "The minority of progressives and near-progressives throughout the South must be kept unified, vocal and increased in number. The two great sources from which this group can be increased are the women and the students."[30]

While the Tenth Man project remained central to their work, CIC leaders also began to look for ways to reach students earlier than high school. At an interracial conference held in Cincinnati in 1925 under the auspices of the CIC and the FCC, a high school principal from Des Moines remarked that young children exhibited little prejudice: "I do not notice that little boys and girls in the lower grades have much trouble playing together." Given the social causes of racial antagonism, "the educational institutions of this country, from kindergarten up, therefore, constitute the strategic centers of approach in developing constructive interracial attitudes." In the South, however, antiprejudice training at first gave little attention to the elementary grades. When a CIC report from 1923 stated that "a person rarely changes his fundamental attitudes after he reaches thirty," it offered an inaccurate account of social science findings. Researchers had emphasized the importance of the very earliest years of life, long before age thirty. This distortion reflected regional differences, for southern institutions offered fewer ways to reach young children. Compared to other areas of the country, the South was slower to embrace the parent education movement, progressive education, and the kindergarten. In 1916–1917, only 1 or 2 percent of four- to six-year-old children were enrolled in kindergartens in seven southern states. Enrollment rates were much higher in the North, reaching over 25 percent in several states.[31]

By the organization's tenth anniversary, compelled by social science findings, the CIC was seeking ways to reach the malleable child. "If racial peace, cooperation and justice are ever to be established, a larger use must be made of the opportunity presented by the education of children," one report declared. "Without doubt the seeds of racial antagonism, suspicion, and fear are sown very early in life, as the result of indirect and more or less unconscious forces at work in the home, in the schools, and even in the churches. This is a field that urgently needs the attention of the best educators and the largest resources that could be put into it."[32] For CIC leaders, teachers colleges marked "the strategic point of attack," since they trained people who would mold the attitudes of future generations. Alexander suggested that white teachers colleges offer courses on race relations, for "in this way we would slowly and safely make white elementary schools avenues for the promotion of better racial attitudes." Mary Church Terrell, a prominent African American author and lecturer, also emphasized the power of the schools to shape public opinion. "If I had money to spend to advance the interests of the Negro, I would work with white children first and with black children second," she wrote.[33]

In 1930, Alexander proposed to conduct summer courses for educators "as the surest way of reaching the mind of the masses in the formative years of childhood." Since prejudices were absorbed early, "the processes of counter education should begin early, also—in high school, certainly, or even in the grammar grades." Funding from the Carnegie Corporation established the Conference on Education and Race Relations, which sponsored summer gatherings at George Peabody College in Nashville under the direction of Robert Eleazar. In attendance at the first conference in 1931 were sixty college presidents, professors, and public school administrators, including representatives from thirty-four teachers colleges. Its purpose, Eleazar stated, was "to inform and inspire these teachers of teachers" in hopes that they would in turn "reach thousands of teachers and prepare them to mediate more intelligent and fair-minded attitudes to the multitudes of children they will teach."[34]

When the Peabody conference reconvened the next year, participants reported on projects they had carried out. A professor from a Christian college for women in Georgia, for example, boasted that "our departments of Bible, sociology, history, and education are committed to the promotion of interracial justice and amity. We believe that the public school teachers are the logical agents through whom to work toward this end; and since about ninety percent of our graduates teach school we are trying to instill these ideals into their minds." Representatives from six other colleges described efforts to promote interracial understanding, some complaining that they were stymied by lack of materials. A faculty member at the state teachers college in Huntsville, Texas, noted that "our text-books have been written by white people primarily for white people" with little attention to black Americans. New materials would "make for open-minded justice and fairness in dealing with this 'tenth man' that we have in our country."[35] To bring the work to a wider audience, Eleazar sent the first conference report to two thousand educators in the South. He also contacted teachers colleges and college departments of education, offering free copies of a shorter summary report. By

1934, he had sent thirteen thousand copies to a hundred southern colleges. Eleazar offered free copies of *America's Tenth Man* as well. He hoped to prepare teachers "to pass on to multitudes of children, from infancy the innocent and helpless victims of traditional misunderstanding, a basis for more intelligent and fair-minded attitudes." Work with teachers was "more direct, less difficult, and at the same time more fundamental and important" than the high school project. The CIC extended its essay competition to include teachers colleges and schools of education, offering one award for the best paper on the responsibility of public school teachers and a second award for the class or college making best use of the conference report.[36] Robert Moton of the Tuskegee Institute reminded the white teachers of their influence: "what will happen twenty years from now will be determined largely by the attitude you and I take with the young people with whom we deal."[37]

Segregation and Racial Attitudes

The CIC's moderate stance aroused skepticism in some black leaders, who feared that the underlying aim was to maintain subordination and prevent black workers from leaving the South. W. E. B. Du Bois, for example, offered a mixed review of the CIC's activities. While he spoke highly of Alexander, he also criticized him for not working with black leaders who demanded integration and equality. He worried that the inclusion of accommodationist blacks would avoid real social change and preempt the work of more radical groups. In 1921, Du Bois called on the organization not to "fill your committees with 'pussy footers' like Robert Moton or 'white-folks' Niggers' like Isaac Fisher." He challenged the CIC to "face the fundamental problems: the Vote, the 'Jim Crow' car, Peonage and Mob-law." In 1930 he praised Alexander as "one of the few white Southerners who has worked to make the interracial movement something more than a gesture and an excuse for inaction." But Du Bois warned that the CIC's funders included whites who prevented blacks from voting, as well as blacks "who continually let themselves be used as catspaws and bell-wethers by enemies of the Negro race." He urged greater effort to repeal offensive legislation on disfranchisement, intermarriage, segregation, and unequal funding for schools. Such an agenda constituted a truly "sane approach to the race problem," he wrote, echoing the title of a CIC report. The CIC should turn its attention "to the final abolition of Negro slavery in the South" through the legislative program he set out.[38]

Yet other black leaders saw the CIC as the most practical way to bring change. In the 1920s, *Opportunity* ran several favorable articles. John Hope gave the organization credit for "preparing a new interracial gospel" in the spirit of brotherhood. According to Mary White Ovington, Will Alexander was "trusted by the Negroes, radicals and conservatives," as "a humane, fair-minded man, without cant and without prejudice."[39] Like their white colleagues, black educators hoped that knowledge would change attitudes. "When scientific analysis reveals new insight, a higher and better way, Negro students expect white students to possess sufficient moral courage to align their conduct and 'mind sets' accordingly," explained Benjamin Mays, then a secretary at the YMCA and an outspoken opponent of segregation. A student from Morehouse College, where Mays later became president, argued that it was "the attitude built up in the youthful mind today that will determine the fate of the country a half century hence."[40]

While the ultimate agenda of these black thinkers may have differed from that of their white colleagues, they agreed that modifying white attitudes was an effective first step. They, too, believed in the transformative power of education. In the interwar South, those few white individuals or organizations who publicly challenged racial subordination earned black support, even if their vision fell short of what African Americans envisaged. Since outspoken white allies were few and far between, many black leaders welcomed the CIC's gestures of racial goodwill as they sought black advancement. They also realized that they could use the CIC's materials for their own purposes. The new textbooks offered a way to instill pride as they introduced students, black as well as white, to the achievements of African Americans. Such knowledge could inspire activism on behalf of a broader vision of racial justice.

Students at black schools took part in CIC activities. They submitted essays to the annual contests, and in 1929, the CIC awarded first prize to Ernestine Banks, a sixteen-year-old black student from Hot Springs, Arkansas, who saw her essay published in the *Arkansas Gazette*. Leaders of the CIC made a few gestures toward training black students to cooperate with liberal-minded whites. They made plans to collaborate with black educators and at one point called together presidents of black colleges to discuss the idea.[41] But this work took lower priority than changing the attitudes of white students. Eleazar may have understood that black schools would need little encouragement to participate, or feared that white teachers would be reluctant to take part in a "black" project. By 1934, the CIC was describing its essay competition as a "south-wide contest in white high schools and colleges." The CIC acknowledged that "white students are getting more preparation for interracial cooperation than Negroes." As W. D. Weatherford explained, those interested in black education "have overlooked the fact that this parallel movement of broadening the sympathy of the white youth is imperative, if the Negro youth is ever to take his place as a real citizen."[42]

Although black schools were not the target of the CIC campaign, teachers there eagerly seized on CIC materials, requesting copies of *America's Tenth Man*. The Calhoun Colored School in Alabama organized special programs on black history, literature, business, science, music, and notable individuals. "Judging by the lively interest your contest aroused here, with the resulting collection of information which has enlightened us on many phases of Negro life, I am sure your Commission is making an [sic] constructive contribution toward interracial understanding and the advance of the Negro," wrote the teacher of English and Latin. "May your success continue." A teacher from Cape Girardeau, Missouri, wrote to the CIC: "Since the use of your project there has been a new spirit among the students about achievements, and advancements of the Negro. Their interest is also on the increase. We are greatly pleased to assist you in your wonderful work. May our dreams not be in vain, when Negro history shall be taught in all schools and colleges."[43]

In fact, the CIC's emphasis on black cultural achievements could obscure patterns of social segregation. Its agenda was defined by contradiction, for even as it promoted progressive and interracial politics, it also followed the status quo, as did most white liberals in the interwar South. Eleazar pursued "some modus vivendi—some plan by which the two groups may be able to live alongside in friendliness and mutual respect." The CIC did not advocate the extension or tightening of Jim Crow, he explained, but neither did its members think it "wise or desirable" to fight it. Woofter warned that challenging segregation would alienate white southerners: "unless those forms of separation which are meant to safeguard the purity of the races are present, the majority of the white people flatly refuse to cooperate with Negroes." Leaders of the CIC imagined a gentler form of segregation, free of brutality and violence.

They worked to improve conditions for blacks within the existing system to bring about gradual, peaceful reform. They hoped that this cautious approach would win approval from southern whites by encouraging tolerance without challenging the structural foundations of white supremacy. The educational campaign gained strength in the 1930s, in part because it offered a low-cost, low-stakes solution to the problems highlighted by the depression.[44]

For the leaders of the CIC, this moderate stance was more practical than ideological, reflecting the dynamics of the South in a period in which segregation was deeply entrenched. Will Alexander himself opposed racial segregation and inequality; his ultimate aims included greater justice and equal status for blacks and whites. He hinted at these larger goals when he asked white teachers to "interpret the aspirations, accomplishments, and rights" of black Americans. As a pragmatist, however, he configured his message to appeal to a broad audience and cautioned against moving too far ahead of popular opinion. A moderate position, he argued, was the most effective way to improve conditions for blacks in the long run and, ultimately, bring about racial equality. (Only in the 1940s did he become an outspoken opponent of segregation.) Arthur Raper, who also objected to segregation, agreed that public opposition could weaken the effectiveness of the CIC. In his survey of the interracial movement, Paul Baker explained the CIC's pragmatic approach: "It plans to keep only a step in advance of the general populace on the race issues," he wrote. "It avoids taking a stand regarding social, economic, or political equality for the Negro. No social functions where the two races meet on a level of social fellowship are held. The commission accepts many of the inequalities and injustices in the race situation in America, stating that, since they are so deeply rooted, it is unwise to attack them now."[45]

The CIC's educational projects followed this gradualist approach. They initially coalesced around the most blatant examples of racial animosity, such as the prevention of lynching. This approach created a gap between the organization's long-range goals and short-term strategies. Woofter assured readers of his textbook that blacks and whites could "dwell peacefully together without the tremendous social cost of amalgamation, each making its own peculiar contribution to the development of the United States," living side by side without violence or prejudice. He advocated fairness in legal protection, education, taxation, living conditions, and health care yet stopped short of "social intermingling." Segregation, in other words, could be equal and just. He counseled patience, explaining that change would take time. He was critical of the group of black leaders—described as northern editors and politicians—that was "insistent in its demands for equality, and constantly agitating and litigating for the immediate realization of its desires." This approach would only lead to "bickering, unrest, litigation, and violence" and would "inevitably impede the progress of race cooperation." He applauded instead the southern teachers, preachers, and businessmen who understood that conditions would improve through "hard work and gradual advancement," a "conciliatory course" he considered most effective. *America's Tenth Man* similarly eschewed integration. Its frontispiece, a quotation by Weatherford, was emblematic of the separationist approach: "Working together for the good of all, each race may have its individual life and yet live in peace and harmony—yes, in helpfulness to the other races which live by its side." Eleazar designed the booklet to appeal to white southerners: "I believe it contains not a single line which could give offense."[46]

In their entries to the essay contests, white students reaffirmed segregation even as they detailed black achievements. In 1928, the CIC awarded second prize to a student from Davidson College who proclaimed: "Brotherhood does not mean intermarriage or social equality." High school students also echoed familiar politics of race and citizenship. "What then should be our attitude?" one essay asked. "Assimilate them? No! They are different in the name of humanity let them stay so." Another student argued that blacks "should have public schools within reach of all of them, but have them separate from the schools of the Whites." Intermarriage or mingling between the races should be "absolutely prohibited," for whites "have many principles of civilization which would be lost or lowered by such intercourse," he believed. "We white people can do the Negroes more good by teaching them the fine points of our civilization, while still keeping our own intact."[47]

The Tenth Man project offered a tacit endorsement of segregation. At Kirksville High School in Missouri, a white school that shared first prize three years in a row, the project affirmed both black accomplishments and segregation. The school-wide project involved class study, assemblies, art, music, drama, and the preparation of a "Negro Year Book" with essays and newspaper clippings on black achievements. Students investigated black life in Kirksville through "observation tours" of black churches and schools, then reported their findings to community groups to plead for better race relations. According to Pauline Knobbs, head of the social science department, the project aimed to foster appreciation and to raise awareness of black community needs. Students used a portion of the prize money to buy books and equipment for the black school. Knobbs assumed the permanence of segregation when she hoped that "the minority may have a chance to develop in the bi-racial system which must come to our nation." Leaders of the CIC endorsed this viewpoint when they distributed Knobbs's account in their publicity materials.[48]

College courses could also reinforce the segregationist outlook. A sociologist from Furman University reported that at the end of his course on race relations, students still considered "social intermixture" undesirable. At the University of North Carolina, a classroom experiment found no proof that prejudice was "yielding greatly to the higher educative processes," while a study at the Georgia State College for Women found that white students who studied black education in the South remained opposed to any social or educational mixing of the races. Knowledge of racial problems, the researcher concluded, had no effect on students' attitudes toward segregation or social rights.[49]

Arthur Raper was the only CIC staff member to question publicly the effectiveness of the courses within a segregated system. In *Opportunity*, a publication aimed at black readers, he pointed out that since colleges were among the most "segregated and sheltered" places in the South, they were problematic for the improvement of racial attitudes. From earliest childhood, students had learned the lessons of their home communities. "To expect the student to shed his racial background upon entering college—itself a racial institution—is to expect the impossible." Raper argued that it was insufficient to be "plastering on the students hastily concocted racial goodwill poultices in the form of unrelated college courses." He urged a more comprehensive approach, from kindergarten through graduate school, but stopped short of advocating an end to segregation.[50]

While Alexander and his colleagues hoped that their educational programs would pave the way for racial equality, some educators used the projects for a different cause. Those who claimed to embrace the CIC's work did not necessarily share its viewpoints, for the language of "cooperation" and "understanding" masked real differences about equality and power. Alexander and his colleagues could not control how their message was understood as it radiated outward across the South. The southern mobilization against prejudice, which originated in Atlanta, took varying form in cities and towns from Texas to Florida.

Some school leaders used the CIC materials to reinforce white supremacy, even as they highlighted black cultural contributions. While Alexander hoped to promote black aspirations as a step toward racial justice, a school project in Arcola, Mississippi, where blacks far outnumbered whites, aimed to furnish "a clearer understanding of the tenant in his relation to the landowner." The project involved typical elements of the cultural gifts approach, including black history, religion, economics, music; it introduced students to black scientists and inventors, poets and musicians. Yet it assumed that blacks would remain in servile roles. "The close contact between whites and negroes in capacities as cooks, nurses, servants, delivery boys" necessitated the study, the project organizer wrote. White students would be interested because of their contact "on the plantations with negroes as servants and tenants," and "as clerks in stores with negroes as customers."[51]

In Atlanta, Willis A. Sutton, superintendent of the public schools and a member of the CIC's Conference on Education and Race Relations, urged teachers to be tolerant and broad-minded, willing to teach children to think without prejudice. With the assistance of the CIC, he boasted, white schoolchildren learned about black contributions to the nation's history. Yet Sutton did not intend this knowledge to undermine the social hierarchy: "we have instilled into the child the attitude of cooperation with the Negro servant in the home or the Negro man who delivers the coal or the Negro child as they meet on the street." For their part, black children would learn to accept subordinate roles: "we are teaching, in the Negro schools, their proper relations to white people," Sutton wrote. "We are showing that the great mass of property in this part of the world is owned and controlled by the white people and that they are willing to tax themselves to give the Negro educational advantages." Thanks to such generosity, "the Negro should have the right attitude toward the white man."[52]

The state teachers college in Conway, Arkansas, whose president had attended the first Peabody conference, defended existing social relations through a romantic portrayal of antebellum life. A display of drawings "portrayed some of the pleasanter features of race relations of plantation life prior to the Civil War," an instructor wrote. Students visited local black schools in order to change attitudes "such that the two races may cooperate harmoniously in lifting the Negro out of a position in which he is more or less of a social and economic liability . . . into one in which he is a decided social and economic asset."[53]

Comments from a junior college in London, Kentucky, reveal the great distance white students still had to travel to reach the "intelligent and sympathetic" attitudes CIC leaders imagined. Despite the CIC's emphasis on research findings, students offered interpretations of race that were very different from those of social scientists. "When I first started this course, I thought of the negro as I would have a mule, but after studying this course it has changed my viewpoints quite a bit," one student marveled. "I still can't see the negro on a level with white people, but I do see him as a human being that should be given an education and taken care of by society." Another student missed the point that blacks had long played important roles in American history and culture. "Since I have taken sociology I have learned that if society reaches its objective it must improve the conditions of the negro. Their environment must be changed in such a way that they in turn may contribute to society instead of being a drawback."[54]

The papers of high school students also revealed the persistence of white supremacy. One began: "The Negro is a little more than a twelve year old child in his actions." Virginia Davidson's prize-winning paper asserted that "the white man owes the black that succor and sympathy which a chivalrous strong man extends to his weaker brother." She considered it a matter of opinion whether slavery was an improvement over conditions in Africa. Another entry declared that blacks "sorely need the guidance and the uplifting hand that the white people, with their superior advancement, are capable to give them." Alexander's concern for black achievements, black aspirations, and civil rights gave way to the familiar paternalism of southern race relations.[55]

That white students could come away from the CIC projects with their sense of superiority intact may have been due to the organization's emphasis on notable African Americans, which substituted class discrimination for racial bigotry and emphasized individual achievements rather than group rights. By teaching respect for "cultured" African Americans, the programs could justify continued prejudice against those black southerners who had not accomplished as much as had notable poets, scientists, and musicians. Students received less guidance in how to approach their black neighbors who had not had the opportunity to gain education or social status. Nor were they encouraged to question the effects of political disfranchisement, unequal school funding, occupational exclusion, or public segregation.

There is little evidence that CIC officials intervened to protest these interpretations. Occasionally they edited the letters and essays they received for publicity purposes. But in general they seem not to have looked carefully at the messages their proxies were sending or recognized the disparities between intention and implementation. Leaders of the CIC were more concerned with increasing the number of school projects than evaluating their content or discovering what instructors were telling their students. "The work is being done in various ways in different institutions," Alexander acknowledged. "Those who direct the courses are open-minded as to methods. No one has brought forward a perfect method or feels that he has found one."[56] Yet the lack of standardization applied to the message as well as to the methods. The gradualist approach sharply circumscribed change, as it allowed the ideal of racial cooperation to coexist with segregation and subordination.

Endorsements and Critiques

Commission leaders exulted when their work became part of southern school curricula. When the 1933 Peabody conference brought together thirty public school administrators from every southern state, including six state superintendents of education, it asked each state department of education to study the treatment of blacks in school textbooks and to make available units on race. The objective, Eleazar reported to the Carnegie Corporation, "is a vast program of popular education involving 35,000,000 people." He sought to expand the program "until it becomes coextensive with the educational system of the South." His figures indicated widespread acceptance: the CIC had sent twenty-five thousand copies of its materials to 116 colleges and universities and had conferred with administrators and faculty. Five hundred high school principals had introduced the Tenth Man project. Thousands of high school students had prepared papers, posters, and community surveys. Yet much work remained. Many colleges were still untouched, and others did "only desultory and superficial work." There was need for more materials and for continued experimentation in methods.[57]

As a result of the 1933 conference, several state departments of education—including Arkansas, Mississippi, Florida, and Tennessee—conducted studies that revealed "a deplorable lack of constructive information" in their textbooks. Studies by graduate students concurred. Eleazar's own survey of textbooks in use in the South, published in 1935, found startling "omissions and inclusions that make for misunderstanding." Of twenty texts in American history, most ignored black patriotism and military service, black leadership, and progress since emancipation; misrepresented the events of Reconstruction and glorified the Ku Klux Klan; included little information about present-day conditions; and portrayed blacks as "unprepared for citizenship and a menace to civilization." Textbooks in civics and literature were little better. To bring his findings to wide attention, Eleazar offered free copies of the survey to educators, publishers, and authors.[58]

The CIC continued to sponsor materials of its own. In 1934, Charles S. Johnson and Willis D. Weatherford published *Race Relations: Adjustment of Whites and Negroes in the United States,* a college textbook written at the recommendation of the Peabody conference. The CIC pamphlets continued to be popular. In 1936, *America's Tenth Man* totaled 135,000 copies. Other titles—including "Recent Trends in Race Relations," "The Quest for Understanding," "Singers in the Dawn" (an anthology of black poetry), and "Southland Spirituals" (a collection of black music)—generated tens of thousands of copies. In 1937 the CIC produced "Population Problems in the South" for civics and social science classes. Teachers colleges ordered twenty-five thousand copies of "Education for Southern Citizenship," published in 1938.[59]

The Conference on Education and Race Relations continued to promote race relations work in the colleges of the South. It sponsored events throughout the 1930s and awarded fellowships for educators to attend summer sessions at Peabody College. As hoped, participants initiated courses in race relations on their return to the state teachers colleges. In the late 1930s, the CIC also held conferences at Mississippi College, Louisiana State University, and the state teachers colleges in Troy, Alabama, and in Blue Ridge, North Carolina. The CIC counted 70 college courses in race relations and 266 courses in history, sociology, literature, and education that included material on race. "Thus the weight of official approval and authority is given to the study of questions which a few years ago would have been absolutely taboo," a CIC report proclaimed in 1938.[60]

Race relations education was becoming more firmly established in public school curricula as well. Seventy public school superintendents agreed to distribute CIC materials to their teachers and place them in school libraries. In 1937, Eleazar reported that five southern state departments of education had issued bulletins "recommending officially the introduction of units of work looking to interracial understanding and justice," which the CIC reprinted in its publicity materials. The Georgia program noted "the challenge to schools for whites to develop an honest and fair-minded attitude toward the other large racial group" and suggested that the schools could help to solve "this difficult and delicate problem." Other southern states issued similar bulletins. The Mississippi unit, for example, suggested the study of black suffrage. A CIC report evaluated these units as "surprisingly frank and thorough-going."[61]

The acceptance of segregation and gradual change may help explain why state departments of education were willing to approve the Tenth Man project. As these superintendents understood, race relations work did not necessarily threaten white interests. When the *Chattanooga Free Press* ran an editorial in support of the participation of a local high school class, it advocated both progressive racial attitudes and the maintenance of social hierarchy. "It is a fine thing that white school children in the South are being trained away from that old product of reconstruction days, hatred of the colored people," the paper opined. "It is impossible to eliminate the prejudice from the old group; the hope is in those who are coming." The editorial faulted both whites, who "have had before them the specter of social equality and the fear that the blacks, through force of numbers, would seize control of local governments," and blacks, who were "wrongly led" by the NAACP and the American Civil Liberties Union, which "taught them that the road to social, political and economic equality is through hating and fighting their white neighbors. Such a course is suicidal to the hopes of the Negro for advancement and makes impossible progress toward harmony between the races." Here again, it appeared that attention to black cultural achievements could substitute for political protest and social change.[62]

Some black leaders continued to endorse the CIC's work in the 1930s.

Even as philosopher Alain Locke, for example, noted that university race relations classes in the Midwest failed to modify social attitudes, he declared that he had "no desire to discourage such efforts." In fact, he explained, he had found such classes to be more effective in southern universities because of "the strong emotional conditioning of the average Southerner on matters of race." In 1936, in *A Preface to Racial Understanding,* Charles Johnson described the CIC as "the one outstanding organization in the South working to improve race relations." According to Johnson, it "has worked for social justice and improved living conditions for Negroes, and has vigorously sought to bring about a more agreeable adjustment between the white and Negro populations in an area in which the traditional pattern demanded segregation." Johnson recounted the organization's achievements, under Alexander's "able direction," in combating lynchings, tenancy, and misdealings. "The Interracial Commission has been criticized at times by certain other groups both for going too far and for not going far enough," he acknowledged, but considered that criticism unfounded. "Working within the mores, it has consistently pursued a policy of change which has not been too radical to weaken seriously its influence within its region."[63]

Yet in the late 1930s, in the context of the lengthening depression, the CIC came under harsher criticism from other black intellectuals, who termed its approach superficial and deceptive and called for stronger action to challenge racial and economic oppression. They questioned whether modifying attitudes would indeed lead to social reform. *Opportunity* disparaged the interracial movement for its unequal status of members, isolation of the races, and little actual achievement. Ralph Bunche, a political scientist at Howard University, criticized Johnson's *Preface to Racial Understanding*—along with the interracial movement in general—for avoiding economic issues. He suspected that Johnson "is talking about 'racial understanding' among the upper classes, black and white, and not among the masses," who rarely enter "the class-snobbish portals of the interracial meetings," Bunche wrote in the *Journal of Negro Education* in 1937. He noted that the book made no mention of black labor organizing and instead fortified "much of the notorious stupidity and confusions" of interracialists. "It may be argued, of course, that this sort of simple, inoffensive, polite analysis is helpful to tender high school and college youth of both races who are evidencing a developing interest in the race problem." But he thought it doubtful that such efforts could reform racial dynamics. Bunche later criticized the CIC's "naive assumptions that when the two races know and understand each other better, the principal incidents of the race problem will then disappear."[64]

A faculty member at Howard, Doxey Wilkerson, also thought it unrealistic to assume that interracial meetings could "counteract the fundamental social and economic forces which move toward a bi-racial caste system." He accused "kindly-spirited whites" of paternalism and caution, following the principle "'Don't-do-anything-to-create-antagonism.'" Wilkerson argued that interracial groups "are not only impotent to aid the Negro in any fundamental manner, but they are also positively vicious. They would lull the Negro into the idealistic belief that real progress is possible without sharp disturbance of existing racial accommodations." Horace Mann Bond, dean of Dillard University, questioned the CIC's effectiveness: "To Negroes it has frequently seemed to be a cunning device to soften, without actually remedying, the harshness of Negro life in

Charles Johnson. (Franklin Library Special Collections, Fisk University)

the South." Bond complained that curricular revisions excluded black teachers, black representatives to boards of education, and black administrators, remarking that "if our children are to be operated on, it is a comfort to know that the family doctor will be present when the patient is laid on the table." He was skeptical about the power of schooling to change attitudes, an approach that had seemed to hold such promise: "Let us confess that the schools have never built a new social order, but have always in all times and in all lands been the instruments through which social forces were perpetuated."[65]

Even as race relations education was becoming established in school curricula, the CIC was losing some of its vitality. In 1935, Alexander went to Washington to serve as assistant administrator of the Resettlement Administration to work for the reduction of farm tenancy, at the same time retaining his position with the CIC and returning to Atlanta each month. In 1937, Howard Odum became president of the CIC. While he endorsed the educational approach, under his leadership the organization focused on regional planning rather than race, to strengthen southern economy and culture for the benefit of both blacks and whites. The CIC dissolved in 1943, replaced by the Southern Regional Council, which stood against segregation in the years after World War II.[66]

In 1937, looking back on the Carnegie grant, Eleazar identified three phases of work. The first step was to make educators aware of the need for interracial education, and the second was to demonstrate that any school subject could improve attitudes. The first two objectives had been achieved, but only a beginning had been made on the third, which was "to root this program so widely and firmly as to make it a permanent part of the educational system, functioning automatically without the aid of constant stimulation," Eleazar explained. "Whether it will be possible to go on until this final and necessary objective is achieved is still to be determined." Alexander lamented that thousands of schools and teachers "are still unprepared for anything so revolutionary" as education for better racial attitudes.[67]

A 1941 survey showed how much work remained to be done. A study of 328 white high school students from across the South found discouraging results. The majority knew nothing of black contributions to the settlement of America or of patriotic service in the nation's wars. Few students had heard of Phillis Wheatley, Matthew Henson, or Jesse Owens or were able to name a single black college. Even graduate students at Peabody College held misconceptions. "To them, therefore, the Negro is not an American in the sense that the rest of us are, but a late comer and an alien," Eleazar lamented. Comments from white college students from South Carolina and Alabama illustrated persistent attitudes of superiority and prejudice, indicating that "the school has failed dismally in its duty of enlightenment and character building." Democratic ideals were at stake, as well as the image of the South in the rest of the country. "As a Georgian and a Southerner I stand shamed before the nation by the lurid stories" of oppression and violence, Eleazar confessed. "We have no hope of escape except by the education of the masses to the point where such things will no longer be tolerated. That, I submit, is a major responsibility of our colleges and public schools."[68]

Despite these dismaying results, Eleazar and his colleagues maintained faith in their approach. The problem, in their view, was not that educational programs had failed, but that they had not gone far enough. In 1941, the CIC continued to reach out to southern educators with optimism, hoping to expand the work and make it permanent. "By such means only may we hope adequately to prepare the youth of today to deal intelligently and fairly with the obligations of tomorrow." Since the state departments of education had approved public school curricula on race relations, "great numbers of children in every Southern state have been enlisted in study of the Negro's history, achievements and contributions to American life, and in the practical problems involved in the bi-racial situation."[69]

Gunnar Myrdal praised the CIC's educational approach in *An American Dilemma*, published in 1944. He noted that some black leaders complained of the insincerity and paternalism of white participants in the interracial movement, and he recognized "the cumulative tendency in the segregation system itself, which continuously drives toward greater spiritual isolation between the two groups." Even so, Myrdal called the CIC's efforts laudable. Compromise was necessary because of the political situation in the South. Since liberal forces were weak, the CIC was compelled to adopt a gradualist approach. "But its main tactics must be condoned. These tactics *are* radical in the South," Myrdal asserted, for education and cooperation would have influence "even if they are slow to develop liberal political power which can force great reforms." He concluded that "one of the most important accomplishments of the Commission—which has a far-reaching cumulative effect—is *to have rendered interracial work socially respectable in the conservative South.*"[70]

As Myrdal recognized, the CIC had succeeded in establishing educational programs designed to ameliorate racial tensions. But this success came at a cost. The approach it adopted did not imply that equality for African Americans would follow from greater tolerance. Most prominently in the South, but also in other regions, the failure to confront racial segregation or socioeconomic inequality limited both the conceptual reach and the political effectiveness of educational work. Indeed, the focus on cultural appreciation, on individual change and psychological attitudes, allowed educators to preach change without defying the institutional foundations of white supremacy or demanding that participants alter their political or social relationships around race. Their challenge to racial prejudice did not necessarily entail a challenge to the structures on which the politics of race and racism were built, and in fact could provide a distraction that subverted the work of civil rights. White southerners could thus attend to cultural appreciation without interrogating the foundations of the social order or imagining relationships of equality with their black neighbors. In the years after World War II, activists who were determined to reform race relations would look to other strategies to bring about full citizenship and democratic participation in the South.

6

Cultural Pride and the Second Generation

By 1934, when Rachel Davis DuBois founded the Service Bureau for Intercultural Education, antiprejudice experiments had found their way into schools across the country. DuBois situated herself at the heart of an increasingly popular educational campaign. At the end of the decade, she gained praise from Eleanor Roosevelt: "This beginning is pointing the way for other school systems throughout the country to do similar work."[1]

Antiprejudice education in the 1930s was in many ways an extension of the experiments begun in the 1920s, for cultural gifts remained the dominant approach. The educational campaign, however, shifted focus. While DuBois and her colleagues had earlier targeted children of the dominant group—the white, native-born, Protestant children they feared would suffer feelings of false superiority—in the 1930s they turned their attention to young people of immigrant backgrounds. In their analysis, the schools should encourage cultural pride as a means both to prevent delinquency and to establish an inclusive American identity. This shift constituted an important expansion of the cultural gifts approach.

A number of social, economic, and intellectual factors came together to inspire this shift in focus. A decade after the passage of the 1924 National Origins Act, as the influx from Europe slowed to a trickle and as the children of immigrants came of age, youth with foreign-born parents became the topic of public debate and social science discussion. Popular anxiety grew over what became known as the "second-generation problem"—the concern that American-born children of immigrants, particularly those from southern and eastern European families, suffered feelings of shame and inferiority, broke family ties, and fell into delinquency and crime.

The onset of the Great Depression also focused attention on the second generation as it highlighted the dangers of disruptive and alienated young people, whose potential for rebellion seemed to threaten American institutions. In the context of the economic crisis, some Americans worried that forced assimilation was at the root of family disintegration, itself the cause of social ills. Others, fearful that the depression would encourage the spread of fascism and Nazism to the United States, hoped that a pluralist approach would dissipate potentially explosive tensions. Efforts to reinforce ties between immigrant parents and their children promised to stabilize social relations. The sympathetic approach to immigrants received reinforcement from New Dealers, who accepted the persistence of ethnic identity in American life.[2]

The entrance of ethnic scholars into the social science professions also brought greater attention to minority group children. In the 1930s, increasing numbers of people from immigrant and minority backgrounds received degrees in such disciplines as sociology, psychology, and education, while others took leadership roles in education, philanthropy, and social reform. Their research into race, ethnicity, and assimilation—and their funding of educational projects—recast the terms of antiprejudice work and influenced the thinking of native-born leaders.

The new focus on the second generation had mixed results for the cultural gifts crusade. It was effective at advocating cultural pride even as the children of European immigrants embraced American identity. But the cultural gifts model was far less effective at explaining the experiences of African American youth, whose ancestors had been in North America for many generations and had arrived through slavery rather than voluntary immigration. DuBois's notion that young people should appreciate the language and folk customs of their Old World parents appeared less applicable to black Americans, who had lost African languages and whose "Old World" was further away in time and memory. Her repeated references to the second generation thus further obscured the experiences of African Americans, who increasingly did not fit into her schema.

The "second-generation problem" could also deflect consideration of socioeconomic issues, even in the midst of the Great Depression. For DuBois, cultural attitudes appeared in psychological terms: feelings of shame and inferiority, a damaged sense of self, the emotional costs of rejecting parents' heritage. She may have reasoned that economic differences were temporary, and in terms of European immigrant groups, she was largely correct—within a generation, economic and political disadvantages would fade as European ethnics, in the American racial schema, merged into an inclusive category of whiteness. But the same was not true for black Americans, whose generations of economic and political oppression were not so easily remedied by praise for musical and artistic traditions. In its refusal to address structural conditions, as in its avoidance of the legacy of slavery and oppression, the cultural gifts movement proved inadequate to account for the place of African Americans. As the movement diverted attention from their pressing needs, black thinkers began to look to other approaches to demand equality and justice.

The Second Generation

Progressive reformers and educators had worried about the second-generation experience at least since the turn of the century. John Dewey, an influence on DuBois's thought, had long expressed concern that rapid assimilation of the younger generation was weakening parental authority. The "immigrant gifts" approach of the social settlements of the Progressive Era had also addressed anxieties over the children of the foreign-born, as did the folk festivals that took place in many cities. In 1921, the "America's Making" exposition in New York City highlighted immigrant participation in the country's agricultural and industrial development, while public schools sponsored two thousand pageants that told "the story of the many races which make up the population of America" though folk songs, dances, and plays. By 1932, more than fifty folk festivals had taken place, events designed to demonstrate the gifts that groups had dedicated to the country before embracing full assimilation. For some, the aim was to incorporate new arrivals into a homogenous population in which national origin no longer played a role.[3] While the leaders of the cultural gifts campaign drew on these earlier projects, they added two important dimensions: they sought to institutionalize such efforts in the schools, and they followed trends in social science, calling on new scholarly findings to lend scientific authority to the celebration of immigrant contributions.

Social scientists of immigrant backgrounds were among the first to study the effects of immigration on family life and cultural adjustment. The claim that too-rapid assimilation caused social ills was a key tenet of the influential Chicago school of sociology. In their study of Polish immigrants in Chicago, published in 1918, William I. Thomas and Florian Znaniecki (himself an immigrant from Poland) advanced the "modernization theory" of immigrant adjustment, arguing that the failure to adapt to modern life caused family disintegration and social disorganization. The abrupt move away from peasant culture, with little time to adjust to New World conditions, led to the decline of family solidarity, parental control, and community oversight and to a host of social problems, including crime, poverty, delinquency, divorce, immorality, and violence.[4]

Sociologist Frederic Thrasher corroborated this argument in his indictment of the Americanization process as the source of criminal behavior. Thrasher's research indicated that youth gangs in New York and Chicago included large numbers of second-generation children, but unlike other observers, he did not attribute this to the innate criminality of the foreign-born. Following modernization theory, he suggested that the assimilation process itself contributed to social disorganization by loosening ethnic ties. Children of immigrants exhibited higher rates of crime "because they are Americans and are no longer controlled by the traditions and customs which keep their parents in the paths of rectitude." In a rejection of scientific racism, Thrasher concluded: "In one important sense it may be said that *Americanization* is one of the chief causes of crime in the United States." The way to correct this antisocial behavior was to strengthen ties between immigrants and their children by boosting the status of minority cultural traditions. Thrasher influenced DuBois when he advised the final stages of her doctoral work and she cited his conclusions in her writings for teachers.[5]

The journalist Louis Adamic brought the "second-generation problem" to widespread public attention. Adamic, who had emigrated from Slovenia to New York City at age fifteen, expressed appreciation for the cultural creativity and ethnoracial diversity he encountered in America. In a widely read article published in *Harper's* in 1934, Adamic worried that "Thirty Million New Americans," children of immigrant parents, were being made ashamed of their ethnic heritage and prevented from participating as full citizens. He suggested that these young people "should be helped to acquire a knowledge of, and pride in, their own heritage." This help should come from social and cultural institutions, including the schools, and from an organization—much like the Service Bureau— that would help teachers learn about the cultural heritage of their students, provide speakers at teachers' conventions and colleges, and revise textbooks to recognize immigrant contributions. Such work would help New Americans "enrich the civilization and deepen the culture of this New World."[6]

Adamic's discussion included a wide range of European ethnic groups: the first sentence of his article mentioned thirty-four nationalities. He envisaged an educational program to teach "that socially and culturally the United States, as it stands today, is an extension not only of the British Isles but, more or less, of all Europe." His repeated use of the term "New Americans," his praise for Old World traditions, his attention to foreign languages and names, and his references to anti-immigrant sentiment focused exclusively on children of the foreign-born. Nowhere did his article mention African American youth, who may also have been "oppressed by feelings of inferiority" and uncertain of their role in American life.[7]

DuBois met Adamic several times and recalled that he "had a great influence on my thinking." Her organization reprinted the *Harper's* article as a pamphlet and distributed thousands of copies to high schools. Thanks in part to this additional publicity, the article "caused a considerable stir," Adamic recounted, generating editorial comments around the country and hundreds of letters from both old-stock and New Americans.[8] Citing his findings, DuBois agreed that Americanization programs exacerbated rather than solved the problems of the second generation. The effects emerged not only in deviant behavior but also in weakening of the creative spirit and disaffection from the democratic process. Drawing a parallel between the cutting down of forests and the suppression of immigrant traditions, she argued that America's cultural resources, like its natural resources, "are being wasted because of the tremendous pressure for everyone to act alike, think alike, *be* alike." In another environmental comparison of the 1930s, which went beyond Adamic in including African Americans, she lamented, "there are millions of young Negroes and second-generation Europeans so ashamed of what they are that our country is as barren culturally as is our dust bowl physically." A dire result was that "America is becoming culturally poorer and poorer."[9]

To DuBois, Adamic's findings showed the dangers of the melting pot theory of Americanization. "Not only did the melting waste our resources; it also failed in its job of melting," she explained. The second generation were "slag-products of our melting pot," outside the mainstream of American life, "inert and even inferior citizens," disproportionately asocial and criminal, "living a hollow, sham culture-existence." When young people were scoffed at for being different, they became shy and self-conscious, as with the six-year-old girl who went home crying to ask, "Mama, am I a god-damn Greek?" DuBois concluded, "Our misplaced confidence in the melting pot has produced not the well-adjusted individuals our country needs, but a tragic group of 'mess of pottage' Americans."[10]

This psychological perspective was influenced by the language of Freudianism and by research into the "inferiority complex" or "oppression psychosis" experienced by minorities. The social psychology of this period, as promoted by scholars Alfred Adler and Floyd Allport, among others, outlined the causes and costs of inferiority. Members of minority groups "are apt to have an oppression psychosis and to manifest it in supersensitivity," DuBois worried. "Only the psychiatrists can tell us the price we are paying for this in soul fiber." DuBois's colleague Ione Eckerson, who helped coordinate Service Bureau projects, expected that "inferiority complexes, sublimated in bravado and mischief, will gradually fall away and become a normal sense of equality when a feeling of status in the community is developed."[11]

The economic crisis of the Great Depression exacerbated these problems, as did developments overseas. DuBois noted that tensions among minority groups increased in times of economic stress. Minority group children, already prone to "social maladjustment" ranging from shyness and stuttering to aggressiveness and delinquency, suffered the rise in prejudice that resulted. To counter their sense of inferiority, second-generation Americans were changing their names, dropping contact with their cultural past, and withdrawing from the mainstream of American life. "Today the fear and the monotony of unemployment or the misery of uncongenial labor has given millions of people an inferiority feeling which makes them all too eager to listen and follow a gospel of race hatred, national chauvinism, or war," DuBois worried. Unemployed youth might overcome feelings of inadequacy "by embracing the unscientific, muddle-headed rationalizations coming from parts of Europe today."[12]

Lasker explained the origins of the inferiority complex in *Race Attitudes in Children,* asserting that children did not have an instinctive sense of the low status of their own group but rather absorbed it from their environment. In some situations, contempt or ridicule could be a stimulus to self-improvement or productive rivalry. But in other cases, children of the excluded group lost ambition and felt hampered in their ability to succeed. Lasker's informants worried that this inferiority complex was "the cause of so much delinquency among foreign-born children" and could even result in race riots, brawls, and the overthrow of law and order. These early experiences had profound and permanent influence, he concluded. Awareness of others' adverse attitudes "is apt to predispose the child to a sense of inferiority that may color his personality for life." Lasker urged schools to preserve self-respect in minority children and to prevent a cleavage between foreign-born parents and their children.[13]

Francis J. Brown and Joseph Slabey Roucek of New York University, the editors of *Our Racial and National Minorities* (1937), addressed their book to "the ever-increasing number who believe that the school must assume responsibility for seeking, honestly and earnestly, to decrease racial and social tensions and build mutual respect and understanding." In his contribution to the book, E. George Payne, dean of the school of education at New York University (where DuBois received her doctorate) endorsed the new approach to preserving ethnic pride. Payne had developed a course entitled "Racial and National Minorities" and had asked DuBois to give a weekly course on intercultural education. He blamed the schools for perpetuating a "naïve" assimilation theory that assumed minority groups would rapidly drop their traditions and integrate completely into American life. The public schools disregarded the cultural backgrounds of immigrant children "and judged their performance by American cultural standards of conduct," he complained. "There was no expectation that American culture should itself be modified or influenced by the various streams of culture represented by the different minority groups." He warned of maladjustment, crime, poverty, and family disorganization.[14]

According to Payne, it was not enough to eliminate prejudice among the children of native-born parents; education should also address children of the foreign-born. He wanted to cultivate pride "in the folkways, mores, customs, conventions, and social patterns, characteristic of the immigrant in his homeland as well as of the Negro and the Indian." The school should discover the characteristics of minority groups, then build the best of these traditions into the larger culture, acquainting each group with the values of the other. "Under this program children of minority groups will be called upon to demonstrate their folkways, their dress, their folk art, their folk dances, their use of leisure, and their occupations." Payne predicted that "children will increase their respect for their non-English speaking parents, while they are at the same time acquiring full appreciation of American cultural backgrounds." Such programs would bring great benefits as "they will tend to eliminate prejudices, will enhance the social status of the members of minority groups, and will tend toward integration and adjustment."[15]

But even educators who shared these aims were unclear how to meet them. While concern for the second generation became a staple of social science and popular literature by the mid-1930s, scholars did not necessarily indicate what programs might look like in practice. A high school principal from Pennsylvania wrote to Adamic to explain the difficulties in devising classroom activities to help children maintain "a proper pride in their own heritage." He taught the history of the European nations where the students' families originated, but recognized the need for more techniques. "Working alone, fumbling for a method, is difficult when the urgent task stares one in the face."[16]

The Assembly Method and Cultural Pride

Rachel Davis DuBois determined that educators would not be left working alone without pedagogical methods. Influenced by her contact with Adamic and Thrasher, as well as with other social scientists grappling with questions of assimilation and with educators from immigrant backgrounds, who were among the first to note the difficulties encountered by the second generation, she searched for ways to bolster minority self-esteem. She hoped to extend into the schools the work of ethnic institutions that sponsored language programs and youth activities to educate American-born children about their cultural heritage.

DuBois proposed the assembly program as an ideal solution to the problem of alienation that social researchers had identified, a means to

Do they ask these people?

help immigrant group children turn to productive citizenship and lively expression and thus create an "American Renaissance" in the arts. She worried that millions of first- and second-generation people "become parts of a dull mass of uncreative citizens" because of being ashamed of their backgrounds. "Our lack of creativity today is caused by our long denial of the experiences of large numbers of individuals who are a part of us." Instead, her method was "so synthesizing our cultural elements in a dynamic and creative way that a renaissance will emerge." DuBois offered frequent accounts of children who flourished in school after witnessing assembly programs about their cultural groups. A typical comment concerned a student who, "practically ostracized for being Jewish, began to lose her shyness and to make higher marks." She observed self-conscious young people "utterly transformed" when teachers and classmates expressed interest in their cultural background. After an assembly program on the Italians in American life, a ninth-grader proudly announced that her parents were Italian and that she could dance the tarantella, a response essential to the sharing of "the Italian spontaneity toward music and art." Flowering of the arts depended on such "conscious sharing of values."[17]

DuBois's concern for minority group children emerged in part from

Students recreating a Mexican market, Sawtelle Boulevard School, Los Angeles. *Progressive Education* 12, March 1935, p. 173.

her own experience as a teacher. At Woodbury High School in New Jersey, where she taught in the 1920s, she empathized with the few minority students at the school. "Though I could not at that time put it into psychological terms," she later recalled, "I sensed intuitively how knowledge of one's own background could benefit the minority group child." Her college courses had not prepared her to consider "the value of self-identity and the blight of alienation," but even so she found herself sensitive to the feelings of the few black, Italian, and Jewish students, who minimized their cultural identity in response to name-calling. DuBois felt moved by the small group of black students, who "were in the school and yet not *of* it. I sensed their potential and yet their misery." She was reminded of how she had not felt fully accepted as a student at Bucknell.[18]

When DuBois moved to New York City to study at Teachers College and brought her program to urban schools, she began to concentrate her efforts on second-generation and minority children. She argued that through the assembly program, minority children could achieve greater sympathy for other minorities as well as for their own experiences. To the readers of *Opportunity,* she suggested that black students could learn of the oppression Jews had suffered for two thousand years and their techniques for preservation, while Jewish children could perceive their own "oppression psychosis" mirrored in some blacks. The student of Italian background learned "that all minority races have the same problems, that 'we're all in the same boat—it's only a difference of degree,'" she wrote (minimizing the long and vicious history of antiblack discrimination in the United States). The student came to see that "America needs more of the Latin temperament, the Latin point of view, that he must not lose his hold on that as he becomes more and more Americanized."[19]

DuBois recognized that such cultural exchange was often unconscious and "goes on in a dynamic society even against our wills." She noted that black folk culture exerted a profound influence on American culture, although white Americans might deny this. Because the black American had close contact with whites in daily life, she explained, "it was inevitable that his song, his dance, his way of looking at the world, should become a part of the social inheritance of white people." In a rare recognition of art's political context, DuBois acknowledged the process of cultural appropriation. "They could take a theme from his music, build a new-world symphony upon it, and then bar the Negro from attending the concert," she observed of white Americans. "They could by their prejudice make the Negro so ashamed of his own folk culture that he would turn his back upon it." It was unusual, however, for DuBois to acknowledge the potential conflict in cultural exchange, for her sunny view of pluralism rarely admitted the possibility of the theft, misappropriation, or depoliticization of a group's cultural expression.[20]

"What are you trying to do to develop enough pride in boys and girls of minority culture groups so that they will try to share their cultural heritage with others?" DuBois asked teachers in an in-service course sponsored by the New York City Board of Education. She advocated the recruitment of teachers from minority groups as another means to foster cultural pride in children. Outside of large cities, she noted, most teachers came from the dominant groups: there were all-white teaching staffs at mostly black schools, and few Italian teachers in schools with large Italian enrollments. Although she counted many Jewish teachers in her courses, DuBois recognized that in many places Jews were not welcome to apply for positions in public schools. Minority group teachers, she thought, would identify with the groups they served and foster the trust of children and parents.[21]

Other liberal educators echoed the focus on self-esteem. A writer for *Religious Education* told of a boy so ashamed of his immigrant background that he denied his knowledge of the Italian language. More widespread teaching of foreign languages, the writer urged, would bring greater approval of other peoples. "Alien children will certainly then not be branded as barbarians because they are the possessors of an unfamiliar speech," and would gain respect for the traditions of their ancestors. "For an American to be ashamed of his European background is as disloyal as for a son to disown his parents."[22]

By the mid-1930s, Louis Adamic would remark in his *Harper's* article: "Of late teachers nearly everywhere, I am told, have advanced so far that they take the trouble to learn the correct pronunciation of difficult Polish, Yugoslav, Lithuanian, Czech, Finnish, and Slovak names, and to caution the old-stock American boys and girls not to call the New American children Hunkies, Wops, and other such names of derision." Some teachers went much further, inviting immigrant parents to school to share their food, music, and dance. In a paper presented at a regional conference of the Progressive Education Association in 1935 and later published in *American Childhood,* a Philadelphia teacher described a program to instill cultural pride among her fifth-graders: "the word *foreign* does not connote *inferior* to us but suggests, rather, an opportunity to widen our horizons." Other authors for the magazine suggested that teachers encourage appreciation for ethnic arts and customs in order to bridge the gap between foreign-born parents and their Americanized children. Similarly, a curriculum guide for the Seattle public schools included an account entitled "I Belong to an Inferior Race," about a student who felt he had "no chance" because of his background. "A few days later, through pictures, poems, and stories, he was surprised to find that his race possessed outstanding qualities and characteristics." According to the guide, the resulting change in attitude improved his schoolwork and carried over to the home. A suggested composition topic, "Where Was Your Dad Born?" further encouraged students to value their immigrant backgrounds.[23]

Parochial school leaders also referred to the second-generation problem. The Diocese of Cleveland, for instance, offered foreign language instruction as a way to meet the "psychological needs" of children from immigrant backgrounds. Failure to recognize immigrant contributions built up in children "a national or racial inferiority complex which is responsible for so many failures in later life," explained the diocese's school report of 1932, and "which produces a feeling of aversion or contempt for their ancestry." The sad result was that young people rejected their origins or embraced "a truculent 'nationalism.'" The parochial school offered materials "which shall make a child feel proud of what his ancestral race has contributed to civilization."[24]

For parents, children's rejection of heritage could bring anxiety and guilt. The CSA, which counted many Jews among its members, paid frequent attention to matters of shame and pride in Jewish children. A question-and-answer column in *Child Study* in 1937, for instance, discussed how a Jewish family could bolster the confidence of its third-grader at Christmastime, when "she feels very much out of it." Although the family celebrated Hanukkah with candles and presents, the parent reported, "somehow, it does not seem to make it all right. She seems to be glad to have it all over with instead of having a good time." In its reply, the journal acknowledged that Jewish children often felt "isolation and separateness." The task of parents from any minority group was to preserve "a spirit of tolerance, free from bitterness," and to show children that their convictions and traditions were worthwhile. Such lessons would not prevent pain and anxiety, but would imbue the child "with the courage to be in the minority when the occasion calls for it."[25]

Rachel Davis DuBois came to consider parents important to the elimination of prejudice and the cultivation of cultural pride. Parents should support the work of the schools, inform themselves about cultural contributions, and provide opportunities for children to meet people of other groups. In 1941 she spoke at a conference of the League of Mothers Clubs in New York City, most of whose members were immigrants from Europe. The intention, she told the group, "is to discover what we as mothers and leaders of groups, responsible for the personality development of our children, can do about the problem of the increasing number of young people whose personality adjustments may be due partially to racial and ethnic group prejudice."[26]

A special issue of *Progressive Education* in 1935, entitled "Minority Groups and the American School," reflected enthusiasm for experiments to inculcate cultural self-esteem. A science teacher at the U.S. Indian School in Santa Fe described a project to bolster ethnic pride, a sharp departure from earlier educational missions to assimilate Indian children. An educator in Los Angeles described how her third-grade unit on Japan improved the self-confidence of Japanese American students and demonstrated that the diversity in her classroom benefited all. The idea was to "enrich our lives and preserve what is rich in their own as well." A teacher at a Denver elementary school reported that attention to Italian and Mexican cultures helped children to see "that they need not feel ashamed of foreign ways or accents" of their parents.[27]

These romantic portrayals did not explain what to do with aspects of immigrant culture that ran counter to Anglo values. Anne Hoppock, a school supervisor in rural New Jersey, proposed in 1933 that the school bridge the gap between foreign-born parents and their children through appreciation of immigrant contributions. But while she approved of the simplicity and creativity of her Ukrainian and Polish neighbors, she was dismayed with their attitudes about gender. "The men seem to have lower standards for their wives than American men have," she complained. Men allowed the women to do the hard work, a model the children followed at school. "In some places the boys show open contempt for the girls, disliking to work with them or to allow them to join in their play." Hoppock hoped that the schools could revise these patterns to resemble those of the children of native-born parents. While she promoted a "curr-iculum that aims definitely to save the national culture," she also wanted one that "plans to set up new attitudes in the minds of men and boys toward womankind." DuBois voiced similar concerns, suggesting that certain cultural traits be "dropped by the wayside" if they were at odds with democratic principles, "such as the domineering attitude toward wives and children of fathers from some European countries." Educa-tors would keep qualities they deemed worthy and reform those they did not.[28]

Cultural pluralists rarely addressed long-term implications. It was unclear whether they expected separate cultures—and cultural pride—to persist for generations or imagined an ultimate merging of once-autonomous groups. E. George Payne, dean of education at New York University, dismissed the question as relatively unimportant. "It does not seem to me that we should be deeply concerned over this matter," he wrote in *Our Racial and National Minorities*. "There certainly could be no harm in preserving intact the best of the various cultures, but, as a mat-

A third-grade class, Bryant-Webster Elementary School, Denver, performing Italian folk songs and dances. *Progressive Education* 12, March 1935, p. 175.

ter of fact, some degree of acculturation is inevitable, and a new and superior culture will emerge. Cultural pluralism then does not imply that the special cultures will continue unchanged in the general stream for all time." In their contribution to the book, Clara A. Hardin and Herbert A. Miller of Bryn Mawr College argued for stimulating interest in Old World traditions to ease adjustment of the second generation. "This furnishes a social bond to hold the rudderless until the transition is complete," they explained, suggesting that pluralism represented a temporary stage. Needed were tolerance "and patience to await inevitable assimilation."[29]

To Benjamin Franklin High School

DuBois's concern for the second generation gave impetus to her work. During the 1934–1935 school year, her Service Bureau undertook an ambitious project in fifteen junior and senior public high schools in the New York metropolitan area. Most of the schools were in suburban New Jersey—Englewood, Fort Lee, Tenafly, Cliffside Park, and Madison—with two urban schools, Benjamin Franklin High School in New York City and Central High School in Newark, also participating. Over the course of the year, the Service Bureau arranged fifty-eight guest assembly programs followed by student-planned programs and related activities. The work reached more than ten thousand high school students and four hundred teachers. The project received funding from the AJC, with a $5,000 donation from Theresa Meyer Durlach, a philanthropist active in the peace movement who had heard DuBois speak at a conference and was impressed by her work in Englewood. Durlach remained a friend of the Service Bureau, serving on its board and providing financial and moral support over the years.[30]

To help with the expanded project, DuBois recruited two field secretaries. Ione Eckerson, a teacher at the Englewood school, would now be in charge of follow-up activities, while social worker Miriam Ephraim, who had organized the Jewish program at Englewood, would invite the guest speakers. Ephraim's attention to the self-perception of Jewish students may have contributed to DuBois's concern for the second generation. Deeply involved in Jewish social welfare activities, Ephraim was concerned about both anti-Semitism and the attitudes of young Jews toward their own heritage. In an account directed to Jewish social service workers, she described one homeroom discussion that "covered all the misconceptions regarding the Jews and money, the Christ story, the

Protocols of Zion and blood libels" and brought out positive facts. She noted that these programs improved attitudes of young people toward their own background as well as toward others, reporting that after the programs, several students "came up and asked where they could join Jewish young people's clubs to learn Jewish history and Hebrew."[31]

The project at Benjamin Franklin High School furthered DuBois's commitment to instilling minority group pride. Benjamin Franklin was a new school for boys in East Harlem with a large Italian American enrollment and students from thirty-four different ethnic groups. Its principal was Leonard Covello, former head of the Casa Italiana Educational Bureau, whom DuBois had come to know while researching Italian culture for her Woodbury programs and had recruited for the Service Bureau's first advisory board. In a doctoral dissertation at New York University, and elsewhere, Covello wrote persuasively about the children of immigrants, and gained prominence as an advocate of cultural education for minority students. At Casa Italiana, he published materials on the contributions of Italians to American life and also worked with the Folk Festival Council of New York City to promote native folk songs and dances.[32]

Covello, who had immigrated to New York as a child, drew on personal experience to understand the difficulties the second generation faced. During his own years at school, he had received little encouragement to appreciate his parents' culture. "I do not recall one mention of Italy or the Italian language or what famous Italians had done in the world," he later wrote. "We soon got the idea that 'Italian' meant something inferior, and a barrier was erected between children of Italian origin and their parents." Young people became Americans "by learning how to be ashamed of our parents." He and his classmates tried to keep their mothers and fathers away from school because of their poor English and European-style dress. "We didn't want these embarrassing 'differences' paraded before our teachers," he recalled, lamenting that the "feeling of scorn and shame" that builds in the children of foreign parents "often produces antisocial attitudes dangerous to the boy and to the community—in short, the delinquent."[33]

Covello had addressed this problem early in his career, when he organized an Italian American youth group that celebrated Italian accomplishments in order to bridge the gap between generations. He impressed on the young men that "theirs was an especially rich heritage, of not only one culture but two—the old and the new." In 1914 he agreed to sponsor a club called *Il Circolo Italiano* at DeWitt Clinton High School, where he taught foreign languages, after a student convinced him that the club would help the student understand "that he does not have to be ashamed that his mother and father are Italian." The club, which continued throughout the 1920s, sponsored musical and dramatic programs, organized students to teach English to new immigrants, and published a magazine on Italian culture. Covello later developed at Benjamin Franklin a similar program for Puerto Rican students. Lasker praised Covello's work: for Italian American students to perform dramatic masterworks lent them "a deserved glory and recognition in the eyes of their fellow pupils as contributors of distinctive cultural values" and made children aware "that the Italian immigrants carry in their blood something of the glory that was Rome."[34]

Like DuBois, Covello was influenced by the work of Frederic Thrasher, the sociologist who argued that Americanization led to criminal behavior. They first met in 1928, when Thrasher had recently arrived at New York University and was beginning a three-year study of the effect of a boys' club on the prevention of delinquency. When Thrasher chose to study a club in East Harlem that served mainly Italian boys, he recruited Covello to help with the project.[35]

Covello agreed with DuBois that the school had an obligation to promote both pluralism and unity. He wrote: "The problem of assimilation and cultural harmony, the development of a wholesome national consciousness in the midst of great cultural diversity, the clash of racial and nationality interests are really basic problems—and they must be the chief concern of the school because to the school is entrusted the education of the future citizens." A pioneer in developing the "community-centered" school, Covello wanted Benjamin Franklin to play an active role in the neighborhood to diminish antagonism between groups and to aid the integration of the foreign-born. Immigrants and their children, he stressed, should realize that knowledge of their cultural heritage was "desirable for themselves, for the America of today, and the America of tomorrow." Such feeling would build a finer citizenship and a stronger democracy. The school should balance cultural pride with national identity, a task Covello admitted was difficult. "We feel that there must be a BLENDING of different cultures into one basic American culture—a reconciliation of conflicting heritages in the creation of a strong American consciousness in which there is a basis of fine pride in the cultural achieve-ments of other lands from which many of our citizens have come."[36]

Covello had been instrumental in the campaign to teach the Italian language in the public schools, an effort that succeeded in 1922 as part of a wave of immigrant language courses that came to the New York City schools in the interwar years, despite isolationist opposition to foreign language instruction in other parts of the country and the general de-cline in language study. In New York, in a dramatic shift away from Americanization trends, Covello and other proponents argued that lan-guage study would help second-generation students appreciate their ethnic heritage and would close the rift between immigrants and their children, thus curbing delinquency and social deviancy. The successful campaign to introduce Hebrew-language classes in the public schools was also justified as a way to instill self-respect in the children of Jewish immigrants.[37]

At Benjamin Franklin, DuBois and Covello decided to emphasize cul-ture groups that predominated in the school: Italian, Puerto Rican, and Slavic. They also added the Japanese, a group not represented, so that "it would not seem as though any particular group was being singled out in the school." African Americans, who made up almost 13 percent of the East Harlem population in 1930 (compared to Puerto Ricans, who ac-counted for 6 percent) were not included as a culture group in the as-sembly program, an omission left unacknowledged. This decision may have been made for political reasons; DuBois hoped that the assemblies would become a permanent feature of all New York City schools, and may have wanted to avoid such a potentially controversial subject as black history as she sought support. But the decision also suggested the invisibility of African Americans in the "second-generation" model. Even thinkers as progressive as DuBois and Covello were slow to recog-nize the growing population of African Americans from the South who were moving to the neighborhood during the thirties. Despite the cul-tural vibrancy of the Harlem Renaissance, which brought black artists and writers to prominence in New York, DuBois and Covello chose to fo-cus on the children of immigrants, a decision that pushed black culture to the margins. Thus it was the black students who were being "singled out" in the school by exclusion from the assembly programs.[38]

For the guest assemblies, DuBois invited "interesting and attractive personalities from each of the four groups." A Japanese American graduate of Cornell offered a talk entitled "Japanese Contributions to Civilization," and members of the Japanese Athletic Association gave a jiujitsu exhibition. The assembly on Puerto Ricans included a music and dance performance. Students later listened to an address entitled "Italy's Gifts to Civilization" and a string ensemble; in another assembly, they heard a talk by a former countess on the culture of Czechoslovakia and a performance of Slavic songs. After the assemblies, students talked with the guests and discussed the groups in class using materials that DuBois distributed.[39]

DuBois boasted of the effectiveness of the program at Benjamin Franklin. The majority group children discovered that the richness of American life resulted from "its gifts from many lands and races." At the same time, minority children took interest in the contributions of their own people to American culture. Attitude tests showed favorable attitudes toward the groups covered, while teachers reported improvement in personal behavior and academic motivation. Covello offered a positive evaluation: "This is a fine work. It is what our schools need. It is vital, alive, real—it makes the students think and reason. It should be a part of the activity of every school in the city." He was pleased that when tensions in East Harlem led to street fighting among Italian American and Spanish-speaking boys, students from Benjamin Franklin took the lead in expressing "friendliness and understanding."[40]

If the leaders of the program were determined to instill cultural pride, they were alert as well to its potential dangers, made apparent by the rise of nationalism overseas. They wanted engagement with, rather than rejection of, the larger American society. In her account of the program, Ephraim noted: "Of course great care was exercised to avoid running into the danger of ethnocentrism," a term in vogue in the 1930s. DuBois saw herself as "striving toward a new, creative, and constructive ethnocentrism—an ethnocentrism *plus* as it were," which would permit each culture group to retain pride in its ways while also seeing good in others. In a 1939 message to the Austrian American League, even as she urged immigrants to share their customs, music, and art with their adopted country, she warned, "none of us must be over-proud of what we have to give. Rather must we be willing to *receive* as well as give."[41] Similarly, Covello warned that programs for minority students "must be handled skillfully in order to avoid the possibility of creating *divisions, instead of harmony*." In a letter written to his students and delivered at the annual dinner of the Service Bureau in 1941, Covello emphasized "that pride in a great racial or cultural heritage should never mean ignoring or minimizing the heritages of other nations." Take pride in your heritage, he urged. "But do not isolate yourself completely in the problems of a single group."[42]

The project at Benjamin Franklin High School did not lead to the immediate incorporation of the assembly program throughout the New York City school system, as DuBois had hoped, but it did inspire teachers at the school to form what they called the Committee for Inter-Racial Cooperation to revise the curriculum. Covello endorsed the assembly program in a letter to the New York City Board of Education, explaining that it would "help to overcome the strains of adjustment for the hundreds of thousands of children of foreign parentage who are to be found in our city schools." The board appeared receptive. In 1935 the board member James Marshall urged schools to give greater recognition to the major ethnic groups in New York City as a means to instill "broad cultural outlook" and overcome feelings of inferiority. Unity, Marshall wrote, "can be achieved by teaching new citizens self-respect through the medium of their old cultures."[43]

Cultural Gifts and American Judaism

In January 1935, halfway through the project at Benjamin Franklin and the other New York–area schools, the AJC decided to discontinue funding the Service Bureau. *"Then one day, the sky fell down!"* DuBois recalled of that time. The decision was a reversal for the AJC, whose leaders had initially looked favorably on the Service Bureau as an effective tool to combat anti-Semitism. In the 1930s, as Jewish organizations grew increasingly alarmed over the rise of Nazism, they had awarded funding to organizations devoted to combating anti-Semitism and upholding democratic ideals. Anxious about negative repercussions if their work were too visible, they tended to finance non-Jewish organizations, including the National Conference of Jews and Christians and the National Council of Churches (formerly the FCC), that worked to overcome prejudice more generally. In 1935, Ephraim told a group of National Association of Jewish Center executives that hostility toward blacks, Asians, and immigrants "is a problem of grave concern to all of us as Jews and Americans." With the spread of nationalism overseas, "there is a grave danger of the development of a state of mind inimical to the most valued ideals of our democratic way of life." Jews had a particular interest in promoting cultural pluralism "as a distinctive characteristic of our nationhood."[44]

But while AJC leaders backed a pluralist orientation, they came to object to DuBois's portrayal of Judaism in cultural terms. DuBois had taken a course under Rabbi Mordecai Kaplan, the founder of the Reconstructionist movement, and had read his book *Judaism as a Civilization*, in which he described Judaism as a set of traditions, customs, and beliefs associated with a people. Like DuBois, Kaplan was troubled by the poor self-esteem of second-generation Jewish youth. Worried that young Jews were moving away from Judaism, he sought ways to make ritual more meaningful in modern terms and to teach young Jews about Jewish history and values. Many of the coworkers DuBois enlisted were followers of Kaplan's ideas: Ephraim, for instance, was a Reconstructionist who had studied with Kaplan, as were some of the rabbis and Jewish representatives whom DuBois invited to be guest speakers at her assembly programs. In the volume that DuBois coedited, *The Jews in American Life*, she defined Jews in Reconstructionist terms, as "a historical, cultural group who once had a nation in Palestine, who evolved the religion of Judaism; who have left a vast literature; who have lived in all the countries of the world; who, today, live among many peoples as loyal citizens of the country in which they dwell, and who hold some degree of loyalty to the traditions of their ancestors." Her memoir recalled Kaplan's explanation that Judaism was a living entity "of which the religion of the Jews is only a part."[45]

Leaders of the AJC, in contrast, wanted Judaism to be presented exclusively in religious terms. As Nicholas Montalto explains, they thought Jews should only be discussed in reference to particular nationalities: as Jews of German, Polish, or English background, for instance, rather than as a distinctive culture of their own. As assimilated Jews of German origin, members of the AJC were uncomfortable with the ethnic orientation of the Service Bureau's approach, fearful that it would lead to the kind of racial discrimination occurring in Germany. From their perspective, safety lay in the sectarian and interdenominational tradition in America. They shied away from a method that would draw attention to Jews or support popular perceptions of Jews as radicals and anarchists, and instead advocated a more cautious strategy for advancement. Their preoccupation was with the anti-Semitism of non-Jews rather than the identity of Jewish young people. An AJC representative informed DuBois: "We don't agree with your philosophy of Judaism as a cultural and ethnic entity. Jews are not a separate ethnic group—we are a religious group. We don't think there should be separate assembly programs on the Jews." He asked her, "You don't have a separate program on the Baptists, why on the Jews?"[46]

DuBois thought it critical to confront anti-Jewish stereotypes directly. She later defended her approach: "since anti-Semitism defines Jews negatively and as a particular group, we feel that positive attitudes toward them are more easily developed by being specific," she explained. Members of ethnic groups were already set off in students' minds—for instance, when Jewish students were absent from public schools during Jewish holidays—so it was important to make those differences appear interesting and attractive rather than negative. In the attempt to change attitudes, "we accomplish nothing when attention is focused only on the concepts *Poles, Germans,* or *Russians.*" Although not a nationality or race, "Judaism may be considered as a subculture within American life." Years later, in reflecting on the AJC's opposition to her work, DuBois recalled the economic crisis of the thirties and the anxiety "that the race hatred of Nazism would spread to America," made real by Nazi groups already functioning in New York City. "What did it feel like to be a Jew in the United States in the thirties and forties?" she wondered. Some Jews were "so filled with fear that they did not even want to feel their Jewish identity." When AJC representatives were unable to alter her point of view, they withdrew funding and, she complained, put up obstacles to prevent the spread of her work.[47]

Despite their differences, DuBois persuaded the AJC to continue funds for the rest of the school year. But without funding beyond that, the Service Bureau was unable to continue work in the high schools the following year. A search for other funding sources in 1935 was unsuccessful. DuBois appealed to the Rosenwald Foundation, asking Will Alexander of the CIC to advocate on her behalf. When her appeal was turned down, she told Alexander that she was "quite discouraged about being able to secure sufficient funds to carry on this work."[48] As she had in the past, DuBois found herself on the margins economically: living on her own apart from her husband, teaching at various universities without a permanent position, relying on grants from foundations and benefactors. Her precarious financial situation may have driven her decision to concentrate on cultural themes rather than political struggles, in order not to alienate the supporters on whom she depended.

DuBois traveled to California that summer to teach a course at Berkeley. She was received warmly by the local AJC representative, who arranged for her to speak over the radio and to local clubs and gatherings. She took a second trip to California in fall 1936, when she taught a course for student teachers at San Francisco State College, gave additional speeches and radio talks, and saw Roosevelt Junior High School in San Francisco adopt her assembly plan. DuBois rejoiced in the cultural diversity she found in California. "San Francisco because of its exciting cultural differences" could lead the way in developing world-mindedness, she told one audience. She also visited Mexico to tour rural schools and discuss intercultural education. On her return to New York she grew ill, underwent surgery, and spent several months recuperating before plunging back in to her activities. She found a way to resume her work when she incorporated her Service Bureau into the Progressive Education Association.[49]

By the middle of the decade, analysis of the second-generation problem had further expanded antiprejudice work into schools and teacher training programs. Concern for the children of immigrants proved an effective means to engage a large audience in the cultural gifts project, for it suggested that all Americans—including those of the majority group—might suffer the costs of cultural crisis. This new attention to the self-esteem of the second generation, however, came at particular cost for the cultural gifts agenda, as it further marginalized the experiences of African Americans. In the second half of the 1930s, as the depression intensified economic concerns, black thinkers would push to incorporate their perspectives into antiprejudice work, analyzing the structural conditions that reinforced attitudes of superiority and prevented some groups from achieving equal citizenship. Over time, the focus on the second generation made the cultural gifts project increasingly irrelevant to the struggle for racial equality. At the same time, the approach highlighted tensions between ethnic identity and national unity. With Americans warily observing the rise of nationalist sentiment overseas, the emphasis on cultural pride came under scrutiny as a threat to the shared values and common culture that appeared to be critical to sustaining both American democracy and loyalty to American institutions.

7

Prejudice and Social Justice

In the second half of the 1930s, racial liberals around the country experimented with programs designed to dispel ethnoracial and religious prejudice. Educational experts, academics and intellectuals, students and teachers debated both means and ends. Even as they shared the language of the cultural gifts vision, they confronted an implicit question: What was the ultimate goal of the antiprejudice crusade? Three key answers emerged over the course of the interwar period. When white educators began the assembly programs in the 1920s, their aim was to instill in dominant group children appreciation for the contributions of other cultures. In the early 1930s, influenced by the work of immigrant thinkers, they added a second goal: to bolster cultural pride in the second generation. During the second half of the 1930s, they gradually began to address economic and social inequalities as well.

The inclusion of economic and social analysis was in large part a response to the lengthening depression and the revival of political liberalism during the New Deal, which highlighted the inequities of the capitalist economy. It also resulted from the efforts of African American educators and those on the political Left, who linked antiprejudice work to a broader agenda for social change. While endorsing the project to teach minority children about their own heritages, black intellectuals expressed ambivalence about its efficacy for ending white prejudice. They offered a mixed response to the cultural gifts agenda, insisting that interracial understanding was not an end in itself but rather a step toward the larger goal of racial equality.

Black intellectuals raised doubts about the power of education to reshape race relations. They were less optimistic than their white counter-parts about the promise of work in the schools, more keenly aware of the entrenched nature of prejudice. As the Great Depression focused attention on economic deprivations, black thinkers questioned whether even the most enlightened curriculum could bring social justice without concurrent changes in material circumstances. Over the course of the decade, they resolved that ending school segregation was the most pressing educational concern. Educators on the Left similarly sought to challenge inequality and discrimination.

Even the black educators who strongly opposed segregation, however, continued to endorse cultural gifts work. They understood educational strategies as critical, though not sufficient, elements of racial progress, and they viewed white cultural gifts advocates as their most reliable allies in the struggle for equality. Their efforts expanded the boundaries of the cultural gifts project beyond its earlier, privatized approach. Cultural gifts proponents now debated whether attitudinal or structural change should come first. In contrast to white liberals, who asserted that the first step was to modify individual attitudes, African American and radical leaders linked the genesis of racial bigotry to policy, law, economic relations, and the courts as they insisted on the need for structural change. Their antiprejudice work demanded the equalization of resources and the intervention of the state to end discrimination.

As the audience expanded to include second-generation and minority children, the discussion raised a set of thorny questions about inequality and mobility. To a certain extent, this discussion also reshaped the viewpoints of the white educators who promoted the cultural gifts message, some of whom now began to incorporate the ideas of their minority colleagues, bringing socioeconomic concerns to the attention of white Americans. Yet even as white liberals engaged new ideas, they insisted that psychological change had to precede, or at least accompany, economic change. In the end, because they remained reluctant to challenge racial inequality or segregation directly, their cultural gifts approach proved insufficient to meet black demands for social justice.

Black History and Economic Reform

When Rachel Davis DuBois initiated her program at Woodbury High School in the 1920s, she planned the assembly on black Americans to coordinate with Negro History Week, which took place in February, commemorating the birthdays of Frederick Douglass and Abraham Lincoln. The originator of Negro History Week was Carter G. Woodson, champion of the black history movement, who founded the Association for the Study of Negro Life and History in 1915, the *Journal of Negro History* in 1916, and the *Negro History Bulletin* in 1937. In many ways, the educational strategies of Woodson and DuBois were similar. Both highlighted minority achievements through speeches, readings, lectures, performances, and exhibits in order to cultivate understanding and pride.[1]

Woodson had long worried about feelings of shame in young people and criticized schools for not educating black students about their own heritage. In both segregated and mixed schools, black students were taught to admire other peoples but to despise their own. "The thought of the inferiority of the Negro is drilled into him directly or indirectly in almost every social science subject which he studies," Woodson complained. The student "has been educated away from himself." Even black schools and colleges did not teach black history. Woodson believed that accurate information about the black past would dispel notions of black inferiority and boost self-esteem. As early as 1915, a black school administrator in the District of Columbia, where Woodson taught high school, praised his efforts: knowledge of black history "gives our children and youth a sense of pride in the stock from which they sprang, an honorable self-confidence, a faith in the future and its possibilities, to know what men and women of Negro blood have actually done."[2]

Woodson focused the annual Negro History Week on the schools as "the seat of the whole trouble." He produced textbooks for schools and colleges, photos and stories of notable blacks, pamphlets on black history in Africa and America, bibliographies and timelines, plays and pageants that dramatized black contributions to civilization. He asked teachers of music, art, and literature to highlight achievements of black artists and writers. He sent promotional literature to state boards of education, schools and colleges, clubs, and newspapers, with suggestions on how to celebrate the event. Since Woodson recognized that most black teachers lacked training in these topics, he offered correspondence courses for teachers and encouraged black colleges to offer courses on black history. In the *Journal,* he described classroom activities and Negro history study clubs. The *Negro History Bulletin,* which popularized scholarly work for teachers, schoolchildren, and the general public, included reports on black history projects, articles by teachers, suggestions of books, and questions for study. Woodson hoped that these activities would extend beyond the initial week to become part of the regular school program.[3]

Like Woodson, black librarians were aware of the scarcity of materials that offered unprejudiced depictions of African Americans. Charlemae Hill Rollins, head of the children's room at the South Side branch of the Chicago Public Library, created in the 1930s a guide to children's literature that included positive images of blacks. When she found only twenty-four such books, Rollins encouraged publishers to include more favorable depictions and reviewed book manuscripts to screen out stereotypes. She also authored books of her own, initiated library clubs, and invited black authors to lecture at the library. Thanks to her efforts, the library acquired an extensive collection on African American life and history. Augusta Baker, a children's librarian at the 135th Street branch of the New York Public Library, established a committee to evaluate depictions of African Americans in books for young people and invited poets and artists to speak to the children and encourage them to write.[4]

For Woodson, as for these black librarians, the primary audience was black youth. Knowledge of their own backgrounds was critical to the psychological well-being of black Americans, he believed. At the same time, he and his colleagues recognized the potential benefit of introducing white students to black history and accomplishments, instilling an awareness that promised to reduce antiblack prejudice. "Experience has shown that white students instructed in Negro life and history have softened in their attitudes toward the Negro," the Association noted in 1934, recommending the teaching of black history in all schools. These efforts met with some success, as boards of education in both white and black communities began to include black history in their curricula, white teachers and administrators wrote for advice, and public libraries purchased books on black history. By the 1940s, white schools had begun to participate in Negro History Week in greater numbers.[5]

Over the years, Woodson entered the network of social scientists and educators engaged in antiprejudice work. He corresponded with Franz Boas and served on a committee with sociologists Charles Johnson, Howard Odum, and Thomas Woofter, all affiliated with the CIC. Funding from the Rockefeller foundations brought him into further contact with liberal white leaders. Woodson also collaborated with leaders in parent education: on the sponsoring committee of the CSA, he worked with the group's Inter-Community Committee, while a CSA staff member served in his organization.[6]

Despite the similarities between Negro History Week and cultural gifts celebrations, Woodson's aims differed from those of his white colleagues, for he hoped not only to reduce antiblack prejudice and instill cultural pride but also to promote black social, political, and economic advancement. He saw education in black history as fundamental to overcoming disfranchisement and oppression. Educational efforts were more effective than the antilynching movement "because there would be no lynching if it did not start in the schoolroom. Why not exploit or enslave a class that everybody is taught to regard as inferior?" In *The Mis-Education of the Negro* (1933), he complained that most teaching prepared blacks for second-class citizenship and argued instead for training to overcome exploitation. An outspoken opponent of segregation in public facilities, he came to reassess interracial cooperation and self-help programs as he grew critical of American democratic institutions during the depression. He believed that history "would dramatize the life of the race and thus inspire it to develop from within a radicalism of its own."[7]

Yet Woodson's pedagogical practices reflected a moderate approach. His instructional materials did not tackle structural injustices directly but rather aimed to build support for racial equality through gradual and deliberate means. His pragmatic view was that black history would bolster black self-esteem and diminish white prejudice, advancing two essential steps toward the dismantling of institutional racism. Study of the black past would inspire action for racial equality. This educational strategy, as it highlighted black achievements, implicitly challenged racial violence and subordination but refrained from direct attacks on social and economic constraints. Although his ultimate goals were more radical, his curricular materials fit comfortably within the cultural gifts framework.

Like Woodson, black educators placed antiprejudice work in the context of socioeconomic change. In 1920, the National Association of Teachers in Colored Schools endorsed universal education, equal salaries for teachers, increased appropriations for school buildings, and improved teacher training. It also resolved "that our colored teachers be urged to introduce the systematic study of the history and literature of the Negro race in their schools, in order that our youth will acquire a pride of race."

Fourteen years later, this association continued to promote both economic and cultural reforms. Its five-point program advocated equal distribution of public tax funds for education, federal subsidies to equalize educational opportunity, equal salary and tenure schedules for all teachers, the provision of adequate numbers of teachers and school buildings, and "the inclusion of stories of Negro life and history in school readers and general literature adopted for use in public and private schools, so as to develop an appreciation of Negro life and of the Negro's contribution to civilization." Black history was thus one tool in a larger struggle for equal education.[8]

Bruno Lasker, whose study *Race Attitudes in Children* helped shape the campaign against prejudice, understood that racial attitudes resulted from unequal relations of power. He reminded readers of *Opportunity* in 1925 that white Americans had an interest in holding onto fixed ideas about the inferiority of other races, for "much of the economic life of America is so firmly built on the exploitation of certain racial groups that those who have their personal prosperity at stake, either directly or indirectly, simply will not see that race capable of reacting to a more humane regime" or of benefiting from education and fair conditions. This economic undercurrent was often unconscious but powerful. "So long as people actually think that underpaid labor is cheap labor, they will stick to the inherited fixed idea that the underpaid workers are inherently inferior," he concluded. John Dewey also traced racial attitudes to material and structural forces, stressing the need for socioeconomic reform. Cultural contacts were important for eradicating prejudice, he argued in 1922, but "without political and economic changes these factors will not go far in solving the problem."[9]

While Lasker endorsed Woodson's efforts, he sounded a cautionary note. Lasker worried that Negro History Week did not develop independent thinking: while its "deliberate one-sidedness in the use of history teaching for racial propaganda" might be justified as an antidote to propaganda in the other direction, it could not claim impartiality. Publicizing the Negro's "glorious" past struck him as instruction "as prejudiced as that which it desires to replace." He warned: "The only possible good that may come from it is that it may make some people sceptical in regard to all historical dogma; but it does nothing to create an attitude of real curiosity as regards the subject of the Negro." He feared that such teaching might "sharpen racial conflict by conditioning the children of two racial groups in opposite directions." Lasker urged teaching children to perform objective analysis to encourage them to evaluate the historical record for themselves.[10]

The political and economic goals of black educators stood in contrast to the cultural aims of many white liberals, who highlighted the achievements of individual African Americans without discussing more complicated—and more bitter—social realities. For white educators, appreciating cultural contributions did not necessarily imply greater economic security for minorities, nor did it demand material sacrifice from the dominant group. Their projects did not examine what white Americans had at stake in the perpetuation of racial bias or what institutional forces kept those prejudices in place. In celebrating successful individuals from each group, they avoided the sticky questions of why others never had the chance to develop their talents, why some groups predominated in menial jobs or were excluded from higher education. Cultural pluralism, in this interpretation, was safe and relatively easy for white audiences, for it required no sharing of political power.[11]

In fact, Rachel Davis DuBois disapproved of emphasis on material advancement. "Many of our citizens born in other countries have lost their artistic values and have taken on the dominant American value of material success," she lamented. She was dismayed by immigrants who abandoned the Old World's "aesthetic attitude toward life" in favor of "a materialistic attitude which they consider American," and denied their heritage in music and art "for the sake of gaining status." Members of the second generation tried to overcome feelings of inferiority "by being cheap imitations of Americans who measure their patriotism by feeling that we have the highest buildings in the world and the most bathtubs." She praised cultures that exhibited her own Quaker appreciation for simplicity and cooperation, as when she looked forward to "sharing of values with the Zuni Indians who have a negative attitude toward wealth, which more of us should have, and a fine cooperative spirit born of group consciousness, but who need to take on some of our qualities, such as alertness."[12]

The celebration of cultural differences offered an antidote to modern American consumerism. Anne Hoppock, a school supervisor in New Jersey, spoke warmly of the creativity and heritage of the Polish and Ukrainian immigrants in her district. Sadly, their folklore, music, and crafts "are in danger of being lost, pushed out of the way by jazz and questionable magazines and tabloids and shoddy machine productions—a simple, devout, warm-hearted, play-loving people with their culture lost and nothing but cheapness to take its place." In a romantic depiction of immigrant culture, Hoppock observed: "They seem to have capacity for enjoyment of simple pleasures which we lack." On entering American society, they were "inclined to choose the shoddy, vulgar, often the evil things, because these are the influences close to them." Like DuBois, she hoped to temper demands for material goods.[13]

Cultural Gifts and the Segregated School

The assumption behind Rachel Davis DuBois's work was that the school was the meeting ground of various cultures. She occasionally acknowledged that this was not always the case. In an article for *Opportunity*, she wondered how to foster constructive attitudes when children attended separate schools, where it was harder to implement antiprejudice education or to dramatize black experience than in "the more natural and therefore better pedagogical situation in a non-segregated school." As she described a mixed class of students—Jewish and Gentile, black and white—who acted out a meeting of the NAACP, she asked how teachers could arrange such situations in segregated schools. It could be done—as when white students visited Howard University—but it required energy, tact, and resourcefulness.[14]

More often, however, DuBois remained silent about racial segregation. While she personally opposed it, she did not make it central to her reformist agenda, suggesting that education alone would be sufficient to dispel prejudice. She thus minimized Lasker's identification of the school's makeup as the strongest influence on children's racial attitudes. He noted "a fundamental American ideal of democracy that must be taught the oncoming generation through the very organization of the school itself." Lasker warned that assemblies on interracial friendship in a segregated school "may serve the excellent purpose of flattering the self-opinion of teachers and pupils, but will not usually be of much effect on their behavior."[15]

The progressive education movement had an uneven record regarding segregation: despite its professed commitment to interracial harmony, progressive schools remained mostly white. Walter White, executive secretary of the NAACP, charged that progressive schools were unwilling to challenge wealthy white parents who wanted to give their children appropriate "social contacts" to help them to "marry favorably" and so resisted the enrollment of black classmates. Nor did they show children the "unpleasant realities"—in working conditions, race riots, and colonial exploitation—beneath what was, for white parents, society's "pleasant superstructure." Progressive education should "be able more courageously and more intelligently to attack, and as far as is humanly possible to eradicate, racial barriers," he declared. Articles in a special 1935 issue of the journal *Progressive Education* entitled "Minority Groups and the American School" all promoted "appreciation" and "friendly relations" but, as the editor admitted, revealed conflicting perspectives on the goals of antiprejudice education. "Some have viewed it as a matter of social justice. Others, sensing deep-lying resentments and antagonisms, have seen it as a problem of bringing about better understanding and greater sympathy" between groups. "Still others have visioned an America enriched by the cultural heritage of all the world in time and space." Quoting Alain Locke's contribution, the editor concluded, "the way is not clear, for we do not thoroughly understand our problem or see our ultimate objectives."[16]

Some contributors to the issue avoided the topic of segregation completely, discussing how to modify attitudes without questioning the composition of the student body. The teachers who described "appreciation units" on China and Mexico never suggested including more Chinese or Mexican students in their classrooms. A teacher in Atlanta, who developed social studies units on African and African American culture for her black fourth- and fifth-graders, wrote that she hoped to instill "respect for their cultural heritage" and "the idea that joy and the true art of living are of far more enduring worth and hold less uncertainty than material gain." Racial pride, in other words, could abate economic dissatisfactions. A social studies teacher from Missouri, describing a program to help white students appreciate black cultural achievements, assumed the inevitability of segregated schools.[17]

Two contributors to the special issue aimed to speed assimilation. A headmaster from Delaware, who made no mention of cultural contributions, thought "the 'out-groups' must be assimilated as quickly and thoroughly as possible." A writer from a private school in Philadelphia, who described his program as "educating for a melting-pot culture," was wary of cultural persistence: "We want no Little Italys, Little Russians, Ghettos;

we want one American people." He grudgingly recognized the limits of Americanization, for "whether we like it or not, those peoples will, in the end, retain something of their ancestral culture and insinuate it into our simon-pure Anglo-Saxon civilization; in fact, they are doing it right under our noses." He thought it best "to welcome contributions—selectively," seeking qualities to enrich "this fine Anglo-Saxon basic culture of ours."[18]

In contrast, other contributors ventured that integrated schools could best combat prejudice. In such a setting, teaching was implicit rather than direct; children learned tolerance by living together and learning about each other. An associate principal in Portland, Oregon, claimed positive results for a student body that included blacks, Japanese, Chinese, European immigrants, Buddhists, Greek and Roman Catholics, and Jews. Amid such diversity, "the school stands as the one unifying social force in the community." The school consulted with black leaders, had parents serve together on committees, and sent teachers to attend services in black and Buddhist churches. Children learned about various groups through classroom projects and daily interactions. "Most of the

Fourth-graders modeling the African continent in sand, Atlanta University Summer School. *Progressive Education* 12, March 1935, p. 175.

work done to inculcate tolerance was incidental and indirect," the principal reported. She held high hopes for children educated in this environment.[19]

The director of a settlement house in Cleveland similarly argued that interactions among people from varied backgrounds developed healthy attitudes. By example, the settlement accomplished what exhortation failed to achieve, Russell Jelliffe explained, for it made segregation appear "unnatural and artificial." Jelliffe's aim was assimilationist: he envisioned "weaving a minority into the major pattern." Although he encouraged study of African and African American heritages "as a basis for racial self-respect," American citizenship came first, for "the purpose is always to keep our minority groups headed into the main stream of American life, rather than to divert them into the racial or national byways through which too much fine leadership is lost to American life. Too many Negro leaders are expert in 'Negroism' only." Such integration would inhibit more confrontational—and potentially more violent—forms of ethnic consciousness. "The more effort expended in this way," Jelliffe reasoned, "the *less* does it become necessary to expend it in protests and a more direct struggle for American minority rights."[20]

In an impassioned discussion in his contribution, Alain Locke—professor of philosophy at Howard University, champion of the Harlem Renaissance, and exponent of cultural pluralism—revealed deep ambivalence regarding the efficacy of intercultural education. Like other black intellectuals, Locke grappled with conflicting strategies for dismantling racism and oppression in American society. His politics of race and culture was complex and evolving, revealing creative tensions between pragmatism and radicalism, between gradual and immediate solutions, between educational and material reforms. Even as he supported curricular improvements as a realistic approach for long-term change, he questioned the value of the cultural gifts model. And he came to question, as well, the efficacy of pedagogical innovations themselves. His internal debates concerned education's potential to effect social justice. In the end, he offered qualified support to antiprejudice education, affirming the importance of both curricular and material change.

Locke awarded the school an important role in ending prejudice. In a presentation to the 1932 meeting of the CSA, he had explained the school's primary responsibility and opportunity as "the extension of the child's experience into sympathetic and yet unpartisan knowledge and appreciation of all sorts of human differences, religious, national, racial and social." Writing for *Progressive Education* several years later, Locke criticized the schools as "strangely silent" on these matters, complaining that "timorousness, temporizing truce, placatory compromise, and apathy or indifference prevail," and called instead for "a progressive and realistic educational approach with respect to minorities." As he embraced social scientific thinking on the acquisition of attitudes, he used the analogy of preventive medicine, another new science, to urge the school to lead in "sterilizing the emotional beds of pride and prejudice" and controlling antipathies "at the sources of original infection." To build resistance to prejudice was "vital and central to the main purposes of education itself."[21]

Locke endorsed the cultural gifts approach as one means to this end, pleased that "a few educational pioneers have had the courage to launch out experimentally" to address racial prejudice, for as people came to appreciate minority achievements, the sources of discrimination would

Alain Locke. (Moorland Springarn Research Center, Howard University)

fade. He thought that pedagogy should look beyond the most admirable qualities of each group: "really intelligent education of this sort will not shirk the problem of unfavorable and unpleasant group characteristics." As a philosopher concerned with placing culture in history, he viewed negative traits as the product of historical forces and thus important topics for analysis and discussion.[22]

Yet even as Locke promoted cultural appreciation, he doubted the effectiveness of cultural gifts programs in separate schools. Without human contact—"a definite antitoxin to the social virus" of prejudice—efforts to build tolerance and respect would fail. Locke saw "flagrant inconsistencies and contradictions" in white Americans' ability to appreciate "the Negro's spiritual products" and at the same time "to despise his person and exclude his normal society," claiming to love black culture but then "oppressing, terrorizing, and lynching him." Locke's ambivalence emerged in his discussion of techniques for combating prejudice. Most expedient, he thought, would be a gradual approach that began with emotional conditioning and intellectual acquaintance with minority groups, then introduced sample social experiences, and finally arranged an integrated environment, in which the white children would have "normal social and personal contact in the school life itself" with children representing minority groups, providing "a basically cosmopolitan experience." Yet while this sequence might be the most attainable scenario, for Locke it represented a compromise. He hesitated to give his full endorsement, noting that if he were to rank the methods in terms of "effectiveness and urgency," he would reverse the order and put integration first.[23]

In this conflict between expediency and urgency, Locke concluded that ending segregation was more critical than pedagogical reform. In phrasing prescient of affirmative action, he wrote that an enlightened school "should be a deliberate composite, with special corrective emphasis in the matter of favorably representing those minorities most likely to be disparaged or misunderstood." "This may be revolutionary," Locke admitted, "but the practical success of a vital principle is at stake." Real transformation would result from modeling the school "on a different human pattern from that of the typically homogenous or snobbishly stratified community." In the end, "the problem cannot be solved by mere educational tinkering," he wrote. "We must either go to the roots of the matter, or let the situation alone."[24]

Locke questioned the role of the school itself in enacting change, cautious about putting too much faith in educational reform. Even integrated schools might be limited in effect. While he sometimes described them as powerful agents of change, elsewhere he minimized their promise. In his presentation to the CSA, he denigrated the "feeble and fatuous belief in the public school as a democratizing agency and class-leveller, as if the mere juxtaposition of children would automatically guarantee such a highly desired result." He pointed out that few communities were sufficiently heterogeneous to offer a wide range of social contacts.[25]

Writing in the *Journal of Negro Education* in 1935, Locke affirmed his belief that "the school is the logical and perhaps the only effective instrument for the corrective treatment" of racial inequality. But to the black readers of the journal, even more than to the largely white readers of *Progressive Education,* he voiced skepticism about the potential for gradual change through education. "This theory of slow accumulative approach, of the slow reform of public opinion, of 'the education of public sentiment' is a fallacy; the lines of social reform are not smooth gradual curves but jagged breaks, sudden advances and inevitable set-backs of reaction." Rather than curricular reform, he argued for "the general educative gains of a democratically organized school system." He saw great potential in legal strategies to end segregation, urging blacks to "resort to the courts to secure any considerable or wholesale improvement of the situation."[26]

Over the next several years, Locke continued to develop his analysis of segregation's pernicious effects. At its best, he wrote in the liberal *Frontiers of Democracy* in 1940, the public school brought together "the children of families involved in creedal, racial and cultural feuds and animosities." But the widespread practice of racial segregation, established through law or public opinion, threatened this function. Locke lambasted the "dangerous inconsistencies" and "undemocratic principles" that made the school "an accessory agent in the perpetuation from one generation to the other of divisive traditions and theoretically un-American practises." He recognized that in practical terms, the disavowal of separate schools might take a long time. "Logically, however, it is the first and most basic of all the possible moves that the schools can and should make" as their contribution to democracy. Americans should realize "the educative effect of having their schools include a representative cross-section of the cultural, racial and religious groups of the general community."[27]

At the same time, Locke intensified his criticism of earlier educational efforts. He explained that tolerance and sympathy "must be by-products of the school instruction and not direct or overt objectives of 'school oratory.'" Intercultural education's reliance on moral appeals made it "well-intentioned but rather ineffectual." He preferred that information be incorporated into a liberal curriculum that addressed "the practical issues of group differences and group maladjustment" and their "social causes and conditions" rather than added separately to induce tolerance. Locke voiced conflicting stances about just what role the school could play in pursuing social justice, for as an institution that reflected the status quo of the larger community, its point of view was inherently conservative. "The school, after all, cannot alone create democracy or be primarily responsible for it," Locke concluded. "At the same time, it has an obligation to contribute vitally toward it."[28]

Despite his ambivalence about pedagogical initiatives, Locke continued to participate in cultural gifts work. He wrote about black cultural achievements, accepted an invitation from Rachel Davis DuBois to join the board of her Service Bureau, coauthored a sourcebook on intercultural education, and reviewed a radio transcript on black contributions to American life, lending his name to cultural gifts projects as a practical step toward racial progress and equality. In 1939 he reassured DuBois that "as always whatever I can do to cooperate or advance the interests of your work, I shall gladly do."[29]

Like Locke, other writers for the *Journal of Negro Education* situated educational reform in the context of social change, urging integration alongside cultural gifts work. The journal's editor, Charles H. Thompson, encouraged the study of blacks in American life and provided an account of Rachel Davis DuBois's program. He insisted that "the *ultimate* solution of the race problem is dependent upon *education*—a change of present attitudes in the older generation, and a development of right attitudes in the younger," a process that could take "a very long time." For Thompson, such education would ensure the eventual success of other strategies for change—such as migration, the ballot, and the courts—that depended on the favorable attitudes of whites. The reformation of racial attitudes was a step "to improve the economic, cultural, recreational, and political conditions of the minority races." At the same time, Thompson consistently argued against school segregation and devoted a special issue to its social, economic, and legislative implications. He published a study that noted the limited effectiveness of brief interracial contacts that "are so far removed from actual community conditions of living that they often do not reach down to practical problems."[30]

The journal's reviews of books for children attended to both cultural pride and social conditions. One book received praise for encouraging appreciation of black achievements and "an understanding of the economic, social, and political problems experienced by Negroes" in work, rural and urban life, schooling, and citizenship. Another was criticized for its emphasis on "the white man's goodwill," while a third came under scrutiny for only granting the white characters the title of "Mr." or "Mrs.," which might "perpetuate the inferiority-complex of Negro children." Research into the attitudes of black students demonstrated the need for new teaching materials, such as a study revealing black youth's lack of confidence in black-owned businesses, which the author worried might undermine economic advancement of black communities.[31]

Instructors at black colleges shared this dual commitment to building racial pride and effecting social change. The *Journal of Negro Education* reported a survey of teachers at black colleges—200 black and 41 white—that showed extensive efforts, among almost 80 percent of the teachers, to incorporate material on black social conditions and history into their courses. The perspectives of these mostly black educators differed from their white counterparts in important ways. While Rachel Davis DuBois and her colleagues aimed to teach minority students about their groups' cultural contributions, instructors at black colleges emphasized material and social conditions: they discussed educational disparities, economic conditions, and race relations more often than topics like folk music and drama. Almost all voiced strong opposition to segregation, advocated the incorporation of blacks into the main currents of American life, and favored the development of race consciousness through the celebration of black history and achievements, agreeing that "Negro youth need to be taught that they have a group heritage and tradition of which they can be proud."[32]

In 1936 the *Journal of Negro Education* published a special issue on black education with articles by some of the most prominent black thinkers of the day, who linked cultural pride with social struggle. Charles S. Johnson, a sociologist at Fisk University and a supporter of progressive education, endorsed efforts to change racial attitudes through the school. Warning that the portrayal of blacks in textbooks could encourage self-disparagement, he proposed that "Negro youth should be provided early with a sound reinterpretation of their own history and traditions." Distortions were possible in many directions, from "glorification of a fanciful racial origin to self-commiseration and apology." He urged a "realism" that would move beyond cultural appreciation to recognize "the fact of an unequal economic struggle." Knowledge of the black past could influence students' behavior and ambitions, and "it is increasingly the school that must render this service." In his outline for a sourcebook on blacks in America, he wrote that his goals included both greater knowledge and "abstract considerations of social justice."[33]

Ralph Bunche, professor of political science at Howard University, advocated social struggle in even stronger terms, asserting that education should offer "a clear understanding of the relation of the Negro to the American political and economic structure and to all groups and classes in it." Education should equip students "to fight the terrific battles which must be waged in order that they may win economic and political justice." W. A. Robinson, principal of the laboratory high school at Atlanta University, similarly urged that teachers train children to seek justice. "We in the Negro schools must be courageous enough to arouse social unrest and a lively dissatisfaction with things as they are," he wrote. Education should make black students aware of their oppression, create a strategy to correct those conditions, and encourage cooperation with other oppressed groups "to improve conditions as they affect the masses generally."[34]

Doxey A. Wilkerson urged "deliberate challenge" to the inferior status assigned to black Americans. According to Wilkerson, an assistant professor at Howard, education "should be for a conflict situation." To prepare black children for the struggle for justice, teachers should address work, civil liberties, health, housing, family, church, education, and mob violence. They should discuss political mobilization and solutions to racial conflict, including interracial conciliation, geographic and economic separatism, political pressure, civil libertarianism, organized labor, and radical political parties.[35] Merl R. Eppse, who taught at Tennessee A and I College, advised colleges to introduce "a clear understanding of the struggles of the Negro people" through discussion of social, economic, and political questions. His list of topics revealed a very different focus from white liberals' focus on cultural gifts. "The Social Studies for Negroes must, by the nature of things, include: Lynching, Jim-Crowism, Discrimination, Low Wages, Denial of the Ballot, Lack of work in city,

State, and National Government, Tenant-Farming, Share Croppers, Personal Service, Unskilled Labor, Lack of Business, Poorly Equipped Schools, and hundreds of other things which cause the Negro to be handicapped in his struggle for his rightful place in the social order," Eppse explained in the *Quarterly Review of Higher Education among Negroes*. He urged a scientific approach to such "injustices and inequalities."[36]

While offering sharp educational critiques, however, these writers did not design curricula themselves. Although Alain Locke suggested that teachers "state problems of a minority in clear, analytical terms," offering for example "a really sound penetrating analysis of slavery, its motives, codes and effects," in order to dissipate antiblack prejudice, he did not author lesson plans or teachers' manuals that would demonstrate what this curriculum would look like in practice.[37] Nor did such thinkers as Bunche or Wilkerson, who advanced theoretical positions on education without offering concrete suggestions on how to implement their ideas. This omission presented a methodological dilemma for teachers. Even teachers who read the *Journal of Negro Education* and agreed with Bunche might have found themselves at a loss as to how to incorporate his analysis into their classrooms. Teachers who embraced Wilkerson's idea that education should prepare students to struggle for justice may have wondered how to structure their lesson plans. Of the prominent black intellectuals of the era, only Carter Woodson made it his mission to disseminate scholarly findings to teachers and to develop concrete programs for school use. In large numbers, instructors turned to Woodson's curricular materials, training programs, and publications—with their more gradualist orientation—because they offered practical guidance for classroom use.

The gap between educational theory and implementation suggested the limitations of curricular reform. Despite their impassioned pleas, black intellectuals rarely made clear just how the content of school lessons might interrogate relations of power or produce the social justice they demanded. Like Locke, they increasingly turned to the makeup of the school as the key to structural change. During and after World War II, they came to argue that the transformative power of the school lay in the interactions among its students. It was school segregation, even more than faulty curricula, that reinforced racist thinking and behavior—and so it was segregation that presented the most pressing need for reform. In 1944 Locke reiterated "the incompatibility of racial segregation as a principle of organization with a system of democratic schools." But he feared that "it will be even more difficult to democratize the public school as an institution than to democratize the curriculum."[38]

The next year Locke sharpened his criticism of intercultural education for its treatment of the individual rather than society. He saw "sporadic and merely palliative effectiveness" in earlier efforts: "like ointments and salves they treat only the superficial symptoms of the situation and have little remedial or lasting effect." He noted that some people might be friendly toward one minority group but still prejudiced toward another, or that minorities might suffer chauvinism themselves. The moralistic approach "diverts attention from the historical and social causes of group antipathies," he complained; this approach paid too little attention to minority views and offered only symbolic interracial contacts. While the school was best equipped to become "the working laboratory and training ground" for improving group relationships, segregation limited its reach. Changes to circumstances needed to accompany curricular innovations in order to bring broader reform.[39]

Antiprejudice Education and the Left

Ties between liberal educators and the radical Left strengthened in the 1930s, when some teachers involved in progressive education were drawn to the Communist Party, which voiced strong opposition to racial discrimination and segregation. The idea of education for social reconstruction, which John Dewey had articulated, seemed to demand radical political change. Communists criticized progressive education for focusing on a small number of children in wealthy schools, but as they sought alliances with liberals during the Popular Front period of the 1930s— which brought together Communists, New Deal activists, and leftists to oppose fascism—they reached out to educators who followed progressive ideas. Many teachers in the New York City schools, for instance, were sympathetic to left-wing movements.

Similarities between radical and liberal educational strategies were apparent in a dramatic performance staged in 1939 at Camp Kinderland, a Communist-run camp in upstate New York devoted to secular Jewish radicalism. One dramatic presentation called "Immigrants All! Americans All!" was reminiscent of the assembly programs and radio series Rachel Davis DuBois developed. The Communist *Daily Worker* described the pageant: "Beginning with a group of beleathered Indians, the kids staged a lively procession of events and peoples and they drove home the point that America is what people from other lands have made it—the French and the Spanish, the English and the Dutch, the Irish and the Russian, the Negro and the Hungarian, the Jew and the Gentile, Lafayette, Kosciusko, and Haim Solomon were all there." The message echoed DuBois's (despite the inaccurate portrayal of Indians as people from other lands): "it was clear that no race or nationality can be excluded from the democracy that they build as Americans."[40]

Despite these similarities, the educational programs of the Communist Party differed markedly from their liberal counterparts. Economic analysis of racial prejudice formed the basis of the radical message that children encountered in after-school programs, summer camps, and youth organizations. The historian Paul Mischler explains that this emphasis reflected the Communist Party's understanding of children's political roles. As a director of the Young Worker's League declared: "We are not only preparing the child for future participation in the class struggle;—we are leading the child in the class struggle now!" Through the Young Pioneers and the junior section of the International Workers Order, children fought for the integration of public facilities, petitioned to free the Scottsboro defendants, assisted striking miners and textile workers, and formed a junior section of the League of Struggle for Negro Rights. One cover of *New Pioneer* pictured black and white children marching together to commemorate the killing of a young organizer. A graphic depicted two boys, one white and one black, holding a banner that read "Workers Children Black and White in the Pioneers Unite." In California, the Young Pioneers organized "a children's demonstration at a park in Los Angeles where Blacks weren't allowed in the swimming pool," a daughter of radical Jewish immigrants recalled, and an interracial hunger march "involving children from all over Northern California—Black, Mexican, Filipino, white."[41]

While the Communist children's movement promoted cooperation between blacks and whites, its position on white ethnic identity was less clear. In the 1920s, American radical movements drew their greatest strength from immigrants, especially eastern European Jews and Finns. Communist Party leaders, however, hoped to discourage ethnic identification in order to appeal to native-born Americans. Many immigrants, disagreeing with this policy, wanted to transmit their cultures to their

American-born children and feared that Americanization would threaten radical values and encourage generational divisions. By the mid-1930s, as Communist Party leaders came to realize that ethnic identification could reinforce political radicalism, they adopted a more tolerant view toward ethnic pluralism, developing activities to help parents pass on both political and ethnic culture to their children. After-school programs incorporated instruction in Yiddish language or Finnish culture as well as radical ideology, and organized troops for the children of radical Slovaks, Germans, Ukrainians, and Russians. In the 1930s, the junior section of the International Workers Order sponsored programs on ethnic culture and history with language instruction, folk dancing, and education about proletarian heroes of various nationalities. Summer camps provided another way for Communist parents to pass on their political radicalism.[42]

Children's literature functioned as an important outlet for the ideas of the organized Left, as Julia Mickenberg has shown. Even as repressive trends limited radicalism in other forms of cultural expression, the children's book field disseminated writings by left-wing authors to schools and public libraries. These books often taught children about racial inequality as well as radical culture through the inclusion of African American, Native American, Hispanic, and international characters. Stories celebrated minority cultures and depicted children as activists in the struggle against racism and class exploitation. Like other progressive thinkers, these leftist authors and publishers targeted children as the best hope for future change.[43]

Communist success in promoting tolerance was illustrated by an experiment conducted in the 1930s. For his doctoral dissertation at Columbia, psychologist Eugene L. Horowitz tested the attitudes of white boys in New York, Tennessee, and Georgia toward African American boys. Horowitz asked the children to look at photographs of white and black faces and to select which ones they would choose as companions in different situations. He found that as early as kindergarten, children demonstrated preference for whites, a prejudice that increased with age. He found little difference among white children who were in New York and in the South, who were in urban and rural areas, who attended mixed schools and all-white schools, or who had contact with a popular black classmate and who did not. Even African American boys showed a preference for white companions, which Horowitz thought indicated the strength of general environmental conditions and the potential for future maladjustment.[44]

The one exception was a group of sixteen children, ranging from fourth through seventh grade, who attended a club in a Communist cooperative dwelling. Horowitz found that these children of Communists showed no antiblack prejudice at all, and even seemed to show a preference for blacks as companions. The children's discussion after taking the test convinced Horowitz that these sentiments were genuine: the boys criticized the test by pointing out that you could not judge personality from faces, and challenged each other by asking "What do you care what other people think?" and "How would you feel if you were a Negro and cousin to a white boy who felt that way?" Horowitz concluded that the social forces that applied with equal pressure among most other children "do not, however, penetrate, or are negated by, the training given to the Communist-trained children." This demonstrated that deliberate intervention, in the context of an ideology of equality, could alter attitudes. "The results from the Communist group seem to indicate that such prejudices are *not* unalterable components of the biological organization of white children," he reported in *Opportunity*. The *Journal of Negro Education* concurred that this finding "would certainly seem to indicate that prejudice is not inherited but is a creation of the social settings in which the child grows." In a setting that critiqued the institutional components of racial inequality, children acquired no racial prejudice.[45]

White Liberal Response

While attention to socioeconomic divisions deepened the understanding of prejudice, it never characterized the mainstream discourse of racial liberalism. Unlike their African American and radical peers, most white liberals continued to describe prejudice as a matter to be resolved by modifying individual attitudes. This depiction brought popular support, for white Americans could embrace the goal of racial harmony without fearing for their own status. Even so, liberal thinkers gave new attention to the matter of just what should be taught to children in place of bigotry and antagonism, raising troublesome questions about how far tolerance would go.

A few white educators did incorporate economic analysis into their antiprejudice work by the second half of the 1930s. Irma Doniger, a librarian in Newark, New Jersey, deplored the "polite evasion" of social conditions in children's literature. "Most of the products of the depression years might well have been written on the planet Mars, for all the picture of the world as it is recreated then," she commented wryly in *Child Study.* Those few books that did mention the depression offered a falsely rosy picture. Doniger faulted, as well, the "quaint, exotic, and picturesque" emphasis of much of the peace literature. Rather than the "countless insipid and futile tales of the windmill and wooden shoes variety" that flooded the market, she sought descriptions of life in countries under fascism and communism as a means to introduce present social realities. She also objected to the "pleasant, nostalgic little tales of plantation life" with their sentimental and condescending portrayals of slavery. Doniger pleaded for "a literature for children deeper in the understanding of our social and economic realities."[46]

At P.S. 61 in the Bronx, Frances B. Mayers introduced her predominantly Jewish class to injustices suffered by Indians and black Americans. In an account written for a course she took with Rachel Davis DuBois in 1939, Mayers reported how she encouraged students to understand "the civilization of the Indians," as well as their "artistic and technical skill." She explained how European settlement hurt Indians, "robbing them of their land and placing them in an inferior position." She hoped to make children aware of "injustice to the Indian, the true American" up to the present day. When she taught the history of Africa and African Americans, Mayers discussed the "exploitation of the negro by the white man" and the cruelties of slavery. Blacks were "forced to become slaves to enrich the White People," she explained. The children listed black contributions to American life, considered ways to "ease the plight of the negro," and discussed what to do "if you are an onlooker during an unjust act toward any race."[47]

By the end of the decade, anthropologist Ruth Benedict had come to link racial prejudice with class conflict. Racism and economic exploitation, she believed, were closely related, and so economic reform was central to the elimination of prejudice. Racist persecution would continue in the absence of full democracy, decent standards of housing and labor, and the regulation of industry. Majorities as well as minorities needed "opportunity to live in security and decency" or else "they will find out a victim and sacrifice him as a scapegoat to their despair." Every effort to eliminate unemployment or raise the standard of living, she wrote in 1940, in an implicit defense of the New Deal, "is a step in the elimination of race conflict."[48]

Benedict concluded that to end racial prejudice, social engineering needed to accompany education. She emphasized the limited effectiveness of school programs designed "to achieve tolerance by special instruction." While important, such efforts should not be ends in themselves. To combat racism, teaching should discuss the participation of different groups in civilization. At the same time, it should promote broader democratic ideals, mutual interdependence, and comparison of social conditions. "We cannot trust to teaching them about the glories of Chinese civilization or the scientific achievements of the Jews. That is worth doing, but if we leave it at that and expect them to become racially tolerant we have deceived ourselves." Several years later, during wartime, Benedict voiced skepticism "that education should shoulder the responsibility for ushering in a new social order." No method of education, she believed, could "make a stable world of an unstable one." To prepare children for a changing world, educators should address not only the curriculum but also the attitudes learned and the institutional organization of the schools, analyzing the transmission of the democratic heritage.[49]

White liberals increasingly challenged segregationist policies. Algernon Black of the Society for Ethical Culture, for instance, believed it critical to bring together children of varied backgrounds to abolish prejudice. Although the progressive Ethical Culture Schools of New York, where he taught, did not enroll African American students until the 1940s, he voiced an integrationist perspective in *Child Study* in 1939: "From an educational point of view, parents, teachers, scout leaders, and ministers should do everything possible so that the school, club, troop, and church, contain a wide diversity of backgrounds and points of view." In December 1942, Black, Benedict, and Locke spoke at Benjamin Franklin High School, where DuBois had brought her programs in 1934. Under Leonard Covello's direction, the school hosted the Greater New York Conference on Racial and Cultural Relations, which received sponsorship from such groups as the NAACP, the American Jewish Congress, and the NCCJ (formerly NCJC). Daniel Patrick Moynihan, then a high school student (and later assistant secretary of labor and U.S. senator), presented a series of resolutions calling for an end to racial segregation in the armed forces and the merging of black and white blood banks by the Red Cross, as well as the appointment of a director of intercultural education for the New York City schools.[50]

Rachel Davis DuBois encountered these views through her contacts with prominent African Americans. At various conference and events she came to know Alain Locke, Charles Johnson, Langston Hughes, and E. Franklin Frazier. She joined the NAACP, which urged the equalization of school terms, teachers' salaries, distribution of funds, and school standards, on the principle that "interracial justice is the only reliable basis for interracial peace and harmony." In 1938 she served on the NAACP's Committee on Textbooks and Current Literature, charged with monitoring the depiction of blacks in books and periodicals, along with such notables as William Pickens, James Weldon Johnson, Arthur Spingarn, Charles H. Thompson, Marion Cuthbert, and Mary White Ovington. She later recalled that "blacks wrote brilliantly about themselves in their journals," citing in particular the *Crisis* and *Opportunity,* both of which published accounts of her programs.[51] The *Crisis* pronounced her a "pioneer in the work of measuring and guiding the thought and prejudice of high-school students in race problems" and briefly listed her as a member of its editorial board. A 1934 article reaffirmed social-scientific findings on the acquisition of attitudes and urged that parents and teachers "interested in the abolition of intolerance should take advantage of these means to counteract the influence of bigotry upon the mind of the coming generation." The magazine optimistically declared that "knowledge has the same power to banish ignorance that light has to dispel darkness."[52]

DuBois's friendships with black leaders and her genuine commitment to racial equality may have shielded her from more intense scrutiny. But hints of criticism did emerge. In a scripted radio program in 1940, Marion Cuthbert, who had authored a book for children that questioned the inequities of separate schools, offered a polite challenge after DuBois described her use of the arts to cultivate understanding. "But isn't that rather superficial?" Cuthbert asked. "We Negroes have been making and singing beautiful music for a long while; but everybody forgets that we have worked hard—and still do—in the building up of American life." Because that work went unacknowledged, "we are often prevented from sharing in this life which we have helped to build." DuBois replied that the intention was not to stop with the arts, but to use them "to open the doors of the closed mind." Cuthbert continued, "hadn't we better be realistic and admit that the real reason for prejudice is that the different groups challenge each others' economic security?"[53]

As mentioned earlier, the apolitical nature of DuBois's program may have been a conscious strategy to appease her critics. She was active in the NAACP and in fact became identified with a left-leaning, labor-oriented faction that urged class consciousness, economic justice, and checks on the power of capitalism. In 1931 she confided to W. E. B. Du Bois that her views made her "too much of a left winger" to appeal to southern Quakers. In 1934, after controversy at the NAACP board, she admitted "my private and personal and subconscious feeling is that it's all a rather hopeless group for this day and age . . . the truth is I'm growing more and more Left but can't see myself fitting into that role."[54] Yet DuBois never mentioned her longtime NAACP affiliation in her antiprejudice materials. Some initial writings from her years at Woodbury did employ the language of civil rights and equality and did encourage teachers and students to support political organizations working to end injustice. But she rarely introduced such analysis into the later literature of the Service Bureau.

After her experience of being attacked at her New Jersey high school, DuBois may have calculated that avoidance of economic and political issues would spare her further attacks and make her work palatable to a wide range of observers. In fact, she continued to face charges of radicalism throughout her career. "Dodging evil names of Bolsheviks etc etc thrown at me in Quincy Mass. where I started to work in a school," she wrote to W. E. B. Du Bois in March 1933. "No permanent harm to me but I had to shift to Somerville High." The next month she told him with discouragement: "I'm being investigated in Washington—my former Supt. of Schools at Woodbury has rec'd a letter asking a lot of questions about me—even who pays me—what organization I'm connected with etc." She joked weakly, "I don't see why I don't go into prison reform so I'll have a decent cell to live in—I'm sure I'll end my days there."[55]

Perhaps influenced by her contacts with leftist thinkers, DuBois increasingly struggled to balance cultural appreciation with economic and social concerns in the mid-1930s. The problem of stereotypes "is of equal importance with our current economic problem. It is, indeed, part of this problem," she explained, for stereotypes justified the exploitation of certain groups. As long as people felt different from each other, "we cannot unite in one common effort to change the economic system."

Economic security, she suggested the next year, was basic to interracial harmony and world peace. She considered ways for her assembly programs "to dramatize the economic competition which underlies much of our race prejudice." DuBois also came to take a stronger stand against segregation, admitting that the successes of antiprejudice programs in mixed schools "force us to see more and more clearly the need for opposing the spread of segregation in our public schools, and for challenging on this point our private schools." Northern schools should hire more minority group teachers, thus offering "more enriching experiences for all children."[56]

Even as DuBois gave greater credence to the structural causes of racial prejudice, she continued to insist on the efficacy of attitudinal change. The world would transform one person at a time. "Must we entrust our social fate to that blind force, economic determinism?" she pleaded. "Must we wait with folded hands and heavy hearts for violent revolution?" In *Adventures in Intercultural Education,* the manual for teachers she published in 1938, DuBois acknowledged claims that "cultural harmony cannot come about until the competitive economic system has been changed, both within and between countries, to a cooperative system." But she placed attitudes first. "We do not need to wait for a new economic system in order to change the psychological factor." She held faith that intergroup amity "would leave us free to devote our energies to the solution of our economic, as well as other, ills."[57]

In her articles, DuBois continued to assert the school's critical role. While she conceded economic factors as a cause of prejudice, she said, "we felt that man is also conditioned by his psychological relationships and that it is in this field that the school can do most at this time." Through valuing cultural differences, DuBois promised at the end of the decade, "we will release an energy which will not only build a richer culture, but which will find ways to cooperate in working out a solution of our economic and political problems." Cultural gifts work now promised to ease economic suffering, "to defend great masses of people from grinding poverty." In addition to cultural sharing, democracy depended partly on "a better distribution of the good things of life, and partly on equal civil and political rights."[58]

In response to the charge that it was useless to change attitudes when economic systems remained in place, DuBois asserted that education could lay the groundwork for larger reform. It was not the teacher's job to secure equal opportunities in jobs, housing, recreation, and voting, she explained in 1945, but by recognizing cultural diversity, the teacher could reduce intergroup conflict. *Build Together Americans*, DuBois's doctoral dissertation, published that year, acknowledged that many factors contributed to prejudice, including the media, legal discrimination, shortcomings of the church, and material inequities. She noted the "extreme economic pressure" affecting black families, who suffered most from discrimination, dating back to the "unmoral conditions" of slavery and the "almost subhuman standards of living" since. Even so, attitude modification was a worthy project: "because people are also conditioned by social-psychological relations that are not affected by economic pressure, the school can develop the kind of attitudes which would enable young people of all groups to co-operate in ways that would finally help to break the vicious cycle." Attitude change could come first, since "we do not need to wait for a new economic system in order to begin to change the social-economic setting in which group relations and attitudes develop." Decades later, DuBois reflected on the limits to this approach. After reading an article in *Teachers College Record* in 1972, in which Walter Feinberg criticized the Service Bureau as conservative, DuBois scribbled in the margins of her copy: "If not focusing on the ec. causes of prejudice is conservative then we were that but we always recognized that cause." Ultimately, she acknowledged, she and her colleagues were "not equipped to deal with it."[59]

Everett Clinchy of the National Conference of Christians and Jews (NCCJ; formerly NCJC), DuBois's longtime colleague in the field, also came to link antiprejudice work with economic reform. "Hate of class, race, creed, or nationality measurably slows up the solution of every economic problem," Clinchy wrote during World War II, and economic depressions exacerbated antagonisms. The schools could help students reject such hatreds and also introduce "the scientific method in attacking economic problems," tolerating diverse views and "encouraging free inquiry and experimentation in economics." But Clinchy, too, affirmed his original goals. In response to a proposal in 1942 for greater activism against racial discrimination in housing and employment—out of recognition that religious bias was not "an isolated problem"—Clinchy countered that his organization's mission was to improve relations among the three faiths, not to fight all forms of intolerance.[60]

By the end of the 1930s, antiprejudice education had undergone a series of reformulations. Initially designed to teach dominant group children to respect the contributions of other cultures, it had evolved to include teaching second-generation and minority children to take pride in their own heritage, and then, at least for some thinkers, bringing about social parity. For African American and radical activists, the focus expanded from the private to the public, from the purely cultural to the economic, the social, and the political. Even as they reiterated the idea that the school had a critical role to play in shaping racial attitudes, they rooted this work in a broader context. They noted limits to the power of curricular reform and called attention to the impact of school segregation. Ending prejudice was a necessary first step toward greater equality, for in addition to cultivating understanding and cultural pride, education could help bring about social justice.

Those who advanced a socioeconomic analysis of prejudice influenced the white liberals who led the antiprejudice campaign but did not ultimately succeed in reshaping the cultural gifts approach. As Rachel Davis DuBois and her colleagues came into contact with black and radical thinkers, they grappled with new tensions over methodology and goals and, to some extent, began to reconceptualize cultural gifts work as part of a larger struggle for socioeconomic change. Yet they were not entirely flexible in their approach. Despite their awareness of how the NAACP and other political organizations understood racial prejudice, white liberals continued to insist on the primacy of psychological change and individual attitudes and to downplay the institutional forces that shaped race relations. They continued to view all minority groups in similar terms, minimizing the structural conditions that penalized African Americans in particular. This oversight limited the viability of the cultural gifts approach in the struggle for racial justice and civil rights during and after World War II.

8

Pluralism in the Shadow of War

Over the course of the 1930s, the antiprejudice crusade gained visibility and influence. While the approach shifted to accommodate concerns for the second generation and greater economic analysis, its core principles remained the same. The spread of racism in Germany inspired efforts to counter racism at home, bringing greater public attention to antiprejudice work, as liberal thinkers contrasted American tolerance with the Nazi persecution of minorities.

Yet by the end of the decade, the methods and aims of the cultural gifts project faced challenges from several sources. The AJC, which had been a chief supporter of cultural gifts work, increasingly objected to the interpretation of Judaism as a culture, not just a religion. Leaders in progressive education grew concerned that group pride would lead to nationalist feelings and cultural fragmentation. A nationally broadcast radio program was torn by dispute over the portrayal of ethnic groups. Rachel Davis DuBois's position became increasingly tenuous, until she was pushed out of her leadership role at the Service Bureau in 1941. Her removal marked the foundering of the cultural gifts approach that she had been developing for seventeen years.

In the context of the looming war overseas, the effort to boost cultural pride came to appear perilous and divisive. Critics called into question the balance between particularism and unity, arguing that the celebration of ethnic pride and national identity too closely echoed fascist thinking. At a moment when treacherous forms of nationalism were gaining strength in Europe and Asia, American Jews in particular—key funders of antiprejudice work—looked with suspicion on a philosophy that emphasized difference among groups. Indeed, the Axis powers represented some of the nationalities that cultural gifts programs had celebrated. To some observers, Italian American youth boasting pride in their parents' homeland resembled youth under Mussolini; the celebration of German achievements seemed to echo Hitler's appeal to "Aryan" heritage. The cultural gifts movement thus became tainted by supposed similarities with the ideologies of the states that became America's enemies in war. Americans had only to look to the totalitarian regimes of Europe to see what might result from excessive cultural pride.

It is ironic that cultural gifts, a pluralist project that celebrated difference, came to be challenged for its perceived connections to fascism, which enforced homogeneity and racial superiority. In part, this paradox lay in the project's narrow vision of cultural identity. One of the project's failures was an inattention to difference within culture groups, a willingness to pigeonhole people according to their ancestry and to reinforce stereotypes of ethnic groups. This narrowness of vision allowed proponents to offer a simple and persuasive way to understand the role of various groups in American life. The rise of Nazism in Germany made the promotion of cultural pride look too much like the ideologies of aggressors who now seemed to threaten American democracy.

At the same time, new social science interpretations of the origins of prejudice reshaped the work of liberal educators. Rather than describing prejudice as the result of ignorance, as they had done in the 1920s, researchers now came to see it as a psychological problem that originated in interpersonal relationships dating back to early childhood. In this new formulation, the solution lay in the reform of family life and personality development.

By the time the United States entered World War II, the cultural gifts approach had fallen from favor. However, the crusade against prejudice expanded rapidly during the wartime years, hailed as a means to boost patriotic sentiment and reinforce democratic traditions so that all citizens would participate fully in the war effort. Even as a fresh burst of educational projects sought to promote tolerance toward racial and religious minorities, such projects adopted new ideological and methodological frameworks. The new tactics came to emphasize national unity rather than pluralism, human similarities and shared ideals rather than ethnic differences. The endeavor now came to be called "intergroup relations" or "human relations," as it moved away from the earlier focus on the contributions of particular cultures.

To the Progressive Education Association

In 1936, after the AJC withdrew funding for her work, Rachel Davis DuBois incorporated the Service Bureau as a commission of the Progressive Education Association (PEA). This association was at the height of its influence at the time, inspiring reforms in public education as well as elite private schools, and had recently expressed a commitment to anti-prejudice education. After hearing talks by DuBois and Louis Adamic at the 1935 annual meeting, members passed a resolution in favor of education for cultural pluralism for both minority group children and for children of the "'old Americans' whose ignorance of other cultures is an equally great menace to our community life." In 1935 the PEA's journal, *Progressive Education,* published its special issue entitled "Minority Groups and the American School," and its New York regional conference held a special session entitled "Education and Cultural Pluralism." The executive secretary declared: "there is no more important program to be initiated during the coming decade." Between 1934 and 1944, *Progressive Education* published more articles on intercultural education than any other magazine. With the support of the NCJC, DuBois asked the PEA to sponsor her work.[1]

To evaluate DuBois's programs, the PEA formed a committee chaired by W. Carson Ryan, former director of education at the U.S Indian Service, and including Ruth Benedict, Frederic Thrasher, who advised DuBois's dissertation, and Goodwin Watson of Teachers College at Columbia, with whom DuBois had taken two courses. The committee's positive review attested to the urgency of the work, especially as "the strains due to racial and minority groups in American life have been intensified recently by the economic situation and by renewed conflicts elsewhere in the world." Thrasher affirmed that the work "can be done best in connection with schools and along the lines developed by the Bureau." No other organization was tackling this educational problem, the committee noted, or had developed appropriate teaching materials. With only meager resources, the Bureau had accomplished much, achieving "one of the best examples of the application of sociology in the field of social control" that one committee member had yet encountered. While the committee acknowledged that the Bureau's materials were "not always in the best literary form or well organized" and may have been lacking in historical scholarship, the committee defended them as products of a new enterprise. In a criticism of DuBois's cultural focus, Watson questioned the assumption that ill will was due to ignorance rather than to "the economic motive" and wanted minority groups "to realize how intimately their welfare is bound up with a broader program of social reconstruction," but he, too, was favorably impressed with the program's "genuine appeal."[2]

DuBois's program seemed to fulfill the PEA's new commitment to cultural pluralism, and the PEA may have hoped that it would draw foundation support. For DuBois, the alliance solved her immediate financial problems and offered potential to extend her reach. The program was renamed the Commission on Intercultural Education—the first time, DuBois later recalled, that the term "intercultural education" was used. She explained that the term aptly described this work, "which was wider than race relations and not so wide as international education, though related closely to both." Members of the commission included Ruth Benedict, Frederic Thrasher, Mabel Carney, and Everett Clinchy. DuBois continued as director. Despite ongoing differences, the AJC, to DuBois's surprise, gave a grant to the PEA to support this work.[3]

DuBois complained that she began with "barely sufficient funds" to pay her salary and an assistant's salary and to cover the office rent and regretted that she had not secured additional support. Even so, she maintained an active schedule. In 1937 she attended regional PEA conferences in St. Louis; Milwaukee; Chicago; Minneapolis; Portland and Eugene, Oregon; San Francisco; Los Angeles; and Fresno, interviewing teachers and school officials in each city. She also gave talks to church and teachers groups in New Jersey, Pennsylvania, New York, and Ohio, consulted with the Home Economics Education Service in Washington, D.C., met with assistant superintendents in the New York City schools, published six magazine articles, and continued teaching her course for teachers at New York University. The next year she produced a manual for secondary school teachers entitled *Adventures in Intercultural Education,* in which she laid out her philosophy and methodology, based on her work in fifty public schools in the metropolitan areas of Philadelphia, New York, San Francisco, and Washington, D.C.[4]

Relations between DuBois and the PEA were rocky, in part because of the same issue that had caused conflict with the AJC. Alice Kelliher, who directed the PEA's Commission on Human Relations, told DuBois that she was wrong to portray the Jews as a cultural group. DuBois refuted the accusation, citing Mordecai Kaplan and her own observations: "in all the schools in which I have worked both here and in California, I've seen how much better the minority group child is able to accept himself when he can see his own group—his own parents—as a significant part of America's cultural diversity. I will not deny the validity of my own experience."[5]

More significantly, critics within the PEA began to argue against the educational theory DuBois had long followed, challenging the cultural gifts approach itself. Leaders of the PEA became increasingly uncomfortable with assembly programs that discussed groups one at a time, concerned that they would harden ethnic and racial divisions, bring cultural fragmentation, and encourage nationalist feelings. Tensions had heightened by early 1938, when DuBois appealed to Alain Locke to attend a meeting. "I do hope that you can come, for it's a life and death struggle," she pleaded in a handwritten note. "We do not have unity on the Commission and until unity is found we can't get funds—It is that a very progressive educator thinks that no special attention should be paid to the different culture groups 'just get them all doing things together'— of course, I say, but something more is needed if we are to be realistic." According to Montalto, the PEA's evaluation committee noted that the separate-groups strategy had come under attack as a "distortion" of American history, while a PEA consultant criticized the commission's materials for the "unwarranted cultivation of group pride" that might undermine the loyalty of the second generation and inspire allegiance to foreign governments.[6]

DuBois thought that tensions among ethnic groups in America reflected the frictions among the European groups from which they came. In 1935, she noted, "an intensified ethnocentrism is growing all over the world, in the South Sea Islands as well as in Germany, in Middletown as well as New York City." Events abroad carried dangerous potential for the United States, she explained the next year, lamenting efforts "to transplant to our shores all the Old World mess of petty prejudices, intolerances, and national antagonisms which caused our ancestors to flee to the New World." Conflicts in the United States mirrored "intense hatreds born of European nationalism,—a social disease which is actually destroying European culture." Sadly, the public schools echoed these group hatreds, sometimes in clashes between students of different backgrounds. She suggested community surveys to examine the impact of recent crisis situations, such as "how Hitler's war on Jews affects relations between Germans and Jews" and "how the present war affects relations between Italians and Negroes." In 1940, she saw conditions worsening, proof that "the Melting Pot is no longer melting." School principals felt that they were "sitting on top of a boiling cauldron." She urged action "before violence breaks out in our communities."[7]

DuBois faulted Americanization programs for contributing to the problem. She detailed the political costs of ignoring cultural contributions, an omission that provided fertile soil for foreign propaganda. "Unrecognized, unappreciated, and therefore in an essential sense unassimilated, many of our citizens, hungry for the feeling that they belong to a cause larger than themselves, thirsting for the prestige which comes through the feeling that they are important to that cause, have turned to their fatherlands for the satisfaction of these needs." She cited the comments of one second-generation girl who said to her, "Ukrainia needs me, America does not." Some were responding to nationalist propaganda from Europe, DuBois said, "because they have not been permitted to feel themselves a part of American life."[8]

DuBois was concerned, as well, that international conflict was fostering prejudice against particular groups in the United States. In a discussion at her in-service course in May 1939, one teacher suggested efforts "showing the difference between Nazis and other Germans; between Fascists and other Italians." By 1940 DuBois had become anxious about young Japanese Americans who expressed loyalty to the United States but faced hardships in finding work "despite their record as good scholars and law-abiding citizens." She had included the Japanese in many of her assembly programs, including in Englewood in 1934, where she had the entire school sing the Japanese national anthem. At Benjamin Franklin High School, DuBois and Leonard Covello had devoted two of their assemblies to the Italians and the Japanese. DuBois completed her book on *The Germans in American Life* (as well as *The Jews in American Life*), despite the risk of promoting the achievements of Germans at a time when war was imminent. Perhaps because of lingering anti-German sentiment after World War I, cultural gifts leaders took pains to highlight German contributions to American life, even as some worried that celebrations of enemy cultures could be used for nationalist purposes or to discredit their organizations. As Lasker recalled, producing projects on German American accomplishments "was rather a daring thing to do just then." In fact, Montalto has found that on at least one occasion, DuBois's appeals for ethnic pride were published in an Italian American newspaper with pro-Fascist leanings.[9]

DuBois began to use the term "cultural democracy" to describe her philosophy, which affirmed "that all our peoples have an equal right and place and value in our country." The emphasis was on the "*conscious sharing of values among the various groups* in America." Not only would this approach prevent the spread of group hatreds, she promised, but also "new values will emerge which have in them the best of those which have gone into the merging." Cultural democracy promised "a unity without monotony, and a healthy political integration without sacrificing our priceless cultural resources." This sharing was especially important at a moment when European cultures were in danger of destruction. In a radio talk, she reassured immigrants "that no matter what happens in their homelands today, they and their children are, or can be, the agents through which may be transplanted into American life the best of the cultural genius of their homelands." She rushed to clarify that she was speaking of cultural loyalties exclusively: "There can be only one political loyalty here, and that is to the flag of the United States."[10]

To DuBois, the cultural gifts ideal was not incidental to America's national identity; in fact, it was what distinguished the United States from its enemies. A teacher who participated in DuBois's project at Roosevelt Junior High School in San Francisco contrasted DuBois's approach with the social theory of other countries. "Italy and Germany, under a philosophy of 'authoritarianism,' exclude elements and persons differing from the accepted cultural norm, and thus isolate themselves from the enriching stream of the interplay of different cultures," this teacher explained in 1937. "Russia, under a policy of 'cultural autonomism,' imposes rigid political and economic doctrines upon its many diverse cultures and peoples, but encourages them to live in separate areas with little cultural contact or exchange between them." In contrast, democratic nations like the United States could incorporate the values of diverse peoples in order to achieve "a healthy personal, social, and political integration."[11]

DuBois asserted that cultural gifts work was germane to relations both at home and abroad, for it offered a step toward international harmony. "France must come to see that she cannot progress without Germany," she contended in 1935. "Germany will come to realize that she cannot build a new culture within a vacuum." In the tradition of American exceptionalism, she painted her efforts as a model for other countries. She proclaimed that America's destiny was "to work out a microcosm of world unity" that would prevail after the war. "From our example there might arise a world which will have learned to allow to each individual, each group, each nation, the cultural patterns most congenial to his or its needs or talents." She still held faith in this ideal forty years later, predicting in her autobiography that as a heterogeneous society, the United States could set the example for other nations. "Because America is heir to the cultures of the world, we can help build a global culture of harmoniously related peoples before it is too late." With her typical romantic denial, she was unwilling to confront the potential conflict between the traits of particular cultures and the standards of the common culture—an ongoing strain on both the international and the domestic stage.[12]

In response to criticisms of her separate-groups strategy, DuBois began to include an introductory and a final program in the year's assembly series to "stress the unity of mankind and portray the groups together in American life." These general programs "offset the danger of developing a feeling of separateness after a series of projects on different groups," she explained. At a culminating pageant, the Spirit of America entered, followed by representatives carrying a symbol of their group's gifts to American life. Speeches, folk music, and dance brought home the message that America was a composite nation. In addition, she was willing to accept a topical approach to highlight similarities, reporting that some schools took a second year for an assembly series that presented the achievements of various groups in fields such as science, literature, art, or industry.[13]

DuBois's attempts to defend her approach were not enough to convince her critics. In a rejection of the cultural gifts approach, the PEA canceled plans for the remaining eight books in the series on ethnoracial groups that had begun with *The Jews in American Life* and *The Germans in American Life*. In September 1938, the PEA dropped DuBois's commission. She was still teaching a weekly course at New York University, but was unsure how else to continue her work. The Mayer family, who had given funds through the AJC in 1934, now agreed to cover her rent. She also received financial help from her Quaker contacts in

Philadelphia and from the NCCJ. The Service Bureau board, which had been suspended during the PEA period, would continue as an independent organization, now called the Bureau for Intercultural Education. The organization cooperated with the conference of the Swarthmore Institute of Race Relations, held in 1938 at New York University under the directorship of Charles Johnson. DuBois arranged social events to introduce members of the Swarthmore Institute to ethnic group leaders in New York City, occasions that reminded her of the importance of personal interactions among people of different backgrounds. The next year, DuBois met Eleanor Roosevelt when a mutual friend arranged for her to visit the first lady's apartment in Greenwich Village. Roosevelt responded warmly to DuBois's account of her work, sent her a check for $500, and devoted a "My Day" column to her endeavors.[14]

Americans All, Immigrants All

After leaving the PEA, DuBois approached John Studebaker, head of the federal Office of Education, to propose an educational radio program that would dramatize the cultural gifts approach. She was disturbed by the racist broadcasts of Father Charles Coughlin and thought that the radio could be effectively enlisted to spread the message of intercultural education to a wide audience. Studebaker agreed to sponsor the program, called *Americans All, Immigrants All,* and produced in collaboration with CBS in 1938–1939 as a series of twenty-six weekly half-hour broadcasts that incorporated dramatizations and music. The writer Gilbert Seldes produced the scripts, and DuBois served as consultant along with a colleague from the Service Bureau. She supervised research activities at the Service Bureau, presented factual and dramatic material to Seldes, and planned educational follow-up activities, with her salary paid, once again, by the AJC—whose on-again, off-again relationship with DuBois revealed deep ambivalence.[15]

In the planning for *Americans All,* DuBois encountered conflicts similar to those she had confronted regarding her assembly programs. While she argued for the separate-groups approach, Seldes wanted to stress the process of immigration and the unity of all groups. Studebaker settled on a compromise that included both segments on particular immigrant groups and general programs on the intermingling of peoples in America. In addition to programs on the English, the Slavs, the Negroes, and the Orientals (among others), the series included episodes on such topics as "opening frontiers," "contributions in industry," and "social progress," which highlighted immigrant Americans. A script on "contributions in science," for example, listed Nobel Prize–winners of Jewish, English, French, and German backgrounds.[16]

The debate over how to portray Jews echoed earlier discussions. DuBois

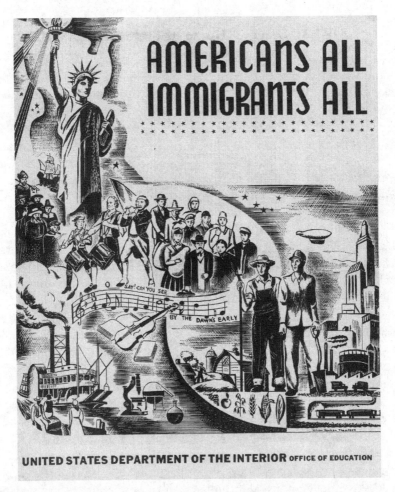

William Norman Thompson, cover illustration, *Americans All, Immigrants All* radio broadcast companion guide, 1939. The Office of Education in the Department of the Interior sponsored the radio series. (Immigration History Research Center, University of Minnesota)

thought it important to have a separate radio program on the Jews in American life, arguing that in public perception Jews constituted a separate group. Some of the series planners and AJC representatives opposed such a program, which they feared might call negative attention to Jews. They insisted that Haym Solomon, who had helped finance the American Revolution, be identified as Polish American. "It did not seem to me to be a realistic application of the principles of social psychology to say that Solomon was a Polish-American if we were trying to develop positive attitudes towards Jews," DuBois complained. Theresa Mayer Durlach, who had funded DuBois's earlier projects through the AJC and who served as chair of the Service Bureau, suggested to Studebaker that if the series included an episode on Jews, it should also include ones on Catholics and Protestants. Iphigene Ochs Sulzberger, wife of the *New York Times* publisher, protested the special program, calling it a mistake to regard "the Jews as a race, when they are merely a religious group," a contention supported by social scientists. "I do not think it is to the interests of the United States or of its Jewish citizens to take Hitler's propoganda [sic] along these lines seriously," she cautioned. After much discussion, Studebaker and his committee decided to include a separate program on Jews (but not other religious groups).[17]

DuBois also encountered conflicts over the participation of African Americans in the program. Soon after accepting her new position, she wrote to Studebaker to express concern that the advisory committee included no black members. While she recognized that it was not practicable to invite representatives from each group, it was imperative to appoint "one Negro leader, not only because it is our largest minority group, but also because I consider it our most important problem, since our democracy, after all, will rise or fall according to the way we treat that group." She had learned the value of including blacks at the policy-making level and nominated Alain Locke. Studebaker denied her request but did promise to include blacks as consultants. DuBois later asked Locke to comment on the draft of the program on African Americans and expressed her dismay when the producers overlooked some suggestions.[18]

The *Americans All* series enjoyed tremendous popular success, winning a number of prizes and bringing national attention to the Service Bureau. Listener response was great: the Office of Education received eighty thousand pieces of mail about the series, many requesting the printed materials that were offered with each broadcast. As the historian

Barbara Savage explains, a large majority of those letters came from people who were interested in the broadcast about their own ethnic group. They considered it significant that the federal government endorsed their role as citizens, and knowledge of their group's accomplishments raised their self-confidence and sense of prestige. Teachers made extensive use of the broadcasts and written scripts, which were made available to schools through the Office of Education. Teachers in New York City requested the programs about Jewish, Italian, and Irish immigrants. According to a teacher in Minnesota, the series helped second-generation students "regain their pride of race and at the same time develop an understanding and toleration of other nationalities." A teacher of black children in Philadelphia had "been very interested in finding 'heroes' for them among their own people, and trying to develop in them the feeling that their people too have contributed in making our land the great country it is." Yet fewer native-born white Americans seemed to be listening to the broadcasts, suggesting that the radio series served DuBois's goal of instilling cultural pride in people from immigrant and minority backgrounds—but did not necessarily succeed in inspiring curiosity or appreciation regarding the contributions of other ethnic groups. To some observers, the response highlighted the potential divisiveness of the separate-groups approach.[19]

The Bureau found itself busy again when the New York City Board of Education passed what it called its Tolerance Resolution in December 1938, soon after the events of *Kristallnacht* highlighted the Nazi persecution of Jews. Concerned with the possible spread of Nazism in American schools, the resolution ordered that all public schools in the city arrange two assembly programs each month devoted "to the promulgation of American ideals of democracy, tolerance and freedom for all men" and "to making the children of our nation aware of the contributions of all races and nationalities to the growth and development of American democracy." When DuBois agreed to help (even though, as she recalled, "We hated the word *tolerance*") the Board of Education encouraged teachers to contact the Bureau for assistance. DuBois hired a teacher to develop activity units for each grade level and to research classroom units done in other school systems. The Bureau produced sixty experimental units and assisted a thousand teachers in planning assembly programs and classroom activities to meet the tolerance mandate.[20]

Despite DuBois's involvement, the assembly programs in New York

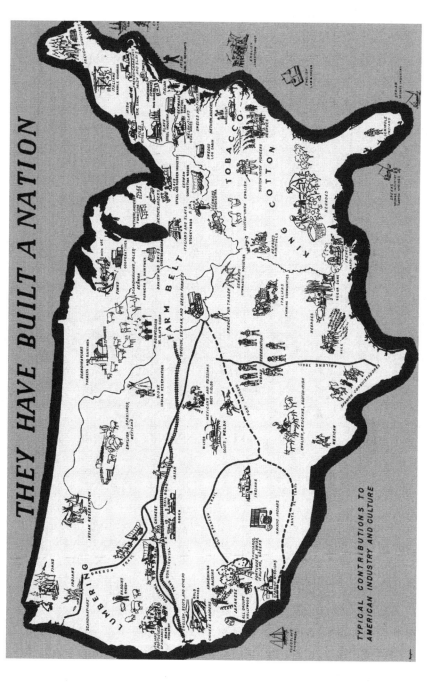

William Norman Thompson, illustrated map, *Americans All, Immigrants All* radio broadcast companion guide, 1939. (Immigration History Research Center, University of Minnesota)

City did not follow her approach but rather reflected the shift that was gathering steam at the end of the 1930s. A critical review of the assemblies, most likely written by DuBois, noted that the programs failed to present the various culture groups at the school, provide opportunities to share experiences, or arrange for social contacts—omissions in keeping with school officials' directives. "Do not stress too much the contributions of any one race," a committee of the Board of Education advised. "This serves to stir atavistic antagonisms not compatible with the 'melting pot'"; it could develop "racial partisanship" in immature minds. The committee urged schools to base their programs "on the cohesive power of all Americans as one nation and one people in furthering the ideals of democracy and tolerance." Teachers frequently emphasized democratic ideals and individual rights rather than intercultural understanding. An assembly at New Utrecht High School, for instance, described the early settlement of America and the adoption of the Bill of Rights, emphasizing the foundational ideals of "religious tolerance, freedom of conscience, human rights."[21]

Teachers in the New York City schools offered mixed responses to the Board's directive. One teacher agreed that "carefully and dramatically prepared programs can be of inestimable value" in teaching democracy, but thought it even more important to "offer our attitudes and behaviors as models of tolerance and good will." Another suggested that "tolerance cannot be taught; it must be lived." Youth needed to see adults practice tolerance "rather than discuss it, preach it, or teach it." A third thought it "very much more effective when taught by indirection." The *New York Times* noted that many of the assemblies discussed tolerance in "superficial, abstract terms" and that "thoughtful educators questioned the value of this approach."[22]

Marie Syrkin, a high school English teacher who wrote about the Board's resolution, found it "easy enough to poke fun at the notion of teaching tolerance." She acknowledged that the idea appeared ludicrous to some: "Tolerance, like castor oil, forced down the throats of the recalcitrant young! 'Love-your-neighbor' pills to be swallowed three times a week for credit!" Syrkin recognized, however, that in the context of the spread of fascist propaganda, it was "important to understand why attempts to teach tolerance have failed." Part of the problem, she thought, was that teachers so adamantly opposed indoctrination that they were reluctant to impose their views or challenge students' biases. Syrkin also noted a "lack of conviction" from teachers and administrators, who turned to other tasks as students became bored by the subject. She worried that when tolerance programs merely repeated "beautiful generalities" and "safe platitudes," timidly avoiding controversial topics, students were unable to apply the doctrine to real situations. "There is no carry-over between sentimental appeal and specific application," she explained. "Teachers should not be afraid to be doctrinaire in regard to democratic ideals."[23]

At the same time that she assisted the tolerance assemblies, DuBois taught in-service courses for teachers in the city schools, held at New York University. Many of the participants were Jews, who were well represented among the New York City teaching staff. Participants wrote that they found the course valuable in understanding cultural contributions and in developing techniques to break down prejudices. At least one teacher in the course, however, complained about the attention to particular groups. "We are tending to emphasize the very things which have caused intolerance such as nationality and religion," wrote Sidney Weinstein, who taught at Abraham Lincoln High School. "I don't want to tolerate a man because he is Italian; I want to like him because he is an American. I want to share what we have in common more than what we differ in!"[24]

Trouble at the Service Bureau

DuBois faced continuing challenges to her philosophy and leadership. The board of the Service Bureau, which included representation from the Bureau's chief funder, the AJC, continued to question her approach. In 1939 the board appointed a new director, Stewart G. Cole, and several new staff members, and assigned DuBois the title of educational director. The newcomers, along with several members of the board, reiterated criticisms of the separate-groups strategy. They wanted to reorient the Bureau's work toward limiting the expression of cultural differences and fostering loyalty to American culture. Cole criticized DuBois's abilities and professional judgment and suggested that the organization adopt a more sophisticated approach. The resulting tension pitted DuBois and her allies against Cole and other board members. The board, chaired by Everett Clinchy, voted DuBois a six-month leave in January 1940, with some members suggesting that she seek psychiatric help. Feeling betrayed, she declined to take the leave, although she did travel to Atlanta for a week to see W. E. B. Du Bois. She thought she was being pushed out because the board no longer wanted a woman to head the organization.[25]

DuBois's work came under further attack when the board hired Bruno Lasker as editorial secretary, in fall 1940, and asked him to review the Bureau's publications. Although DuBois considered Lasker a longstanding friend, he strongly criticized the materials she and her colleagues had developed. Years later he recalled "that many of the publications struck me as being rather shoddy, intellectually speaking, and sentimental rather than realistic." (He did not think much of Stewart Cole's work either, recalling that "he could not write at all, and his ideas were either confused or borrowed from other people.") This was not the first occasion on which Lasker questioned the intellectual value of DuBois's work. In 1934, he had called her pamphlet on Japanese culture "entirely inadequate" and noted, "I have for two years tried to discourage Mrs. DuBois from attempting to publish any of the pamphlets which she has prepared. They are all sentimental and second-rate."[26]

On arriving at the Service Bureau, Lasker issued a steady stream of memos, letters, and reviews assessing the curriculum materials. He soon advised Cole to call a "complete moratorium on the sale of any of this material for one year" to allow time to replace it. Each unit for study required revision, and most were so inadequate "that even revision is hopeless." Several days after appearing before the Board, Lasker wrote to DuBois to apologize for "the extreme candor, not to say rudeness or brutality, with which I attacked the whole body of the Bureau's mimeographed materials." The classroom units, he told her, did not meet a sufficiently high standard, and although teachers had responded positively, authorities in their fields had not reviewed the material. Lasker did not agree with critics who feared that attention to cultural groups would accentuate differences. But he felt strongly that the priority needed to be "the soundest possible historical and analytical basis of subject treatment." He urged: "Let's get all the facts first, before we consider what schools can do with them."[27]

Lasker found most of the Service Bureau materials to be unsatisfactory "on grounds of inadequacy, frequency of misinformation, sentimentalism, false emphasis, lack of clarity, poor style, or insufficient pertinence to the major educational purposes of the Bureau." They treated ethnicity in superficial ways by reducing complicated histories to a few pages. The Bureau's strategy of "teaching about the cultural heritage brought by immigrant groups to the United States is more or less bunk," he asserted. It was wrong to exaggerate the contributions of groups that often had only minor cultural impact on first arrival. Cultural traits commonly attributed to ethnic groups were not actually ones that immigrants brought with them from their countries of origin: some were "purely fictitious," others were formed in America, and yet others were associated with the most educated residents of other nations, not with the peasants who made up the bulk of immigrants and were "too poor and too ignorant to share to any large extent in those cultural heritages of their home country which are associated with these groups in retrospect."[28]

Lasker also thought it inaccurate to credit groups with the achievements of a few individuals. For one thing, such accomplishments often came at the expense of group loyalty or communal responsibilities. In a review of Louis Adamic's book *From Many Lands,* Lasker had praised Adamic for telling tales "different from the old success stories of individual immigrants who, all too often, were admired for their skill in climbing up and out of the common lot over the bodies of their countrymen." In his review of Service Bureau publications, Lasker noted that singular accomplishments were not indicative of a group's contributions and rarely derived from their particular heritage. "The effort to credit ethnic groups as such with the individual achievements of persons of renown is fictitious, fails in its purpose of raising respect or liking for the particular group, and should be abandoned." Overall, he wanted the materials to be less nostalgic and to encourage more realistic analysis of cultural interaction. He recommended that emphasis be on "the joint working out by members of many ethnic groups of many tasks before the American people" and on "the processes of cultural change." Intellectual honesty and scientifically correct information should guide the Bureau's publications.[29]

DuBois's work at the Service Bureau came under even broader criticism from an assessment committee established when the Bureau received a grant of $8,000 from the General Education Board of the Rockefeller Foundation for an extensive evaluation of its program, including its classroom work, in-service courses for teachers, and publications. DuBois opposed accepting the money, noting that the PEA had conducted an evaluation just a few years earlier, but the Service Bureau board decided to proceed. A committee of eight experts, chaired by Otto Klineberg and including such notables as E. Franklin Frazier and Donald

Young, oversaw the investigation, which was conducted by a researcher from Columbia University, Genevieve Chase, who spent a year analyzing the Bureau's operations. DuBois pointed out acerbically, "as usual, the men got a woman to do the actual work."[30]

The resulting report, completed in January 1941, offered a detailed account of the Bureau's activities. The report praised "the pioneering nature" of the work, acknowledging that "significant accomplishment has been made in the right direction." But it also noted important shortcomings. Regarding the in-service courses DuBois conducted in New York, the report remarked on "the defensive reactions of the teachers," many of whom were themselves members of minority groups—meaning they were Jews—and as such were "insecure" and "particularly sensitive to criticisms or suggestions" about how they might alter their teaching. One Jewish principal complained that most of the teachers enrolled were Jewish, even though "the purpose of the course is to make non-Jews more tolerant of Jews. Non-Jews won't take the course." The report recommended including a more representative group of teachers. It also found fault with the concentration of work in the New York metropolitan area. While the Bureau responded to requests from other eastern states and the Midwest, as well as California, the bulk of materials remained in the New York region, and few curriculum units reached the South or elsewhere in the West.[31]

A more serious criticism concerned the guiding principle behind the Bureau's work. The report questioned whether the cultural contributions approach did in fact dispel prejudice. The Bureau's programs, it charged, made students overly conscious of differences and estranged them from each other, accentuating divisions that menaced American unity. "Children remind us that they are not interested in their different contributions, but in ways they are alike," the report asserted. It quoted one student as saying: "When you talk about general ideals, I feel enthusiastic, but when you talk about *my* people, or *my* religion, I feel set apart." While the evaluators acknowledged the enthusiastic response of many teachers, they claimed that others objected to DuBois's methods. One doubted what attitudes would result: "The direct approach points out what one does not want pointed out. Tolerance is built out of a wide variety of *common* experiences. Other methods only raise antagonisms." Teachers feared that programs built on the contributions of various groups "will bring about an increased consciousness of differences among children," Klineberg and Chase reported. "This the teachers feel is contrary to American ideals and encourages adherence to old-world habits rather than adaptations to American life."[32]

Experts consulted for the evaluation similarly doubted the emphasis on cultural contributions. While acknowledging that the approach raised status and self-esteem, they were less convinced that it improved relationships among groups. A social scientist questioned "the superficiality and ineffectiveness of attacking prejudice through appreciations," arguing that it was inadequate to rely on aesthetic and intellectual experiences "while general economic and social conditions continue to develop prejudice." One consultant faulted the Service Bureau's programs as "unnatural and artificial interpretations," while another called them a "mixture of unscientific statements and irrelevant fancy." They asked for a more "realistic" attempt to discuss problems and weaknesses as well as positive contributions. In a challenge to DuBois's educational philosophy, they wrote: "We are led to wonder why the method of dealing with prejudices has heretofore placed so much emphasis upon cultural pluralism." They recommended greater attention to essential similarities and "common heritages and responsibilities," replacing expression of cultural difference with affirmation of shared democratic ideals.[33]

DuBois complained that the report represented her work unfairly. "Never was I asked to explain in detail what we were doing in the schools or the philosophy on which it was based," she recalled with frustration. Her goal of fostering cultural pride in the second generation was largely absent from the report. She wrote a lengthy response in defense of her position but doubted that the members of the evaluation committee ever read it. The depth of her hurt was still apparent in her recollections of the event forty years later. "Oh, so delicately and intellectually, from their professional ivory towers, they shredded our efforts," she lamented. She wondered at the committee members' change of heart: Frazier, she recalled, had endorsed her approach five years earlier, when he told a group of black children that they "needed a good dose of ancestors, and [to] find some people in our group to be proud of, for we Negroes have a role to play in American life."[34]

DuBois defended her materials against the accusations from the General Education Board evaluation committee and from Lasker. She admitted some mistakes, such as the exaggeration of a group's contributions, or the denial of its actual characteristics, or an emphasis on the achievements of particular individuals. But such minor flaws, she claimed, were inevitable in pioneering work. Gaps and oversights were simply evidence of the need for greater knowledge and institutional support. The translation of social science theory for an audience of teachers involved practical considerations. She later wrote: "Yes, some of our curriculum materials may have been written hastily and perhaps were not scholarly enough. But after all, some had to be prepared from Saturday to Saturday to meet the needs of the classroom teachers coming to us each week for help, and referred to us by the New York Board of Education." Despite the criticisms, she knew from her experience in the schools and from the results of attitude tests "that we were on the right track." She and her staff went on with their work "as best we could in spite of the interferences."[35]

DuBois continued to insist on the value of the cultural contributions approach. "Our country is made up of many people who are Americans but are still group-conscious," she explained in a 1941 article, "Intercultural Education and Democracy's Defense." Cultural differences endured, despite what assimilationists had predicted, as was evidenced by the prevalence of foreign-language publications, schools, and organizations, "all of which tend to produce distinct culture groups with unique practices and corresponding attitudes." She argued, as she had in the past, for the need to confront directly the prejudices against particular groups. She was hurt by accusations of fostering disloyalty, protesting that her two goals—appreciation for other peoples and for one's own cultural heritage—worked in concert to bring about a lively cultural exchange and an inclusive democratic process.[36]

DuBois's critics, however, disagreed. To her opponents on the Service Bureau board, the celebration of ethnic contributions was intellectually weak and potentially divisive. Cole and some board members, including the new chair, the progressive educator William Heard Kilpatrick, wanted to reduce ethnic consciousness and instead promote individual identity. They were less concerned about the inferiority complexes of the children of immigrants and more concerned with speeding their progress toward becoming American. Like other liberal thinkers with an eye on Hitler's rise to power, they worried that cultural allegiance could engender nationalist sentiment. At a moment when a strong sense of national unity became paramount, the attempt to celebrate cultural groups and to bolster minority self-confidence no longer appeared wise.

In the struggles within a bitterly divided Service Bureau, several of

DuBois's supporters resigned in protest of her treatment. The board then asked her to resign, which she did in the spring of 1941. With her estrangement from the Service Bureau, her visibility and influence among liberal thinkers declined. The next year she learned that New York University had canceled her course, along with others, because of wartime conditions.[37] Although DuBois had poured her heart into antiprejudice education for fifteen years, she now found herself marginalized from the field she had helped to establish.

World War II and American Unity

As the United States drew closer to war, educators continued to experiment with antiprejudice projects in school, home, and church, drawing on the findings and institutional structures of fifteen years of experimentation. In the context of wartime, the task of incorporating all Americans into national life gained even greater urgency. Yet even as the war intensified efforts to eliminate prejudice, it hastened the shift away from the cultural gifts approach. In part, this trajectory reflected a more general decline of interest in immigration identity. By the late 1930s, white ethnic groups were less visible as newcomers and their children had taken their places in American society. Franklin and Eleanor Roosevelt's friendly attitudes toward immigrants may also have influenced public opinion. Beginning in the World War II period, cultural relations work came to focus more on antiblack prejudice and anti-Semitism rather than on attitudes toward European ethnic groups. In the armed services and on the homefront, the exigencies of war brought together Americans from various backgrounds to work together in a common cause.

Nevertheless, liberal Americans feared that the war would reignite the nativist sentiment of the 1920s. Conservative groups might use the war to justify suppression of foreign-born Americans, as they had in World War I, by citing the possibility of internal subversion from Nazi agitators. The passage of the 1940 Alien Registration Act (known as the Smith Act), which mandated that all aliens be fingerprinted and made it easier to deport those suspected of radicalism, seemed to portend further difficulties for foreign-born Americans. Liberal thinkers looked to the antiprejudice campaign as a way to prevent the return of the xenophobia that had accompanied World War I. As Clara Savage Littledale reminded the readers of *Parents' Magazine* in December 1940, "appreciation of the diversities that characterize our population is a patriotic necessity." Each religion and nationality "has made a particular contribution to the life of the country, and the country belongs to them all. This we must teach our children." The message was critical at a moment when the world was engulfed by war. "It is a philosophy diametrically opposed to that of totalitarianism. It is a belief in the possibility and desirability of unity in diversity," Littledale asserted. Maintaining an atmosphere friendly to each group would foster a broad patriotism and "defend the essentials of democracy."[38]

In the context of the war, racial and religious prejudice appeared a threat to the national unity so desperately needed. Observers feared that foreign enemies would exploit tensions within the United States to weaken resolve and destabilize social relations, using prejudice to open the door to fascism. Events in Europe underscored the dangers of racial hatred and further discredited biological theories of race. To distinguish American race relations from the antagonisms in Europe, liberals argued that prejudice was contrary to American values of inclusiveness. Indeed, the increased public tolerance for minority rights was due in part to the wartime emphasis on American unity in the face of a common enemy. The "double victory" campaign waged by racial minorities linked the struggle for democracy abroad with the struggle against racism at home and set the stage for the postwar civil rights movement. "Cultural democracy" became the new catch phrase in liberal circles. In contrast to doctrines gaining strength in Europe, democracy offered *An American Answer to Intolerance,* as proclaimed the title of a leading teachers' manual of the period, published by the newly formed Council Against Intolerance in America.[39]

Liberal educators in the war years adopted new strategies to combat racial prejudice, describing Americans as individuals deserving full rights of citizenship rather than as members of certain ethnic groups. This marked a shift from particularism to universalism, from a pluralist to a cosmopolitan perspective. Educators aimed to defend individual rights and democratic participation, to speed cultural integration and minimize ethnic identity. The Service Bureau, a report from 1941 asserted after DuBois's departure, should highlight "the basic human similarities of the people of every race, sect, and culture represented in this country, and thus solidify the abiding forces of national unity." New programs tended to follow a thematic approach as they described the achievements of all peoples on particular topics. Such a strategy represented a sympathetic melting pot more than pure pluralism—though its assimilationist impulse was far more respectful of difference than had been the forced Americanization of earlier decades. The new philosophy of intergroup relations held "that differences of a religious or ethnic character should not be called to the attention of others," stated a representative of the NCCJ (formerly NCJC). "The emphasis should be primarily upon common interests and activities with the belief that as people live together they will come to know and appreciate each other as people and that cultural differences would be emphasized only after attitudes of goodwill have been created."[40]

A proliferation of new projects to end prejudice involved greater numbers of scholars and educators. Even a brief survey of important publications suggests the extent of the field and the range of its participants. Between 1939 and 1940, the *Journal of Educational Sociology, Frontiers of Democracy, American Teacher,* and *Scholastic* all devoted special issues to racial and religious understanding; toward the end of the war, special issues of the *Harvard Educational Review, Child Study, Educational Leadership,* the *International Journal of Religious Education,* and the *Annals of the American Academy of Political and Social Science* examined means to control group prejudice. In 1942, the PEA published *When Peoples Meet,* edited by Alain Locke and Bernhard J. Stern, and the National Education Association's fourteenth yearbook was entitled *Americans All: Studies in Intercultural Education.* The following year, the Bureau of Intercultural Education published *Intercultural Education in American Schools.* These publications emphasized national unity, democracy, and individual rights rather than ethnic identity.[41]

The shadow of war advanced the agenda of organizations that had pioneered antiprejudice work in the 1920s and 1930s. The CSA established an award to recognize a book that faced "real problems in our children's world—a strong, realistic picture translating democratic ideals into everyday terms." Its 1943 award went to a story that offered "a strong plea for team work among all creeds and races in American life" through a "courageous handling of questions of racial and religious prejudice."[42] The NCCJ developed programs for schools, assisted teachers, and worked with PTAs, Sunday schools, and colleges. It organized trio teams to speak before entire companies at army training camps and to reach army chaplains, whom the NCCJ hoped would return to their hometowns to spread interfaith goodwill. The AJC continued to fund intergroup work, offering $400,000 to various organizations (including the NCCJ and the Bureau of Intercultural Education) between 1939 and 1942 and encouraging publications to carry articles on tolerance. A number of new agencies also emerged.[43]

In 1939 the NCCJ initiated a project in Springfield, Massachusetts, that received widespread publicity as a model for instilling tolerance. Springfield, a middle-sized industrial city with a diverse population, undertook a community-wide project to foster democratic living and "education for citizenship." The Springfield Plan, as it became known, invited students to experience democracy through "living, learning, working, and thinking together." In the schools, they took part in map fairs, city surveys, student councils, and school meetings; rather than focusing on particular cultural groups, they studied such topics as religious contributions to democracy and anthropological understandings of race. Adult education classes, teacher training, parent-teacher organizations, and cooperation with employers and civic organizations broadened the program beyond the school system to make this "one community's total war against prejudice."[44]

After DuBois's departure, the Bureau for Intercultural Education continued to distribute materials and work with community agencies. During the war the Bureau's leaders expressed concern over heightened antagonism toward people of German, Italian, and Japanese background in the United States. To view immigrants from Axis countries with suspicion was to "contribute indirectly to the cause of our enemies." The Bureau offered its educational expertise to the War Relocation Authority, the Office of Army Education, and the Office of Civilian Defense. It also proposed a program in the New York City schools to promote the principles of American democracy.[45]

The cultural gifts focus continued to draw criticism. During wartime, Ruth Benedict became an outspoken opponent, although she had earlier served as a member of the Commission on Intercultural Education. In the *Americans All* yearbook, Benedict claimed that the majority of children from immigrant groups then entering the schools were of the third generation, who faced universal—not specifically immigrant—difficulties. "Therefore we do not need to single out their problems as special or unique," for young people would find it humiliating to be considered as a special case. It was "sociologically false" to treat the problems of any one group as separate from others. Conditions had changed, she believed, so that "intercultural education in 1942 does not have to face the extreme conditions of cultural separatism and the extreme antagonisms which marked the days when immigration was unrestricted." She thought the melting pot and the retention of cultural traits presented "two false alternatives," for despite efforts to preserve traditions, "special folkways will be sloughed off gradually." In America, immigrant groups gave up their idiosyncrasies voluntarily. She faulted programs "emphasizing quaint, surface, and easily exhibited cultural products," whose patronizing message young people would resent. Intercultural perspectives should permeate the entire life of the school and not be confined to special programs, "what are so often intolerably named the 'tolerance' courses."[46]

Benedict recognized that not all groups had been able to advance equally. "We cannot gloss over the disabilities enforced by law and custom against 13,000,000 Negro Americans," she urged. In addition to showing the history of slavery, "we must stress the step-by-step changes in law and custom which will make Negroes *de facto* citizens of this Republic." Intercultural education should promote opportunity, civil liberties, and equality before the law. Its aim was "a national unity based on freedom and security for all." Echoing—and then altering—the original idea that had inspired Rachel Davis DuBois two decades earlier, Benedict instructed, "Do not concentrate 'across the tracks' and let intercultural education 'on the hill' go by default," for it was the privileged who held the power. It was just as important to reach the school whose students were old-stock Americans as it was to reach the school of many nationalities. Benedict advocated a broad curriculum that emphasized the diversity of American life, the importance of full opportunity, and the shortsightedness of discrimination.[47]

Rachel Davis DuBois continued to defend her approach against such criticism. In her assembly programs, she explained in her own contribution to *Americans All*, teachers assured "that all the programs suggested and emphasized the fundamental unity of the human race," even as they helped students gain pride in their own cultural backgrounds and those of others. In answer to charges that the assemblies developed a sense of separateness, DuBois asked: "If members of culture groups are already set off in a negative way, do we not need to be realistic and set them off in a positive way in order to counteract that negative influence?" She acknowledged in 1945 that ethnic allegiance was voluntary; she allowed that individuals should not be "confined within the limits of their own culture groups" but rather should be free to lose their cultural identities if they desired. But they should be encouraged to maintain those identities if they wanted to benefit themselves and the country as a whole. The separate-groups strategy could "make difference appear interesting and attractive." She reiterated that her programs did not encourage "separation which would come from isolated cultural islands" but rather "a sharing of the ethnic richness from all of us."[48]

For Everett Clinchy of the NCCJ, world conflict underscored the urgent importance of religious goodwill. Anti-Semitism appeared to be "an instrument of Nazism, Fascism and anti-democratic forces generally which seeks to disrupt the unity of the American people and distract Americans from a genuine solution of problems by singling out a special group as a scapegoat," he wrote in 1939. He noted that Americans increasingly supported interfaith cooperation as they realized the urgency of the need for goodwill. The unity the NCCJ had long worked for "has become essential to victory in the global war America is fighting" and would be all-important in postwar society, a publicity pamphlet stated in 1942. Goodwill was indispensable to victory. "We Americans cannot successfully defend a cause whose essence is human freedom and equal opportunity for all unless our own national life is cleansed of the stain of intolerance, of racial and religious prejudice."[49]

Leaders in the interfaith goodwill movement were unwilling to minimize the importance of group identity—which would have implied a diminishment of religious allegiance and the gradual disappearance of sectarian customs, a scenario clearly unacceptable to clergy and lay religious leaders. Clinchy continued to invoke the cultural pluralism of Horace Kallen, referring to America's subgroups as a symphony orchestra. But he increasingly insisted that pluralism would not exacerbate religious or ethnoracial divisions, defending it through the concept of "unity without uniformity." Clinchy asked people to draw on their cultural background "that you may contribute it to the common wealth of America, *as an American.*" This liberal vision sought to create "a democracy of cultures as well as a free society of individuals." Clinchy affirmed "the right to be different" toward the end of the war. "The cooperation of religious groups in America builds a nation united and strong," he wrote. "We can be united without being alike."[50]

Even as he continued to endorse pluralism, Clinchy was wary of an approach that singled out prejudice toward particular groups, especially Jews. He worried that calling attention to anti-Jewish sentiment might unintentionally intensify it. The repetition of libels might "sow the seeds of anti-Semitism among the lowest levels of intelligence." Similarly, repeated references to anti-Catholicism might contribute to its growth. Instead, Americans should focus on safeguarding broad democratic principles of tolerance, justice, and cooperation.[51] .

Prejudice as Pathology

New developments in social science also challenged the cultural gifts approach during World War II. In the interwar period, racial liberals had assumed that misinformation was the cause of prejudice. At the end of the 1930s, however, social scientists began to reinterpret the problem in more complex terms. Prejudice came to indicate a far deeper problem: personality damage rather than misinformation, psychological disease rather than faulty instruction. In light of this new paradigm of prejudice as pathology, researchers questioned whether a cultural contributions curriculum, with its faith in reason and persuasion, could address the deep psychological roots of racial attitudes.[52]

The work that first popularized this approach was *Frustration and Aggression*, published in 1939 by John Dollard and his colleagues at the Yale Institute of Human Relations. Its central claim was that irrational frustration, dating back to childhood experiences, was the cause of aggressive behavior in adulthood. Dollard and his coauthors described racial prejudice as an outlet for displaced aggression, in which minorities served as scapegoats. Such outlets differed in democracies and in authoritarian regimes, which helped explain recent aggressions in fascist countries. For healthy personality formation and citizenship, the solution was to provide acceptable outlets for frustration. In the 1940s this model influenced the work of social scientists who explored how frustration contributed to a range of social problems.[53]

This psychodynamic theory was developed more fully in the Studies in Prejudice series the Institute for Social Research published in 1949–1952. Like many of the earlier activities on prejudice, this research received funding from the AJC. The well-known study *The Authoritarian Personality*—whose preliminary reports appeared during the war years—described prejudice as a psychological response to early childhood experiences. Its authors were Theodor Adorno and other members of the Frankfurt School, émigré scholars (many of them Jews) who began their work in Germany and fled to the United States in 1933 after Hitler came to power. Along with American researchers, these left-wing scholars combined psychology and Marxist analysis in a critical theory approach.[54]

The research question behind *The Authoritarian Personality* reflected pressing concerns of the wartime period. Adorno and his colleagues identified distinct personality types; authoritarian personalities—rigid and frightened of difference—were easily exploited by demagogues who tapped into latent frustration and hostilities. Democratic personalities, in contrast, were more flexible and tolerant. Bigots were not bigots because they lacked full information, but rather because of deep-seated psychological disorders, for prejudice was "the defense system of an insecure ego." These personality types emerged through childhood experience. In an interpretation of the research published in the *New York Times Magazine,* Samuel H. Flowerman, coeditor of the series and research director at the AJC, noted the importance of family background and social environment: "personality is developed in the crucible of interpersonal relationships, the most important of which is the relationship between parent and child." As a youngster, the typical authoritarian "was usually subjected to harsh discipline and was given little affection in a home in which the father was a tough boss." When the parent was "menacing, punitive and overpowering," the child responded with submission and fear, qualities that carried over into later life. As an adult, he might admire authoritarian figures, who would trigger his unconscious conflicts, and feel threatened by people who seemed different.[55]

Adorno and his coauthors blamed certain kinds of mothers for the excessive frustration that led to prejudice. Mothers who were too strict as disciplinarians—or, in the other extreme, were overly sacrificing and submissive—could foster antagonistic attitudes, and were often at fault for crippling the father's healthy self-expression and making him either too stern or too unassertive. In contrast, the mother who raised the child for democratic citizenship struck a careful balance; she was loving and understanding, but not all-consumed by her children. According to Flowerman, the democratic individual grew up in a home that emphasized affection, equality, and independence. In a study of prejudice in children themselves, Else Frenkel-Brunswik, one of the authors of *The Authoritarian Personality,* found that the "ethnocentric child" submitted to parents and teachers but retained underlying resentment against authority, which later emerged in hostile tendencies. The "liberal child" emphasized cooperation and, in later life, did not long for strong authority or assert his strength against those who were weaker.[56]

In *Dynamics of Prejudice,* another in the Studies in Prejudice series, psychoanalyst Bruno Bettelheim and sociologist Morris Janowitz agreed that anti-Semitism and antiblack prejudice were expressions of aggression that were rooted in childhood deprivations and took irrational form. In interviews, "a *significant* association was found between tolerance toward minority groups and the recollection of love and affection on the part of the parents, while intolerance toward minority groups was associated with the recall of lack of parental love and harsh discipline." Through improved education, fewer children would mature into intolerant adults. "Education for better ethnic relations must reach deeper levels than can be touched by factual information," they urged. It must influence basic personality traits, "such as tendencies to view life experiences as rewarding rather than deprivational." The control of personality development would form happier individuals who would be able to live successfully with one another.[57]

The fact that authoritarian types were found within the United States, not just in fascist countries, was frightening to consider, as it suggested that authoritarianism had the potential to take hold. But this finding was not entirely pessimistic, for it seemed possible to direct personality development toward democracy and tolerance instead. The solution lay not in the dissemination of knowledge about minority groups, or in the careful monitoring of a parent's or teacher's expression of racial attitudes, but rather in the reform of family dynamics and parent-child relationships. "We must reach parents so that they can learn the importance of affection and equality in the home," Flowerman wrote, and select better teachers and train them "as engineers of human relations" in order to check the authoritarian personality at its source.[58]

These psychological perspectives called into question the cultural gifts approach that racial liberals had followed since the 1920s. If prejudice was a disease emerging from misplaced frustration and aggression, it could not be cured through greater awareness of a group's contributions to American life. Curricular reform no longer offered the promise it had two decades earlier. As a result of this shift in scientific thinking, the AJC and other groups concerned with tolerance—already wary of the pluralist approach because of its potentially divisive implications—rejected the cultural gifts model more definitively. Overcoming the illness of prejudice would require new strategies of psychological intervention.

Yet important continuities remained. Social scientists continued to understand bigotry as an individual matter and to insist that it was not an innate reaction to difference. Analysis of prejudice's causes—and solutions—still focused on childhood experience. The NCCJ, for instance, continued to remind its representatives that attitudes were acquired: "Prejudice is not natural or inborn. It is a product of social life," in the words of a wartime memorandum. The family and other early influences were still critical; the reform of early childhood training still promised to create tolerant adults.[59]

Attention to democracy within the family marked an about-face from the behaviorist theories promulgated by John Watson. In the 1920s, Watson had asserted that rigid child-rearing practices offered the best training for a productive adult life. Two decades later, social scientists feared that overly strict discipline would lead toward totalitarianism. The behaviorist ideas that had earlier promised to end prejudice were now blamed for inciting it. Affection, the very quality Watson had scorned, now appeared critical to the development of tolerant and democratic citizenship. As Flowerman noted, "Love has chased the behaviorists from the nursery; modern parents are less ashamed of loving their children." Bettelheim and Janowitz noted that parents were "discarding the rigid feeding schedules imposed by so-called experts, for more flexible behavior in which they follow the natural leads given by the child." Such flexibility would protect the child "from a source of possibly permanent anxiety" that might prejudice him against racial and religious minorities. In this way, evolving concepts of prejudice advanced changing notions about the needs of the child.[60]

The Studies in Prejudice reports exerted a powerful influence on the liberal racial ideology of the wartime and postwar years. Educators in a range of venues looked for ways to abolish authoritarian practices and promote democratic ones. While they continued to insist that education could instill habits of racial and religious tolerance, they paid increasing attention to the roots of prejudice in personality development and family dynamics.

Parents' Magazine interpreted the new psychological model for its readers through articles and study guides on how to raise democratically minded children and guide them to healthy outlets for their hostilities. Parents should be tolerant and moderate, the magazine explained, and should respect the dignity of the individual through discipline that was sound and just, authority that was kind and reasonable, so that the child would not "fall easy prey to the totalitarian propaganda which abounds in our world today." A "democracy test for parents" considered whether the home upheld the Bill of Rights. Without respect and appreciation, "an inevitable sense of inferiority and frustration leads certainly to personality disorders."[61] *Child Study* similarly explained that intolerant people were "psychologically hostile," while Anna Wolf of the CSA described how aggressive attitudes resulted from a psychiatric record that extended back to "the nursery years." Preventing later grudges depended on "a contented, satisfied, bountiful infancy."[62] The endorsement of affection was part of a larger shift toward a more child-centered, emotionally expressive, and individualized style of child rearing—popularized with the publication of Benjamin Spock's *Baby and Child Care* in 1946.

The pathology model of prejudice influenced the religious goodwill movement as well. At one session of a 1941 gathering sponsored by the NCCJ, a psychiatrist and an educator depicted intolerance "not merely as a matter of misguided emotion, but as a sickness to be treated with the same techniques as any other medical and health problem of the community." Descriptions of psychological malady replaced the references to contagious infection that had characterized discussions fifteen years earlier. Two years later, NCCJ materials reported: "intolerance may also lead to violent hatred which psychiatrists say is a mental disease." It now seemed clear that "individuals who are ill with hate need treatment by specialists." The organization's educational ambitions were now twofold: to disseminate facts that would counter misinformation, and to reconstruct the "warped emotional patterns" that also caused prejudice. In recognition of the authoritarian tendencies that underlay anti-Semitism and religious prejudice, the NCCJ considered expanding its efforts to combat intolerance in general, but decided to retain its religious focus.[63]

The school-based campaign against prejudice reflected the new thinking. Alice Keliher of the PEA explained that anger and hatred derived from excessive restraint and domination. Since people learned from childhood "not to strike back directly at the person who defeats us"—who at the youngest age was the mother or father—they took out repressed feelings on a scapegoat, who might be a minority or a distant nation.

Keliher worried that the "antiseptic neglect" behaviorist experts prescribed would create anxiety that might signal the beginnings of hatred. She recommended that parents and teachers treat children with affection and direct their feelings toward solving problems. This perspective infused the educational literature. A 1945 survey of articles on intercultural education described "prejudice as a psychological process" and advocated "recognition of the operation of the scapegoat mechanism, projection and frustration in explaining prejudice and its evils."[64]

Rachel Davis DuBois acknowledged, to a degree, these new theories on the origins of prejudice. In *Build Together Americans,* her doctoral dissertation, published in 1945, she included a chapter on "prejudice and its relation to personality maladjustment," in which she adopted the language of frustration and aggression and cited John Dollard. "May I say in passing that of course I do not believe the problem of personality maladjustment is as simple as this," she admitted in an outline of her assembly approach. "Race and culture group prejudice is only one phase of a very complex phenomenon." But until new theoretical developments resulted in practical suggestions, she thought it critical to continue educational efforts. With a hint of impatience, she suggested, "while our psychiatrists are doing their experiments and research may not we, the average classroom teacher, and community leader, do what we can to bring first aid to the personalities injured by our present world's madness?" As she had throughout her career, she saw her central task as the inclusion of antiprejudice work in the school curriculum.[65]

Despite shifting intellectual currents, DuBois continued to believe firmly in the cultural gifts approach. She interpreted the new psychological narrative as a complement, rather than a contradiction, to her philosophy. "The essence of democracy is the recognition of the importance of the individual personality," she wrote in 1941, as well as "the part that each group has played in the building of our country." Healthy personality development included pride in one's cultural heritage. Yet to other observers, DuBois's methods came to seem outdated in their emphasis on cultural gifts. Her reliance on social science had ultimately ironic implications: while social science provided the initial direction and justification for her work, it later led to her marginalization in the field that was now called "human relations." For instance, neither the *Harvard Educational Review* nor the *Annals* included an article by DuBois—the pioneer in the field—in their special issues on intergroup education in 1945 and 1946.[66]

By the end of the war, antiprejudice work had undergone significant reformulations. In the 1930s, cultural pride had provided a major impetus for this work's expansion. Fears of delinquency and disorder among the second generation, backed by scientific research and intellectual trends, had offered a powerful justification for the cultural gifts model, allowing advocates to extend their reach to children of the minority as well as the dominant group. But with the rise of racial nationalism in Europe and fears of its incursion in the United States, the notion of cultural gifts—with its stress on ethnic pride and group identity—appeared to threaten American unity. Wartime intensified the criticism DuBois had faced in her work at the PEA, on the radio series *Americans All, Immigrants All,* and at the Service Bureau for Intercultural Education. As Nazi doctrine took hold overseas, American liberals rejected cultural particularism as a model for American identity and instead stressed similarities among peoples and shared aspirations and common humanity that united all citizens.

Because cultural gifts advocates had offered a narrow definition of cultural identity that avoided larger political and social frameworks, they could not make a case for their approach as a democratic alternative to fascism. Despite their efforts, DuBois and her colleagues had not succeeded in casting it as an effective means to strengthen civic participation, national unity, and individual freedom. The cultural gifts project faded from view as new psychodynamic theories offered powerful explanations for the origins and consequences of racial prejudice, linking tolerance to democratic personalities. In the urgency of war, social scientists and liberal thinkers looked for new ways to address the country's cultural diversity. After the war, when activists again turned their attention to racial difference in American life, they looked to new strategies to effect social change.

Epilogue:
The Fall and Revival
of Cultural Gifts

By the end of World War II, the enthusiasm for national unity and the psychodynamic interpretations of personality had reshaped antiprejudice education. Aspects of the cultural gifts model endured: educational programs continued to celebrate the contributions of many peoples to the building of America, in belief that the schools could dispel prejudice and produce an open-minded citizenry. But efforts to overcome ignorance tended to emphasize a general tolerance and respect for individual rights. Rather than examine cultural groups one by one, programs applauded the participation of *all* groups in various fields of endeavor and in the institutions of American democracy.

Discussions of prejudice increasingly concerned attitudes toward African Americans rather than European immigrant and ethnic groups, who were well on their way toward acculturation and acceptance. While the cultural gifts approach had achieved impressive successes—advancing its central principles that each group contributed to the larger community, that ethnicity was compatible with American identity, that difference could be a source of strength for the nation—its limitations appeared increasingly salient. Despite the critiques of black thinkers in the 1930s, the approach had failed to articulate ways to remove the legal, social, and economic barriers that prevented racial minorities from achieving full political participation and equal citizenship. The model's focus on cultural contributions now appeared too narrow to support the emerging movement for civil rights and racial equality. Because cultural gifts advocates had never fully addressed the experience of African Americans, their model appeared inadequate for the struggles of the postwar period.

268

The model's blindness to entrenched forms of economic and political oppression—the very omission that had given it widespread appeal among whites in the 1920s and 1930s—spelled its irrelevance in later years.

The decline of the cultural gifts movement accompanied a redefinition of racial liberalism in the post–World War II period. Due in part to the institutional reach of the New Deal, with its commitment to an expanded welfare state, racial liberalism came to embrace government intervention as a means to achieve the promise of equal opportunity. Activists struggled to enact civil rights legislation that would remove barriers to individual freedoms and social mobility. They transferred their optimism from education to law, hopeful that the state would assume a role as the guarantor of political and economic rights. At the same time, they embraced economic reform, promising security and opportunity through economic reorganization. They argued that the amelioration of conditions of industrial capitalism would improve relations between capital and labor and revitalize American democracy.[1]

During the Great Depression, some activists had brought together these two sides of liberalism, as when Ruth Benedict explored the links between racism and economic exploitation to explain why bigotry intensified in moments of class conflict. "Until we have 'made democracy work' so that the nation's full manpower is drafted for its common benefit, racist persecution will continue in America," she asserted in 1940. "Until the regulation of industry has enforced the practice of social responsibility, there will be exploitation of the most helpless racial groups, and this will be justified by racist denunciations." Since racial minorities became scapegoats in times of economic crisis, the kinds of reform brought by the New Deal promised to cure the problems of prejudice.[2] Some black intellectuals shared this interpretation of racism, declaring that economic inequalities reinforced racial bigotry. In wartime this analysis gained adherents as liberals depicted racism and material deprivations as undemocratic, as problems that threatened to weaken American patriotism and unity. Racial progress and a redistribution of resources, they asserted, needed to proceed hand in hand.

But in the wake of World War II, fewer thinkers connected problems of race and class. As the economic crisis receded, poverty now seemed to concern a few Americans on the margins rather than the nation as a whole. Bigotry, less prevalent against European immigrant groups, now appeared a regional concern largely confined to the South. Racial and economic reforms came to inhabit distinct spheres in the postwar liberal agenda, championed by different activists in different realms. Liberal attention shifted between addressing the problems of diversity and racial discrimination on the one hand and the problems of capitalist excess and market regulation on the other. While both strands were central to liberal ideology and each achieved important goals in promoting civic ideals and the public good, this divide helps explain why liberalism as a whole was unable to implement the larger communal progress it envisaged or to maintain its strength through the end of the century. On their own, neither racial nor economic reform programs could reconstruct American society to achieve, and sustain, the equal opportunity and expansive democracy liberals imagined. The story of the cultural gifts movement suggests the dangers of pursuing ethnoracial equality without attending to economic divisions as well.

The decline of ethnic consciousness unified whites from various national backgrounds while sharpening the divide between whites and blacks. This black-white emphasis gained widespread attention with *An American Dilemma,* published in 1944 by Swedish economist Gunnar Myrdal, the most influential analyst of American race relations in the 1940s, who understood white racial attitudes in psychological and moral terms. Like earlier liberal thinkers, he expressed faith in the power of education to change attitudes. His massive study, funded by the Carnegie Corporation and written in collaboration with white and black American social scientists, described the education of whites as a key strategy for reducing antiblack prejudice. Myrdal had no doubt "that a great majority of white people in America would be prepared to give the Negro a substantially better deal if they knew the facts." He wrote: "We do not share the skepticism against education as a means of mitigating racial intolerance which recently has spread among American sociologists as a reaction against an important doctrine in the American creed. *The simple fact is that an educational offensive against racial intolerance, going deeper than the reiteration of the 'glittering generalities' in the nation's political creed, has never seriously been attempted in America.*" The extent of past educational efforts, he maintained, had been relatively insignificant compared to the scope of the problem. Myrdal proposed a *"deliberate and well-planned campaign of popular education."*[3]

Although writers and educators in the postwar period were less likely to promote ethnic pride and more likely to situate their analysis in psychological perspective, they continued to remind Americans of the insights that had first inspired the cultural gifts campaign. Ideas that had seemed revolutionary in the years after World War I were reiterated during and after World War II: that racial and religious prejudices were not instinctive and that children played together without regard for difference until they absorbed the biased attitudes of adults in the world around them.[4] Rodgers and Hammerstein reflected the consensus on the learned nature of prejudice in these popular lyrics from their 1949 Broadway musical *South Pacific:* "You've got to be taught to hate and fear."

Many of the individuals and institutions of the interwar crusade remained active in the post–World War II years. Clara Savage Littledale, an early popularizer of the cultural gifts approach in parent education, served as editor of *Parents' Magazine* until her death in 1956. She continued to publish articles on how to raise children to seek peace, cooperation, and interracial understanding, for example "Teaching Children Religious Tolerance," and "One Little Boy Meets Prejudice." In 1953, Littledale gave an address, "Parental Responsibility for Better Race Relations," at the Abyssinian Baptist Church in New York City, at a luncheon for "those interested in Racial Goodwill." Her topic was one she had considered throughout her professional life but had rarely discussed with a predominately black audience.[5]

The NCCJ, under the leadership of Everett Clinchy, pursued its educational approach to religious goodwill. "For the young child, too young to have acquired prejudices, the proper course is to shield him from wrong education at the hands of his elders," Clinchy wrote in 1945. The past decade had seen "a surprising and promising development in both methods and materials for education in human relations." This work needed to proceed on many levels. "It is a task for home and school and church. It must start with the individual himself: the parent in the home, the teacher in the school, the clergyman in the church."[6] In 1946 the NCCJ consulted on intergroup relations for *Superman,* a radio show that promoted racial and religious tolerance. In one episode, Superman used his powers on behalf of an interfaith council, proclaiming against acts of "hating people and trying to destroy them because they don't go to the same church you do." In another episode he battled the "Hooded Klan" who were trying to run a Chinese family out of town. A third story line involved a veteran who protested job discrimination by introducing wounded soldiers from Protestant, Catholic, and Jewish backgrounds.

The show's producers succeeded in their efforts to combine entertainment with social conscience: the series enjoyed high ratings, unprecedented audience mail, citations from civic groups, and imitators. When the CSA brought together fifty experts to discuss how children's radio programs could combat prejudice, the group listened to several recordings that dramatized themes of tolerance.[7]

After leaving the Service Bureau for Intercultural Education in 1941, Rachel Davis DuBois formed a new organization, the Intercultural Education Workshop (later called the Workshop for Cultural Democracy), with the support of such longstanding allies as W. E. B. Du Bois, Leonard Covello, Mordecai Kaplan, Mabel Carney, Eduard C. Lindeman, E. Franklin Frazier, and Frederic Thrasher. She developed a technique called "group conversation," which brought together people from varied backgrounds to recount childhood memories as a way to appreciate both diversity and commonality. She divorced her husband, who had remained in New Jersey during the previous decade, and completed her long-delayed doctoral dissertation, which she published in 1945 as *Build Together Americans*. Despite their earlier conflict, she thanked Bruno Lasker for help in developing the manuscript. Lasker in turn praised the book's emphasis "on the growth of democracy through the pursuit of common interests and aspirations by persons of varied cultural and racial background" and noted that DuBois aspired to more than mutual acquaintance or tolerance: "there also has to be a sincere conviction of our oneness." In 1958, he wrote a positive account of group conversation, in which he noted his long admiration for her devices "for bringing people with different social backgrounds into mutually enlightening exchanges of ideas," methods that resulted in heightened mutual respect and responsibility. In an implicit reference to his earlier accusations, he also admired how she had responded to criticisms of her methodology "by further refining it and by branching out into new techniques to fit diverse circumstances." In her programs, "diversity, even controversy, lost its menace to unity."[8]

During her later career, which extended for many more years, DuBois continued to advocate intercultural education in the schools and to teach university courses. In 1951 she traveled to Germany under the auspices of the State Department to assist in postwar reconstruction. Over the course of five months, she led group conversations designed to integrate ethnic German refugees who had been expelled from their homes in eastern Europe into their new communities in Germany, and trained local leaders in her methods. On her return home, she promoted techniques for interracial understanding among adults, including the "neighborhood-home festival." In 1953 she was called to appear before Senator Joseph McCarthy's Committee on Government Operations. When the brief questioning revealed no incriminating evidence, she was excused. She also became active in the civil rights movement. After the Workshop dissolved in the late 1950s, she worked with the Southern Christian Leadership Conference, at the invitation of Martin Luther King Jr. and Bayard Rustin, to lessen tensions between white and black southerners. She organized a training workshop for community leaders in Atlanta, attended the 1963 March on Washington, and greeted marchers in Montgomery. She received two honorary doctorates, including one from her alma mater, Bucknell University, as well as an award from the Reconstructionist Rabbinical College for her interfaith work. Active until the end of her life, she died in 1993 at the age of 101.[9]

The image of the child continued to shape efforts against prejudice. In his "I Have a Dream" speech of 1963, King envisaged a day when the racial hostility of a place like Alabama "will be transformed into a situation where little black boys and black girls will be able to join hands with little white boys and white girls and walk together as sisters and brothers." The Children's Campaign of the Birmingham movement offered a compelling moral call for equality, as did the Children's Defense Fund, founded in the 1970s, which enlisted sympathy and aid for the most innocent victims of racism and poverty. Indeed, early efforts against prejudice laid the groundwork for the civil rights movement. Because antiprejudice activists targeted young people, their work reverberated for decades. Some Americans who came of age in the 1940s and 1950s had grown up hearing the cultural gifts message.

Historians have recently traced civil rights activism back to the 1940s, yet the story of the antiprejudice campaign suggests that its foundations were laid even earlier. While there were other currents at work as well, the popularization of pluralism in the interwar years may help to explain why civil rights initiatives could go forward in the 1940s and beyond. The landmark *Brown v. Board of Education* Supreme Court decision of 1954 called on old as well as new interpretations of prejudice to outlaw segregation in the public schools. In its famous footnote 11, the decision invoked the research of social scientists Kenneth and Mamie Clark, who investigated the effect of prejudice on the self-esteem of black children. The Clarks' work followed the agenda laid out in the 1930s by cultural gifts activists concerned about the cultural pride of second-generation and minority children. At the same time, *Brown* took inspiration from the attention to democracy and the new understandings of personality that emerged from World War II. It was the wartime shift toward individual rights that pointed the way toward a legal strategy to remedy the problems of racial prejudice.[10]

Despite these connections, the postwar civil rights movement diverged from the cultural gifts model. To a new generation of activists, educational strategies, while essential for shaping attitudes, were not sufficient by themselves to meet the urgent calls for social change. As the civil rights agenda articulated black demands for equality before the law, economic justice, the political franchise, and desegregation, cultural gifts liberalism came to seem outdated. It had failed to address the economic and political oppression that gave rise to prejudice, to suggest means to organize resistance, or to imagine a truly different racial order. The cultural gifts campaign could promote respect—no small aim for black Americans—but was too politically weak to address institutional inequities. Although King did call on DuBois to share what she had learned, her approach was largely tangential for activists who were striving to register voters or desegregate schools. Its easy, romantic ideal, which promised to eliminate prejudice through individual attitudes, was inadequate to meet the demands to reform social institutions and the law. It did not cost anything material for white Americans to recognize cultural contributions—but it would cost something for them to correct the maldistribution of resources and to provide equal opportunities regardless of race.

Activists thus turned to new methods to attend to matters of difference and diversity. Their goals required a philosophy that would address socioeconomic exploitation and would confront, head on, the discrepancies of power and privilege that favored some groups at the expense of others. Civil rights activists called on group identity in the interest of political mobilization as well as cultural pride. They looked to the courts, to mass mobilization, and to political protest to tackle enduring racial inequalities. When they discussed the schools, it was in the context of desegregation rather than curricular instruction, so that the schools became the target of change, rather than the vehicle to bring it about. Their demands for social justice—as well as for cultural recognition—signaled the continued influence of the African American and radical scholars of the interwar period who had linked antiprejudice efforts to broader social transformations.

Beginning in the 1970s, partly in response to perceived entitlements brought by the civil rights movement, the tide shifted back toward the cultural gifts vision. Pluralism again became the dominant expression of diversity, and the schools again served as the battleground for cultural struggles. Ethnic educators, unpersuaded by the claims for cultural democracy that had pervaded the post–World War II period, pointed out the continued exclusion of minorities from the "common cause" of American life. The new multiculturalism they devised harkened back to earlier times in its notions of group identity and its celebration of cultural difference. The ethnic studies programs of the 1970s, for example, were ideological descendants of the cultural gifts projects. Like earlier efforts, ethnic studies initiatives embraced cultural distinctiveness and preservation. They sought to instill in students appreciation of their own cultural heritage as a means to bolster self-esteem and to challenge the cultural hegemony of white America. The ethnic revival, with its reclaiming of European immigrants as "white ethnics," demonstrated that cultural particularism persisted in late-twentieth-century America.[11]

The multiculturalism that emerged in the 1970s suffered from limitations similar to those of the cultural gifts approach of the interwar years. Certain versions of multiculturalism, as it was now called, promoted positive stereotypes and generalizations, allowed for superficial depictions that denied complexity within groups or the realities of mixed identity, and minimized cultural change over time. It depicted group boundaries as fixed rather than shifting and obscured the process of racialization that affected groups in different ways. And like the earlier efforts, multicultural curricula tended to mask questions of socioeconomic class, power, and privilege, focusing instead on the "heroes and holidays" each group had contributed to American life. The message was again cheerful and nonthreatening, suggesting few social consequences to appreciating diversity.

Multiculturalism flourished in the 1990s and continues today. Modern multiculturalism differs from the cultural gifts vision in important ways, most notably in the moral force it has come to exert on American society. Our ethnoracial categories have changed—from dozens of groups in the 1920s that factored in religious and ethnic affiliations to the major races usually acknowledged in the United States today—thanks in part to the acculturation of European ethnics and to the increase in immigration from Asia and Latin America after 1965. New attention to such characteristics as gender, physical ability, and sexual orientation, as well as to adherents of Islam, Buddhism, Hinduism, and other religions, has shifted the categories of difference.

Yet the similarities are striking as well. Indeed, the vision of modern multiculturalism has much in common with earlier notions of cultural gifts. The modern approach is still eager to celebrate cultural traditions, still reluctant to examine the socioeconomic systems that buttress racism or to suggest that members of the dominant group might have to relinquish advantages in the interest of equal opportunity. Multiculturalism's support for diversity has expanded Americans' understanding of national identity and inclusion while continuing to mask the dynamics of class and race. School programs today, for example, tend to recall King's advocacy of racial respect and dignity rather than his demands for economic equality: they highlight his dream of children joining hands rather than his support for striking sanitation workers. Affirmative action programs emphasize the cultural contributions members of minority groups bring to educational institutions but fail to address economic discrepancies or to equalize school funding. As with the earlier movement, the narrow focus on cultural diversity obscures inequities in class, power, and privilege and can thus co-opt attempts for broader social change.[12] Despite claims of enhancing citizenship, recent multiculturalism has appeared inadequate to resolve the deeper divisions that plague American life. Fault lines in the earlier cultural gifts model can alert us to these potential pitfalls.

The pluralist vision established in the years between the world wars continues to shape our understanding of racial identity and cultural diversity. Today, as in the 1920s, our racial categories divide the population into communities of descent as a way to organize cultural diversity. A distinct classification system attempts to fit people into fixed and clear-cut groups. Only in the past few years has a "new cosmopolitanism" arisen to challenge the dominance of the pluralist viewpoint. The United States census of 2000, which for the first time allowed citizens to indicate more than one racial affiliation, may signal a nascent trend away from ethnoracial particularism.[13]

Over the past seventy-five years, the specifics of antiprejudice education have changed many times in response to impassioned debate. The battle has been over the aims and methods of antiprejudice work: over questions of culture and politics, separation and integration, tolerance and equality—issues we still grapple with today. What has remained consistent, in both scholarship and popular culture, is the reliance on the education of the child as the best hope for new racial attitudes. "Tragically, our children are often the first to reap the consequences of what we as a society have sown," the Anti-Defamation League stated. "They learn to hate before they can comprehend why. As parents and caregivers, we must teach our children not only to accept but to celebrate diversity. Intolerance is learned. Therefore it can be unlearned."[14] This assertion—published at the turn of the twenty-first century—could have been written in 1930 or in 1950. Today, as earlier, liberal educators seek ways to teach children to respect the vision of a common civic culture whose vitality emerges from its diversity.

Notes

Abbreviations

Benedict Papers	Ruth Benedict Papers, Archives and Special Collections, Vassar College Libraries
BIE	Bureau for Intercultural Education Records, Immigration History Research Center, University of Minnesota
CIC	*Commission on Interracial Cooperation Papers, 1919–1944,* Microfilm Edition (Ann Arbor: University Microfilms International, 1984)
Clinchy Papers	Everett Clinchy Papers, American Heritage Center, University of Wyoming
CSA	Child Study Association of America Records, Social Welfare History Archives, University of Minnesota
GEB	General Education Board Archives, Rockefeller Archive Center, North Tarrytown, New York
Lasker Papers	Bruno Lasker Papers, Columbia University Rare Book and Manuscript Library, New York
Littledale Papers	Clara Savage Littledale Papers, Schlesinger Library, Radcliffe College, Cambridge, Massachusetts
Locke Papers	Alain Locke Papers, Moorland-Spingarn Research Center, Howard University, Washington, D.C.
LSRM	Laura Spelman Rockefeller Memorial Archives, Rockefeller Archive Center, North Tarrytown, New York
NCCJ	National Conference of Christians and Jews Records, Social Welfare History Archives, University of Minnesota
PEA	Progressive Education Association Records, Archives Research Center, University of Illinois, Urbana-Champaign

RDD Papers	Rachel Davis DuBois Papers, Immigration History Research Center, University of Minnesota
"Reminiscences of Bruno Lasker"	Interview by Louis M. Starr, 1956, Oral History Research Office, Butler Library, Columbia University
WEBD Papers	W. E. B. Du Bois Papers, Special Collections and Archives, W. E. B. Du Bois Library, University of Massachusetts, Amherst

Introduction

1. See James A. Banks, "Multicultural Education: Historical Development, Dimensions, and Practice," in Banks, ed. *Handbook of Research on Multicultural Education* (San Francisco: Jossey-Bass, 2001), 7, and Fred Schultz, ed., *Annual Editions: Multicultural Education 06/07* (Guilford, Conn.: McGraw-Hill, 2006), iv. To date, the most thorough accounts of early antiprejudice work examine the schools. Particularly valuable are Nicholas V. Montalto, *A History of the Intercultural Education Movement, 1924–1941* (New York: Garland, 1982), and Jonathan Zimmerman, *Whose America? Culture Wars in the Public Schools* (Cambridge: Harvard University Press, 2002).

2. Matthew Frye Jacobson, *Whiteness of a Different Color: European Immigrants and the Alchemy of Race* (Cambridge: Harvard University Press, 1998), especially chap. 3. While I build on Jacobson's analysis, I put greater emphasis on conscious efforts to maintain European ethnic identities. In this regard, I follow Eric Arnesen's suggestion that historians include concrete evidence and empirical archival work as they study the concept of whiteness and specify the agents identifying racial categories. See Arnesen, "Whiteness and the Historians' Imagination," and responses by six scholars, *International Labor and Working-Class History* 60 (Fall 2001).

3. Rachel Davis DuBois, *Adventures in Intercultural Education* (New York: Progressive Education Association, 1938), 2–3.

4. My use of the term "ethnoracial" follows David Hollinger in "American Ethnoracial History and the Amalgamation Narrative," *Journal of American Ethnic History* 25 (Summer 2006): 153–159.

5. For depictions of the 1920s as a reactionary decade, see John Higham, *Strangers in the Land: Patterns of American Nativism, 1860–1925* (New Brunswick, N.J.: Rutgers University Press, 1955), and Stanley Coben, *Rebellion against Victorianism: The Impetus for Cultural Change in 1920s America* (New York: Oxford University Press, 1991). On varied responses to cultural conflicts of the era, see Lynn Dumenil, *The Modern Temper:*

American Culture and Society in the 1920s (New York: Hill and Wang, 1995), and David J. Goldberg, *Discontented America: The United States in the 1920s* (Baltimore: Johns Hopkins University Press, 1999).

6. David Hollinger, "Ethnic Diversity, Cosmopolitanism, and the Emergence of the American Liberal Intelligentsia," in Hollinger's *In the American Province: Studies in the History and Historiography of Ideas* (Bloomington: Indiana University Press, 1985), 56–73; John Higham, "Ethnic Pluralism in Modern American Thought," in Higham's *Send These to Me: Immigrants in Urban America* (1975), rev. ed. (Baltimore: Johns Hopkins University Press, 1984), 198–232.

7. Rachel Davis DuBois, "What American Culture Might Become," draft of League of Women Voters speech, San Francisco, 1935, box 12, folder 10, RDD. (Rachel Davis DuBois was no relation to W. E. B. Du Bois.)

8. Bruno Lasker, notes for lecture, "Race Attitudes in Children," Albany, 28 January 1928, notebook 5, 33–34, Lasker Papers. John Higham notes that the passage of restriction laws lessened anti-immigrant sentiment and facilitated the process of assimilation. See "The Politics of Immigration Restriction," in Higham's *Send These to Me*, 58–60.

9. Quoted in Katherine Gardner, "Changing Racial Attitudes," *Crisis* 38 (October 1931): 336.

10. Akira Iriye, *Cultural Internationalism and World Order* (Baltimore: Johns Hopkins University Press, 1997).

11. Gary Gerstle, *American Crucible: Race and Nation in the Twentieth Century* (Princeton, N.J.: Princeton University Press, 2001).

12. Gary Gerstle, "The Protean Character of American Liberalism," *American Historical Review* 99 (October 1994): 1043–1073.

13. Ellsworth Faris, "Racial Attitudes and Sentiments," *Southwestern Political and Social Science Quarterly* 9 (March 1929): 485.

14. R. B. Eleazar, form letter, n.d. [c. 1931], file V:122, CIC.

15. DuBois, *Adventures*, 11.

16. Patricia Sullivan, *Days of Hope: Race and Democracy in the New Deal Era* (Chapel Hill: University of North Carolina Press, 1996); Richard Weiss, "Ethnicity and Reform: Minorities and the Ambiance of the Depression Years," *Journal of American History* 66 (December 1979): 566–585.

17. In *American Crucible*, Gerstle terms this competing tradition "racial nationalism."

18. On the silence of both Americanizers and their critics in regard to black Americans, see Nathan Glazer, *We Are All Multiculturalists Now* (Cambridge: Harvard University Press, 1997), chap. 6.

19. Bruno Lasker, *Race Attitudes in Children* (New York: Holt, 1929), 63–78, 115–135.

20. Charles S. Johnson, "On the Need of Realism in Negro Education," *Journal of Negro Education* 5 (July 1936): 375–382.

21. John Dollard et al., *Frustration and Aggression* (New Haven, Conn.: Yale University Press, 1939); T. W. Adorno et al., *The Authoritarian Personality* (New York: Norton, 1950).

1. Searching for the Origins of Prejudice

1. Bruno Lasker, *Race Attitudes in Children* (New York: Holt, 1929), 56–57.

2. George M. Fredrickson, *The Black Image in the White Mind: The Debate on Afro-American Character and Destiny, 1817–1914* (Middletown, Conn.: Wesleyan University Press, 1971), chap. 4; Edward W. Blyden, *Christianity, Islam and the Negro Race* (1887; reprint, Edinburgh: University Press, 1967), 277–278; Wilson Jeremiah Moses, *The Golden Age of Black Nationalism, 1850–1925* (Hamden, Conn.: Archon, 1978).

3. John Dewey, "The School as Social Center," *Elementary School Teacher* 3 (October 1902): 78; Raymond A. Mohl, "The International Institutes and Immigrant Education, 1910–40," in *American Education and the European Immigrant: 1840–1940*, ed. Bernard J. Weiss (Urbana: University of Illinois Press, 1982), 117–141, and "Cultural Pluralism in Immigrant Education: The International Institutes of Boston, Philadelphia, and San Francisco, 1920–1940," *Journal of American Ethnic History* 1 (Spring 1982): 35–58.

4. Jane Addams, *Twenty Years at Hull-House* (1910; reissue, Chicago: University of Illinois Press, 1990), 136–150; *Tenth Annual Report of the College Settlements Association* (Boston: A. Y. Bliss, 1899), 49.

5. On changing views of the child, see Paula S. Fass and Mary Ann Mason, eds., *Childhood in America* (New York: New York University Press, 2000), and Steven Mintz, *Huck's Raft: A History of American Childhood* (Cambridge: Harvard University Press, 2004).

6. Lyford P. Edwards, "Religious Sectarianism and Race Prejudice," *American Journal of Sociology* 41 (September 1935): 173.

7. Lee D. Baker, *From Savage to Negro: Anthropology and the Construction of Race, 1896–1954* (Berkeley: University of California Press, 1998), chap. 5; Vernon J. Williams Jr., *Rethinking Race: Franz Boas and His Contemporaries* (Lexington: University Press of Kentucky, 1996); Richard Handler, "Boasian Anthropology and the Critique of American Culture," *American Quarterly* 42 (June 1990): 252–273; Marshall Hyatt, "Franz Boas and the Struggle for Black Equality: The Dynamics of Ethnicity," *Perspectives in American History*, new ser. 2 (1985): 269–295.

8. W. E. B. Du Bois, "The Conservation of Races," in *The Oxford W. E. B. Du Bois*

Reader, ed. Eric J. Sundquist (New York: Oxford University Press, 1996), 38–47, and *The Souls of Black Folk* (1903; reprint, New York: Random House, 1998), 265; Baker, *From Savage to Negro,* chap. 5; Matthew Pratt Guterl, *The Color of Race in America, 1900–1940* (Cambridge: Harvard University Press, 2001), chap. 3.

9. W. E. B. Du Bois, *The Gift of Black Folk* (Boston: Stratford, 1924; reprint, Millwood, N.Y.: Kraus-Thomson, 1975), ii, 135, 320.

10. Joseph C. Carroll, "The Race Problem," *Journal of Applied Sociology* 11 (January–February 1927): 266–271.

11. On Hall, see Ann Hulbert, *Raising America: Experts, Parents, and a Century of Advice about Children* (New York: Knopf, 2003); Sheldon H. White, "Child Study at Clark University, 1894–1904," *Journal of the History of the Behavioral Sciences* 26 (April 1990): 131–150; Dorothy Ross, *G. Stanley Hall: The Psychologist as Prophet* (Chicago: University of Chicago Press, 1972).

12. William I. Thomas, "The Psychology of Race-Prejudice," *American Journal of Sociology* 9 (March 1904): 607–611; Alfred Holt Stone, "Is Race Friction between Blacks and Whites in the United States Growing and Inevitable?" *American Journal of Sociology* 13 (March 1908): 676–697 (of eight responses in the following issue, none challenged Stone's assertion); Franklin Henry Giddings, *The Principles of Sociology* (1896) (New York: Macmillan, 1916), 18. Not all social scientists accepted the instinctive view in full; see George W. Ellis, "The Psychology of American Race Prejudice," *Journal of Race Development* 5 (January 1915): 297–315. Ellis described a "natural antipathy" to strangers that became more permanent through social forces. Also see Jerome Dowd, "Race Segregation in a World of Democracy," *Publications of the American Sociological Society* 14 (December 1919): 189–203, and Robert Park's response.

13. John B. Watson, *Behaviorism* (New York: Norton, 1924), 74, emphasis in original. See Hamilton Cravens, "Behaviorism Revisited: Developmental Science, the Maturation Theory, and the Biological Basis of the Human Mind, 1920s–1950s," in *The Expansion of American Biology,* ed. Keith R. Benson, Jane Maienschein, and Ronald Rainger (New Brunswick, N.J.: Rutgers University Press, 1991), 133–163.

14. Watson, *Behaviorism,* 131–139, 157–158, 239–242, emphasis in original.

15. Ibid., 38, 76, 82, 240, 248.

16. John B. Watson with Rosalie Rayner Watson, *Psychological Care of Infant and Child* (New York: Norton, 1928), 9, 38–45.

17. *Ibid.,* 81–87.

18. On Watson, see for example Hulbert, *Raising America,* chap. 5, and Kerry W. Buckley, *Mechanical Man: John Broadus Watson and the Beginnings of Behaviorism* (New York: Guilford, 1989).

19. On mothers' responses to behaviorism see Julia Grant, *Raising Baby by the Book: The Education of American Mothers* (New Haven, Conn.: Yale University Press, 1998), chap. 5.

20. For example, Ann Hulbert details Watson's "routinized, depersonalized approach," his "extreme theory," and his "harsh ban on intimacy," all of which aimed "to intimidate, infuriate, and titillate mothers," in *Raising America*, 140–144; Fred Matthews describes Watson's "horror of affection and stridently mechanical view of human nature" in "The Utopia of Human Relations: The Conflict-Free Family in American Social Thought," *Journal of the History of the Behavioral Sciences* 24 (October 1988): 346.

21. Kelly Miller, "Is Race Prejudice Innate or Acquired?" *Journal of Applied Sociology* 11 (July–August 1927): 516–524.

22. Ellsworth Faris, "Racial Attitudes and Sentiments," *Southwestern Political and Social Science Quarterly* 9 (March 1929): 479–490. Also see John P. Jackson Jr., *Social Scientists for Social Justice: Making the Case against Segregation* (New York: New York University Press, 2001), chap. 2, and Hamilton Cravens, *The Triumph of Evolution: The Heredity-Environment Controversy, 1900–1941* (Baltimore: Johns Hopkins University Press, 1988), chap. 6.

23. J. Hayden Kershner, "Race Prejudice a Form of Group Prejudice," *Journal of Applied Sociology* 11 (May–June 1927): 446–452.

24. Emory S. Bogardus, *Immigration and Race Attitudes* (Boston: D. C. Heath, 1928), 44, 65–66, 94, 174–183, "Social Distance and Its Origins," *Journal of Applied Sociology* 9 (January–February 1925): 216–226, "Measuring Social Distances," *Journal of Applied Sociology* 9 (March–April 1925): 299–308, and "Race Friendliness and Social Distance," *Journal of Applied Sociology* 11 (January–February 1927); Daniel Katz and Kenneth Braly, "Racial Prejudice and Racial Stereotypes," *Journal of Abnormal and Social Psychology* 30 (July–September 1935): 175–193.

25. Rhoda E. McCulloch, *And Who Is My Neighbor? An Outline for the Study of Race Relations in America* (New York: Association, 1924); Bruno Lasker, ed., *Jewish Experiences in America: Suggestions for the Study of Jewish Relations with Non-Jews* (New York: Inquiry, 1930); Julius Drachsler, "Prejudice as a Social Phenomenon," transcript and abstract of presentation, 30 January 1925, notebook 3, 39–40, 50–51, Lasker Papers.

26. Bruno Lasker, "As I See It," *Brooklyn Central*, notebook 6, 346–348, Lasker Papers. On Lasker, see *Who's Who in America*, vol. 17, 1932–33 (Chicago: A. N. Marquis, 1932), 1375.

27. "Reminiscences of Bruno Lasker," 246–247; Lasker, *Race Attitudes in Children*, xvi; "A Meeting of the Race Commission's Subcommittee on Children and Race Prejudice," 29 January 1925, letter 16 March 1925 and

questionnaire on "Race Attitudes in Children" and "Some Illustrative Incidents," all in notebook 3, 19–26, 101–108, Lasker Papers.

28. Minutes of committee meetings, 29 January 1925, 12 November 1925, notebook 3, 23 and 67; "Race Attitudes in Children: A History of the Study Project," 13 November 1928, notebook 5, 266; B. L. to A. D. S., 20 August 1926, notebook 4, 111–113; Bruno Lasker to Rose Zeligs, 8 December 1930, notebook 7, 131, all in Lasker Papers.

29. "Minutes of Third Meeting, Committee on Race Attitudes in Children," 12 November 1925, notebook 3, 234–235; "And Who Is My Neighbor?" Yorkville Neighborhood Council, 8 February 1926, notebook 4, 5–10; "Race Attitudes in Children: A History of the Study Project," 267, all in Lasker Papers.

30. "A Meeting of the Race Commission's Subcommittee," 23.

31. Lasker, *Race Attitudes in Children,* 17–18, 253–257, and *Jewish Experiences in America,* ix–x.

32. Lasker, *Race Attitudes in Children,* 35, 42, 48, 55–62, 262, 370.

33. Drachsler, "Prejudice as a Social Phenomenon"; Lasker, *Race Attitudes in Children,* 63–78, 94, 270–277, 370–377. This conclusion agreed with Bogardus's research, which showed that contact did not necessarily increase tolerance.

34. "A Meeting of the Race Commission's Subcommittee," 20; Bruno Lasker, "Race Attitudes in Children," *Woman's Press* (May 1926): 332–334.

35. Lasker, "Race Attitudes in Children," *Woman's Press,* 334.

36. Bruno Lasker, "Can Race Tolerance Be Taught?" *Woman's Press* (September 1926): 608–611; "Childhood Prejudices," (radio talk), 22 March 1929, notebook 6, 10; Bruno Lasker to Mary Frances Hedges, 13 September 1938, notebook 15, 65–66, both in Lasker Papers.

37. Lasker, "Can Race Tolerance Be Taught?" 611; "Childhood Prejudices" (radio talk), 8; "And Who Is My Neighbor?" 10.

38. Lasker, *Race Attitudes in Children,* 115–124.

39. Lasker, "Race Attitudes in Children," *Woman's Press,* 332; "And Who Is My Neighbor?" 10.

40. Lasker, *Race Attitudes in Children,* 63–78, 94, 125–135, 298–299; "Childhood Prejudices" (radio talk).

41. Ralph D. Minard, "Race Attitudes of Iowa Children," *University of Iowa Studies in Character* 4 (1931): 20, 60–63, 97–98.

42. Bruno Lasker to Rose Zeligs, 8 December 1930, notebook 7, 131, Lasker Papers.

43. See the following by Rose Zeligs and Gordon Hendrickson in *Sociology and Social Research:* "Racial Attitudes of Two Hundred Sixth-Grade Children" 18 (September–October 1933): 26–36, "Checking the Social Distance

Technique through Personal Interviews" 18 (May–June 1934): 420–430, and "Factors Regarded by Children as the Basis of Their Racial Attitudes" 19 (January–February 1935): 225–233. Also see Rose Zeligs, "Racial Attitudes of Children as Expressed by Their Concepts of Races," *Sociology and Social Research* 21 (March–April 1937): 361–371, and "Children's Intergroup Attitudes," *Journal of Genetic Psychology* 72 (March 1948): 101–110.

44. Rose Zeligs, "Tracing Racial Attitudes through Adolescence," *Sociology and Social Research* 23 (September–October 1938): 45–54, and *Glimpses into Child Life* (New York: Morrow, 1942), 250–276.

45. Lasker, *Race Attitudes in Children,* 377–378; emphasis in original.

46. See for example Robert L. Duffus, "Where Do We Get Our Prejudices?" *Harper's* 153 (September 1926): 503–508; Beatrice M. Hinkle, "Psychological Tendencies of the Pre-school Child and Its Relation to the New World Order," *Progressive Education* 2 (April–May–June 1925): 62–67; James Weldon Johnson, "A Negro Looks at Race Prejudice," *American Mercury* 14 (May 1928): 54.

2. Parent Education and the Teaching of Tolerance

1. "Tolerant Childhood," *Children* 1 (October 1926): 51, from *Woman's Home Companion.* The publication *Children* changed its name to *Parents' Magazine* in 1929.

2. Helen L. Kaufmann, "Should We Hand-Pick Our Children's Friends?" *Parents' Magazine* 4 (August 1929): 17.

3. Lasker, *Race Attitudes in Children* (New York: Holt, 1929), 93, 371–372.

4. Ibid., 116, 273–291; Bruno Lasker, "What Shall I Do as a Parent?" Note on talk to Committee on Race Relations, Society of Friends, Philadelphia, 22 October 1929, notebook 6, 381–382, Lasker Papers.

5. "Minutes of Third Meeting, Committee on Race Attitudes in Children," 12 November 1925, notebook 3, 235–236, Lasker Papers; Bruno Lasker, "Race Attitudes in Children," *Woman's Press* (May 1926): 333, and *Race Attitudes in Children,* xi, 277–290; Lyford P. Edwards, "Religious Sectarianism and Race Prejudice," *American Journal of Sociology* 41 (September 1935): 174–175.

6. Lawrence K. Frank, "Childhood and Youth," in *Recent Social Trends in the United States* in the report of the President's Research Committee on Social Trends (New York: McGraw Hill, 1933), 751–800.

7. On the parent education movement see Julia Grant, *Raising Baby by the Book: The Education of American Mothers* (New Haven, Conn.: Yale University Press, 1998); Ann Hulbert, *Raising America: Experts, Parents, and a Century of Advice about Children* (New York: Knopf, 2003); Hamilton

Cravens, "Child-Saving in the Age of Professionalism, 1915–1930," in *American Childhood: A Research Guide and Historical Handbook*, ed. Joseph M. Hawes and N. Ray Hiner (Westport, Conn.: Greenwood, 1985), 415–488; and three articles by Steven L. Schlossman: "The Formative Era in Parent Education: Overview and Interpretation," in *Parent Education and Public Policy*, ed. Ron Haskins and Diane Adams (Norwood, N.J.: Ablex, 1983), 7–39, "Philanthropy and the Gospel of Child Development," *History of Education Quarterly* 21 (Fall 1981): 275–299, and "Before Home Start: Notes toward a History of Parent Education in America, 1897–1929," *Harvard Educational Review* 46 (August 1976): 426–467.

8. Judith Clark, "Extent and Scope" in White House Conference on Child Health and Protection, *Parent Education* (New York: Century, 1932), 41.

9. *Developing Attitudes in Children*, Proceedings of the Mid-West Conference of the Chicago Association for Child Study and Parent Education, March 1932 (Chicago: University of Chicago Press, 1932), 20–40, 67–83; "Child Study Conference of 1932," *Religious Education* 27 (April 1932): 300.

10. On the CSA, see Grant, *Raising Baby by the Book*, 48–54, and Judith Sealander, *Private Wealth and Public Life: Foundation Philanthropy and the Reshaping of American Social Policy from the Progressive Era to the New Deal* (Baltimore: Johns Hopkins University Press, 1997), chap. 3.

11. For examples, see Sidonie Matsner Gruenberg, "How New Psychologies Affect Parental Practices," and Joseph Jastrow, "What Have the New Psychologies to Offer Parents?" *Child Study* 6 (October 1928): 3–6, 11–13.

12. Lasker, *Race Attitudes in Children*, 331; "Parents' Questions," *Child Study* 8 (December 1930): 109; notes on interview with Mrs. Benjamin C. Gruenberg, 25 November 1924, notebook 1, 173–174, Lasker Papers; Sidonie Matsner Gruenberg, "Twigs of Prejudice," *Survey* 56 (1 September 1926): 586–588, and "Parents as Interpreters in a Changing World," *Child Study* 6 (February 1929): 118.

13. "Race Prejudices in Children," conference, 12 March 1929, and "Childhood Prejudices," (radio talk), 22 March 1929, both in notebook 6, 61–73, Lasker Papers; Bruno Lasker, "Childhood Prejudices," *Child Study* 6 (February 1929): 107–109; Dorothy Crane Vaughan, review of *Race Attitudes in Children*, by Bruno Lasker, *Child Study* 7 (January 1930): 120; V. T. Thayer, "Children in a Changing World," *Child Study* 11 (November 1933): 35–36.

14. "Parents' Questions," *Child Study* 5 (October 1927): 13; "News and Notes," *Child Study* 6 (April 1929): 185; "Study Material: The Development of Social Attitudes," *Child Study* 11 (November 1933): 48; Bruno Lasker, "How to Correct Anti-Semitism among Jewish Children," in *Jewish Experiences in America: Suggestions for the Study of Jewish Relations with Non-Jews*, ed. Bruno Lasker (New York: Inquiry, 1930), 111–120.

15. Child Study Association of America, *Parents' Questions* (New York: Harper, 1936), 207–208; Gruenberg, "Twigs of Prejudice," 587; "Parents' Questions," *Child Study* 7 (January 1930): 118, and "Parents' Questions," *Child Study* 16 (May 1939): 194.

16. Gruenberg, "Twigs of Prejudice," 587; "Parents' Questions," *Child Study* 6 (February 1929): 126.

17. Bruno Lasker, "And Who Is My Neighbor?" Yorkville Neighborhood Council, 8 February 1926, notebook 4, 8, Lasker Papers.

18. Ibid., 10, and "Childhood Prejudices" (radio talk), 69.

19. "And Who Is My Neighbor?" 10–11; Lasker, "Can Race Tolerance Be Taught?" 610.

20. "Widening the Circle of Understanding," *Child Study* 2 (December 1925): 8; Gruenberg, "Twigs of Prejudice," 586; "Study Material," 48.

21. Gruenberg, "Twigs of Prejudice," 588; Child Study Association, *Parents' Questions*, 201–202.

22. Child Study Association, *Parents' Questions*, 202–203.

23. Grant, *Raising Baby by the Book*, 95–107.

24. "Child Study and Race Relationships," *Child Study* 7 (December 1929): 81; "Inter-community Child Study Committee," *Child Study* 7 (July 1930): 309; Grant, *Raising Baby by the Book,* 99.

25. "Parents' Questions," *Child Study* 6 (February 1929): 126; Lasker, "Childhood Prejudices," *Child Study,* 107.

26. "Study Material," 48.

27. Lasker, "Childhood Prejudices," *Child Study,* 108.

28. Charles E. Carson, "An Antidote for Racial Prejudice," *Crisis* 41 (June 1934): 163.

29. Spelman College Progress Report, 8 December 1931, folder 414, box 39, series 3.5, LSRM; W. McKinley Menchan, "Parent Education in a Negro College," *School and Society* 37 (3 June 1933): 713; Grant, *Raising Baby by the Book,* 107.

30. William Pickens, "Racial Segregation," *Opportunity* 5 (December 1927): 364. Also see Jennifer Ritterhouse, *Growing up Jim Crow: How Black and White Southern Children Learned Race* (Chapel Hill: University of North Carolina Press, 2006).

31. Eva Knox Evans, "Truth or Evasion for the Negro Child?" *Opportunity* 15 (June 1937): 172; Mary White Ovington, "Revisiting the South," *Crisis* 34 (April 1937): 60.

32. Evans, "Truth or Evasion for the Negro Child?" 173–174.

33. Cecelia Eggleston, "What a Negro Mother Faces," *Forum* 100 (August 1938): 59, emphasis in original; "The White House Conference," *Opportunity* 8 (March 1930): 71.

34. Clara Savage Littledale, "Then and Now," *Parents' Magazine* (October 1946): 18; Steven Schlossman, "Perils of Popularization: The Founding of *Parents' Magazine* in *History and Research in Child Development: Monographs of the Society for Research in Child Development* 50 (1986), 65–77.
35. Martha L. Fischer, "Character Education in Magazines for Parents," *Religious Education* 27 (November 1932): 785–792; graph of subscription growth, *Children* 2 (October 1927): 10. See the following in *Parents' Magazine:* George J. Hecht, "Re-Dedication" 6 (October 1931): 10; "We Celebrate Our Ninth Birthday" 10 (October 1935): 15; George J. Hecht, "A Re-Dedication" 11 (October 1936): 15; Mary E. Buchanan, "Our First Twenty Years" 21 (October 1946): 168.
36. "Publisher's Statement: Period Ending Dec. 31, 1930," folder 393, box 37, series 3.5, LSRM. The political affiliations of the magazine's readers can be inferred from results of a "junior poll" in 1936. The magazine instructed readers to tell their children about the presidential campaign and have them vote for a candidate. Landon received 58 percent of the children's votes, while Roosevelt received only 39 percent. If children's political views reflected those of their parents—who had described the issues to their offspring—the majority of subscribers were probably the white, native-born, middle-class Republicans and conservative Democrats who opposed the New Deal. In an election unusually focused on class, the children's preference indicates the conservative leanings and middle-class status of the magazine's readership. See "Let Your Youngsters Vote!" *Parents' Magazine* 11 (September 1936): 28 and "Landon Leads!" *Parents' Magazine* 11 (November 1936): 14.
37. Cravens, "Child-Saving in the Age of Professionalism"; Schlossman, "Before Home Start," 452, and Grant, *Raising Baby by the Book,* chap. 2.
38. On Hecht, see Schlossman, "Perils of Popularization," 65–77. Hecht served as publisher and president for over fifty years; see *Parents' Magazine* 51 (October 1976): 10.
39. For more on Littledale, see *Who's Who in America 1946–47* (Chicago: A. N. Marquis, 1947); Ellen Condliffe Lagemann, "Littledale, Clara Savage" in *Notable American Women: The Modern Period,* ed. Barbara Sicherman and Carol Hurd Green (Cambridge: Harvard University Press, 1980), 421–423; obituary, *New York Times,* 10 January 1956.
40. Clara Savage Littledale, "We Celebrate Fourth of July," *Parents' Magazine* 12 (July 1937): 151; Margaret Mead, "South Sea Hints on Bringing up Children," *Parents' Magazine* 4 (September 1929): 20; "Water Babies of the South Seas," *Parents' Magazine* 5 (September 1930): 20; "South Sea Tips on Character Training," *Parents' Magazine* 7 (March 1932): 13; "Five Decades of Writing for *Parents' Magazine,*" *Parents' Magazine* 51 (October 1976): 44.

41. "Tolerant Childhood," 51. *Parents' Magazine* published an interview with Watson, "What to Do When Your Child Is Afraid," 2 (March 1927), and an article by his wife, Rosalie Rayner Watson, "I Am the Mother of a Behaviorist's Sons" 5 (December 1930), as well as pieces by other behaviorists. Littledale repudiated the emphasis on habit training in "Can We Make Them Good?" *Parents' Magazine* 12 (August 1937): 15, and "Then and Now," *Parents' Magazine* 21 (October 1946): 18.

42. Bruno Lasker, "How Children Acquire Race Prejudice," *Children* 3 (March 1928): 23; "Books for Parents," *Parents' Magazine* 4 (December 1929): 76; John Palmer Gavit, "Plain Talk about Race Prejudice," *Parents' Magazine* 13 (February 1938): 82.

43. Littledale to Marion Savage Sabin, 2 December 1918, folder 56, box 3, Littledale Papers; Clara Savage Littledale, "How Teach Peace?" *Parents' Magazine* 12 (January 1937): 13. On world-thinking, see the following in *Parents' Magazine:* Florence Brewer Boeckel, "Education Races with Catastrophe" (May 1927): 13; editorial, "Young Citizens of the World" (August 1927): 7; Norman Thomas, "Mothers, Fathers, and World Peace" (May 1928): 11; Walter Van Kirk, "Will Our Sons Go to War?" (January 1932): 9. Also see Akira Iriye, *Cultural Internationalism and World Order* (Baltimore: Johns Hopkins University Press, 1997), and Diana Selig, "World Friendship: Children, Parents, and Peace Education in America between the Wars," in *Children and War,* ed. James Marten (New York: New York University Press, 2002), 135–146.

44. Helen K. Champlin, "Will Our Children Outlaw War?" *Parents' Magazine* 8 (July 1933): 14; Elizabeth Cleveland, "If Parents Only Knew—" *Children* 3 (April 1928): 17.

45. Rachel Dunaway Cox, "World Friendship among Children," *Parents' Magazine* 5 (July 1930): 16; Sophia Lyon Fahs, "Enlarging Our Children's World," *Parents' Magazine* 12 (June 1937): 27.

46. For examples see Champlin, "Will Our Children Outlaw War?" and the following in *Parents' Magazine:* Gustavus S. Paine, "Youth and the New Patriotism" (July 1928): 9; Cox, "World Friendship," 16; Frances Frisbie O'Donnell, "Educating for Peace" (July 1931): 15; Solomon B. Freehof, "These Things a Child Should Know" (February 1936): 11; Margaret Stroh Hipps, "Mothers Can Work for Peace" (May 1938): 21. The "Felt-O-Gram Mishe" is in "Playthings of the Month" (February 1936): 85.

47. Transcription of radio talk, n.d., folder 39, box 3, Littledale Papers; Mrs. Franklin D. Roosevelt, "Books I Loved as a Child," *Children* 3 (December 1928): 15. Also see Clara Savage Littledale, "Give Your Child Happy Memories," 30 September 1932, and reply from Ella C. Quest, 18 November 1932, folder 42, box 2, Littledale Papers. Littledale's writings on travel in-

clude "Invitation to Travel," *Parents' Magazine* 13 (April 1938): 15, and "Travel Together," *Parents' Magazine* 14 (April 1939): 17.

48. Joyce Evans Green, "A Tribute to My Mother," *Parents' Magazine* 8 (March 1933): 29; Mildred W. Stillman, "The Home Altar," *Parents' Magazine* 2 (October 1927): 15, and "Living the Christmas Spirit," *Parents' Magazine* 8 (December 1933): 13.

49. Rose Zeligs, "Teach Your Child Tolerance," *Parents' Magazine* 9 (August 1934): 15; Fahs, "Enlarging Our Children's World," 26; Ernest Osborne, "The Family's Contributions to Democracy," *Parents' Magazine* 12 (November 1937): 84.

50. Gavit, "Plain Talk about Race Prejudice," 15; Hester Cushing Daly, "What Happens to Our Children?" *Parents' Magazine* 14 (November 1939): 15; Marion LeBron, "Mothers Need to Get Together," *Parents' Magazine* 13 (September 1938): 26; Kaufmann, "Should We Hand-Pick Our Children's Friends?" 16.

51. Anna W. M. Wolf, "Study Course on the School-Age Child," *Parents' Magazine* 12 (June 1937): 105 and 14 (March 1939): 97.

52. For example, see the *Parents' Magazine* column "Pointers for Parents," with submissions from Mrs. E. E. E. (May 1930): 60, and from L. P. S. (April 1932): 44.

53. Champlin, "Will Our Children Outlaw War?" 51. On how "mothers make wars," see Ezra Kempton Maxfield, "Education and World Peace," *Religious Education* 26 (September 1931): 550. On mother-blaming see Ruth Feldstein, *Motherhood in Black and White: Race and Sex in American Liberalism, 1930–1965* (Ithaca, N.Y.: Cornell University Press, 2000).

54. Janet M. Knopf, "Worthwhile Play," *Parents' Magazine* 6 (June 1931): 30, 70–71.

55. Constance Lindsay Skinner, "Our Children's Indian Heritage," *Parents' Magazine* 8 (October 1933): 16–17, 54–55; Philip J. Deloria, *Playing Indian* (New Haven, Conn.: Yale University Press, 1998), chap. 4. Recapitulation theory asserted that the stages of individual development mirrored the evolution of the species from primitive to civilized life.

56. "Playthings of the Month," *Parents' Magazine* 11 (March 1936): 65; Mrs. J. P. W., in "Pointers for Parents," *Parents' Magazine* 8 (November 1933): 55; A. P. C., Denver, Colo., in "Family Fun and Things for Children to Do and Make," *Parents' Magazine* 5 (August 1930): 55.

57. Beatrice Black, "Motion Pictures for Children," *Children* 3 (January 1928): 30; Daly, "What Happens to Our Children?" 15.

58. Photo by H. Armstrong Roberts, "Americans in the Making," *Children* 2 (July 1927): 26; also see Elizabeth McFadden, "Dey's All Got Debbils!" *Parents' Magazine* 4 (October 1929): 22. Lasker, "Childhood Prejudices"

(radio talk), 70; "Parents' Magazine Honors Three Youth Leaders," *Parents' Magazine* 15 (May 1940): 101; C. Madeleine Dixon, "Democracy before Five!" *Parents' Magazine* 17 (August 1942): 24–25.

59. See the following in *Parents' Magazine*: Ruth Sapin, "For Better or Worse— Servants Influence Children" (January 1929): 20; illustration by Walter Van Arsdale for Mary Ormsbee Whitton, "So Early Monday Morning" (November 1930): 28; ad for Ivory Soap (October 1934): 13; "Childhood Problems and Ways to Meet Them" (August 1935): 66; Mary French Caldwell, "The Commonest Thing" (December 1935): 50; "Things for Children to Do and to Make" (November 1929): 90, and "Things for Them to Do" (January 1935): 65.

60. Bruno Lasker to Rose Zeligs, 8 December 1930, notebook 7, 131, Lasker Papers.

3. Cultural Gifts in the Schools

1. David Tyack, *Seeking Common Ground: Public Schools in a Diverse Society* (Cambridge: Harvard University Press, 2003); Paula S. Fass, *Outside In: Minorities and the Transformation of American Education* (New York: Oxford University Press, 1989).

2. My understanding of DuBois is indebted to the work of Nicholas V. Montalto, especially *A History of the Intercultural Education Movement, 1924–1941* (New York: Garland, 1982). Also see his articles "The Intercultural Education Movement, 1924–41: The Growth of Tolerance as a Form of Intolerance," in *American Education and the European Immigrant: 1840–1940,* ed. Bernard J. Weiss (Urbana: University of Illinois Press, 1982), 142–160, and "Multicultural Education in the New York City Public Schools, 1919–1941," in *Educating an Urban People: The New York City Experience,* ed. Diane Ravitch and Ronald Goodenow (New York: Teachers College Press, 1981), 67–83. Other discussions of DuBois include Cherry A. McGee Banks, *Improving Multicultural Education: Lessons from the Intergroup Education Movement* (New York: Teachers College Press, 2005); George A. Crispin, "Rachel Davis DuBois: Founder of the Group Conversation as an Adult Educational Facilitator for Reducing Intercultural Strife" (Ed.D. diss., Temple University, 1987); O. L. Davis Jr., "Rachel Davis DuBois: Intercultural Education Pioneer," in *"Bending the Future to Their Will": Civic Women, Social Education, and Democracy,* ed. Margaret Smith Crocco and O. L. Davis Jr. (Lanham, Md.: Rowman and Littlefield, 1999), 169–183; Shafali Lal, "1930s Multiculturalism: Rachel Davis DuBois and the Bureau for Intercultural Education," *Radical Teacher* 69 (Spring 2004): 18–22.

3. Rachel Davis DuBois with Corann Okorodudu, *All This and Something*

More: Pioneering in Intercultural Education (Bryn Mawr, Pa.: Dorrance, 1984), chap. 1, 105.

4. On DuBois's peace work see Melinda Ann Plastas, "'A Band of Noble Women': The WILPF and the Politics and Consciousness of Race in the Women's Peace Movement, 1915–1945" (Ph.D. diss., State University of New York, Buffalo, 2001).

5. Edward Yeomans, "The Undernourished Soul," *Progressive Education* 2 (April–May–June 1925): 57–62; Thomas Woody, "Nationalistic Education and Beyond," *Educational Review* 76 (September 1928): 99–110; "Education and Nationalism," special issue, *Journal of Educational Sociology* 9 (March 1936); "The Study of International Relations within Formal Education," in *The Study of International Relations in the United States: Survey for 1937,* ed. Edith E. Ware (New York: Columbia University Press, 1938), 141–149.

6. DuBois, *All This,* 30–37. The article most likely was W. E. B. Du Bois, "The Dilemma of the Negro," *American Mercury* 3 (October 1924): 179–184. Rachel DuBois's memory was faulty, for the article was not published (or the magazine established) until several years after she recalled reading it.

7. DuBois, *All This,* 32–61, 69; Rachel Davis DuBois to W. E. B. Du Bois, 9 September 1927, WEBD Papers.

8. Paul M. Limbert, "What Children Think about War," *Progressive Education* 10 (February 1933): 67; Anne Biddle Stirling, "Interracial Teaching in the Schools," *Opportunity* 1 (March 1923): 7–8.

9. DuBois, *All This,* 47. On Rugg and textbook debates, see Joseph Moreau, *Schoolbook Nation: Conflicts over American History Textbooks from the Civil War to the Present* (Ann Arbor: University of Michigan Press, 2003), and Gary B. Nash, Charlotte Crabtree, and Ross E. Dunn, *History on Trial: Culture Wars and the Teaching of the Past* (New York: Knopf, 1997).

10. Desmond King, *Making Americans: Immigration, Race, and the Origins of the Diverse Democracy* (Cambridge: Harvard University Press, 2000), chap. 4; Diane Ravitch, "On the History of Minority Group Education in the United States," *Teachers College Record* 78 (December 1976): 213–228; M. J. Heale, *American Anticommunism: Combating the Enemy Within, 1830–1970* (Baltimore: Johns Hopkins University Press, 1990), 81–89; Jonathan Zimmerman, *Whose America? Culture Wars in the Public Schools* (Cambridge: Harvard University Press, 2002), 13.

11. Rachel Davis DuBois, "Hunters of the Reds," *Pax International* 2 (September 1927): 6.

12. DuBois, *All This,* 56–58; W. E. B. Du Bois to Rachel Davis DuBois, 7 June 1927, WEBD Papers; Rachel Davis DuBois to W. E. B. Du Bois, 13 July 1927, WEBD Papers; A. Philip Randolph to Rachel Davis DuBois, 15 November

1928, reprinted in Crispin, "Rachel Davis DuBois," 591–592; "Legion to Question Teacher on Loyalty," *New York Times* (21 May 1927): 22; "Teacher to Fight Legion's Charges," *New York Times* (22 May 1927): 24; "Will Ask Teacher About Patriotism," *New York Times* (24 May 1927): 14.

13. Rachel Davis DuBois, "The Value of Keeping Peace," *Friends Intelligencer* (Sixth Month 11, 1927): 474, and "The New Frontier," *Opportunity* 12 (February 1934): 40–41. For DuBois's accounts of the assembly program, also see "Developing Sympathetic Attitudes towards Peoples," *Journal of Sociology* 9 (March 1936): 387–396; "Practical Problems of International and Interracial Education," *Clearing House* 10 (April 1936): 486–490; "Intercultural Education at Benjamin Franklin High School," *High Points* 19 (December 1937): 23–29; "The Role of Home Economics in Intercultural Education," *Journal of Home Economics* 30 (March 1938): 145–149; *Build Together Americans* (New York: Hinds, Hayden, and Eldredge, 1945), 56–68.

14. Rachel Davis DuBois, "Building Tolerant Attitudes in High School Students," *Crisis* 38 (1931): 334; *Adventures in Intercultural Education* (New York: Progressive Education Association, 1938), 22–25; "Shall We Emotionalize Our Students?" *Friends Intelligencer* (Twelfth Month 3, 1932): 973–974; and "Our Enemy—The Stereotype," *Progressive Education* 12 (March 1935): 146–147.

15. DuBois, "The New Frontier," 40–41, and *All This,* 51–52.

16. DuBois, *Adventures,* 28–30, 52–60.

17. DuBois, "Shall We Emotionalize Our Students?" 974, *Adventures,* 30–31, "Developing Sympathetic Attitudes," 391, and "The New Frontier," 40.

18. DuBois, *Adventures,* 15. On ethnic responses to textbooks see Jonathan Zimmerman, *Whose America?* chap. 1, and "'Each "Race" Could Have Its Heroes Sung': Ethnicity and the History Wars in the 1920s," *Journal of American History* 87 (June 2000): 92–111.

19. Rachel Davis DuBois, "Danger or Promise?" speech at San Francisco Teachers College, 1936, 3–4, box 12, folder 10, RDD. Versions of this story appeared in DuBois, "Developing Sympathetic Attitudes," 387, "Sharing Cultural Values," *Journal of Educational Sociology* 12 (April 1939): 483, and "A Philosophy of Intercultural Relations," *World Order* 4 (April 1938): 138–142.

20. DuBois, "Developing Sympathetic Attitudes," 390, 392. DuBois repeated these examples elsewhere, including "The Role of Home Economics," 148, and *Adventures,* 33.

21. DuBois, "The Role of Home Economics," 147, "Developing Sympathetic Attitudes," 394, and *Adventures,* 17, 26–27.

22. Rachel Davis DuBois, "Shall We Emotionalize Our Students?" 974; "Danger or Promise," 5–6; "Americanizing Our American Public Schools," ra-

dio program, San Francisco, 6 November 1936, box 12, folder 10, RDD; "Appreciating Other Cultures," radio program, New York City, 17 April 1940, 4, box 13, folder 1, RDD.

23. Countee Cullen, "Incident," in *Color* (New York: Harper, 1925); Rachel Davis DuBois, "The Need for Sharing Cultural Values," *Friends Intelligencer* (Second Month 11, 1939): 84; "Sharing Cultural Values," 483; "The Role of Home Economics," 145; *All This,* 54; "The New Frontier," 41; *Adventures,* 6.

24. Rachel Davis DuBois, "The Value of Keeping Peace," 473–474; "Friends Schools and Sacred Cows," *Friends Intelligencer* (Sixth Month 13, 1931), 506–507.

25. Rachel Davis DuBois, *A Program in Education for World Mindedness* (Philadelphia: Women's International League for Peace and Freedom, n.d. [c. 1927]), box 2, folder 5, RDD; *Education in Worldmindedness* (Philadelphia: American Friends Service Committee, n.d. [c. 1928]), box 16, folder 1, RDD.

26. DuBois, *All This,* 6, 295; correspondence, box 3, folder 1, RDD; Rachel Davis DuBois, *Pioneers of the New World* (Philadelphia: Women's International League for Peace and Freedom, 1930), 10–21, box 16, folder 1, RDD.

27. Rachel Davis-DuBois, *Some Racial Contributions to America: A Study Online for Secondary Schools,* Philadelphia: Committee on Interests of the Colored Race, (Philadelphia Yearly Meeting of Friends, n.d. [c. 1928]), box 2, folder 5, RDD.

28. Rachel Davis DuBois to W. E. B. Du Bois, 10 March 1933, WEBD Papers.

29. Rachel Davis DuBois, autobiography, notes and drafts, box 9, folder 8, RDD; review of *Race Attitudes in Children,* by Bruno Lasker, *World Tomorrow* 12 (September 1929): 375.

30. Bruno Lasker, "Some Obstacles of Race Co-operation," *Opportunity* 3 (April 1925): 101–104; "Can Race Tolerance Be Taught?" *Woman's Press* (September 1926), 611; *Race Attitudes in Children* (New York: Holt, 1929), 146–170, 302–307, 334–336.

31. Bruno Lasker to Rachel Davis DuBois, 10 January 1929, box 3, folder 1, RDD; Bruno Lasker to Daniel H. Kulp, 13 December 1932, box 3, folder 2, RDD.

32. "Address of President Wilson," *Immigrants in America Review* 1 (1915): 30–32; Horace Kallen, "Democracy versus the Melting Pot," *Nation* 100 (18–25 February 1915): 190–194; Kallen, *Culture and Democracy in the United States* (New York: Boni and Liveright, 1924). On Kallen and cultural pluralism, see John Higham, "Ethnic Pluralism in Modern American Thought" in Higham, *Send These to Me: Immigrants in Urban America*

(1975), rev. ed. (Baltimore: Johns Hopkins University Press, 1984), 198–232, and writings by David A. Hollinger, including "Ethnic Diversity, Cosmopolitanism, and the Emergence of the American Liberal Intelligentsia" in Hollinger, *In the American Province: Studies in the History and Historiography of Ideas* (Bloomington: Indiana University Press, 1985), 56–73, and "Cultural Pluralism and Multiculturalism," in *A Companion to American Thought,* ed. Richard Wightman Fox and James T. Kloppenberg (Cambridge, England: Blackwell, 1995), 162–165.

33. Rachel Davis DuBois, "The Role of Home Economics," 145; *Adventures,* 3; "What American Culture Might Become," draft of speech to League of Women Voters, San Francisco, 1935, 17, box 12, folder 10, RDD.

34. Rachel Davis DuBois, "Appreciating Other Cultures," radio program, 3; "Our Enemy—The Stereotype," 146–147; "Can We Help to Create an American Renaissance?" *English Journal* 27 (November 1938): 733–740.

35. Rachel Davis DuBois, "Fitting the Child for the Modern World," address to Lehigh Valley Child Helping Conference, 19 May 1934, box 12, folder 10, RDD; "Practical Problems," 487; "Danger or Promise?" 9.

36. Rachel Davis DuBois, *All This,* 50–55, 88; "Sharing Cultural Values," 482; "Intercultural Education and Democracy's Defense," *Friends Intelligencer* (Second Month 1, 1941): 69; "Developing Sympathetic Attitudes," 391, emphasis in original.

37. Chang-Peng-Chun, "Inter-cultural Contacts and Creative Adjustment," *Progressive Education* 13 (November 1936): 515–520.

38. DuBois, "What American Culture Might Become," 16; "Danger or Promise?" 10.

39. DuBois, *Adventures,* 11–12. Also see Zimmerman, "'Each "Race" Could Have Its Heroes Sung,'" and *Whose America?* chap. 1.

40. DuBois, "What American Culture Might Become," 17.

41. Ibid., 16.

42. DuBois, "Danger or Promise?" 3; "Practical Problems," 490.

43. Rachel Davis DuBois to W. E. B. Du Bois, 30 December 1925, WEBD Papers; DuBois, *All This,* 68–69; "Why the Opposition to Our Work?" chapter draft for *All This,* box 9, folder 7, RDD.

44. William W. J. Dinwoodie, "Teaching Tolerance in the Public Schools," *School and Society* 30 (23 November 1929): 715–716; "Teaching Tolerance," *Survey* 63 (15 February 1930): 590; Katharine H. Spessard, "Appreciating China in America," and Katharine Shaw, "Understanding Our Southern Neighbor," *Progressive Education* 12 (March 1935): 202–206 and 163–167.

45. American Historical Association, *Report of the Commission on the Social Studies* (New York: Scribner's, 1934), 24–26.

46. Lasker, *Race Attitudes in Children,* 317; Zimmerman, *Whose America?* 18–24.

47. Beatrice M. Hinkle, "Psychological Tendencies of the Pre-school Child and Its Relation to the New World Order," *Progressive Education* 2 (April–May–June 1925): 62–67.

48. Richard Watson Gilder, "The Kindergarten: An Uplifting Social Influence in the Home and the District," *National Education Association, Journal of Proceedings and Addresses of the Forty-Second Annual Meeting* (1903): 390; Bessie Locke, "Children's Year and Kindergartens," *Social Service Review* 7 (June 1918): 13; White House Conference on Child Health and Protection, *The Young Child in the Home* (New York: Appleton-Century, 1936), 266–267, 331–332; Barbara Beatty, "'The Letter Killeth': Americanization and Multicultural Education in Kindergartens in the United States, 1856–1920," in *Kindergartens and Cultures: The Global Diffusion of an Idea,* ed. Roberta Wollons (New Haven, Conn.: Yale University Press, 2000), 42–58, and *Preschool Education in America: The Culture of Young Children from the Colonial Era to the Present* (New Haven, Conn.: Yale University Press, 1995), 105–108.

49. Margarette Willis Reeve, "The Habit of World Friendship," *Childhood Education* 9 (December 1932): 115–118; Mary Chaplin Shute, "We Who Desire Peace," *Childhood Education* 2 (February 1926): 269–278. Also see Lovisa C. Wagoner, "The Development of Learning in Relation to International Mindedness," *Childhood Education* 10 (June 1934): 451–453.

50. DuBois, *All This,* 63, 104–105.

51. Ibid., 60–61.

52. Quoted in Robert Westbrook, *John Dewey and American Democracy* (Ithaca, N.Y.: Cornell University Press, 1991), 213–214.

53. John Dewey, "Nationalizing Education," *Journal of Proceedings and Addresses of the National Education Association* 54 (1916): 185, and "The School as a Means of Developing a Social Consciousness and Social Ideals in Children," *Journal of Social Forces* 1 (1923): 513–517.

54. Rachel Davis DuBois, "Peace and Intercultural Education," *Journal of Educational Sociology* 12 (March 1939): 420; "Building Tolerant Attitudes," 335; *Adventures,* 14; "Practical Problems," 490; "What American Culture Might Become," 23; "Developing Sympathetic Attitudes," 387–396.

55. John Dewey, *Art as Experience* (New York: Minton, Balch, 1934), 334; DuBois, "Developing Sympathetic Attitudes," 392.

56. DuBois, *Some Racial Contributions to America,* 2; *Adventures,* 2–3; Matthew Frye Jacobson, *Whiteness of a Different Color: European Immigrants and the Alchemy of Race* (Cambridge: Harvard University Press, 1998), chap. 3.

57. Rachel Davis DuBois, *All This,* 100; "Shall We Emotionalize Our Stu-

dents?" 973–974. Also see Harry Overstreet, "Forming First Habits for Internationalism," *Progressive Education* 2 (April–May–June 1925): 68–71.

58. DuBois, *Build Together Americans,* 47.

59. Rachel Davis DuBois, "Measuring Attitudes," *Friends Intelligencer* (Sixth Month 14, 1930), 467–468; *All This,* 64; Montalto, *Intercultural Education,* 88–91.

60. Goodwin Watson, *The Measurement of Fair-Mindedness* (New York: Teachers College, 1925); G. B. Neumann, *International Attitudes of High School Students* (New York: Teachers College, 1926). Also see Emory S. Bogardus, "Social Distance and Its Origins," *Journal of Applied Sociology* 9 (January–February 1925): 216–226; "Measuring Social Distances," *Journal of Applied Sociology* 9 (March–April 1925): 299–308, and "Race Friendliness and Social Distance," *Journal of Applied Sociology* 11 (January–February 1927): 272–287; L. L. Thurstone, "An Experimental Study of Nationality Preferences," *Journal of General Psychology* 1 (July–October 1928): 405–425, "The Measurement of Social Attitudes," *Journal of Abnormal and Social Psychology* 26 (1931–1932): 249–269, and "The Measurement of Change in Social Attitudes," *Journal of Social Psychology* 2 (1931): 230–235; E. D. Hinckley, *Attitude toward the Negro* (Chicago: University of Chicago Press, 1930).

61. Paul W. Schlorff, "An Experiment in the Measurement and Modification of Racial Attitudes in School Children" (thesis, New York University, 1930), quoted in E. George Payne, "Education and Cultural Pluralism," in *Our Racial and National Minorities,* ed. Francis J. Brown and Joseph Slabey Roucek (New York: Prentice-Hall, 1937), 767–768; James M. Reinhardt, "Students and Race Feeling," *Survey* 61 (15 November 1928): 239–240; Daniel Katz and Floyd Henry Allport, *Students' Attitudes: A Report of the Syracuse University Reaction Study* (Syracuse, N.Y.: Craftsman, 1931), 380; Daniel Katz and Kenneth Braly, "Racial Stereotypes of One Hundred College Students," *Journal of Abnormal and Social Psychology* 28 (October–December 1933): 281–290, and "Racial Prejudice and Racial Stereotypes," *Journal of Abnormal and Social Psychology* 30 (July–September 1935): 175–193.

62. DuBois, "Measuring Attitudes," 467; "Building Tolerant Attitudes in High School Students," 334; "Developing Sympathetic Attitudes," 394–395.

63. DuBois, "The Role of Home Economics," 148–149; Walter C. Reckless and Harold L. Bringen, "Racial Attitudes and Information about the Negro," *Journal of Negro Education* 2 (April 1933): 128–138; D. D. Droba, "Education and Negro Attitudes," *Sociology and Social Research* 17 (November–December 1932): 137–141; Ruth E. Eckert and Henry C. Mills, "International Attitudes and Related Academic and Social Factors," *Journal of Educational Sociology* 9 (November 1935): 142–153; Austin L. Porterfield,

"Education and Race Attitudes," *Sociology and Social Research* 21 (July–August 1937): 538–543; Donald Young, "Some Effects of a Course in American Race Problems on the Race Prejudice of 450 Undergraduates at the University of Pennsylvania," *Journal of Abnormal and Social Psychology* 22 (October–December 1927): 235–242; Marie Butts, "International Cooperation in Education," *Childhood Education* 12 (June 1936): 389–391; Marie Elizabeth Carpenter, *The Treatment of the Negro in American History School Textbooks* (Menasha, Wisc.: George Banta, 1941), 6–7.

64. DuBois, "The New Frontier," 40; *Adventures*, ii, 42–43.

65. DuBois, "Developing Sympathetic Attitudes," 394; "Intercultural Education at Benjamin Franklin High School," 25, *Adventures*, 41–43; "The Role of Home Economics," 149.

66. Katz and Braly, "Racial Prejudice and Racial Stereotypes," 178; DuBois, "Our Enemy—The Stereotype," 149, and *All This*, 83–86; Rachel Davis DuBois and Rosie Nelson, *Methods of Achieving Racial Justice: Discussion Outline for Church, School, and Adult Education Groups* (New York: Service Bureau for Education in Human Relations, 1936).

67. Abraham F. Citron, Collins J. Reynolds, and Sarah W. Taylor, "Ten Years of Intercultural Education in Educational Magazines," *Harvard Educational Review* 15 (March 1945): 129–132; DuBois, *Adventures*, 44.

68. DuBois, *All This*, 56–65; *The Contributions of Racial Elements to American Life* (Philadelphia: Women's International League for Peace and Freedom, 1930); Montalto, *Intercultural Education,* 95–96, and "The Intercultural Education Movement," 146. On Englewood, see Rachel Davis DuBois, *Changing Attitudes towards Other Races and Nations* (New York: Service Bureau for Education in Human Relations, 1934), box 9, folder 11, RDD.

69. DuBois, "The New Frontier," 40.

70. DuBois, *All This*, 51–55, 68–79. Correspondence with Randolph, Pickens, and Johnson, box 3, folder 1, RDD.

71. DuBois, *All This*, 69–73; letters from W. E. B. Du Bois, 29 June 1925, and W. E. B. Du Bois to Rachel Davis DuBois, 4 July 1950, reprinted in Crispin, "Rachel Davis DuBois," 588–589; Rachel Davis DuBois to W. E. B. Du Bois, 30 December 1925 and 28 February 1933, both in WEBD Papers. On the friendship between the two DuBoises, see David Levering Lewis, *W. E. B. Du Bois, 1919–1963: The Fight for Equality and the American Century* (New York: Holt, 2001).

72. DuBois, *All This*, 72, 81, 90; Rachel Davis DuBois to W. E. B. Du Bois, 23 May 1934 and 15 June 1934, both in WEBD Papers.

73. Ibid., 66–68; "Practical Problems," 488; *Changing Attitudes toward Other Races and Nations;* Montalto, *Intercultural Education,* 90–92, 112–113.

74. DuBois, *Adventures,* 104–174; "The Role of Home Economics," 148;

Rachel Davis DuBois and Emma Schweppe, eds., *The Jews in American Life* (New York: Thomas Nelson, 1935), 13–15, and *The Germans in American Life* (New York: Thomas Nelson, 1936); DuBois, *All This,* 71–72.

75. Emory S. Bogardus, *Immigration and Race Attitudes* (Boston: D. C. Heath, 1928), 69, 243; W. W. Charters, "Developing the Attitudes of Children," *Education* 53 (February 1933): 353–357. Also see Ruth C. Peterson, "The Effect of Motion Pictures on the Social Attitudes of High-School Children," in *Developing Attitudes in Children: Proceedings of the Midwest Conference of the Chicago Association for Child Study and Parent Education* (Chicago: University of Chicago Press, 1933), 84–106.

76. Rachel Davis DuBois, "Our Enemy—The Stereotype," 149–150; "Rediscovering America by Films," *4-Star Final* 2 (December 1937), 2, box 10, folder 1, RDD. On the potential of film, see Alain Locke, "The Child's Social Attitudes—Whose Responsibility?" n.d. [c. 1932], box 41, folder 443, CSA.

77. "Requests for Materials: Guidance by Mail, October 1934–March 1935," enclosure in Rachel Davis DuBois to Will W. Alexander, 5 April 1935, file I:91, CIC; DuBois, *Adventures.*

78. DuBois, "Can We Help to Create an American Renaissance?" 733–740; *Adventures,* 43; "Shall We Emotionalize Our Students?" 973–974.

79. "The Service Bureau for Education in Human Relations: What It Offers to American Schools and Communities," flyer, n.d., box 29, folder 1, RDD; DuBois, "Developing Sympathetic Attitudes," 391; *Adventures,* 9.

80. DuBois, *Adventures,* 8, 44; "The New Frontier," 40.

81. Lasker, *Race Attitudes in Children,* 142, 303, 337; Mapheus Smith, "A Study of Change of Attitudes toward the Negro," *Journal of Negro Education* 8 (January 1939): 64; Maurice S. Hammond, "Some Experiments in Cultural Pluralism," *Journal of Educational Sociology* 12 (April 1939): 477; Ruth Wanger, "Improving Race Relations through Social Studies," *Progressive Education* 12 (March 1935): 192–197; Katherine Gardner, "Changing Racial Attitudes," *Crisis* 38 (October 1931): 336.

82. "Parents' Questions," *Child Study* 16 (May 1939): 194; Shute, "We Who Desire Peace," 270–276.

83. DuBois, "Our Enemy—The Stereotype," 147–148; "Practical Problems," 490.

84. John J. Mahoney to Rachel Davis DuBois, 22 November 1932, box 3, folder 2, RDD; Rachel Davis DuBois to Alain Locke, 19 September 1934, Locke Papers; Francis J. Brown, "Sociology and Intercultural Understanding," *Journal of Educational Sociology* 12 (February 1939): 328–331; DuBois, *All This,* 65–67, *Adventures,* 46; Montalto, *Intercultural Education,* 96–97.

85. DuBois, *Build Together Americans,* 150–163, *All This,* 65.

86. "What Mrs. DuBois' Students Say of the Course for Teachers," n.d., box 14,

folder 6, RDD; interview with Elba F. Garzau by George A. Crispin, 28 August 1986, in Crispin, "Rachel Davis DuBois," 562–575.

87. "Criticism of Course in Education in Human Relations," handwritten forms, n.d. [c. 1934], box 14, folder 4, RDD.

88. Rachel Davis DuBois to W. E. B. Du Bois, 10 March 1933, WEBD Papers, emphasis in original.

89. "Criticism of Course in Education in Human Relations" and "Criticism on the Course in World-Mindedness for Constructive Purposes," Englewood, N.J., 24 January 1934, box 14, folder 4, RDD.

90. "Criticism of Course in Education" and "Course in World-Mindedness."

91. "Criticism of Course in Education."

92. Ibid.

93. Ibid., and "Course in World-Mindedness."

94. "Current Events of Importance in Negro Education," *Journal of Negro Education* 2 (April 1933): 230.

4. Religious Education and the Teaching of Goodwill

1. Bruno Lasker, *Religious Liberty and Mutual Understanding: An Interpretation of the National Seminar of Catholics, Jews and Protestants* (New York: National Conference of Jews and Christians, 1932), 29–31.

2. Will Herberg, *Protestant-Catholic-Jew: An Essay in American Religious Sociology* (New York: Doubleday, 1955).

3. Throughout the 1920s, the *Federal Council Bulletin* carried articles on international peace. For other examples see Will Irwin, "The Churches Can Stop War!" *Christian Century* 41 (13 March 1924): 329; Florence Brewer Boeckel, *The Turn toward Peace* (New York: Friendship, 1930), 162–168; "Peace through Religious Education," *Religious Education* 26 (October 1931): 595.

4. Everett Clinchy, *All in the Name of God* (New York: John Day, 1934), 95–128, 138; Isaac Landman, ed., *Christian and Jew: A Symposium for Better Understanding* (New York: Liveright, 1929), 371–374.

5. See Benny Kraut: "Towards the Establishment of the National Conference of Christians and Jews: The Tenuous Road to Religious Goodwill in the 1920s," *American Jewish History* 77 (March 1988): 388–412, and "A Wary Collaboration: Jews, Catholics, and the Protestant Goodwill Movement," in *Between the Times: The Travail of the Protestant Establishment in America, 1900–1960,* ed. William R. Hutchison (New York: Cambridge University Press, 1989), 193–230. Also see John A. Hutchison, *We Are Not Divided: A Critical and Historical Study of the Federal Council of Churches of Christ in America* (New York: Round Table Press, 1941), 138–142.

6. "A Joint B'nai B'rith–Christian Program for Tolerance," *B'nai B'rith* 39, supp.

(February 1925): 1–2; John W. Herring, "Jewish Christian Co-operation," *B'nai B'rith* 42 (November 1927): 13; Kraut, "Towards the Establishment," 401–402, and "A Wary Collaboration," 204.

7. Kraut, "Towards the Establishment," 403–409.

8. Kraut, "A Wary Collaboration," 212–224; Martin E. Marty, *Modern American Religion*, vol. 2, *The Noise of Conflict: 1919–1941* (Chicago: University of Chicago Press, 1991), 145–154. The goodwill movement also included the Amos Society, founded by Isidor Singer, and the Permanent Commission on Better Understanding between Christians and Jews, established by Rabbi Isaac Landman.

9. Kraut, "Towards the Establishment," 410–411, and "A Wary Collaboration," 203–212; Nicholas V. Montalto, *A History of the Intercultural Education Movement, 1924–1941* (New York: Garland, 1982), 200–201. An in-house history of the NCJC claimed that Protestants were majority contributors: James E. Pitt, *Adventures in Brotherhood* (New York: Farrar, Straus, 1955), 135.

10. "Advance Step in Jewish-Christian Goodwill: Everett Clinchy Joins Federal Council's Staff," *Federal Council Bulletin* 11 (September 1928): 14; Pitt, *Adventures in Brotherhood*, 17–19.

11. Claris Edwin Silcox and Galen M. Fisher, *Catholics, Jews and Protestants* (New York, Harper, 1934), 313; Pitt, *Adventures in Brotherhood*, 26–30; J. Elliot Ross, *How Catholics See Protestants* (New York: Inquiry, 1928).

12. Pitt, *Adventures in Brotherhood*, 40–62.

13. Louis Minsky, "The National Conference of Christians and Jews," in *The Universal Jewish Encyclopedia*, vol. 8, ed. Isaac Landman (New York: Universal Jewish Encyclopedia, 1942), 114–115; Montalto, *Intercultural Education*, 188–207.

14. John W. Herring, "Goodwill and Democracy," *B'nai B'rith* 42 (August 1928): 375; John Haynes Holmes, "Converting Our Emotions," *Christian Century* 48 (21 January 1931): 112.

15. Clinchy, *All in the Name of God*, 149. Also see Edward Frank Humphrey, ed., *Liberty Documents* (New York: National Conference of Jews and Christians, 1936); Joseph M. Proskauer, "Can Prejudice Be Overcome?" and Roger W. Straus, "An Organized Approach," both in *Christian Century* 48 (21 January 1931): 116, 120.

16. Clinchy, *All in the Name of God*, 4–5, 152, 163–179; publicity in *Christian Century* 53 (22 January 1936): 176; Lasker, *Religious Liberty*, 30. Also see Clinchy, *Education and Human Relations*, Personal Growth Leaflet no. 149 (Washington, D.C.: National Education Association, n.d. [1943]), 3.

17. Clinchy, *All in the Name of God*, 165, and "Can Minorities Protect Themselves?" *Christian Century* 51 (28 March 1934): 418.

18. "National Council of Forums," *B'nai B'rith* 40 (February 1926): 144; Clinchy, *All in the Name of God,* 176; Lasker, *Religious Liberty,* 50, 66; Robert C. Dexter, "Beyond Toleration," *Federal Council Bulletin* 15 (April 1932): 23.

19. Roger W. Straus, "Youth and Good Will," in Straus, *Religious Liberty and Democracy: Writings and Addresses* (Chicago: Willett, Clark, 1939), 74; Silcox and Fisher, *Catholics, Jews and Protestants,* 347; "The Schools" in *The American Way: A Study of Human Relations among Protestants, Catholics, and Jews,* ed. Newton Diehl Baker, Carlton J. H. Hayes, and Roger Williams Straus (Chicago: Willett, Clark, 1936), 75–76.

20. Lasker, *Religious Liberty,* 66.

21. Everett R. Clinchy, *All in the Name of God,* 21, 160–162; "Seminars of Christians and Jews," *Religious Education* 26 (April 1931): 310–313, and "Are Christian Missions Menacing Judaism?" *B'nai B'rith* 45 (March 1931): 192, 212; Pitt, *Adventures in Brotherhood,* 156.

22. Kirby Page, "Building Tomorrow's World," *World Tomorrow* 10 (January 1927): 28; William H. Kilpatrick, "Thinking in Childhood and Youth," *Religious Education* 23 (February 1928): 132; "And Now the Children Are Accused," *Literary Digest* 3 (17 October 1931): 20; Albert John Murphy, *Education for World-Mindedness* (New York: Abingdon, 1931), 30–32.

23. Clinchy, "Seminars of Christians and Jews," 312, and *All in the Name of God,* 168; John Haynes Holmes, "Converting Our Emotions," 112; Helen Elizabeth Hughes, "Overcoming Prejudice as an Aim of Religious Education" (M.A. thesis, Pacific School of Religion, 1932), 33–43.

24. Lasker, *Religious Liberty,* 27, 66–67.

25. Ibid., 66–67; Clinchy, *All in the Name of God,* 147–149.

26. David Goldberg, "This Good-Will Question," *B'nai B'rith* 44 (June 1931): 351; "Women's Organizations," in Baker, Hayes, and Straus, *The American Way,* 69; Pitt, *Adventures in Brotherhood,* 128–129; Silcox and Fisher, *Catholics, Jews and Protestants,* 346.

27. "Roger W. Straus Reviews Program," NCJC pamphlet (September 1932), box 1, folder 3, and "Building Tolerant Attitudes in Schools," *NCJC Information Bulletin* 9 (July 1931): 5, box 1, folder "Historical," both in NCCJ; Pitt, *Adventures in Brotherhood,* 156–157.

28. Everett R. Clinchy to Rachel Davis DuBois, 5 October 1932, and Everett R. Clinchy to John J. Mahoney, 23 November 1932, both in box 3, folder 2, RDD.

29. Rachel Davis DuBois, notes and drafts for *All This and Something More,* box 9, folder 8, RDD.

30. Everett Clinchy, "Prejudice and Minority Groups," in *Our Racial and National Minorities,* ed. Francis J. Brown and Joseph Slabey Roucek (New

York: Prentice-Hall, 1937), 545; "Conference on Intercultural Education for Teachers," n.d. [1938], box 3, folder 10, NCCJ; Rachel Davis DuBois and Rosie Nelson, *Methods of Achieving Racial Justice: Discussion Outline for Church, School, and Adult Education Groups* (New York: Service Bureau for Education in Human Relations, 1936), 3; Rachel Davis DuBois, "Church and School: Intercultural Relations," *Church Woman* 4 (February 1938): 3–4.

31. Lasker, *Race Attitudes in Children*, 183–187, 343; "And Who Is My Neighbor?" Yorkville Neighborhood Council, 8 February 1926, notebook 4, 6–7, Lasker Papers.

32. Clinchy, "Seminars of Christians and Jews," 310–311.

33. Lasker, *Race Attitudes in Children*, 252; Abram Simon, "Can Jew and Christian Understand Each Other?" in Landman, *Christian and Jew*, 246. Also see Max Hunterberg, "Anti-Semitism, the Disease and Its Cure," *B'nai B'rith* 45 (December 1930): 80; Morris S. Lazaron, *Common Ground: A Plea for Intelligent Americanism* (New York: Liveright, 1938), 223.

34. Frank Gavin, "Christians and Anti-Semitism," *Federal Council Bulletin* 13 (May 1930): 10. Also see Henry M. Edmonds, "The Christian Speaks to the Jew," *Federal Council Bulletin* 14 (June 1931): 10, and Karen Monrad Jones, "Because Jesus Was a Jew," *Religious Education* 31 (July 1936): 171–177.

35. Clinchy, "The Borderland of Prejudice," *Christian Century* 47 (14 May 1930): 623–627.

36. Lasker, *Religious Liberty*, 29–30; T. Aaron Levy, "The Fruits of Goodwill," *B'nai B'rith* 45 (August–September 1931): 388; Everett Clinchy, "Understanding between Christian and Jew," *World Unity* 12 (June 1933): 148–153.

37. Silcox and Fisher, *Catholics, Jews and Protestants*, 51–52, 346; "Human Relations in the United States" in Baker, Hayes, and Straus, *The American Way*, 35.

38. Clinchy, *All in the Name of God*, 136, 159; Lasker, *Religious Liberty*, 27; Lazaron, *Common Ground*, 137.

39. Everett R. Clinchy, "The Borderland of Prejudice," 623–627; Lasker, *Religious Liberty*, 59.

40. Murphy, *Education for World-Mindedness*, 261; Jessie Eleanor Moore, "Meeting One's Neighbor," *Pilgrim Elementary Teacher* 19 (November 1935): 408–412.

41. "A Proposed Plan for the Study of Educational Literature Used by Sunday Schools," 18 March 1932; Everett Clinchy to Morris Waldman, 13 May 1932; Clinchy to Waldman, 29 May 1932, all in box 7, folder 32, NCCJ; BL to ECC, "Re Conference of Jews and Christians," notebook 5, 237–238, Lasker Papers; Naomi W. Cohen, *Not Free to Desist: The American Jewish*

Committee, 1906–1966 (Philadelphia: Jewish Publication Society of America, 1972), 458–460; Kraut, "A Wary Collaboration," 205, and "Towards the Establishment," 410.

42. "A Study of Official Protestant Church School Periodicals for Children, Young People and Adults, as Related to Inter-racial Inter-cultural Attitudes," 1934–1935, box 20, folder "Reports—B," Clinchy Papers; "Contributions of Religious Education to Better Human Relations" in Baker, Hayes, and Straus, *The American Way*, 57–59, 143; James V. Thompson, "Can We Learn to Be Brotherly?" *Christian Century* 53 (22 January 1936): 169.

43. Silcox and Fisher, *Catholics, Jews and Protestants*, 310; "The Textbook Revision Program of the National Conference of Christians and Jews," n.d. [c. 1944], box 6, folder 25, NCCJ.

44. "Contributions of Religious Education," in Baker, Hayes, and Straus, *The American Way*, 57; Lazaron, *Common Ground*, 224; "Textbook Revision Program."

45. Estelle M. Sternberger, "Specific Problems in Cooperation," *Christian Century* 48 (21 January 1931): 111; Bruno Lasker, "Run of the Shelves," for *Survey Midmonthly*, 5 December 1932, notebook 9, 131, Lasker Papers.

46. Lasker, *Race Attitudes in Children*, 181, 339–341; Clinchy, "Understanding between Christian and Jew," 148–153; Newton D. Baker, "For the Triumph of Democracy," *Christian Century* 48 (21 January 1931): 117. Also see John W. Herring, "Education in Understanding and Goodwill," *Federal Council Bulletin* 10 (June 1927): 6.

47. Silcox and Fisher, *Catholics, Jews and Protestants*, 283, 288. Also see Kraut, "Towards the Establishment," and "A Wary Collaboration."

48. Samuel S. Cohon, "The St. Louis Seminar on Good Will," *B'nai B'rith* 44 (June 1930): 350; Lasker, *Religious Liberty*, 28.

49. Clinchy, "Are Christian Missions Menacing Judaism?" 192; "Christian Disavowal of Anti-Semitism," *Federal Council Bulletin* 15 (January 1932): 21.

50. Silcox and Fisher, *Catholics, Jews and Protestants*, 338; "Contributions of Religious Education" in Baker, Hayes, and Straus, *The American Way*, 54–55; Roger William Straus, "Judaism and the Youth of Tomorrow," in Straus, *Religious Liberty and Democracy*, 92.

51. Lasker, *Religious Liberty*, 30–32.

52. Sternberger, "Specific Problems in Cooperation," 112; Cohon, "The St. Louis Seminar," 350; Silcox and Fisher, *Catholics, Jews and Protestants*, 202.

53. Lasker, *Religious Liberty*, 32; Rachel Davis DuBois, "Our Enemy—The Stereotype," *Progressive Education* 12 (March 1935): 148–149.

54. Abram Simon, "The Extent of Discrimination and What We Can Do about It," *Religious Education* 26 (April 1931): 306; Heywood Broun and George

Britt, *Christians Only: A Study in Prejudice* (New York: Vanguard, 1931), 7; Lasker, *Religious Liberty,* 33.

55. East Bay Religious Fellowship and the National Conference of Jews and Christians, *Report of the 1931 Oakland-Berkeley Seminar on Human Relations,* 15–18, Archives, Graduate Theological Union, Berkeley, California; Lasker, *Religious Liberty,* 32; Silcox and Fisher, *Catholics, Jews and Protestants,* 39–40. See also Samuel Tenenbaum, "Jewish Teachers," in *Jewish Experiences in America,* ed. Bruno Lasker (New York: Inquiry, 1930), 75–80.

56. Israel Goldstein to Everett R. Clinchy, 10 September 1952, box 1, folder 9, NCCJ.

57. Silcox and Fisher, *Catholics, Jews and Protestants,* 352–353; Kraut, "A Wary Collaboration," 206, 224–225.

58. Silcox and Fisher, *Catholics, Jews and Protestants,* 353–354.

59. Pitt, *Adventures in Brotherhood,* 36.

60. Silcox and Fisher, *Catholics, Jews and Protestants,* 19–22, 32; Ellsworth Faris, "The Sociology of Religious Strife" in Faris's *The Nature of Human Nature* (New York: McGraw Hill), 338–349.

61. Montalto, *Intercultural Education,* 200–202.

62. Stuart Svonkin, *Jews against Prejudice: American Jews and the Fight for Civil Liberties* (New York: Columbia University Press, 1997); Marty, *Modern American Religion,* 149–152.

63. Montalto, *Intercultural Education,* 199–205.

64. Edward Sapir, "The Application of Anthropology to Human Relations," Donald Young, "Some Contributions of Social Psychology and Sociology to Intergroup Relations in the United States" and comments by Frank Kingdon in Baker, Hayes, and Straus, *The American Way,* 121, 132, 144.

65. "Widening Group Friendship," *Commonweal* 16 (10 August 1932): 359.

66. Silcox and Fisher, *Catholics, Jews and Protestants,* 165–173, 201; "Human Relations," in Baker, Hayes, and Straus, *The American Way,* 36.

67. Silcox and Fisher, *Catholics, Jews and Protestants,* 354–357; Kraut, "A Wary Collaboration," 221–225.

68. Lazaron, *Common Ground,* 268–270; Kraut, "A Wary Collaboration," 225.

69. Cohon, "The St. Louis Seminar," 350; East Bay Religious Fellowship and the National Conference of Jews and Christians, *Report of the 1931 Oakland-Berkeley Seminar,* 16; Lasker, *Religious Liberty,* 29.

70. "Human Relations" in Baker, Hayes, and Straus, *The American Way,* 36; Silcox and Fisher, *Catholics, Jews and Protestants,* 165, 182–184.

71. Silcox and Fisher, *Catholics, Jews and Protestants,* 332–333, 339, 344; Lucy P. [Mrs. Abel J.] Gregg, *New Relationships with Jews and Catholics* (New York: Association, 1934), and Everett Clinchy to Rhoda E. McCulloch, 26 October 1934, both in box 7, folder 21, NCCJ; "Contributions of Religious Ed-

ucation" in Baker, Hayes, and Straus, *The American Way,* 59. Also see "Books for Parents," *Parents' Magazine* 10 (June 1935): 85. The FCC also issued a guide for young people, "Better Understanding between Jews and Christians," 1938, box 1, folder 13, NCCJ.

72. Clinchy, "Understanding between Christian and Jew," 148; East Bay Religious Fellowship and the NCJC, *Report of the 1931 Oakland-Berkeley Seminar,* 17; Straus, "Youth and Good Will," 74–79.

73. Pitt, *Adventures in Brotherhood;* "*Fortune's* Survey of Attitudes on Religion and Tolerance," *Journal of Educational Sociology* 12 (April 1939): 506; "Report of the Director," 2 November 1939, 6–7, box 1, folder 3, NCCJ.

74. Clinchy, *All in the Name of God,* 147.

75. Pitt, *Adventures in Brotherhood,* 57.

76. National Interracial Conference, "Toward Interracial Cooperation: What Was Said and Done at the First National Interracial Conference Held Under the Auspices of the Commission on the Church and Race Relations of the Federal Council of the Churches and the Commission on Interracial Cooperation, Cincinnati, Ohio, March 25–27, 1925," Federal Council of the Churches of Christ in America, book no. 1 (New York: J. J. Little and Ives, 1926); Paul E. Baker, *Negro-White Adjustment: An Investigation and Analysis of Methods in the Interracial Movement in the United States* (New York: Association, 1934), 24–27, 226–230; Hutchison, *We Are Not Divided,* 131–138; F. Ernest Johnson, "The Educational Program of the Federal Council of Churches," *Religious Education* 29 (April 1934): 168; "Choir Festival of Interracial Goodwill," *Federal Council Bulletin* 19 (February 1936): 9; Svonkin, *Jews against Prejudice,* 26; "Race Relations," *Religious Education* 26 (February 1931): 99. Also see Herring, "Education in Understanding and Goodwill," 6.

77. Baker, *Negro-White Adjustment,* 150, 231–232; Francis J. Brown, "The Meaning of Minorities," in Brown and Roucek, *Our Racial and National Minorities,* 4.

78. W. E. B. Du Bois, "Will the Church Remove the Color Line?" *Christian Century* 48 (9 December 1931): 1554; "A Modern Crusade," *Opportunity* 12 (August 1934): 230.

79. Bruno Lasker, "Race Attitudes in Children," *Woman's Press* (May 1926): 332–334, and "Can Race Tolerance Be Taught?" *Woman's Press* (September 1926): 608–611.

80. Lasker, *Race Attitudes in Children,* 119, 171–179, 263, 341–345.

81. Ibid., 343–345; Bruno Lasker, "Childhood Prejudices" (radio talk), 22 March 1929, notebook 6, 71, Lasker Papers; "Reminiscences of Bruno Lasker," 251–252. Also see Bruno Lasker, "Race Relations and the Church School," *International Journal of Religious Education* 7 (January 1930): 11–12.

82. S. Ralph Harlow, "The Color Bar in the Churches," *Christian Century* 47 (28 May 1930): 683; Andrew J. Allison, "Youths Get Together," *Opportunity* 2 (April 1924): 108; "American Youth and Youth Movements," *Opportunity* 4 (May 1926): 143; "Northwestern Student Conference Takes Bold Stand," *Christian Century* 41 (28 February 1924); "The Race Issue at Detroit," *Christian Century* 48 (14 January 1931): 49; "Race Relations," *Opportunity* 15 (May 1937): 156. Also see B. E. Mays, "Realities in Race Relations," *Christian Century* 48 (25 March 1931): 404; "Methodist Youth Declare Themselves," *Social Frontier* 1 (December 1934): 4; George A. Coe, "The Educational Frontier of the Churches," *Social Frontier* 2 (December 1935): 80.

83. Clinchy, *All in the Name of God,* 173; Comments by Carleton J. H. Hayes, in Baker, Hayes, and Straus, *The American Way,* 152.

84. "Basic Conviction," flyer (n.p.: NCCJ, 1942). Also see Matthew Frye Jacobson, *Whiteness of a Different Color: European Immigrants and the Alchemy of Race* (Cambridge: Harvard University Press, 1998).

5. A New Generation in the South

1. Wilma Dykeman and James Stokely, *Seeds of Southern Change: The Life of Will Alexander* (Chicago: University of Chicago Press, 1962); Charles Kirk Pilkington, "The Trials of Brotherhood: The Founding of the Commission on Interracial Cooperation," *Georgia Historical Quarterly* 69 (Spring 1985): 55–80; Morton Sosna, *In Search of the Silent South: Southern Liberals and the Race Issue* (New York: Columbia University Press, 1977), chap. 2; George Brown Tindall, *The Emergence of the New South, 1913–1945* (Baton Rouge: Louisiana State University Press, 1967), 177–183; Willis D. Weatherford and Charles S. Johnson, *Race Relations: Adjustments of Whites and Negroes in the United States* (Boston: D. C. Heath, 1934), 512.

2. Paul E. Baker, *Negro-White Adjustment: An Investigation and Analysis of Methods in the Interracial Movement in the United States* (New York: Association, 1934), 19. For critical assessments see Jacquelyn Dowd Hall, *Revolt against Chivalry: Jessie Daniel Ames and the Women's Campaign against Lynching* (New York: Columbia University Press, 1979), and John H. Stanfield, "Northern Money and Southern Bogus Elitism: Rockefeller Foundations and the Commission on Interracial Cooperation Movement, 1919–1929," *Journal of Ethnic Studies* 15 (Summer 1987): 1–22.

3. Pilkington, "The Trials of Brotherhood," 64; Baker, *Negro-White Adjustment,* 18.

4. For an overview of the CIC's programs, see "History of the CIC and ASWPL," in Mitchell F. Ducey, ed., *The Commission on Interracial Cooper-*

ation Papers, 1919–1944 and the Association of Southern Women for the Prevention of Lynching Papers, 1930–42: A Guide to the Microfilm Edition, 1–7, CIC.

5. Will Alexander, "Building Better Attitudes: Work of Interracial Commission in Colleges and Schools," report to F. S. Keppel of the Carnegie Corporation, 1930, file VI:21, CIC; "Progress in Race Relations: A Survey of the Work of the Commission on Interracial Cooperation for the Year 1923–24," 13–14, folder 978, box 97, series 3.8, LSRM.

6. "A General Survey of the Work of the Commission on Interracial Cooperation for 1922–23," 4, folder 975, box 96, series 3.8, LSRM.

7. "Progress in Race Relations," 1923–24; "Report for 1927–28: Commission on Interracial Organization," 3, folder 976, box 96, series 3.8, LSRM; Mary White Ovington, "Revisiting the South," *Crisis* 34 (April 1927): 42.

8. Will W. Alexander, "The Changing South," *Opportunity* 5 (October 1927): 296; "Talks to Southern White Students," *Fisk University News,* n.d. [c. 1923], 10–11, folder 980, box 97, series 3.8, LSRM.

9. Arthur Raper, "College Graduates and Race Relations," *Opportunity* 15 (December 1937): 371; "Summary of Work for 1925–26, Commission on Interracial Cooperation," folder 975, box 96, series 3.8, LSRM; CIC, "Race Relations in 1927," folder 978, box 97, series 3.8, LSRM; Ovington, "Revisiting the South," 61. Also see Cranston Clayton, "College Interracialism in the South," *Opportunity* 12 (September 1934): 267–269, and articles by R. B. Eleazar, Mabel R. Bell, and W. W. Alexander in *Southern YMCA Intercollegian* 2 (February 1929).

10. Dykeman and Stokely, *Seeds of Southern Change,* 120; Alexander, "Southern White Schools Study Race Question," *Journal of Negro Education* 2 (April 1933): 139–146; W. C. Jackson, "College Instruction in Race Relations," *Religious Education* 26 (February 1931): 124–126; Baker, *Negro-White Adjustment,* 217.

11. R. B. Eleazar, form letter, n.d. [c. 1931], file V:122, CIC; T. J. Woofter Jr., "The Status of Racial and Ethnic Groups," in *Recent Social Trends in the United States,* Report of the President's Research Committee on Social Trends (New York: McGraw-Hill, 1933), 592.

12. "General Survey of the Work of the Commission on Interracial Cooperation for 1922–23," 4; Dykeman and Stokely, *Seeds of Southern Change,* 120; T. J. Woofter Jr., *The Basis of Racial Adjustment* (Boston: Ginn, 1925), 12–13.

13. "College Entries" and "Colleges Represented in Essay Competition," 1927–28, file VI:96; Charles H. Brown, "The Quest for Understanding: A Personal Record," 1931–32, file VI:85; DeMila Sanders Lonsberry, "The Quest for Understanding," file VI:85, also published in *Tuskegee Messenger,* 10 July 1934, 5, file VI:17, all in CIC.

14. Alexander, "The Changing South," 295; "Progress in Race Relations," 1923–24; Jackson, "College Instruction in Race Relations," 125–126; Dykeman and Stokely, *Seeds of Southern Change,* 182; Conference on Education and Race Relations, "College Courses in Race Relations," pamphlet (Atlanta: Conference on Education and Race Relations, 1939), file VI:119, CIC.

15. Woofter, "The Status of Racial and Ethnic Groups," 593; Jackson, "College Instruction in Race Relations," 124; "Extracts from Special Campaign Presentation," n.d., file VI:87, CIC; Vann Woodward, "An Incident from the Career of Judge Lynch," file VI:85, CIC. This essay, on the Atlanta riot of 1906, is an early example of Woodward's distinctive literary style.

16. "Notes on Atlanta—October 18 to 20, 1923," notebook 1, 1–5, Lasker Papers; William B. Thomas, "Conservative Currents in Howard Washington Odum's Agenda for Social Reform in Southern Race Relations, 1930–36," *Phylon* 45 (June 1984): 121–134; Sosna, *In Search of the Silent South,* 51.

17. "Summary of Work for 1925–26," 5; Alexander quoted in Tindall, *Emergence of the New South,* 182; "Race Relations and Negro Work, 1926–27," folder 996, box 98, series 3.8, LSRM; "A Sane Approach to the Race Problem," 1930, folder 977, box 97, series 3.8, LSRM; Stanfield, "Northern Money and Southern Bogus Elitism."

18. "Proceedings of the Inter-racial Conference," New Haven, Conn., 19–21 December 1927, 44, 147–148, folder 1001, box 98, series 3.8, LSRM.

19. Will W. Alexander to Dr. Beardsley Ruml, 16 February 1929, folder 976, box 96, series 3.8, LSRM.

20. Rachel Davis DuBois to Will Alexander, 11 March 1935; DuBois to Edwin Embree, 11 March 1935; DuBois to Alexander, 5 April 1935, file I:91, CIC; "A Statement to the Carnegie Corporation," 25 December 1933, file VI:21, CIC.

21. Tindall, *Emergence of the New South,* 198–199; Sosna, *In Search of the Silent South,* 23; Dykeman and Stokely, *Seeds of Southern Change,* 113. One Alabama teacher did include study of Asians and Native Americans; see Ralph W. Stonier to Conference on Education and Race Relations, 30 April 1937, file VI:3, CIC.

22. George L. Collins, "How Prejudice Is Overcome," *World Tomorrow* 11 (October 1928): 410; "General Survey of the Work of the Commission on Interracial Cooperation for 1922–23," 4; Dykeman and Stokely, *Seeds of Southern Change,* 162; "Summary of Work for 1925–26," 4; "Commission on Interracial Cooperation: Brief Statement of Work for 1927 and Brief Suggestions for 1928," folder 975, box 96, series 3.8, LSRM; "Report for 1927–28," 3–4; Alexander, "Southern White Schools Study Race Question," 144; R. B. Eleazar, "A Realistic Approach to the Race Problem," *Religious Education* 26 (February 1931): 119–122.

23. "General Survey of the Work, 1922–23," 3; "Notes on Atlanta—October 18

to 20, 1923"; Alexander, "The Changing South," 295; W. W. Alexander, "Spiritual Values in Teachers' Work," in Second Peabody Conference on Education and Race Relations, "Education and Racial Adjustment" (Atlanta: Executive Committee of the Conference, 1932), folder 978, box 97, series 3.8, LSRM.

24. "Review of Ten Years' Work," 1928, 13, folder 976, box 96, series 3.8, LSRM; "'America's Tenth Man': A High School Project in Human Understanding," 1931, file VI:87, CIC; Robert B. Eleazar, *America's Tenth Man: A Brief Survey of the Negro's Part in American History* (Atlanta: CIC, 1928; reprint, May 1932); *Crisis* (February 1925): 181, cited in Bruno Lasker, *Race Attitudes in Children* (New York: Holt, 1929), 158.

25. Eleazar, *America's Tenth Man;* R. B. Eleazar, form letter, n.d. [c. 1931], file V:122, CIC; *Some Recent Trends in Race Relations* (Atlanta: CIC, 1932), 15; Will W. Alexander to the Members of the CIC, 10 August 1943, folder 1819, box 193, series 1, RG 1.2, GEB.

26. "Papers Submitted in 1932–33 'Tenth Man' Contest," file VI:86, CIC; Virginia Davidson, "America's Tenth Man," 1932, file VI:18, CIC.

27. "Schools Participating in Tenth Man Project," file VI:86, CIC; Dykeman and Stokely, *Seeds of Southern Change,* 120; "Suggestions for 'Tenth Man' Project," n.d., file VI:87, CIC; Flora Y. Hatcher (Prattville, Ala.) to CIC, 31 March 1931, file VI:3, CIC; "A Few Typical High School Projects, Reported May 1937," file VI:21, CIC; *Education for Southern Citizenship* (Atlanta: Conference on Education and Race Relations, n.d. [1939]), 7–8, folder 1818, box 193, series 1, RG 1.2, GEB.

28. Comment from Grace Whitfield Lovelace, in "Clinton High School Race Relations Unit," file VI:3, CIC; Sarah Clancy, preface to "The Negro Problem," 1930, file VI:14, CIC.

29. Decora Adams to R. B. Eleazar, 25 March 1930, file VI:21, CIC; George L. Blackwell, "'Tenth Man' Project in Central High School, St. Joseph, Mo.," file VI:22, CIC.

30. Alexander, "The Changing South," 296.

31. National Interracial Conference, "Toward Interracial Cooperation: What Was Said and Done at the First National Interracial Conference Held Under the Auspices of the Commission on the Church and Race Relations of the Federal Council of the Churches and the Commission on Interracial Cooperation, Cincinnati, Ohio, March 25–27, 1925," Federal Council of the Churches of Christ in America, book no. 1 (New York: J. J. Little and Ives, 1926): 150–159; "General Survey of the Work, 1922–23," 4; Barbara Beatty, *Preschool Education in America: The Culture of Young Children from the Colonial Era to the Present* (New Haven, Conn.: Yale University Press, 1995), 107–108.

32. "Race Relations in 1927."

33. "The Interracial Front: Annual Report of the Commission on Interracial Cooperation, 1933," 10, file I:58, CIC; Will W. Alexander to Anson Phelps Stokes, 28 January 1929, and Mary Church Terrell to Anson Phelps Stokes, 22 January 1929, both in folder 1021, box 101, series 3.8, LSRM. Also see Ullin W. Leavell, "Trends of Philanthropy in Negro Education: A Survey," *Journal of Negro Education* 2 (January 1933): 50–51.

34. "Building Better Attitudes," 4; Peabody Conference on Dual Education in the South, "Education and Racial Adjustment," (Atlanta: Executive Committee of the Conference, 1931), folder 977, box 97, series 3.8, LSRM; R. B. Eleazar to Isaac Fisher, 13 June 1931, file VI:30, CIC.

35. R. L. Brantley, "Interracial Emphasis at Bessie Tift College" and J. L. Clark, "The Chairman Explains" in Second Peabody Conference, "Education and Racial Adjustment" (1932), 19, 51.

36. R. B. Eleazar, form letter, 1 January 1932, file VI:22, CIC; "'The Quest for Understanding': An Educational Project for Teachers Colleges and Schools of Education," 1934, file VI:119, CIC; R. B. Eleazar, form letter, n.d., file V:122, CIC; "Comments on 'America's Tenth Man,'" n.d., file VI:87, CIC; *Some Recent Trends in Race Relations*, 17; "Awards for Teachers' Colleges and Schools of Education," 1932, file VI:87, CIC.

37. Robert R. Moton, "What the Negro Thinks," in Second Peabody Conference, "Education and Racial Adjustment" (1932), 44.

38. W. E. B. Du Bois, "Inter-racial Comity," *Crisis* 22 (May 1921): 6–7; quoted in Pilkington, 65; W. E. B. Du Bois, "Postscript: The Commission of Interracial Co-operation," *Crisis* 37 (July 1930): 245. Du Bois offered a positive assessment in "Will W. Alexander and the South," *Crisis* 32 (August 1926): 164–165. Also see W. O. Brown, "Interracial Cooperation: Some of Its Problems," *Opportunity* 11 (September 1933): 272.

39. James Bond, "The Inter-racial Commissions of the South," *Opportunity* 1 (February 1923): 13–14; Ruth Wysor Atkinson, "Inter-racial Co-operation," *Opportunity* 1 (September 1923): 275–277; Ovington, "Revisiting the South," 43.

40. B. E. Mays, "What Negro Students Expect of White Students," *Southern YMCA Intercollegian* 2 (February 1929): 4; J. Neal Hughley, "Justice in Race Relations," n.d., file VI:85, CIC.

41. "Hot Springs Negro Girl Wins Contest," *Arkansas Gazette,* 9 May 1929, file VI:17, CIC; "A Statement to the Carnegie Corporation"; "Work of Conference on Education and Race Relations, 1935, Under Grant of Carnegie Corporation to Commission on Interracial Cooperation," 3, file VI:21, CIC.

42. W. D. Weatherford to Beardsley Ruml, 27 April 1929, folder 1043, box 103, series 3.8, LSRM.

43. Helen Harding to CIC, 30 March 1931, and Theodore R. Lee to Eleazar, 24 March 1931, both in file VI:3, CIC.

44. Eleazar, "A Realistic Approach to the Race Problem," 119; Dykeman and Stokely, *Seeds of Southern Change,* 79; Woofter, *The Basis of Racial Adjustment,* 240.

45. Alexander, "Southern White Schools Study Race Question," 143, and "Our Conflicting Racial Policies," *Harper's* 190 (January 1945): 172–179; Baker, *Negro-White Adjustment,* 19. Other CIC members voiced ideological commitment to segregation: see Sosna, *In Search of the Silent South,* 25–26, 40, 111, 154.

46. Woofter, *Basis of Racial Adjustment,* 3, 16, 23–28, 235–242; Eleazar, *America's Tenth Man,* frontispiece; R. B. Eleazar, (form letter, n.d. [c. 1931]), file V:122, CIC.

47. A. C. Ray, "Even-Handed Justice and Equal Opportunity," *Southern YMCA Intercollegian* 2 (February 1929): 5; "America's Tenth Man," no author, n.d., and Carl Reed, "The Status of the American Negroes," n.d., both in file VI:18, CIC.

48. "K. H. S. Again First in Negro Study Contest," *Kirksville (MO) Daily Express and News,* 14 (April 1932), file VI:17, CIC; Pauline D. Knobbs, "Remarkable Program in Missouri School" in Second Peabody Conference, "Education and Racial Adjustment" (1932), 29; "Educating for a Bi-racial Community," *Progressive Education* 12 (March 1935): 181–184, and "Toward Racial Understanding in the South," in *Americans All: Studies in Intercultural Education,* National Education Association, Department of Supervisors and Directors of Instruction, fourteenth yearbook (Washington, D.C.: National Education Association, 1942), 132–139.

49. E. J. Trueblood, "Effect of Race Relations Course" in Second Peabody Conference, "Education and Racial Adjustment" (1932), 21–26; Lee M. Brooks, "Racial Distance as Affected by Education," *Sociology and Social Research* 21 (November–December 1936): 128–133; Euri Belle Bolton, "Effect of Knowledge upon Attitudes towards the Negro," *Journal of Social Psychology* 6 (February 1935): 68–90.

50. Raper, "College Graduates and Race Relations," 370–373. On lessons absorbed outside the classroom, see Jennifer Ritterhouse, *Growing up Jim Crow: How Black and White Southern Children Learned Race* (Chapel Hill: University of North Carolina Press, 2006).

51. A. L. Chapman, "A High School Unit," *Mississippi Educational Advance* (April 1937): 222–224, file VI:3, CIC.

52. Willis A. Sutton, "Correct Racial Attitudes in the Public Schools," *Religious Education* 26 (April 1931): 296–297.

53. Maude Carmichael, "A Program for 'A Better Understanding Between the Races,'" *Journal of Negro History* 2 (April 1933): 151–156.

54. "Extracts from Papers of Junior College Students," Sue Bennett College, March 1932, CIC.

55. Herman Hudson, "The Negro as I Know Him," Virginia Davidson, "America's Tenth Man," Carl Reed, "The Status of the American Negro," file VI:18, CIC. See also other examples from the high school essay contest in the same location.

56. Alexander, "Southern White Schools Study Race Question," 145.

57. "Findings and Recommendations, Meeting of State Public School Administrators, Nashville, Tennessee, August 3–4, 1933," file VI:22, CIC, reprinted in "Current Events of Importance in Negro Education," *Journal of Negro Education* 2 (October 1933): 520–521; "The Quest for Understanding: Extracts from the Peabody Conference on Education and Race Relations," 23–24, file VI:119, CIC; "Education and Racial Adjustment: Report of Work in Colleges and Public Schools under Grant of Carnegie Corporation," 1933, file VI:21, CIC.

58. "Work of Conference on Education and Race Relations, 1935," 2; R. B. Eleazar, "School Books and Racial Antagonism," pamphlet, 2 ed., 1935, file VI:119, CIC, summary of pamphlet (possibly press release), file VI:144, CIC; "Work of Conference on Education and Race Relations, Under Grant of the Carnegie Corporation to the Commission on Interracial Cooperation, 1935–36," 2, file VI:21, CIC; "Educational Program: Commission on Interracial Cooperation," n.d. [c. 1938], 4, file VI:84, CIC. Also see Mary Elizabeth Carpenter, *The Treatment of the Negro in American History School Textbooks* (Menasha, Wisc.: George Banta, 1941).

59. Weatherford and Johnson, *Race Relations*. For a critique of Weatherford's chapters see Horace Mann Bond, "The Curriculum and the Negro Child," *Journal of Negro Education* 4 (April 1935): 166. On the pamphlets see "Work of Conference on Education and Race Relations, 1935–36," 3; "Work of Conference on Education and Race Relations, 1934–37," 1, file VI:21, CIC; and "Educational Program," 4–5.

60. "Work of Conference on Education and Race Relations, 1935," "Work of Conference on Education and Race Relations, 1935–36," "Work of Conference on Education and Race Relations, 1934–37"; "Work of Conference on Education and Race Relations, Supplementary Report, December 1, 1937," file VI:21, CIC, and "Educational Program," 5–6.

61. "Work of Conference on Education and Race Relations, 1935," 1, "Work of Conference on Education and Race Relations, 1935–1936," 2, and "Supplementary Report," 1937, 2; "Educational Program," 6; "Extracts from Bulletins of State Departments of Education," file VI:21, CIC.

62. "A School Contest of Great Value," *Chattanooga Free Press*, 24 (April, n.d.), file VI:3, CIC.

63. Alain Locke, "The Child's Social Attitudes:—Whose Responsibility?" n.d.

[c. 1932], box 41, folder 443, CSA; Charles Johnson, *A Preface to Racial Understanding* (New York: Friendship, 1936), 168–169, 174–175.

64. Brown, "Interracial Cooperation: Some of Its Problems"; Clayton, "College Interracialism in the South"; R. J. Bunche, "Interracial Beacon," review of *A Preface to Racial Understanding,* by Charles S. Johnson, *Journal of Negro Education* 6 (January 1937): 76–78; Bunche quoted in Gunnar Myrdal, *An American Dilemma: The Negro Problem and American Democracy* (New York: Harper, 1944), 848.

65. Doxey Wilkerson, "American Caste and the Social Studies Curriculum," *Quarterly Review of Higher Education among Negroes* 5 (April 1937): 67–74; Bond, "The Curriculum and the Negro Child," 165.

66. Howard W. Odum to A. R. Mann, 9 November 1942, folder 1819, box 193, series 1, RG 1, GEB; Sosna, *In Search of the Silent South,* 115–120; Linda Reed, *Simple Decency and Common Sense: The Southern Conference Movement, 1938–1963* (Bloomington: Indiana University Press, 1991).

67. "Supplementary Report," 1937, 2–3; Will W. Alexander to Raymond B. Fosdick, 8 June 1938, folder 1818, box 193, series 1, RG 1.2, GEB.

68. R. B. Eleazar, "A Challenge to Southern Schools," opening address, Conference on Education for Southern Citizenship, Blue Ridge, North Carolina, August 25–30, 1941, file VI:119, CIC.

69. "Preliminary Report by Mr. E. for Rosenwald," April 1941, file I:65, CIC.

70. Myrdal, *An American Dilemma,* 842–850, emphasis in original.

6. Cultural Pride and the Second Generation

1. Eleanor Roosevelt, "My Day," 1939, quoted in Rachel Davis DuBois with Corann Okorodudu, *All This and Something More: Pioneering in Intercultural Education* (Bryn Mawr, Pa.: Dorrance, 1984), 91.

2. See Richard Weiss, "Ethnicity and Reform: Minorities and the Ambiance of the Depression Years," *Journal of American History* 66 (December 1979): 566–585.

3. John Dewey, "The School as Social Center," *Elementary School Teacher* 3 (October 1902): 78; Jane Addams, *Twenty Years at Hull-House* (1910); reprint, Chicago: University of Illinois Press, 1990), 136–510; Allen H. Eaton, *Immigrant Gifts to American Life* (New York: Russell Sage, 1932), 90–93, 104–106, 171.

4. William I. Thomas and Florian Znaniecki, *The Polish Peasant in Europe and America* (1918), ed. Eli Zaretsky (reprint; Urbana: University of Illinois Press, 1996).

5. Frederic M. Thrasher, "Are Our Criminals Foreigners?" in *Our Racial and National Minorities,* ed. Francis J. Brown and Joseph Slabey Roucek (New

York: Prentice-Hall, 1937), 697–710; DuBois, *All This,* 104–105, and *Adventures in Intercultural Education: A Manual for Secondary School Teachers* (New York: Progressive Education Association, 1938), 5–6.

6. Louis Adamic, "Thirty Million New Americans," *Harper's* 169 (November 1934): 648–693.

7. Ibid., 648–693.

8. DuBois, *All This,* 68; Adamic, *My America: 1928–1938* (New York: Harper, 1938), 222–223; Rachel Davis DuBois to Louis Adamic, 30 June 1938, box 3, folder 3, RDD.

9. Rachel Davis DuBois, "The Need for Sharing Cultural Values," *Friends Intelligencer* (Second Month 11, 1939): 84, and "Practical Problems of International and Interracial Education," *Clearing House* 10 (April 1936): 487. Also see "Peace and Intercultural Education," *Journal of Educational Sociology* 12 (March 1939): 419.

10. Rachel Davis DuBois, "Danger or Promise?" speech at San Francisco State College, 1936, box 12, folder 10, RDD.

11. Rachel Davis DuBois, "Our Enemy—The Stereotype," *Progressive Education* 12 (March 1935): 147, and "Practical Problems," 487–488. On the inferiority complex, see Floyd Allport, *Social Psychology* (New York: Houghton Mifflin, 1924), 368–372. Eckerson quoted in Nicholas V. Montalto, "Multicultural Education in the New York City Public Schools, 1919–1941," in *Educating an Urban People: The New York City Experience,* ed. Diane Ravitch and Ronald K. Goodenow (New York: Teachers College Press, 1981), 72.

12. Rachel Davis DuBois, "What American Culture Might Become," draft of speech to League of Women Voters, San Francisco, 1935, 5–8, box 12, folder 10, RDD.

13. Bruno Lasker, *Race Attitudes in Children* (New York: Holt, 1929), 17, 253–257.

14. Francis J. Brown and Joseph Slabey Roucek, preface, xii–xiii, and E. George Payne, introduction, "The School and the Immigrant," and "Education and Cultural Pluralism," xxi, 601–602, 760–762, all in Brown and Roucek, *Our Racial and National Minorities.* On the courses at New York University, see Robert Whitney Peebles, *Leonard Covello: A Study of an Immigrant's Contribution to New York City* (New York: Arno, 1968), 173–180, and DuBois, *All This,* 67.

15. Payne, "Education and Cultural Pluralism," 762–768.

16. Adamic, *My America,* 223.

17. Rachel Davis DuBois, "Can We Help to Create an American Renaissance?" *English Journal* 27 (November 1935): 733–741, "The Need for Sharing Cultural Values," 84, and "What American Culture Might Become," 14.

Also see Nicholas V. Montalto, *A History of the Intercultural Education Movement, 1924–41* (New York: Garland, 1982), chap. 4.

18. DuBois, *All This*, 52.
19. Rachel Davis DuBois, "The New Frontier," *Opportunity* 12 (February 1934): 41.
20. DuBois, "Can We Help to Create an American Renaissance?" 736–737.
21. DuBois, *Build Together Americans: Adventures in Intercultural Education for the Secondary School* (New York: Hinds, Hayden, and Eldredge, 1945), 161–163, and "Our Enemy—The Stereotype," 147; Montalto, "Multicultural Education," 73–74.
22. Ezra Kempton Maxfield, "Education and World Peace," *Religious Education* 26 (September 1931): 552.
23. Adamic, "Thirty Million New Americans," 691; Ethel M. Duncan, "The Incidental Approach in Attitude Building," and Anne Merriman Peck and Enid Johnson, "The Peoples That Make America," both in *American Childhood* 23 (September 1937): 21, 45; *Successful Living* (Seattle: Seattle Public Schools, 1935), 46, 157; quoted in Yoon K. Pak, *Wherever I Go, I Will Always Be a Loyal American: Schooling Seattle's Japanese Americans during World War II* (New York: RoutledgeFalmer, 2002), 82, 91, 177.
24. Claris Edwin Silcox and Galen M. Fisher, *Catholics, Jews and Protestants* (New York: Harper, 1934), 183–184.
25. "Parents' Questions and Discussion," *Child Study* 15 (December 1937): 77.
26. Rachel Davis DuBois, "Fitting Your Child for the Modern World," address, Lehigh Valley Child Helping Conference, 19 May 1934, box 12, folder 10, RDD, and "Intercultural and Interracial Contributions of the Women of a Community to the Club," outline of discussion, 20 January 1941, box 3, folder 4, RDD.
27. Max Kramer, "An Experiment in Indian Education," 155–59; La Von Whitehouse, "Sharing Cultures in California," 206–209; Vivienne S. Worley, "Italy and Mexico Come to Denver," 160–163, all in *Progressive Education* 12 (March 1935).
28. Anne Hoppock, "Schools for the Foreign Born in a New Jersey County," *Progressive Education* 10 (April 1933): 189–193; Rachel Davis DuBois, introduction to Ethel M. Duncan, *Democracy's Children* (New York: Hinds, Hayden, and Eldredge, 1945), xii.
29. Payne, "Education and Cultural Puralism," 763–764, and Clara A. Hardin and Herbert A. Miller, "The Second Generation," 720–721, both in Brown and Roucek, *Our Racial and National Minorities*.
30. DuBois, *Build Together Americans*, xvi, 54; *Methods of Achieving Racial Justice*, 49.

31. Miriam R. Ephraim, "An Experiment in Education for Human Relations," *Jewish Social Service Quarterly* 12 (June 1936): 357–364.

32. DuBois, *All This*, 54. On Covello, see Michael C. Johanek and John L. Puckett, *Leonard Covello and the Making of Benjamin Franklin High School: Education as If Citizenship Mattered* (Philadelphia: Temple University Press, 2007); Peebles, *Leonard Covello*; Cherry A. McGee Banks, *Improving Multicultural Education: Lessons from the Intergroup Education Movement* (New York: Teachers College Press, 2005), chap. 3; Vito Perrone, *Teacher with a Heart: Reflections on Leonard Covello and Community* (New York: Teachers College Press, 1998).

33. Leonard Covello with Guido D'Agostino, *The Heart Is the Teacher* (New York: McGraw Hill, 1958), 43–47, 195.

34. Ibid., 104, 109; Lasker quoted in Peebles, *Leonard Covello*, 140.

35. Covello, *The Heart Is the Teacher*, 170–171; Peebles, *Leonard Covello*, 168–175.

36. Leonard Covello, "A High School and Its Immigrant Community—A Challenge and an Opportunity," *Journal of Educational Sociology* 9 (February 1936): 331–346, and "Intercultural Understanding among Young Adults," n.d., box 29, folder 1, RDD.

37. Leonard Covello, "Language as a Factor in Social Adjustment," in Brown and Roucek, *Our Racial and National Minorities*, 681–696; Peebles, *Leonard Covello*, 114, 129–130; Montalto, "Multicultural Education," 70.

38. Rachel Davis DuBois, "Intercultural Education at Benjamin Franklin High School," *High Points* 19 (December 1937): 23–29. On the school demographics see Peebles, *Leonard Covello*, 196, 204.

39. DuBois, "Intercultural Education," 23–29.

40. DuBois, "Intercultural Education at Benjamin Franklin," 23–29; Covello, "Intercultural Understanding among Young Adults," 4–6.

41. Ephraim, "An Experiment in Education for Human Relations," 363; Rachel Davis DuBois, "Developing Sympathetic Attitudes toward Peoples," *Journal of Educational Sociology* 9 (March 1936): 387–396, and "Sharing Cultural Values," *Journal of Educational Sociology* 12 (April 1939): 485; statement from Rachel Davis DuBois to Dr. Grunebaum, 14 September 1939, box 3, folder 3, RDD; "Intercultural Education: A Statement by Rachel Davis-DuBois," n.d. [c. 1940], box 2, folder 10, RDD.

42. Covello, "Intercultural Understanding among Young Adults," 2, emphasis in original; Peebles, *Leonard Covello*, 266.

43. Peebles, *Leonard Covello*, 271, 275, 299, appendix HH; quotations from Montalto, *Intercultural Education*, 121, and "Multicultural Education," 68.

44. DuBois, *All This*, 72; Miriam Ephraim, "Service for Education in Human Relations," 14 June 1935, box 29, folder 1, RDD.

45. DuBois, *All This,* 72, 80, 97; Rachel Davis DuBois and Emma Schweppe, eds., *The Jews in American Life* (New York: Thomas Nelson, 1935), 23.

46. DuBois, *All This,* 72; Montalto, *Intercultural Education,* chap. 7. On this debate in the post–World War II period see Svonkin, *Jews against Prejudice.*

47. DuBois, *Adventures,* 10, *Build Together Americans,* 105–106, *All This,* 96–97, and "Why the Opposition to Our Work?" chap. draft for *All This,* box 9, folder 7, RDD.

48. Rachel Davis DuBois to Will Alexander, 11 March 1935; DuBois to Edwin R. Embree, 11 March 1935; DuBois to Alexander, 5 April 1935; all in file I:81, CIC.

49. DuBois, *All This,* 72–76; course announcement, San Francisco State College, 19 October 1936, box 14, folder 5, RDD; DuBois, "What American Culture Might Become," 3, 22; DuBois, "Danger or Promise," 17; Bertha Melkonian, "America's Cultural Heritage," *San Francisco Teachers Bulletin* 20 (February 1937): 7–11, box 17, folder 12, RDD.

7. Prejudice and Social Justice

1. On Woodson, see Jacqueline Goggin, *Carter G. Woodson: A Life in Black History* (Baton Rouge: Louisiana State University Press), 1993, and Pero Gaglo Dagbovie, "Making Black History Practical and Popular: Carter G. Woodson, the Proto Black Studies Movement and the Struggle for Black Liberation," *Western Journal of Black Studies* 27 (2003): 263–274.

2. "Negro History Week the Fifth Year," *Journal of Negro History* 16 (April 1931): 125–131; "Annual Report of the Director," *Journal of Negro History* 16 (October 1931): 354–357; Goggin, *Carter G. Woodson,* 31.

3. Goggin, *Carter G. Woodson,* 87, 114, 118; "Negro History Week Explained," file VI:144, CIC.

4. Stephanie J. Shaw, *What a Woman Ought to Be and to Do: Black Professional Women Workers during the Jim Crow Era* (Chicago: University of Chicago Press, 1996), 204–206, 229, 328n111. Also see Effie Lee Newsome, "Child Literature and Negro Childhood," *Crisis* 34 (October 1927): 260.

5. "Proceedings of the Annual Meeting of the Association for the Study of Negro Life and History," *Journal of Negro History* 19 (January 1934): 11; Goggin, *Carter G. Woodson,* 118, 120, 156–157.

6. Goggin, *Carter G. Woodson,* chap. 3; "Surveying Negro Life Today," *Child Study* 9 (December 1931): 120.

7. "Negro History Week the Fifth Year," 127; "History of the Association," file VI:144, CIC; Carter G. Woodson, *The Mis-Education of the Negro* (Washington, D.C.: Associated, 1933); Goggin, *Carter G. Woodson,* chap. 5, 85, 119.

8. "Resolutions," and "Declarations," *National Note-Book Quarterly* 2 (October 1920): 5–7; "Coordination of National Organizations," *Journal of Negro Education* 4 (April 1935): 157.

9. Lasker, "Some Obstacles of Race Co-operation," *Opportunity* 3 (April 1925): 102; John Dewey, "Racial Prejudice and Friction," *Chinese Social and Political Science Review* 6 (1922): 1–17.

10. Bruno Lasker, *Race Attitudes in Children* (New York: Holt, 1929), 154–155.

11. See for example Mary W. Heffernan, "My Attempt to Interpret Some of the Negro Poets to My Class," *Opportunity* 7 (July 1929): 219; Charles A. Daly, "Racial Enrichment of the Curriculum," *Journal of the National Education Association* 27 (November 1938): 235; Anne Biddle Sterling, "Interracial Teaching in the Schools," *Opportunity* 1 (March 1923): 7; Edgar C. Bye, "Inter-racial Bridge Building," *Opportunity* 4 (April 1926): 116.

12. Rachel Davis DuBois, "Practical Problems of International and Interracial Education," *Clearing House* 10 (April 1936): 486–489; "Church and School: Intercultural Relations," *Church Woman* 4 (February 1938): 3–4; "What American Culture Might Become," draft of speech to League of Women Voters, San Francisco, 1935, 8, box 12, folder 10, RDD; "Sharing Cultural Values," *Journal of Educational Sociology* 12 (April 1939): 485.

13. Anne Hoppock, "Schools for the Foreign Born in a New Jersey County," *Progressive Education* 10 (April 1933), 189–193.

14. Rachel Davis DuBois, "The New Frontier," *Opportunity* 12 (February 1934): 40.

15. Lasker, *Race Attitudes in Children,* 299.

16. Walter White, "The Progressive School and the Race Problem," *School and Home* 15 (November 1932): 33–36; editorial, *Progressive Education* 12 (March 1935): 140.

17. Helen Adele Whiting, "Negro Children Study Race Culture," and Pauline D. Knobbs, "Educating for a Bi-racial Community," both in *Progressive Education* 12 (March 1935): 172–181.

18. Rev. Walden Pell II, "Manners, Morals, and Minorities," and Henry C. Fenn, "Educating for a Melting-Pot Culture," both in *Progressive Education* 12 (March 1935): 151–155 and 198–202.

19. Julia A. Spooner, "The Minority Question in a Demonstration School," *Progressive Education* 12 (March 1935): 185–191.

20. Russell W. Jelliffe, "Weaving a Minority into the Major Pattern," *Progressive Education* 12 (March 1935): 168–171.

21. Alain Locke, "Minorities and the Social Mind," *Progressive Education* 12 (March 1935): 141–146; "The Child's Social Attitudes: —Whose Responsibility?" n.d. [c. 1932], box 41, folder 443, CSA.

22. Locke, "Minorities and the Social Mind," 143–144.

23. Ibid., 143–145.

24. Ibid.

25. Locke, "The Child's Social Attitudes," 2.

26. Locke, "The Dilemma of Segregation," *Journal of Negro Education* 4 (July 1935): 406–411.

27. Alain Locke, "With Science as His Shield," *Frontiers of Democracy* 6 (15 April 1940): 208–210.

28. Ibid., 208–210.

29. Alain Locke to Rachel Davis DuBois, 28 March 1939, Locke Papers; Alain Locke and Bernhard Stern, *When Peoples Meet: A Study of Race and Culture Contacts* (New York: Progressive Education Association, 1942).

30. "Current Events of Importance in Negro Education," and "Race Relations and the Education of Negroes," *Journal of Negro Education* 2 (April 1933): 121–127, 230, 252; "The Courts and the Negro Separate School," *Journal of Negro Education* 4 (July 1935); Paul E. Baker, "Negro-White Adjustment in America," *Journal of Negro Education* 3 (April 1934): 194–204.

31. John T. Phillips Jr., review of *We Sing America,* by Marion Cuthbert, *Journal of Negro Education* 6 (January 1937): 85; Anne O'H. Williamson, review of *The Negro American Series of Supplementary Readers,* by Emma E. Aiken, *Journal of Negro Education* 8 (April 1939): 214; Vishnu V. Oak and Eleanor H. Oak, "Children's Literature Dealing with Negro Life," *Journal of Negro Education* 8 (January 1939): 77; Thomas E. Davis, "Some Racial Attitudes of Negro College and Grade School Students," *Journal of Negro Education* 6 (April 1937): 157–165.

32. Irwin V. Shannon, "The Teaching of Negro Life and History in Relation to Some Views of Educators on Race Adjustment," *Journal of Negro Education* 2 (January 1933): 53–64.

33. Charles S. Johnson, "On the Need of Realism in Negro Education," *Journal of Negro Education* 5 (July 1936): 375–382; "Current Events of Importance," 228. Also see Johnson, "The Education of the Negro Child," *Opportunity* 14 (February 1936): 38.

34. Ralph J. Bunche, "Education in Black and White," and W. A. Robinson, "What Peculiar Organization and Direction Should Characterize the Education of Negroes?" both in *Journal of Negro Education* 5 (July 1936): 351–358, 399.

35. Doxey A. Wilkerson, "A Determination of the Peculiar Problems of Negroes in Contemporary American Society," *Journal of Negro Education* 5 (July 1936): 327, 346–350, and "American Caste and the Social Studies Curriculum," *Quarterly Review of Higher Education among Negroes* 5 (April 1937): 67–74.

36. Merl R. Eppse, "Social Studies and the Struggles of the Negro People,"

Quarterly Review of Higher Education among Negroes 6 (October 1938): 268–275.

37. Alain Locke, "The Negro in the Schools—Minority Rights in a Democracy," talk delivered to Annual Educational Conference of Teachers Union, Local 5, American Federation of Teachers, New York, 2 April 1938, Locke Papers, box 164–120, folder 9.

38. Alain Locke, "Whither Race Relations? A Critical Commentary," *Journal of Negro Education* 13 (Summer 1944): 398–406.

39. Alain Locke, "The Minority Side of Intercultural Education," *Education for Cultural Unity* 17 (1945): 60–64.

40. Quoted in Paul C. Mishler, *Raising Reds: The Young Pioneers, Radical Summer Camps, and Communist Political Culture in the United States* (New York: Columbia University Press, 1999), 93.

41. Mishler, *Raising Reds,* chaps. 2 and 3; Lillian Carlson, "A California Girlhood," in *Red Diapers: Growing up in the Communist Left,* ed. Judy Kaplan and Linn Shapiro (Chicago: University of Illinois Press, 1998), 20–26.

42. Mishler, *Raising Reds;* Judy Kaplan and Linn Shapiro, introduction to Kaplan and Shapiro, *Red Diapers,* 5–6.

43. Julia L. Mickenberg, *Learning from the Left: Children's Literature, the Cold War, and Radical Politics in the United States* (New York: Oxford University Press, 2006).

44. Eugene L. Horowitz, "The Development of Attitude toward the Negro," *Archives of Psychology* 194 (January 1936): 8–37. Also see Eugene L. Horowitz, "The Social Roots of Prejudice," *Frontiers of Democracy* 6 (15 April 1940): 206.

45. Horowitz, "The Development of Attitude toward the Negro," 8–37; Eugene Horowitz, "Race Prejudice in Children," *Opportunity* 13 (May 1935): 145–147; Howard H. Long, "A Genetic Study of Race Prejudice," *Journal of Negro Education* 6 (April 1937): 199–201.

46. Irma Doniger, "Our Protected Children," *Child Study* 14 (December 1936): 75.

47. Frances B. Mayers, evaluation of in-service course, Fall 1939, box 14, folder 7, RDD.

48. Ruth Benedict, *Race: Science, and Politics* (New York: Modern Age Books, 1940), 245.

49. Ibid., 253–255, and "Transmitting Our Democratic Heritage in the Schools," *American Journal of Sociology* 48 (May 1943): 722–727.

50. Algernon Black, "Concerning Children's Prejudices," *Child Study* 17 (Fall 1939): 12; Robert Whitney Peebles, *Leonard Covello: A Study of an Immigrant's Contribution to New York City* (New York: Arno, 1978), 272–275.

51. Program for "Conference on Intercultural Education for Teachers," 16–17

July 1939, box 3, folder 10, NCCJ; Rachel Davis DuBois with Corann Okorodudu, *All This and Something More: Pioneering in Intercultural Education* (Bryn Mawr, Pa.: Dorrance, 1984), 80–81; William Pickens, "To the Committee on Textbooks and Current Literature," 21 January 1938; "Note for Committee on Textbooks and Current Literature," 19 January 1938; Rachel Davis DuBois to members of the committee, 17 May 1938, box 17, folder 3, RDD.

52. DuBois, "Building Tolerant Attitudes in High School Students," and Katherine Gardner, "Changing Racial Attitudes," *Crisis* 38 (October 1931): 334–336; Charles E. Carson, "An Antidote for Racial Prejudice," *Crisis* 41 (June 1934): 163.

53. "Culture Groups in Community Life," suggested plans for radio broadcast, 10 November 1940, 9–10, box 13, folder 1, RDD; Marion Cuthbert, *We Sing America* (New York: Friendship, 1936).

54. Raymond Wolters, *Negroes and the Great Depression* (Westport, Conn.: Greenwood, 1970), 313–318; Rachel Davis DuBois to W. E. B. Du Bois, 24 December 1931 and n.d. [1934], both in WEBD Papers.

55. Rachel Davis DuBois to W. E. B. Du Bois, 10 March 1933 and 22 April 1933, both in WEBD Papers.

56. Rachel Davis DuBois, "Our Enemy—The Stereotype," *Progressive Education* 12 (March 1935): 147; "Practical Problems," 486–489.

57. DuBois, "What American Culture Might Become," 19; Rachel Davis DuBois, *Adventures in Intercultural Education* (New York: Progressive Education Association, 1938), 13.

58. Rachel Davis DuBois, "The Role of Home Economics in Intercultural Education," *Journal of Home Economics* 30 (March 1938): 148; "Greetings to the Japanese-American Courier," January 1938, box 3, folder 3, RDD; "The Need for Sharing Cultural Values," *Friends Intelligencer* (Second Month 11, 1939): 84; "Intercultural Education and Democracy's Defense," *Friends Intelligencer* (Second Month 1 1941): 69.

59. Rachel Davis DuBois, introduction to Ethel M. Duncan, *Democracy's Children* (New York: Hinds, Hayden, and Eldredge, 1945), xiii; *Build Together Americans: Adventures in Intercultural Education for the Secondary School* (New York: Hinds, Hayden, and Eldredge, 1945), 41–45; handwritten response to Walter Feinberg, "Progressive Education and Social Planning," *Teachers College Record* 72 (May 1972): 497, box 1, folder 6, RDD.

60. Everett R. Clinchy, *Education and Human Relations*, Personal Growth Leaflet no. 149 (Washington, D.C.: National Education Association, n.d. [c. 1943]), 14: James E. Pitt, *Adventures in Brotherhood* (New York: Farrar, Straus, 1955), 144–148.

8. Pluralism in the Shadow of War

1. Nicholas V. Montalto, "The Intercultural Education Movement, 1924–41: The Growth of Tolerance as a Form of Intolerance," in *American Education and the European Immigrant, 1840–1940,* ed. Bernard J. Weiss (Urbana: University of Illinois Press, 1982), 142–160; Abraham F. Citron, Collins J. Reynolds, and Sarah W. Taylor, "Ten Years of Intercultural Education in Educational Magazines," *Harvard Educational Review* 15 (March 1945): 129–132.

2. Rachel Davis DuBois with Corann Okorodudu, *All This and Something More: Pioneering in Intercultural Education* (Bryn Mawr, Pa.: Dorrance, 1984), 76; "The Service Bureau for Intercultural Education," report of an evaluation committee, 9 March 1936, box 29, folder 4, RDD.

3. DuBois, *All This,* 76–77; *Build Together Americans: Adventures in Intercultural Education for the Secondary School* (New York: Hinds, Hayden, and Eldredge, 1945), xvi.

4. Rachel Davis DuBois, "Report of Work during 1937, Commission on Intercultural Education," 20.13, Benedict Papers, and *Adventures in Intercultural Education* (New York: Progressive Education Association, 1938).

5. DuBois, *All This,* 80.

6. Rachel Davis DuBois to Alain Locke, 9 February 1938, Locke Papers; Nicholas V. Montalto, *A History of the Intercultural Education Movement, 1924–1941* (New York: Garland, 1982), 136–137.

7. Rachel Davis DuBois, "What American Culture Might Become," draft of speech to League of Women Voters, San Francisco, 1935, 18, box 12, folder 10; "Americanizing Our American Public Schools," (radio talk), San Francisco, 6 November 1936, 3, box 12, folder 10; "Danger or Promise?" speech to San Francisco State College, 1936, 2–3, box 12, folder 10; "Tentative Plans for Work in New York City High Schools," n.d. [c. 1936], box 17, folder 13; "Culture Groups in Community Life," suggested plans for radio broadcast, 10 November 1940, 7–8, box 13, folder 1, all in RDD.

8. Rachel Davis DuBois, "A Philosophy of Intercultural Relations," *World Order* 4 (April 1938): 140–141, and "What American Culture Might Become," 18.

9. "Notes Taken at Mrs. DuBois Class, May 24, 1939," box 14, folder 6, RDD; *Changing Attitudes toward Other Races and Nations* (New York: Service Bureau for Education in Human Relations, 1934), 11, box 9, folder 11, RDD; "Culture Groups in Community Life," 6; "Reminiscences of Bruno Lasker," 439–440; Montalto, *Intercultural Education,* 266n90.

10. DuBois, "Danger or Promise?" 3, 8–9; "Peace and Intercultural Educa-

tion," *Journal of Educational Sociology* 12 (March 1939): 418–424; "A Philosophy of Intercultural Relations," 140–142; "Appreciating Other Cultures," radio program, 17 April 1940, box 13, folder 1, RDD.

11. Bertha Melkonian, "America's Cultural Heritage," *San Francisco Teachers Bulletin* 20 (February 1937): 8.

12. Rachel Davis DuBois, "Intercultural Education and Democracy's Defense," *Friends Intelligencer* (Second Month 1, 1941): 69–71; "What American Culture Might Become," 22; *Adventures,* 13; *All This,* 98.

13. Rachel Davis-DuBois, "The Role of Home Economics in Intercultural Education," *Journal of Home Economics* 30 (March 1938): 147; *Adventures,* 19–20, 61; *Build Together Americans,* 57.

14. DuBois, *All This,* 81, 91; report, no title, n.d. [c. 1938], 22b, box 29, folder 4, RDD.

15. DuBois, *All This,* 86–91; J. W. Studebaker, "Scaling Cultural Frontiers," *Journal of Educational Sociology* 12 (April 1939): 487–498; Barbara Dianne Savage, *Broadcasting Freedom: Radio, War, and the Politics of Race, 1938–1948* (Chapel Hill: University of North Carolina Press, 1999), chap. 1; Montalto, *Intercultural Education,* chap. 6.

16. DuBois, *Build Together Americans,* 198–211; Savage, *Broadcasting Freedom,* 25–26; Montalto, *Intercultural Education,* 159–162.

17. DuBois, *All This,* 87; Mrs. Arthur Hays Sulzberger to Arthur Derounian, 24 February 1939, box 3, folder 3, RDD; Savage, *Broadcasting Freedom,* 45–52; Montalto, *Intercultural Education,* 209–212.

18. Rachel Davis DuBois and Alain Locke, correspondence, October–December 1938, Locke Papers.

19. Savage, *Broadcasting Freedom,* 34, 44, 56–57; Montalto, *Intercultural Education,* 165–168.

20. Benjamin Fine, "Schools Fight Racial Hatred," *New York Times,* 12 February 1939, 58; "Schools to Expand Tolerance Study," *New York Times,* 5 October 1939, 19; DuBois, *All This,* 88; Nicholas V. Montalto, "Multicultural Education in the New York City Public Schools, 1919–1941," in *Educating an Urban People: The New York City Experience,* ed. Diane Ravitch and Ronald K. Goodenow (New York: Teachers College Press, 1981), 72–73.

21. "Summary and General Statement of the Reports on Democracy and Tolerance in the High School," n.d. [c. 1939], box 17, folder 13, RDD; "Report of the Committee; Assemblies on Democracy," 8 February 1939, box 3, folder 3, RDD; Anna Paisner, "A Script for a Tolerance Program," *High Points* 21 (April 1939): 15–23.

22. Clara Colla, "Toleremus," *High Points* 22 (March 1940): 76–78; "Tolerance," *High Points* 22 (February 1940): 21–24; M. M. Mandl, "Teaching

Tolerance in the High Schools," *High Points* 23 (June 1941): 61–64; Benjamin Fine, "Tolerance Aim in School Plan," *New York Times,* 31 December 1939, 28. On teachers' responses also see Jonna Perrillo, "White Teachers and the 'Black Psyche': Interculturalism and the Psychology of Race in the New York City High Schools, 1940–1950," in *When Science Encounters the Child: Education, Parenting, and Child Welfare in 20th-Century America,* ed. Barbara Beatty, Emily D. Cahan, and Julia Grant (New York: Teachers College Press, 2006), 157–174.

23. Marie Syrkin, *Your School, Your Children* (New York: L. B. Fischer, 1944), 189–207.

24. List of teachers enrolled in in-service course, 1939, box 14, folder 6; Frances B. Mayers, evaluation of in-service course and report, Fall 1939, box 14, folder 7; "Criticisms of Intercultural Education Course at N.Y.U.," box 14, folder 10; Sidney Weinstein, "Criticism of Course," box 14, folder 6, all in RDD; Robert Shaffer, "Multicultural Education in New York City during World War II," *New York History* 77 (July 1996): 307.

25. DuBois, *All This,* 92; *Build Together Americans,* xvii; Montalto, *Intercultural Education,* 218–234.

26. "Reminiscences of Bruno Lasker," 437–439; Lasker, "Textbook Study," memorandum, 27 June 1934, notebook 11, 128, Lasker Papers.

27. B. L. to S. G. C., 22 November 1940; Bruno Lasker to Rachel Davis DuBois, 25 November 1940; both in notebook 17-3, 115–119, Lasker Papers.

28. "Theme for a Ph.D. Dissertation, submitted (not too respectfully) by BL," n.d. [c. March 1941], and Bruno Lasker, "A Draft Statement of Certain Principles Affecting Publication Policy," 6 March 1941, notebook 18-1, 29, 41–48, Lasker Papers.

29. Bruno Lasker, review of *From Many Lands,* by Louis Adamic, for *Survey* 1940, notebook 17-2, 118–119, Lasker Papers; Lasker, "A Draft Statement of Certain Principles."

30. DuBois, *All This,* 89, 93; Montalto discusses the GEB evaluation in detail in *Intercultural Education,* 235–250.

31. "Report of the Committee for Evaluation to the General Education Board," report B, 33–34, 69, 70, box 31, folder 7, RDD.

32. Ibid., 34, 52; Montalto, *Intercultural Education,* 243.

33. "Report of the Committee for Evaluation," 34, 68–69, 72; DuBois, *All This,* 89–94; Montalto, *Intercultural Education,* 235–250.

34. DuBois, *All This,* 93–94.

35. Ibid., 93–95; *Build Together,* 106–107.

36. Rachel Davis DuBois, "Intercultural Education and Democracy's Defense," *Friends Intelligencer* (Second Month 1, 1941): 69–71.

37. DuBois, *All This,* 95.

38. Clara Savage Littledale, "Good Will toward Men," *Parents' Magazine* 15 (December 1940): 13.

39. Council Against Intolerance in America, *An American Answer to Intolerance* (New York: Council Against Intolerance in America, 1939); Richard Weiss, "Ethnicity and Reform: Minorities and the Ambiance of the Depression Years," *Journal of American History* 66 (December 1979): 566–585; Ronald Takaki, *Double Victory: A Multicultural History of World War II* (New York: Little, Brown, 2000).

40. Annual Report 1940–41, 19, box 1, folder 7, BIE; Herbert L. Seamans, "Schools and the Jews," *Frontiers of Democracy* 6 (15 April 1940): 211. On pluralism and cosmopolitanism see David Hollinger, *Postethnic America: Beyond Multiculturalism,* rev. ed. (New York: Basic Books, 2006).

41. Alain Locke and Bernhard J. Stern, eds., *When Peoples Meet: A Study of Race and Culture Contacts* (New York: Progressive Education Association, 1942); *Americans All: Studies in Intercultural Education,* National Education Association, Department of Supervisors and Directors of Instruction, fourteenth yearbook (Washington, D.C.: National Education Association, 1942); William E. Vickery and Stewart G. Cole, *Intercultural Education in American Schools* (New York: Harper, 1943).

42. Mrs. Hugh Grant Straus, form letter, 16 June 1943; press releases, November 1943 and December 1943, box 11, folder 104, CSA.

43. Everett R. Clinchy, *Semi-annual Report of the Director* (New York: NCCJ, 15 May 1939); James E. Pitt, *Adventures in Brotherhood* (New York: Farrar, Straus, 1955), chap. 7. On wartime efforts see Richard W. Steele, "The War on Intolerance: The Reformulation of American Nationalism, 1939–1941," *Journal of American Ethnic History* 9 (Fall 1989): 9–35; Sherry L. Field, "Intercultural Education and Negro History during the Second World War," *Journal of the Midwest History of Education Society* 22 (1995): 75–85; Shaffer, "Multicultural Education in New York City."

44. Clarence I. Chatto and Alice L. Halligan, *The Story of the Springfield Plan* (New York: Barnes and Noble, 1945), 51, 154; Alexander Alland and James Waterman Wise, *The Springfield Plan* (New York: Viking, 1945).

45. "The Service Bureau and the War," "A Program of Intercultural Education in Wartime: Annual Report 1941–42," and "Suggested Program of Intercultural Education," RS 10/6/20, box 2, PEA.

46. Ruth Benedict, "American Melting Pot, 1942 Model," in *Americans All,* 14–24.

47. Ibid., 14–24. Also see Ruth Benedict, "Differences vs. Similarities," *Frontiers of Democracy* 9 (15 December 1942): 81.

48. Rachel Davis DuBois, "Conserving Cultural Resources," in *Americans All,* 155, 158; *Build Together Americans,* 18, 105, and *All This,* 68.

49. Clinchy, *Semi-annual Report,* and *Sowing the Seeds of Goodwill* (New York: NCCJ, 1942).

50. Everett R. Clinchy, *Education and Human Relations,* Personal Growth Leaflet no. 149 (Washington, D.C.: National Education Association, n.d. [1943]), 3–5; foreword, to Benson Y. Landis, ed., *Religion and the Good Society* (New York: Association, 1942), 5–8; "The Right to be Different," in *Religion and Our Racial Tensions,* ed. Clyde Kluckhohn et al. (Cambridge: Harvard University Press, 1945), 28–39.

51. Clinchy, *Semi-annual Report.*

52. See Ruth Feldstein, *Motherhood in Black and White: Race and Sex in American Liberalism* (Ithaca, N.Y.: Cornell University Press, 2000), 44–49; Ellen Herman, *The Romance of American Psychology: Political Culture in the Age of Experts* (Berkeley: University of California Press, 1995), 58–60, 184–186; John P. Jackson Jr., *Social Scientists for Social Justice: Making the Case against Segregation* (New York: New York University Press, 2001), chap. 3.

53. John Dollard et al., *Frustration and Aggression* (New Haven, Conn.: Yale University Press, 1939).

54. T. W. Adorno, Else Frenkel-Brunswik, Daniel J. Levinson, and R. Nevitt Sanford, *The Authoritarian Personality* (New York: Norton, 1950). On the AJC's role see Stuart Svonkin, *Jews against Prejudice: American Jews and the Fight for Civil Liberties* (New York: Columbia University Press, 1997), 32–40.

55. Adorno et al., *The Authoritarian Personality*; Samuel H. Flowerman, "Portrait of the Authoritarian Man," *New York Times Magazine,* 23 April 1950, 9.

56. Adorno et al., *The Authoritarian Personality,* 366–367; Flowerman, "Portrait of the Authoritarian Man"; Else Frenkel-Brunswik, "A Study of Prejudice in Children," *Human Relations* 1 (August 1948): 295–306, and "Differential Patterns of Social Outlook and Personality in Family and Children," in *Childhood in Contemporary Cultures,* ed. Margaret Mead and Martha Wolfenstein (Chicago: University of Chicago Press, 1955), 369–402; Miriam Reimann, "How Children Become Prejudiced," *Commentary* 11 (January 1951): 88–94.

57. Bruno Bettelheim and Morris Janowitz, *Dynamics of Prejudice: A Psychological and Sociological Study of Veterans* (New York: Harper, 1950), 105, emphasis in original, 178, 186.

58. Flowerman, "Portrait of the Authoritarian Man," 31.

59. "Memorandum," from the NCCJ to speakers dealing with prejudice, n.d. [c. 1943], 1.

60. Flowerman, "Portrait of the Authoritarian Man," 31; Bettelheim and Janowitz, *Dynamics of Prejudice,* 184.

61. Evelyn Emig Mellon, "Democracy Should Begin at Home," *Parents' Magazine* 16 (December 1941): 20; Frances Lee, "Learning the Ways of Democracy," *Parents' Magazine* 14 (December 1939): 12.

62. David M. Levy, "Intolerance—Its Toll upon the Intolerant," *Child Study* 19 (Winter 1941–42): 42; Anna W. M. Wolf, *Our Children Face War* (Boston: Houghton Mifflin, 1942), 180–183.

63. Pitt, *Adventures in Brotherhood*, 77, 144–148; "Memorandum," 3.

64. Alice V. Keliher, "What Shall We Do about Hatred?" *Progressive Education* 16 (November 1939): 485–487, and "Understanding Themselves and Others," *Parents' Magazine* 16 (September 1941): 23; Citron, Reynolds, and Taylor, "Ten Years of Intercultural Education," 129–132.

65. DuBois, *Build Together Americans*, 21–49, 142, "The Need for Sharing Cultural Values," *Friends Intelligencer* (Second Month 11, 1939): 84–85, and "Sharing Cultural Values," *Journal of Educational Sociology* 12 (April 1939): 485.

66. DuBois, "Intercultural Education and Democracy's Defense," 69.

Epilogue

1. For examples of the extensive literature on twentieth-century American liberalism, see James T. Kloppenberg, *The Virtues of Liberalism* (New York: Oxford University Press, 2000); Alan Brinkley, *The End of Reform: New Deal Liberalism in Recession and War* (New York: Knopf, 1995); Gary Gerstle, "The Protean Character of American Liberalism," *American Historical Review* 99 (October 1994): 1043–1073; Ruth Feldstein, *Motherhood in Black and White: Race and Sex in American Liberalism, 1930–1965* (Ithaca, N.Y.: Cornell University Press, 2000).

2. Ruth Benedict, *Race: Science, and Politics* (New York: Modern Age Books, 1940), 247.

3. Gunnar Myrdal, *An American Dilemma: The Negro Problem and American Democracy* (New York: Harper, 1944), 48–49, 109–110, 383–385, emphasis in original. Also see Walter A. Jackson, *Gunnar Myrdal and America's Conscience: Social Engineering and Racial Liberalism, 1938–1987* (Chapel Hill: University of North Carolina Press, 1990).

4. On postwar intercultural education see Stuart Svonkin, *Jews against Prejudice: American Jews and the Fight for Civil Liberties* (New York: Columbia University Press, 1997), Cherry A. McGee Banks, *Improving Multicultural Education: Lessons from the Intergroup Education Movement* (New York: Teachers College Press, 2005), and Michael R. Olneck, "The Recurring Dream: Symbolism and Ideology in Intercultural and Multicultural Education," *American Journal of Education* 98 (February 1990): 147–174.

5. Florence Mary Fitch, "Teaching Children Religious Tolerance," *Parents' Magazine* 21 (June 1946): 42; Ophelia Settle Egypt, "One Little Boy Meets Prejudice," *Parents' Magazine* 31 (February 1956): 50; Invitation and program for Abyssinian Parent-Teacher Association, 31 October, n.d. [c. 1953], folio folder, Littledale Papers.

6. Everett Clinchy, "The Right to Be Different," in *Religion and Our Racial Tensions,* ed. Clyde Kluckhohn, et. al. (Cambridge: Harvard University Press, 1945), 38–39.

7. Willard Johnson to Robert Maxwell, 4 March 1946, and clippings from the *New York Times, PM, New York Herald Tribune,* and *World Telegram,* n.d. [1946], box 24, folder 240, CSA; Josette Frank, "Children's Radio Programs," *Child Study* 22 (Summer 1945): 120; "Further Discussion of Social Attitudes," and press release, n.d. [c. 1946], box 24, folder 236, CSA.

8. Rachel Davis DuBois with Corann Okorodudu, *All This and Something More: Pioneering in Intercultural Education* (Bryn Mawr, Pa.: Dorrance, 1984), 95, 106; Bruno Lasker, review of *Build Together Americans,* by Rachel Davis DuBois, n.d. [c. 1945], box 8, folder 9, and "Social Education through Happy Memories," *Adult Leadership* 6 (March 1958): 247–248, box 41, folder 8, RDD. On group conversation see George A. Crispin, "Rachel Davis DuBois Founder of the Group Conversation as an Adult Educational Facilitator for Reducing Intercultural Strife" (Ed.D. diss., Temple University, 1987).

9. DuBois's later books include *Get Together Americans: Friendly Approaches to Racial and Cultural Conflicts through the Neighborhood-Home Festival* (New York: Harper, 1943); *Build Together Americans: Adventures in Intercultural Education for the Secondary School* (New York: Hinds, Hayden, and Eldredge, 1945); *Neighbors in Action: A Manual for Local Leaders in Intergroup Relations* (New York: Harper and Row, 1950); and with Mew-Soong Li, *The Art of Group Conversation* (New York: Association, 1963), and *Reducing Social Tension and Conflict* (New York: Association, 1971). She describes her later career in *All This.* For DuBois's obituary see *New York Times,* 2 April 1993, LB7.

10. See Daryl Michael Scott, "Postwar Pluralism, *Brown v. Board of Education,* and the Origins of Multicultural Education," *Journal of American History* 91 (June 2004): 69–82, and Jonathan Zimmerman, "*Brown*-ing the American Textbook: History, Psychology, and the Origins of Modern Multiculturalism," *History of Education Quarterly* 44 (Spring 2004): 46–69.

11. See Michael Novak, *The Rise of the Unmeltable Ethnics* (New York: Macmillan, 1971), and Desmond King, *Making Americans: Immigration, Race, and the Origins of the Diverse Democracy* (Cambridge: Harvard University Press, 2000), chap. 9.

12. The literature on contemporary multiculturalism is extensive. For an analysis of its avoidance of issues of class, see John Higham, "Multiculturalism and Universalism: A History and Critique," *American Quarterly* 45 (June 1993): 195–219. Also see David Hollinger, *Postethnic America: Beyond Multiculturalism,* rev. ed. (New York: Basic Books, 2006).

13. See, for example, Pheng Cheah and Bruce Robbins, eds., *Cosmopolitics: Thinking and Feeling beyond the Nation* (Minneapolis: University of Minnesota Press, 1998), Joshua Cohen, ed., *For Love of Country: Debating the Limits of Patriotism* (Boston: Beacon Press, 1996), and David Hollinger, "Not Universalists, Not Pluralists: The New Cosmopolitans Find Their Own Way," *Constellations* 8 (June 2001): 236–248.

14. Abraham H. Foxman and Leonard Riggio, "Dear Readers," Caryl Stern-LaRose and Ellen Hofheimer Bettmann, *Hate Hurts: How Children Learn and Unlearn Prejudice* (New York: Scholastic, 2000), flyleaf.

Bibliography

Archival Sources

American Heritage Center, University of Wyoming, Laramie, Wyoming
   Everett Clinchy Papers

Friends Historical Library, Swarthmore College, Swarthmore, Pennsylvania
   Rachel Davis DuBois Papers

Graduate Theological Union Archives, Berkeley, California

Immigration History Research Center, University of Minnesota, Minneapolis
   Bureau for Intercultural Education Records
   Stewart Cole Papers
   Rachel Davis DuBois Papers
   George Graff Papers

Moorland-Spingarn Research Center, Howard University, Washington, D.C.
   Alain Locke Papers

Oral History Research Office, Butler Library, Columbia University, New York
   The Reminiscences of Bruno Lasker (interview by Louis M. Starr, 1956)

Rare Book and Manuscript Library, Columbia University, New York
   Bruno Lasker Papers

Rockefeller Archive Center, North Tarrytown, New York

>   General Education Board Archives
>   Laura Spelman Rockefeller Memorial Archives

Schlesinger Library, Radcliffe College, Cambridge, Massachusetts

>   Clara Savage Littledale Papers

Social Welfare History Archives, University of Minnesota, Minneapolis

>   Child Study Association of America Records
>   National Conference of Christians and Jews Records

Special Collections and Archives, W. E. B. Du Bois Library, University of Massachusetts, Amherst

>   W. E. B. Du Bois Papers

Swarthmore College Peace Collection, Swarthmore, Pennsylvania

University Microfilms International, Ann Arbor, Michigan

>   Commission on Interracial Cooperation Papers, 1919–1944 (microfilm ed. 1984)

Vassar College Libraries, Archives and Special Collections, Poughkeepsie, New York

>   Ruth Benedict Papers

Selected Primary Sources

Adamic, Louis. "Thirty Million New Americans." *Harper's* 169 (November 1934): 648–693.

———. *My America, 1929–38*. New York: Harper, 1938.

Addams, Jane. *Twenty Years at Hull-House*. 1910. Reprint, Chicago: University of Illinois Press, 1990.

Adler, Florence C. "Toward Good Will." *High Points* 26 (June 1944): 17–28.

Adorno, T. W., Else Frenkel-Brunswik, Daniel J. Levinson, and R. Nevitt Sanford. *The Authoritarian Personality*. New York: Norton, 1950.

Alexander, Will W. "The Changing South." *Opportunity* 5 (October 1927): 296.

———. "History of Student Inter-racial Interest." *Southern YMCA Intercollegian* 2 (February 1929). Copy in CIC.

———. "Southern White Schools Study Race Question." *Journal of Negro Education* 2 (April 1933): 140.

———. "Our Conflicting Racial Policies." *Harper's* 190 (January 1945): 172–179.

Alland, Alexander, and James Waterman Wise. *The Springfield Plan*. New York: Viking, 1945.

Americans All: Studies in Intercultural Education. National Education Association, Department of Supervisors and Directors of Instruction, fourteenth yearbook. Washington, D.C.: National Education Association, 1942.

"And Now the Children Are Accused." *Literary Digest* 3 (17 October 1931): 20.

Baker, Newton Diehl, Carlton J. H. Hayes, and Roger Williams Straus, eds. *The American Way: A Study of Human Relations among Protestants, Catholics, and Jews*. Williamstown Institute of Human Relations. Chicago: Willett, Clark, 1936.

Baker, Paul E. *Negro-White Adjustment: An Investigation and Analysis of Methods in the Interracial Movement in the United States*. New York: Association, 1934.

———. "Negro-White Adjustment in America." *Journal of Negro Education* 3 (April 1934): 197.

Benedict, Ruth. *Race: Science, and Politics*. New York: Modern Age Books, 1940.

———. "American Melting Pot, 1942 Model." In *Americans All: Studies in Intercultural Education*. National Education Association, Department of Supervisors and Directors of Instruction, fourteenth yearbook. Washington, D.C., National Education Association, 1942.

Bettelheim, Bruno, and Morris Janowitz. *Dynamics of Prejudice: A Psychological and Sociological Study of Veterans*. New York: Harper, 1950.

Black, Algernon. "Concerning Children's Prejudices." *Child Study* 17 (Fall 1939): 12.

Black, Irma Simonton. "Let Them Know the People of the World." *Progressive Education* 21 (March 1944): 116–118.

Blefield, Maurice. "A Biology Unit Dealing with Racial Attitudes." *American Biology Teacher* 2 (October 1939): 7–9.

Boeckel, Florence Brewer. "Education Races with Catastrophe." *Parents'* 2 (May 1927): 13.

———. *The Turn toward Peace*. New York: Friendship, 1930.

Bogardus, Emory S. "Social Distance and Its Origins." *Journal of Applied Sociology* 9 (January–February 1925): 216–226.

———. "Measuring Social Distances." *Journal of Applied Sociology* 9 (March–April 1925): 299–308.

————. "Race Friendliness and Social Distance." *Journal of Applied Sociology* 11 (January–February 1927): 272–287.

————. *Immigration and Race Attitudes.* Boston: D. C. Heath, 1928.

Bolton, Euri Belle. "Effect of Knowledge upon Attitudes towards the Negro." *Journal of Social Psychology* 6 (February 1935): 68–90.

Bond, Horace Mann. "The Curriculum and the Negro Child." *Journal of Negro Education* 4 (April 1935): 166.

Bristow, William H. "Intercultural Education: Problems and Solutions." *High Points* 25 (October 1943): 14–26.

Brooks, Lee M. "Racial Distance as Affected by Education." *Sociology and Social Research* 21 (November–December 1936): 128–133.

Broun, Heywood, and George Britt. *Christians Only: A Study in Prejudice.* New York: Vanguard Press, 1931.

Brown, Francis J. "Sociology and Intercultural Understanding." *Journal of Educational Sociology* 12 (February 1939): 328–331.

Brown, Francis J., and Joseph Slabey Roucek, eds. *Our Racial and National Minorities.* New York: Prentice-Hall, 1937.

Brown, Spencer. *They See for Themselves.* New York: Harper, 1945.

Brown, W. O. "Interracial Cooperation: Some of Its Problems." *Opportunity* 11 (September 1933): 272.

Bunche, Ralph J. "Education in Black and White." *Journal of Negro Education* 5 (July 1936): 351–358.

Bye, Edgar C. "Inter-racial Bridge Building." *Opportunity* 4 (April 1926): 116.

Cahill, Daniel J. "Some Thoughts on Intercultural Education." *High Points* 26 (October 1944): 5–11.

Caliver, Ambrose. "Developing Racial Tolerance in America." *Harvard Educational Review* 11 (October 1941): 447–458.

Carmichael, Maude. "A Program for 'A Better Understanding between the Races.'" *Journal of Negro History* 2 (April 1933): 151–156.

Carpenter, Marie Elizabeth. *The Treatment of the Negro in American History School Textbooks.* Menasha, Wisc.: George Banta, 1941.

Carroll, Joseph C. "The Race Problem." *Journal of Applied Sociology* 11 (January–February 1927): 266–271.

Carson, Charles E. "An Antidote for Racial Prejudice." *Crisis* 41 (June 1934): 163.

Chaimas, Herbert M., and Samuel Wallach. "More Than Good Will Is Needed." *High Points* 26 (October 1944): 11–20.

Champlin, Helen K. "Will Our Children Outlaw War?" *Parents'* 8 (July 1933): 14.

Chang-Peng-Chun. "Inter-cultural Contacts and Creative Adjustment." *Progressive Education* 13 (November 1936): 515–520.

Chapman, A. L. "A High School Unit." *Mississippi Educational Advance* (April 1937): 222–224. Copy in CIC.

Charters, W. W. "Developing the Attitudes of Children." *Education* 53 (February 1933): 353–357.

Chatto, Clarence I., and Alice L. Halligan. *The Story of the Springfield Plan.* New York: Barnes and Noble, 1945.

Child Study Association of America. *Parents' Questions.* New York: Harper, 1936.

Citron, Abraham F., Collins J. Reynolds, and Sarah W. Taylor. "Ten Years of Intercultural Education in Educational Magazines." *Harvard Educational Review* 15 (March 1945): 129–132.

Clayton, Cranston. "College Interracialism in the South." *Opportunity* 12 (September 1934): 267.

Cleveland, Elizabeth. "If Parents Only Knew—" *Children* 3 (April 1928): 17.

Clinchy, Everett R. "The Borderland of Prejudice." *Christian Century* 47 (14 May 1930): 623–627.

———. "Human Relations," *Christian Century* 48 (21 January 1931): 106.

———. "Are Christian Missions Menacing Judaism?" *B'nai B'rith* 45 (March 1931): 192.

———. "Seminars of Christians and Jews." *Religious Education* 26 (April 1931): 310–313.

———. "Understanding between Christian and Jew." *World Unity* 12 (June 1933): 148–153.

———. *All in the Name of God.* New York: John Day, 1934.

———. "Can Minorities Protect Themselves?" *Christian Century* 51 (28 March 1934): 418–419.

———. "Prejudice and Minority Groups." In Brown and Roucek, *Our Racial and National Minorities.*

———. Foreword to Benson Y. Landis, ed., *Religion and the Good Society.* New York: Association, 1942.

———. *Education and Human Relations.* Personal Growth Leaflet no. 149. Washington, D.C.: National Education Association, n.d. [1943].

———. "The Right To Be Different." In Clyde Kluckhohn, Everett R. Clinchy, Edwin R. Embree, Margaret Mead, and Bradford S. Abernethy, eds., *Religion and Our Racial Tensions.* Cambridge: Harvard University Press, 1945.

———. "The Effort of Organized Religion." *Annals of the American Academy of Political and Social Science* 244 (March 1946): 128–136.

———. *Intergroup Relations Centers.* New York: Farrar, Straus, 1949.

———. ed. *The World We Want to Live In.* Garden City, N.Y.: Doubleday, Doran, 1942.

Cohen, Morris R. "Minimizing Social Conflicts." *Annals of the American Academy of Political and Social Science* 203 (May 1939): 114–123.

Colla, Clara. "Toleremus." *High Points* 22 (March 1940): 76–78.

Collins, George L. "How Prejudice Is Overcome." *World Tomorrow* 11 (October 1928): 410.

"Controlling Group Prejudice." Special issue, *Annals of the American Academy of Political and Social Science* 244 (March 1946).

Council Against Intolerance in America. *An American Answer to Intolerance.* New York, Council Against Intolerance in America, 1939.

Covello, Leonard. "A High School and Its Immigrant Community—A Challenge and an Opportunity." *Journal of Educational Sociology* 9 (February 1936): 331–346.

———. "Language as a Factor in Social Adjustment." In Brown and Roucek, *Our Racial and National Minorities.*

Covello, Leonard, with Guido D'Agostino. *The Heart Is the Teacher.* New York: McGraw Hill, 1958.

Cox, Rachel Dunaway. "World Friendship among Children." *Parents'* 5 (July 1930): 16.

"Culture Conflicts and Education." Special issue, *Journal of Educational Sociology* 12 (April 1939).

Daly, Charles A. "Racial Enrichment of the Curriculum." *Journal of the National Education Association* 27 (November 1938): 235.

Daly, Hester Cushing. "What Happens to Our Children?" *Parents'* 14 (November 1939): 15.

Davis, Thomas E. "Some Racial Attitudes of Negro College and Grade School Students." *Journal of Negro Education* 6 (April 1937): 157–165.

"Declarations." *National Note-Book Quarterly* 2 (October 1920): 7.

Developing Attitudes in Children. Proceedings of the Mid-West Conference of the Chicago Association for Child Study and Parent Education, March 1932. Chicago: University of Chicago Press, 1932.

Dewey, John. "The School as Social Center," *Elementary School Teacher* 3 (October 1902): 73–86.

———. "Nationalizing Education." *Journal of Proceedings and Addresses of the National Education Association* 54 (1916): 183–184.

———. *Democracy and Education.* New York: Macmillan, 1916.

———. "Racial Prejudice and Friction." *Chinese Social and Political Science Review* 6 (1922): 1–17.

———. "The School as a Means of Developing a Social Consciousness and Social Ideals in Children." *Journal of Social Forces* 1 (1923): 513–517.

Dinwoodie, William W. J. "Teaching Tolerance in the Public Schools." *School and Society* 30 (23 November 1929): 715–716.

Dixon, C. Madeleine. "Democracy before Five!" *Parents'* 17 (August 1942): 24–25.

Dollard, John, et al. *Frustration and Aggression.* New Haven, Conn.: Yale University Press, 1939.

Doniger, Irma. "Our Protected Children." *Child Study* 14 (December 1936): 75.

Droba, D. D. "Education and Negro Attitudes." *Sociology and Social Research* 17 (November–December 1932): 137–141.

DuBois, Rachel Davis. "The Value of Keeping Peace." *Friends' Intelligencer* (Sixth Month 11, 1927): 473–474.

———. "Hunters of the Reds," *Pax International* 2 (September 1927): 6.

———. *A Program in Education for World Mindedness.* Philadelphia: Women's International League for Peace and Freedom. [c. 1927?]. Copy in RDD.

———. *Education in Worldmindedness.* Philadelphia: American Friends Service Committee. [c. 1928?]. Copy in RDD.

———. *Some Racial Contributions to America: A Study Outline for Secondary Schools.* Philadelphia: Committee on Interests of the Colored Race, Philadelphia Yearly Meeting of Friends [c. 1928?]. Copy in RDD.

———. Review of *Race Attitudes in Children. World Tomorrow* 12 (September 1929): 375.

———. *The Contributions of Racial Elements to American Life.* Philadelphia: Women's International League for Peace and Freedom, 1930. Copy in RDD.

———. *Pioneers of the New World.* Philadelphia: Women's International League for Peace and Freedom, 1930. Copy in RDD.

———. "Measuring Attitudes." *Friends Intelligencer* (Sixth Month 14, 1930): 467–468.

———. "Building Tolerant Attitudes in High School Students." *Crisis* 38 (October 1931): 334–335.

———. "Friends' Schools and Sacred Cows." *Friends Intelligencer* (Sixth Month 13, 1931): 506–507.

———. "Shall We Emotionalize Our Students?" *Friends Intelligencer* (Twelfth Month 3, 1932): 973–974.

———. *Changing Attitudes toward Other Races and Nations.* New York: Service Bureau for Education in Human Relations, 1934. Copy in RDD.

———. "The New Frontier." *Opportunity* 12 (February 1934): 40–41.

———. "New Racial Ideas Taught." *New York Times* (20 May 1934): 24.

———. "Our Enemy—The Stereotype." *Progressive Education* 12 (March 1935): 146–147.

———. "Developing Sympathetic Attitudes toward Peoples." *Journal of Sociology* 9 (March 1936): 387–396.

———. "Practical Problems of International and Interracial Education." *Clearing House* 10 (April 1936): 486–490.

———. "Intercultural Education at Benjamin Franklin High School." *High Points* 19 (December 1937): 23–29.

———. "Rediscovering America by Films," *4-Star Final* 2 (December 1937): 2. Copy in RDD.

————. "Leader in Cultural Work Says Young Japanese Are Refreshing." *Japanese-American Courier* 10 (1 January 1938): 3.

————. *Adventures in Intercultural Education.* New York: Progressive Education Association, 1938.

————. "Church and School: Intercultural Relations." *Church Woman* 4 (February 1938): 3–4.

————. "The Role of Home Economics in Intercultural Education." *Journal of Home Economics* 30 (March 1938): 145–149.

————. "A Philosophy of Intercultural Relations." *World Order* 4 (April 1938): 138–142.

————. "Can We Help to Create an American Renaissance?" *English Journal* 27 (November 1938): 733–740.

————. "The Need for Sharing Cultural Values." *Friends Intelligencer* (Second Month 11, 1939): 84–85.

————. "Peace and Intercultural Education." *Journal of Educational Sociology* 12 (March 1939): 420.

————. "Sharing Cultural Values." *Journal of Educational Sociology* 12 (April 1939): 482–486.

————. "Intercultural Education and Democracy's Defense." *Friends Intelligencer* (Second Month 1, 1941): 69–71.

————. "Conserving Cultural Resources." In *Americans All: Studies in Intercultural Education.* National Education Association, Department of Supervisors and Directors of Instruction, fourteenth yearbook. Washington, D.C.: National Education Association, 1942.

————. *Get Together Americans: Friendly Approaches to Racial and Cultural Conflicts through the Neighborhood-Home Festival.* New York: Harper, 1943.

————. *Build Together Americans: Adventures in Intercultural Education for the Secondary School.* New York: Hinds, Hayden, and Eldredge, 1945.

————. Introduction to Ethel M. Duncan, *Democracy's Children.* New York: Hinds, Hayden, and Eldredge, 1945.

————. *Neighbors in Action: A Manual for Local Leaders in Intergroup Relations.* New York: Harper and Row, 1950.

DuBois, Rachel Davis, and Rosie Nelson. *Methods of Achieving Racial Justice: Discussion Outline for Church, School, and Adult Education Groups.* New York: Service Bureau for Education in Human Relations, 1936.

DuBois, Rachel Davis, and Mew-Soong Li. *The Art of Group Conversation.* New York: Association, 1963.

————. *Reducing Social Tension and Conflict.* New York: Association, 1971.

DuBois, Rachel Davis, and Emma Schweppe, eds. *The Jews in American Life.* New York: Thomas Nelson, 1935.

————. *The Germans in American Life.* New York: Thomas Nelson, 1936.

DuBois, Rachel Davis, with Corann Okorodudu. *All This and Something More: Pioneering in Intercultural Education.* Bryn Mawr, Pa.: Dorrance, 1984.

Du Bois, W. E. B. "The Conservation of Races" (1897). Edited by Eric J. Sundquist. *The Oxford W. E. B. Du Bois Reader.* Reprint, New York: Oxford University Press, 1996.

———. "Inter-racial Comity." *Crisis* 22 (May 1921): 6–7.

———. *The Gift of Black Folk.* Boston: Stratford, 1924. Reprint, Millwood, N.Y.: Kraus-Thomson, 1975.

———. "The Dilemma of the Negro." *American Mercury* 3 (October 1924): 179–184.

———. "Will W. Alexander and the South." *Crisis* 32 (August 1926): 164–165.

———. "Postscript: The Commission of Interracial Cooperation." *Crisis* 37 (July 1930): 245.

———. "Will the Church Remove the Color Line?" *Christian Century* 48 (9 December 1931): 1554.

Duffus, Robert L. "Where Do We Get Our Prejudices?" *Harper's* 153 (September 1926): 503–508.

Duncan, Ethel M. "The Incidental Approach in Attitude Building." *American Childhood* 23 (September 1937): 21.

———. *Democracy's Children.* New York: Hinds, Hayden, and Eldredge, 1945.

Eaton, Allen H. *Immigrant Gifts to American Life.* New York: Russell Sage, 1932.

Eckert, Ruth E., and Henry C. Mills. "International Attitudes and Related Academic and Social Factors." *Journal of Educational Sociology* 9 (November 1935): 142–153.

"Education and the Cultural Process." Special issue, *American Journal of Sociology* 48 (May 1943).

"Education and Nationalism." Special issue, *Journal of Educational Sociology* 9 (March 1936).

"Education for Racial Understanding." Special issue, *Journal of Negro Education* 13 (Summer 1944).

Edwards, Lyford P. "Religious Sectarianism and Race Prejudice." *American Journal of Sociology* 41 (September 1935): 167–179.

Eggleston, Cecelia. "What a Negro Mother Faces." *Forum* 100 (August 1938): 59.

Egypt, Ophelia Settle. "One Little Boy Meets Prejudice." *Parents'* 31 (February 1956): 50.

Eleazar, Robert B. *America's Tenth Man: A Brief Survey of the Negro's Part in American History.* Atlanta: Commission on Interracial Cooperation, 1928. Reprint, 1932.

———. "A Realistic Approach to the Race Problem." *Religious Education* 26 (February 1931): 119–122.

Ellenwood, James Lee. "Are You a Dictator?" *Parents'* 13 (November 1938): 16.

Ellis, George W. "The Psychology of American Race Prejudice." *Journal of Race Development* 5 (January 1915): 297–315.

Ephraim, Miriam R. "An Experiment in Education for Human Relations." *Jewish Social Service Quarterly* 12 (June 1936): 357–364.

Eppse, Merl R. "Social Studies and the Struggles of the Negro People." *Quarterly Review of Higher Education among Negroes* 6 (October 1938): 268–275.

Evans, Eva Knox. "Truth or Evasion for the Negro Child?" *Opportunity* 15 (June 1937): 172.

Fahs, Sophia Lyon. "Enlarging Our Children's World." *Parents'* 12 (June 1937): 27.

Faris, Ellsworth. "Racial Attitudes and Sentiments." *Southwestern Political and Social Science Quarterly* 9 (March 1929): 485.

Fenn, Henry C. "Educating for a Melting-Pot Culture." *Progressive Education* 12 (March 1935): 198–202.

Fine, Benjamin. "Schools Fight Racial Hatred." *New York Times* (12 February 1939): 58.

———. "Tolerance Aim in School Plan." *New York Times* (31 December 1939): 28.

Fisher, Pearl M. "English, Democracy, and Color." *High Points* 24 (May 1942): 5–10.

Fitch, Florence Mary. "Teaching Children Religious Tolerance." *Parents'* 21 (June 1946): 42.

Flowerman, Samuel H. "Portrait of the Authoritarian Man." *New York Times Magazine* (23 April 1950): 9.

"*Fortune's* Survey of Attitudes on Religion and Tolerance." *Journal of Educational Sociology* 12 (April 1939): 506.

Freehof, Solomon B. "These Things a Child Should Know." *Parents' Magazine* 11 (February 1936): 11.

Frenkel-Brunswik, Else. "A Study of Prejudice in Children." *Human Relations* 1 (August 1948): 295–306.

———. "Differential Patterns of Social Outlook and Personality in Family and Children." In Margaret Mead and Martha Wolfenstein, eds., *Childhood in Contemporary Cultures*. Chicago: University of Chicago Press, 1955.

Gallant, Joseph. "Approaches to Intercultural Education." *High Points* 26 (November 1944): 39–45.

Gardner, Katherine. "Changing Racial Attitudes." *Crisis* 38 (October 1931): 336.

Garrison, K. C., and Viola S. Burch. "A Study of Racial Attitudes of College Students." *Journal of Social Psychology* 4 (May 1933): 230.

Gavit, John Palmer. "Plain Talk about Race Prejudice." *Parents'* 13 (February 1938): 82.

Gell, Kenneth E. "What the Rochester Schools Are Doing about Internationalism." *Journal of Educational Sociology* 9 (March 1936): 397–407.

Gregg, Lucy P. [Mrs. Abel J.] *New Relationships with Jews and Catholics.* New York: Association, 1934. Copy in NCCJ.

Gruenberg, Sidonie Matsner. "Twigs of Prejudice." *Survey* 56 (1 September 1926): 586–588.

———. "Parents as Interpreters in a Changing World." *Child Study* 6 (February 1929): 118.

Hammond, Maurice S. "Some Experiments in Cultural Pluralism." *Journal of Educational Sociology* 12 (April 1939): 477.

Hardin, Clara A., and Herbert A. Miller. "The Second Generation." In Brown and Roucek, *Our Racial and National Minorities.*

Heffernan, Mary W. "My Attempt to Interpret Some of the Negro Poets to My Class." *Opportunity* 7 (July 1929): 219.

Herring, John W. "Education in Understanding and Goodwill." *Federal Council Bulletin* 10 (June 1927): 6.

———. "Goodwill and Democracy." *B'nai B'rith* 42 (August 1928): 375.

Hinckley, E. D. *Attitude toward the Negro.* Chicago: University of Chicago Press, 1930.

Hinkle, Beatrice M. "Psychological Tendencies of the Pre-school Child and Its Relation to the New World Order." *Progressive Education* 2 (April–May–June 1925): 62–67.

Hipps, Margaret Stroh. "Mothers Can Work for Peace." *Parents' Magazine* 13 (May 1938): 21.

Holmes, John Haynes. "Converting Our Emotions." *Christian Century* 48 (21 January 1931): 112.

Hoppock, Anne. "Schools for the Foreign Born in a New Jersey County." *Progressive Education* 10 (April 1933): 189–193.

Horowitz, Eugene L. "Race Prejudice in Children." *Opportunity* 13 (May 1935): 145–147.

———. "The Development of Attitude toward the Negro." *Archives of Psychology* 194 (January 1936): 8–37.

———. "The Social Roots of Prejudice." *Frontiers of Democracy* 6 (15 April 1940): 206.

Hughes, Helen Elizabeth. "Overcoming Prejudice as an Aim of Religious Education." M.A. thesis, Pacific School of Religion, 1932.

Hunterberg, Max. "Anti-Semitism, The Disease and Its Cure." *B'nai B'rith* 45 (December 1930): 80.

"Intergroup Education." Special issue, *Harvard Educational Review* 15 (March 1945).

Jackson, W. C. "College Instruction in Race Relations." *Religious Education* 26 (February 1931): 124–126.

Jelliffe, Russell W. "Weaving a Minority into the Major Pattern." *Progressive Education* 12 (March 1935): 168–171.

Johnson, Charles S. *A Preface to Racial Understanding.* New York: Friendship, 1936.

———. "The Education of the Negro Child." *Opportunity* 14 (February 1936): 38.

———. "On the Need of Realism in Negro Education." *Journal of Negro Education* 5 (July 1936): 375–382.

Johnson, James Weldon. "A Negro Looks at Race Prejudice." *American Mercury* 14 (May 1928): 54.

Jones, Karen Monrad. "Because Jesus Was a Jew." *Religious Education* 31 (July 1936): 171–177.

Kaiser, Leon S., and Leonora S. Ratner. "A Program for Intercultural Education—The Road to Peace and Victory." *High Points* 26 (March 1944): 19–29.

Kallen, Horace. "Democracy versus the Melting Pot." *Nation* 100 (18–25 February 1915): 190–194.

———. *Culture and Democracy in the United States.* New York: Boni and Liveright, 1924.

Katz, Daniel, and Floyd Henry Allport. *Students' Attitudes: A Report of the Syracuse University Reaction Study.* Syracuse, N.Y.: Craftsman, 1931.

Katz, Daniel, and Kenneth Braly. "Racial Stereotypes of One Hundred College Students." *Journal of Abnormal and Social Psychology* 28 (1933): 280–290.

———. "Racial Prejudice and Racial Stereotypes." *Journal of Abnormal and Social Psychology* 30 (1935): 175–193.

Kaufmann, Helen L. "Should We Hand-Pick Our Children's Friends?" *Parents'* 4 (August 1929): 17.

Keliher, Alice V. "What Shall We Do about Hatred?" *Progressive Education* 16 (November 1939): 485–487.

Kershner, J. Hayden. "Race Prejudice a Form of Group Prejudice." *Journal of Applied Sociology* 11 (May–June 1927): 446–452.

Kilpatrick, William H. "Thinking in Childhood and Youth." *Religious Education* 23 (February 1928): 132.

Kirshner, Alfred. "Scientific Approach to the Development of Tolerance." *High Points* 23 (September 1941): 11–23.

Knobbs, Pauline D. "Educating for a Bi-racial Community." *Progressive Education* 12 (March 1935): 181.

———. "Toward Racial Understanding in the South." In *Americans All: Studies in Intercultural Education.* National Educational Association, Department of Supervisors and Directors of Instruction, fourteenth yearbook. Washington, D.C.: National Education Association, 1942.

Landman, Isaac, ed. *Christian and Jew: A Symposium for Better Understanding.* New York: Horace Liveright, 1929.

Lasker, Bruno. "Some Obstacles of Race Co-operation." *Opportunity* 3 (April 1925): 101–104.

———. "Race Attitudes in Children." *Woman's Press* 20 (May 1926): 332–334.

———. "Can Race Tolerance Be Taught?" *Woman's Press* 20 (September 1926): 608–611.

———. "How Children Acquire Race Prejudice." *Children* 3 (March 1928): 23.

———. *Race Attitudes in Children.* New York: Holt, 1929.

———. "Childhood Prejudices." *Child Study* 6 (February 1929): 107–109.

———. "Race Relations and the Church School." *International Journal of Religious Education* (January 1930): 11–12.

———. *Religious Liberty and Mutual Understanding: An Interpretation of the National Seminar of Catholics, Jews and Protestants.* New York: National Conference of Jews and Christians, 1932.

———, ed. *Jewish Experiences in America: Suggestions for the Study of Jewish Relations with Non-Jews.* New York: Inquiry, 1930.

Lazaron, Morris S. *Common Ground: A Plea for Intelligent Americanism.* New York: Liveright, 1938.

Lee, Frances. "Learning the Ways of Democracy." *Parents'* 14 (December 1939): 12.

"Legion to Question Teacher on Loyalty." *New York Times* (21 May 1927): 22.

Levy, T. Aaron. "The Fruits of Goodwill." *B'nai B'rith* 45 (August–September 1931): 388.

Limbert, Paul M. "What Children Think about War." *Progressive Education* 10 (February 1933): 67.

Littledale, Clara Savage. "The 1935 Needs for Children." *Friends Intelligencer* (Fifth Month 4, 1935): 277–278.

———. "How Teach Peace?" *Parents'* 12 (January 1937): 13.

———. "Democracy by Discussion." *Parents'* 12 (April 1937): 17.

———. "We Celebrate Fourth of July." *Parents'* 12 (July 1937): 15.

———. "Invitation to Travel." *Parents'* 13 (April 1938): 15.

———. "Travel Together." *Parents'* 14 (April 1939): 17.

Locke, Alain. "Minorities and the Social Mind." *Progressive Education* 12 (March 1935): 141–146.

———. "The Dilemma of Segregation." *Journal of Negro Education* 4 (July 1935): 406–411.

———. "With Science as His Shield." *Frontiers of Democracy* 6 (15 April 1940): 208–210.

———. "Whither Race Relations? A Critical Commentary." *Journal of Negro Education* 13 (Summer 1944): 398–406.

———. "The Minority Side of Intercultural Education." *Education for Cultural Unity* 17 (1945): 60–64.

Locke, Alain, and Bernhard J. Stern, eds. *When Peoples Meet: A Study of Race and Culture Contacts*. New York: Progressive Education Association, 1942.

Mandl, M. M. "Teaching Tolerance in the High Schools." *High Points* 23 (June 1941): 61–64.

Maxfield, Ezra Kempton. "Education and World Peace." *Religious Education* 26 (September 1931): 552.

Mays, B. E. "What Negro Students Expect of White Students." *Southern YMCA Intercollegian* 2 (February 1929): 4. Copy in CIC.

McCulloch, Rhoda E. *And Who Is My Neighbor? An Outline for the Study of Race Relations in America*. New York: Association, 1924.

Melkonian, Bertha. "America's Cultural Heritage." *San Francisco Teachers Bulletin* 20 (February 1937): 7–11.

Mellon, Evelyn Emig. "Democracy Should Begin at Home." *Parents'* 16 (December 1941): 20.

Menchan, W. McKinley. "Parent Education in a Negro College." *School and Society* 37 (3 June 1933): 713.

Meras, Edmond A. "World-Mindedness." *Journal of Higher Education* (May 1932): 246–252.

Miller, Kelly. "Is Race Prejudice Innate or Acquired?" *Journal of Applied Sociology* 11 (July–August 1927): 516–524.

Miller, Marion M. "What the Family Thinks—" *Child Study* 11 (November 1933): 36.

———. "Study Material: The Development of Social Attitudes." *Child Study* 11 (November 1933): 62.

Minard, Ralph D. "Race Attitudes of Iowa Children." *University of Iowa Studies in Character* 4 (1931).

"Minority Groups and the American School." Special issue, *Progressive Education* 12 (March 1935).

Mitchell, Lucy Sprague, and Johanna Boetz. *The People of the U.S.A.: Their Place in the School Curriculum*. New York: Progressive Education Association, 1942.

Moore, Jessie Eleanor. "Meeting One's Neighbor." *Pilgrim Elementary Teacher* 19 (November 1935): 408–412. Copy in RDD.

Murphy, Albert John. *Education for World-Mindedness*. New York: Abingdon, 1931.

Myrdal, Gunnar. *An American Dilemma: The Negro Problem and American Democracy*. New York: Harper, 1944.

National Association of Teachers in Colored Schools. *Program of the Seventeenth Annual Meeting, Baltimore, July 1920*. National Note-Book Quarterly 2, supp. (July 1920).

Neumann, G. B. *International Attitudes of High School Students*. New York: Teachers College, 1926.

Niebuhr, Reinhold. "When Virtues Are Vices." *Christian Century* 48 (21 January 1931): 114.

Nurnberg, Rose. "Children of Freedom." *High Points* 25 (September 1943): 15–18.

O'Donnell, Frances Frisbie. "Educating for Peace." *Parents'* 6 (July 1931): 15.

Osborne, Ernest. "The Family's Contributions to Democracy." *Parents'* 12 (November 1937): 84.

Overstreet, Harry A. "Forming First Habits for Internationalism." *Progressive Education* 2 (April–May–June 1925): 68–71.

Ovington, Mary White. "Students Eager for Inter-racial Forums." *Crisis* 41 (June 1934): 181.

———. "Revisiting the South." *Crisis* 34 (April 1937): 42.

Page, Kirby. "Building Tomorrow's World." *World Tomorrow* 10 (January 1927): 28.

Paine, Gustavus S. "Youth and the New Patriotism." *Parents'* 3 (July 1928): 9.

Paisner, Anna. "A Script for a Tolerance Program." *High Points* 21 (April 1939): 15–23.

Patrick, James G. "Interracial Friendship Circles." *Sociology and Social Research* 18 (May–June 1934): 462–469.

Payne, E. George. Introduction to Brown and Roucek, *Our Racial and National Minorities*.

———. "Education and Cultural Puralism." In Brown and Roucek, *Our Racial and National Minorities*.

———. "The School and the Immigrant." In Brown and Roucek, *Our Racial and National Minorities*.

Peck, Anne Merriman, and Enid Johnson. "The Peoples That Make America." *American Childhood* 23 (September 1937): 45.

Pell, Rev. Walden, II. "Manners, Morals, and Minorities." *Progressive Education* 12 (March 1935): 151–155.

Pickens, William. "Racial Segregation." *Opportunity* 5 (December 1927): 364.

Porterfield, Austin L. "Education and Race Attitudes." *Sociology and Social Research* 21 (July–August 1937): 538–543.

Powdermaker, Hortense. *Probing Our Prejudices*. New York: Harper, 1944.

"The Problem of Minorities." Special issue, *Frontiers of Democracy* 6 (15 April 1940).

Proskauer, Joseph M. "Can Prejudice Be Overcome?" *Christian Century* 48 (21 January 1931): 116.

"Race Relations." *Religious Education* 26 (February 1931): 99.

"Race Relations and the Education of Negroes." *Journal of Negro Education* 2 (April 1933): 121–127.

"Racial Minorities." *Nation's Schools* 33 (May 1944): 30–32.

Raper, Arthur. "College Graduates and Race Relations." *Opportunity* 15 (December 1937): 371.

Ray, A. C. "Even-Handed Justice and Equal Opportunity." *Southern YMCA Intercollegian* 2 (February 1929): 5. Copy in CIC.

Reckless, Walter C., and Harold L. Bringen. "Racial Attitudes and Information about the Negro." *Journal of Negro Education* 2 (April 1933): 128–138.

Reeve, Margarette Willis. "The Habit of World Friendship." *Childhood Education* 9 (December 1932): 115–118.

Reimann, Miriam. "How Children Become Prejudiced." *Commentary* 11 (January 1951): 88–94.

Reinhardt, James M. "Students and Race Feeling." *Survey* 61 (15 November 1928): 239–240.

"Resolutions." *National Note-Book Quarterly* 2 (October 1920): 5–6.

Robinson, W. A. "What Peculiar Organization and Direction Should Characterize the Education of Negroes?" *Journal of Negro Education* 5 (July 1936): 399.

Roosevelt, Mrs. Franklin D. "Books I Loved as a Child." *Children* 3 (December 1928): 15.

"School Children and Their Teachers." *Opportunity* 15 (February 1937): 37.

"Schools to Expand Tolerance Study." *New York Times* (5 October 1939): 19.

Seamans, Herbert L. "Schools and the Jews." *Frontiers of Democracy* 6 (15 April 1940): 211.

Shannon, Irwin V. "The Teaching of Negro Life and History in Relation to Some Views of Educators on Race Adjustment." *Journal of Negro Education* 2 (January 1933): 53–64.

Shaw, Katharine. "Understanding Our Southern Neighbor." *Progressive Education* 12 (March 1935): 163–167.

Shute, Mary Chaplin. "We Who Desire Peace." *Childhood Education* 2 (February 1926): 269–278.

Siegler, Celia. "Intercultural Education Vitalized." *High Points* 26 (April 1944): 19–26.

Silcox, Claris Edwin, and Galen M. Fisher. *Catholics, Jews, and Protestants.* New York: Harper, 1934.

Simon, Abram. "The Extent of Discrimination and What We Can Do about It." *Religious Education* 26 (April 1931): 306.

Skinner, Constance Lindsay. "Our Children's Indian Heritage." *Parents'* (October 1933): 16–17.

Smith, Mapheus. "A Study of Change of Attitudes toward the Negro." *Journal of Negro Education* 8 (January 1939): 64–70.

Solovay, Ethel F. "Neither Border nor Breed nor Birth." *High Points* 23 (September 1941): 31–35.

Spessard, Katharine H. "Appreciating China in America." *Progressive Education* 12 (March 1935): 202–206.

Spooner, Julia A. "The Minority Question in a Demonstration School." *Progressive Education* 12 (March 1935): 185–191.

Stanford Workshop on Intercultural Education. *Charting Intercultural Education, 1945–55.* Stanford, Calif.: Stanford University Press, 1946.

Sternberger, Estelle M. "Specific Problems in Cooperation." *Christian Century* 48 (21 January 1931): 111.

Stillman, Mildred W. "The Home Altar." *Parents'* 2 (October 1927): 15.

———. "Living the Christmas Spirit." *Parents'* 8 (December 1933): 13.

Stirling, Anne Biddle. "Interracial Teaching in the Schools." *Opportunity* 1 (March 1923): 7–8.

Straus, Roger W. "An Organized Approach." *Christian Century* 48 (21 January 1931): 120.

———. *Religious Liberty and Democracy: Writings and Addresses.* Chicago: Willett, Clark, 1939.

Studebaker, J. W. "Scaling Cultural Frontiers." *Journal of Educational Sociology* 12 (April 1939): 487–498.

Sutton, Willis A. "Correct Racial Attitudes in the Public Schools." *Religious Education* 26 (April 1931): 296–297.

Syrkin, Marie. *Your School, Your Children.* New York: L. B. Fischer, 1944.

"Teacher to Fight Legion's Charges." *New York Times* (22 May 1927): 24.

"Teaching Tolerance." *Survey* 63 (15 February 1930): 590.

Thayer, V. T. "Children in a Changing World." *Child Study* 11 (November 1933): 35–36.

Thomas, Norman. "Mothers, Fathers, and World Peace." *Parents'* 3 (May 1928): 11.

Thomas, William I., and Florian Znaniecki. *The Polish Peasant in Europe and America.* (1918). Ed. Eli Zaretsky. Reprint, Urbana: University of Illinois Press, 1984.

Thompson, James V. "Can We Learn to Be Brotherly?" *Christian Century* 53 (22 January 1936): 169.

Thrasher, Frederic M. "Are Our Criminals Foreigners?" In Brown and Roucek, *Our Racial and National Minorities.*

Thurstone, L. L. "An Experimental Study of Nationality Preferences." *Journal of General Psychology* 1 (July–October 1928): 405–425.

———. "The Measurement of Social Attitudes." *Journal of Abnormal and Social Psychology* 26 (1931–32): 249–269.

———. "The Measurement of Change in Social Attitudes." *Journal of Social Psychology* 2 (1931): 230–235.

"Tolerance." *High Points* 22 (February 1940): 21–24.

"Tolerant Childhood." *Children* 1 (October 1926): 51.

Vickery, William E., and Stewart G. Cole. *Intercultural Education in American Schools*. New York: Harper, 1943.

Wagoner, Lovisa C. "The Development of Learning in Relation to International Mindedness." *Childhood Education* 10 (June 1934): 451–453.

Wanger, Ruth. "Improving Race Relations through Social Studies." *Progressive Education* 12 (March 1935): 192–197.

Ware, Edith E., ed. *The Study of International Relations in the United States: Survey for 1934*. New York: Columbia University Press, 1934.

———, ed. *The Study of International Relations in the United States: Survey for 1937*. New York: Columbia University Press, 1938.

Watson, Goodwin. *The Measurement of Fair-Mindedness*. New York: Teachers College, 1925.

Watson, John B. *Behaviorism*. New York: Norton, 1924.

Watson, John B., with Rosalie Rayner Watson. *Psychological Care of Infant and Child*. New York: Norton, 1928.

Weatherford, Willis D., and Charles S. Johnson. *Race Relations: Adjustments of Whites and Negroes in the United States*. Boston: D. C. Heath, 1934.

"We, the Children . . . Boys and Girls Discuss Intercultural Understanding." Special issue, *Educational Leadership* 2 (March 1945).

White, Walter. "The Progressive School and the Race Problem." *School and Home* 15 (November 1932): 33–36.

Whiting, Helen Adele. "Negro Children Study Race Culture." *Progressive Education* 12 (March 1935): 172–181.

"Widening Group Friendship." *Commonweal* 16 (10 August 1932): 359.

Wilkerson, Doxey A. "A Determination of the Peculiar Problems of Negroes in Contemporary American Society." *Journal of Negro Education* 5 (July 1936): 327–350.

———. "American Caste and the Social Studies Curriculum." *Quarterly Review of Higher Education among Negroes* 5 (April 1937): 67–74.

"Will Ask Teacher about Patriotism." *New York Times* (24 May 1927): 14.

Wolf, Anna W. M. "Educating for Peace." *Child Study* 15 (May 1938): 231.

———. *Our Children Face War*. Boston: Houghton Mifflin, 1942.

Woofter, T. J., Jr. *The Basis of Racial Adjustment*. Boston: Ginn, 1925.

———. "The Status of Racial and Ethnic Groups." In *Recent Social Trends in the United States*. New York: McGraw-Hill, 1933.

"Workshops in Intergroup Education." Special issue, *Journal of Educational Sociology* 18 (May 1945).

Young, Donald. "Some Effects of a Course in American Race Problems on the Race Prejudice of 450 Undergraduates at the University of Pennsylvania."

Journal of Abnormal and Social Psychology 22 (October–December 1927): 235–242.

Young, Kimball. "Prejudice and Education." *Educational Trends* 6 (October–November 1938): 7–13.

Young, Otis. "Some Educational Implications of Behaviorism." *Education* 51 (February 1931): 351–355.

Zeligs, Rose. "Teach Your Child Tolerance." *Parents'* 9 (August 1934): 15.

———. "Racial Attitudes of Children as Expressed by Their Concepts of Races." *Sociology and Social Research* 21 (March–April 1937): 361–371.

———. "Tracing Racial Attitudes through Adolescence." *Sociology and Social Research* 23 (September–October 1938): 45–54.

———. *Glimpses into Child Life.* New York: Morrow, 1942.

———. "Children's Intergroup Attitudes." *Journal of Genetic Psychology* 72 (March 1948): 101–110.

Zeligs, Rose, and Gordon Hendrickson. "Racial Attitudes of Two Hundred Sixth-Grade Children." *Sociology and Social Research* 18 (September–October 1933): 26–36.

———. "Checking the Social Distance Technique through Personal Interviews." *Sociology and Social Research* 18 (May–June 1934): 420–430.

———. "Factors Regarded by Children as the Basis of Their Racial Attitudes." *Sociology and Social Research* 19 (January–February 1935): 225–233.

Index

Abolitionist writings, 7

Adamic, Louis, 10; Lasker's praises of, 251; on second-generation problem, 186–189; teachings of, 190; writings of, 193

Adams, Abigail, 81

Addams, Jane, 8, 21, 72, 81

Adler, Alfred, 188

Adorno, Theodor, 262–263

Adventures in Intercultural Education (Rachel Davis DuBois), 104, 232, 238

African American educators and scholars: antiprejudice work by, 24–25, 29, 210–211; and black history, 207–210; criticism of churches by, 147; doubts of, on power of education, 206–207; opposition to segregation, 167–169, 207; political and economic goals of, 15, 177–180, 212

African Americans: as affiliates of Commission on Interracial Cooperation, 154; Alexander on achievements of, 174; cultural achievements of, 88–89, 169–170; depictions of, in *Parents' Magazine*, 63–65; education programs for, 172–173; Harlem Renaissance and, 4, 21, 93, 200, 216; as parents, 50–53; participation of, in *Americans All, Immigrants All*, 245; racial prejudice and, 2–3, 40, 82, 146–150; segregation and, 4, 35–36, 152, 169–175, 213–224, 229; in social sciences, 25; and southern colleges, 155–159

Alexander, Will W., 160, 172–173, 174, 175; as assistant administrator of Resettlement Administration, 180; as director of Commission on Interracial Cooperation, 153, 156–157, 158, 159, 160–162, 164–167, 170, 172–173, 178; DuBois, Rachel Davis, and, 204; Du Bois, W. E. B., on, 167;

Lasker and, 162; Ovington on, 168; on race relations, 159, 165–166; work in language of Protestant liberalism, 162

Alien Registration Act (1940), 255

Allport, F. H., 122, 188

American Answer to Intolerance, An (teachers' manual), 256

American Association of University Women, 99

American Childhood (magazine), 194

American Civil Liberties Union, 177

American Dilemma, An (Myrdal), 181, 270

American Friends Service Committee, 81

American Historical Association, 90

American Indian Movement, 17

American Indians. *See* Native Americans

Americanization, 8, 68, 93; concerns about, 91, 215; DuBois, Rachel Davis, on, 85, 240; melting pot theory of, 2, 4, 120, 137, 188; process of, 186

American Jewish Committee (AJC), 11, 101; backing of pluralist orientation, 203; funding of work by, 130–131, 258; leaders of, 203–204; loss of funding for work of DuBois, Rachel Davis, 237; objections on interpretation of Judaism as culture, 235

American Jewish Congress, 139–140, 229

American Judaism, cultural gifts and, 202–205. *See also* Jews

American Legion, 68, 75, 76

American Mercury, 38

Americans All, Immigrants All (radio program), 243–249, 258, 259, 267

Americans All: Studies in Intercultural Education (yearbook), 257

American Teacher, 257

"America's Making" exposition in New York City, 185